Constructing postmodernism

"Postmodernism is not a found object, but a manufactured artifact."
Beginning from this constructivist premise, Brian McHale develops a series
of readings of problematically postmodernist novels – Joyce's *Ulysses*,
Pynchon's *Gravity's Rainbow* and *Vineland*, Eco's *The Name of the Rose*
and *Foucault's Pendulum*, the novels of Joseph McElroy and Christine
Brooke-Rose, avant-garde works such as Kathy Acker's *Empire of the
Senseless*, and works of cyberpunk science-fiction by William Gibson,
Bruce Sterling, Lewis Shiner, Rudy Rucker and others. Although mainly
focused on "high" or "elite" cultural products – "art" novels – *Constructing Postmodernism* relates these products to such phenomena of postmodern popular culture as television and the cinema, paranoia and nuclear
anxiety, angelology and the cybernetic interface, and death, now as always
(in spite of what Captain Kirk says) the true Final Frontier.

McHale's previous book, *Postmodernist Fiction*, had seemed to propose a
single, all-inclusive inventory of postmodernist poetics. This book, by
contrast, proposes multiple, overlapping and intersecting inventories –
not a construction of postmodernism, but a plurality of constructions.
Constructing Postmodernism will be essential reading for all students of
contemporary literature and culture.

Brian McHale is Senior Lecturer in Poetics and Comparative Literature
at Tel-Aviv University, and Co-Editor of *Poetics Today*.

Constructing postmodernism

Brian McHale

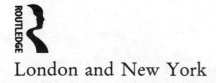

London and New York

First published 1992
by Routledge
11 New Fetter Lane, London EC4P 4EE

Simultaneously published in the USA and Canada
by Routledge
29 West 35th Street, New York, NY 10001

© 1992 Brian McHale

Phototypeset in 10 on 12 point Garamond by
Intype, London
Printed in Great Britain by
T.J. Press (Padstow) Ltd, Padstow, Cornwall.

British Library Cataloguing in Publication Data
McHale, Brian
    Constructing Postmodernism
    I. Title
    306

Library of Congress Cataloging in Publication Data

McHale, Brian,
    Constructing postmodernism / Brian McHale.
    p.   cm.
    Includes bibliographical references and index.
    1. Fiction—20th century—History and criticism.
    2. Postmodernism (Literature)
    3. Science fiction—20th century—History and
    criticism. I. Title.
    PN3503.M37 1992
    809.3′04—dc20   92–16210

ISBN 0–415–06013–3   ISBN 0–415–06014–1 (pbk)

For Clara Siepmann and Dorothy McHale Chambers
and in memory of
Herman A. Siepmann 1900–89

Contents

Part 3 Reading postmodernists

Part 4 At the interface

Acknowledgments

My debts are many; the space in which to acknowledge them, confined; the chances of my acknowledging them as they deserve to be acknowledged, slight.

In the case of essays already published elsewhere (in every case in a different version from the present one), I wish to thank the respective editors for having accepted the essays in the first place, and for granting permission to reprint them here:

Chapter 1, originally published in *Poetics Today* 9, 3 (1988), 545–71. Another, shorter version has appeared under the title, "Some Postmodernist Stories," in Theo D'Haen and Hans Bertens (eds) (1988) *Postmodern Fiction in Europe and the Americas*, Amsterdam: Rodopi, 13–25.

Chapter 2, originally published in *Style* 24, 1 (Spring 1990), 1–21.

Chapter 3, originally published in *Poetics Today* 1, 1–2 (Autumn 1979), 85–110. Reprinted in Arno Heller (ed.) (1987) *Der Amerikanische Roman nach 1945*, Darmstadt: Wissenschaftliche Buchgesellschaft, 415–45.

Chapter 4, originally published in *Language and Style* 18, 1 (Winter 1985), 93–118.

Chapter 6, originally published in *Hebrew University Studies in Literature and Art* 17 (1989), 1–35.

Chapter 8, originally published in *Review of Contemporary Fiction* 10, 1 (Spring 1990), 227–47.

Chapter 10, originally published in Larry McCaffery (ed.) (1991), *Storming the Reality Studio: A Casebook of Cyberpunk and Postmodern Science Fiction*, Durham, NC: Duke University Press, 308–23.

Chapter 11, originally published in *Critique* 33, 3 (1992), under the title "Elements of a Poetics of Cyberpunk," 149–75.

Chapters 5 and 8 began as book-reviews of Pynchon's *Vineland* and McElroy's *Women and Men*, commissioned by Ron Sukenick for *The American Book Review*. Chapters 7 and 9 have never before appeared in print in any version.

The publishers and I would like to acknowledge gratefully permission to use the following copyright material:

Pages 38–41. "Post-Modernism" from *Free Agents* by Max Apple. Copyright © 1984 by Max Apple. Reprinted by permission of HarperCollins Publishers.

Page 95. From "Paradoxes and Oxymorons" in *Shadow Train* by John Ashbery (New York: Viking Penguin, 1981). Copyright © 1980, 1981 by John Ashbery. Reprinted by permission of Georges Borchardt, Inc. for the author.

Page 115. From "Tower of Song" from the album *I'm Your Man* by Leonard Cohen. Copyright © 1988 by Leonard Cohen Stranger Music, Inc. Used by permission. All rights reserved.

Pages 239, 240–1. From *Neuromancer* by William Gibson. Copyright © 1984 by William Gibson. Reprinted by permission of the Berkley Publishing Group.

Pages 240, 241–2. From *Empire of the Senseless* by Kathy Acker. Copyright © 1988 by Kathy Acker. Reprinted by permission of Grove Weidenfeld.

Every attempt has been made to obtain permission to reproduce copyright material. If there are any omissions please contact Janice Price at Routledge's London Office.

For invitations to speak on topics that later became the subjects of some of these essays, I wish to thank Wladimir Krysinski (Chapter 2), Dennis Kurzon (Chapter 6), and Richard Kaplan and Joris Vlasselaers (Chapter 10).

For information, insight, encouragement and assistance of more varied kinds than I can easily enumerate, I wish to thank all of the following people: Sonja Bašić, Richard Lehan, and Yael Renan (Chapter 2); Ron Hankison and Douglas Young (Chapter 3); Sally Jacoby and Colin Nicholson (Chapter 4); Richard Shusterman (Chapter 5); Lilach Lachman, Joseph McElroy, Steven Moore, and Tamar Yacobi (Chapter 8); Christine Brooke-Rose and Richard Martin (Chapter 9); Thomas Disch (Chapter 10); Martin Melaver (Chapters 2, 5 and 7); John Cartmell (Chapters 3, 10 and 11); Randall Stevenson (Chapters 3 and 4); Tamar Hager (Chapters 6 and 7); Clem Robins (Chapters 7 and 10); Larry McCaffery and James Douglas McHale (Chapters 10 and 11). The usual disclaimer applies: these people can only be held responsible for whatever, if anything, might be of value in these essays; the stupidities are all my own.

Two of these essays were written under extraordinary circumstances, away from home; so I wish especially to thank, for hospitality, change of venue, and safe haven, Ziva and Haimke Ben-Porat and the members of Kibutz Re'im, Northern Negev, who hosted us during the time I was drafting Chapter 4; and the Ravino family, especially Haim, Ora, and Shai, and their fellow townspeople of Yesud Hama'ala, Upper Galilee, who gave us sanctuary in the emergency of January through March 1991, during which I somehow drafted Chapter 5.

Finally, my thanks to George Milner and Claire McHale Milner for taking us to an exhibition at Penn State that they rightly guessed would appeal to our postmodernist sensibilities, thereby introducing me to the paintings of Robert Yarber; and to Sanford Sivitz Shaman, organizer of that exhibition and author of the exhibition catalogue, for further information and insight into the painter I have come to regard as the best of his (and my) generation.

It seems redundant somehow to acknowledge Esther, Alma, and Lily, since we're all in this together – never more so than during those strange, anxious hours of January and February 1991 when, breathing through gasmasks, we sat listening to radio broadcasts harder to believe than reports of an invasion from Mars, and waited for the all-clear to sound. This is one postmodernist experience I do not recommend: writing about Pynchon during the day, spending the night listening for air raid sirens . . .

Introducing constructing

CONSTRUCTIVISM, OR, DOES POSTMODERNISM EXIST?

No doubt there "is" no such "thing" as postmodernism. Or at least there is no such thing if what one has in mind is some kind of identifiable object "out there" in the world, localizable, bounded by a definite outline, open to inspection, possessing attributes about which we can all agree. But postmodernism's failure to satisfy the criteria of objecthood is one it shares with other interesting and valuable cultural artifacts, such as, for example, "the Renaissance" or "American literature" or "pastoral elegy" or "Shakespeare." Like these other artifacts, postmodernism exists discursively, in the discourses we produce *about* it and *using* it. The word "postmodernism," as Alan Thiher says, "has become a counter in our language games" (Thiher 1984:227), and in that sense, if in no other, postmodernism does indeed exist.

One such language game in which the word "postmodernism" figured as a counter was a book called *Postmodernist Fiction* (McHale 1987). There the present writer sought to invest the term with a certain definite semantic substance, and to persuade others to understand the concept in the way he had come to understand it and to use the term as he used it. In that book, too, I insisted on the discursive and constructed character of postmodernism, though perhaps not often enough or memorably enough, since some readers (see, e.g., Connor 1989:124–6) seem to have come away thinking I had attributed to postmodernism the kind of "fixed essence" that Alan Thiher rightly denies to it. This is a rhetorical problem (though not a "merely" rhetorical one): how to persuade the reader to entertain a particular construction of postmodernism while at the same time preserving a sense of the provisionality, the "as if" character, of all such constructions? Inevitably (or so it seems), in the course of an exposition devoted to substantiating one particular construction of postmodernism, the constructivist emphasis itself tends to get lost. There is a delicate balance to be maintained between advocating a particular version of constructed reality and entertaining a plurality of versions, and it may be that *Postmodernist Fiction* failed to maintain that balance.

The present book aspires to get the balance right; or at least to make explicit what evidently remained too implicit in its predecessor. To this end it wears its constructivism on its sleeve – or rather, in its title. By "constructivism" I mean something like the constructivist epistemology whose consequences for literary study Siegfried Schmidt has explored (Schmidt 1984, 1985; for other, more or less compatible versions, see, e.g., Berger and Luckmann 1966; Goodman 1978; Rorty 1982). Constructivism's basic epistemological principle is that *all* our cognitive operations, including (or especially) perception itself, are theory-dependent. This means, first of all, that data do not exist independently of a theory that constitutes them *as* data; they are not so much "given" as "taken," seized. "A datum," writes Schmidt, " . . . is but a datum 'in the light of' the theoretical framework of a particular observer" (1985:282). Or, as Goodman puts it, facts "are theory-laden; they are as theory-laden as we hope our theories are fact-laden" (1978:96–7).

Granted the theory-dependency of "facts," it follows that faithfulness to objective "truth" cannot be a criterion for evaluating versions of reality (since the truth will have been produced by the version that is being evaluated by its faithfulness to the truth, and so on, circularly). The appropriate criteria for evaluation now are, for instance, the explicitness of the version; its intersubjective accessibility; its "empirical-mindedness," i.e. its aspiration to be as empirical as possible, where empiricism is not a method but a *horizon* to be approached only asymptotically; and, above all, the adequacy of the version to its intended purpose (Schmidt 1985:285, 292, 298). In other words, constructions, or what I have been calling versions of reality, are *strategic* in nature, that is, designed with particular purposes in view.

In the particular case of those constructs we call literary histories (of which the present book and its predecessor are both, in different ways, examples), the constructivist approach focuses our attention on the problem of *concatenating* data into coherent larger units, such as "periods," "schools," "genres," etc. (Schmidt 1985:282). These too, of course, are constructs; "postmodernism" is one of them. So, too, for that matter is "literature" itself.[1] Literary histories, Schmidt concludes, "are *constructions* and not reconstructions, and . . . the work of the literary historian is constructive through and through." Moreover, "literary histories exist but not *literary history*" (Schmidt 1985:294); that is, literary-historical versions cannot be reduced to a single, univocal version, but must remain irreducibly plural.

Postmodernist Fiction perhaps seemed to propose a single, all-inclusive inventory of features or characteristics of postmodernist writing, and a single corpus of texts, and seemed to aspire (however inadequately) to encyclopedic exhaustiveness. By contrast, *Constructing Postmodernism* proposes multiple, overlapping and intersecting inventories and multiple corpora; not *a* construction of postmodernism, but a plurality of constructions; constructions that, while not necessarily mutually contradictory, are not fully integrated, or perhaps even integrable, either. In other words, the present book, much more so than its predecessor, tries to acknowledge (however feebly) what Robert Venturi (1977) has called "the obligation toward the difficult whole."

I choose to regard the "imperfect" integration of these essays as illustration and corroboration of the point I have tried to make throughout this book about the plurality of possible constructions in literary history (and cultural studies generally) and the strategic nature of construction. I wish I could pretend that I set out programmatically to produce a plurality of constructions; unfortunately, it was not as deliberate as that. However, having recognized *post factum* that these essays *do* possess this kind of plurality, I have not sought to reduce multiplicity by imposing upon it some (arbitrary) uniformity of model; rather, I have let the multiplicity stand, as appropriate to the book's thesis. In fact, not only have I not tried to suppress or resolve inconsistencies or contradictions (apparent or real) between chapters, I have occasionally even called attention to them.[2]

If literary-historical "objects" such as postmodernism are constructed, not given or found, then the issue of *how* such objects are constructed, in particular the genre of discourse *in which* they are constructed, becomes crucial. For, as Schmidt observes (1985:283–4), the relations to be constructed among the "data" depend intimately on the genre of their presentation. Narrative, Schmidt reminds us, has been the preferred genre of literary histories, but it is not the only possible genre of literary history, and one could imagine literary history that used some alternative mode of discourse (e.g. collage or montage, argumentation, etc.; Schmidt 1985:283–4, 297).

Nevertheless, I have come to prefer narrative constructions of literary history, here and elsewhere. In *Postmodernist Fiction*, I told a story about how, through a change in the structuring of texts, the modernist poetics of fiction gave way to postmodernist poetics. In the present introduction, I have been telling a story about how the book before you continues and extends the preoccupations of its predecessor, while also aspiring to correct some of the latter's shortcomings. I propose to keep right on telling stories until the end of this book. Schmidt, however, has suggested that narrative, just because it is the normative mode for constructing history, including literary history, ought perhaps to be abandoned in favor of alternative genres (Schmidt 1985:297). So, before going any further, I must pause to defend my decision to narrate.

NARRATIVE TURNS

Once upon a time there used to be narratology, which had aspirations to be the science of narrative. Whatever happened to it? "It got swallowed into story," Christine Brooke-Rose answers (Brooke-Rose 1991:16). And therein lies a tale.

For something like two decades, beginning with the ferment of Parisian structuralist narratology in the sixties (Barthes, Bremond, Genette, Greimas, Todorov) and parallel developments elsewhere (e.g. in Israel), narrative was a favored, perhaps *the* favored, object of literary theorizing. The passing of that era seems to have been signalled by the consolidation of narratology in the eighties in a series of handbooks[3] and synoptic surveys of the state of the art.[4] The appearance of such publications indicates, at the very least, the end of the exciting phase of paradigm-building and the onset of "normal science." Lately the tables have been turned, and instead of narrative being the object of narratological theory, it is theory that has become the object of narrative: where once we had theories about narrative, we begin now to have stories about theory.

But that is not the whole story (so to speak), because while narrative has tended to displace narratology in its "home" discipline, namely literary studies, narratology has responded to its displacement by leaving home, emigrating to adjacent disciplines where the findings of narratological research, far from seeming outdated, still make news (see Bal 1990; Barry 1990; Nash 1990). So story, in one form or another, whether as object *of* theory or as the alternative *to* theory, seems to be everywhere. Historiography (LaCapra 1985; White 1987), psychology (Spence 1982; Bruner 1986), philosophy (Rorty 1982, 1985, 1989), sociology (Brown 1987), economics (McCloskey 1990), and many other fields and disciplines of the human sciences – all have recently been affected by what Christopher Norris (1985) has called the "narrative turn" of theory. It is indicative that the editors of a recent volume of conference papers on "Objectivity and Science" (Lawson and Appignanesi 1989) would choose to use "stories" in titles where once they would have used "theories": "Stories About Science," "Stories About Truth," "Stories About Representation," even (what else?) "Stories About Stories." A number of theorists (or what we would once have called theorists), some from within the literary discipline, others "outsiders," have been influential in getting us to think in terms of "telling stories" rather than "doing theory," among them Richard Rorty, Fredric Jameson, and Jean-François Lyotard.

The narrative turn would seem to be one of the contemporary responses to the loss of metaphysical "grounding" or "foundations" for our theorizing. We are no longer confident that we can build intellectual structures upward from firm epistemological and ontological foundations. We suspect, with Nelson Goodman (1978), that, while there may well be somewhere a "world" underlying all our disparate versions of it, that world is finally inaccessible, and all we have are the versions; but that hardly matters, since it is only the versions that are of any use to us anyway, and the putative world-before-all-versions is, as Rorty (1982) says, "well lost." Nevertheless, there is a problem here: lacking foundations, how are we to proceed? "A postmodernist cannot build a foundation before constructing a construction," writes William S. Wilson; paradoxically, "foundation is constructed and strengthened by what is built upon it" (Wilson 1989:27, 14). Narrative in particular recommends itself as a means of building foundations by constructing constructions because storytelling (at least in its traditional forms) bears within it its own (provisional) self-grounding, its own (local, limited) self-legitimation (Lyotard 1984b; cf. Brown 1987:170–1; Tyler 1987:216).

It is in the spirit of this response to the so-called legitimation crisis that Stephen Tyler has made his extraordinary claim that today ethnography is the "superordinate discourse to which all other discourses are relativized and in which they find their meaning and justification" (1987:199). In a postmodern situation in which science, in particular, is no longer able to legitimate itself by appealing to metaphysical foundations, it is only through the ethnographic context of scientific practice that science can hope to ground itself, and that context is available to us only through the discourse of ethnography, the foundational discourse of the postmodern world (Tyler 1987:200) – or, at any rate, what the postmodern world has in lieu of foundational discourse. However, when Tyler speaks of ethnographic discourse he is clearly thinking not of present models of "scientific" ethnography, but something different, a postmodern ethnography which would be a good deal more like story-telling: "a story of sorts," "cooperative story making" (Tyler 1987:203). This ethnographic narrative discourse, stories about theorizing and in place of theorizing, would nevertheless be local and provisional, not some kind of all-mastering meta-narrative or "story of stories" (Tyler 1987:208) in which postmoderns have found they can no longer believe.[5]

For the narrative turn of theory has also provoked a counter-reaction, the most conspicuous symptom of which is what might be called the "anxiety of metanarratives." It all begins with Lyotard, who has persuaded us that metanarratives or master-narratives ("grands récits"), the various stories (Enlightenment, Marxist, Hegelian) about human emancipation and progress that once served to ground and legitimate knowledge, are no longer credible (1984b). In the hands of epigonic thinkers, Lyotard's description has been turned into a prescription: avoid at all costs the appearance of endorsing metanarratives (since nobody believes in them any more); or, more briefly: avoid story; don't narrate. Moreover, the thesis of "incredulity toward metanarratives" has been turned against its originator. Linda Hutcheon, for instance, accuses Lyotard of having produced "an obviously meta-narrative theory of postmodernism's incredulity to meta-narrative" (Hutcheon 1988:198). In a similar vein, though more cruelly, John Mepham has written that Lyotard "tells a simple tale about the naivety of tale-telling, grandly narrativizes his incredulity towards grand narratives" (Mepham 1991:147).

In a situation in which we are being urged to "just say no" to narrative, and where even attempting to describe the situation is likely to draw accusations of metanarrating, it is hard to see how one is to avoid succumbing to a paralyzing anxiety *not to be seen to narrate*. One corrective to this anxiety would be simply to deny that there are now or have ever been metanarratives (see Montag 1988:95). In others words, despite what it may claim about itself, no self-professed metanarrative (including, e.g., the Marxist one) has ever been other than a first-order narrative with pretensions above its station, just one more story like all the others and not any kind of masterful "story of stories." Just like all the other stories, every putative metanarrative is conditioned by the situation of its telling, the identity and interests of its tellers and audience, the purpose for which it was told, and so on.

Another approach would be to learn to "tolerate the anxiety" (Barthelme 1976:119). This would involve admitting that, since there is no escaping metanarratives anyway, one might as well go ahead and tell one's story. To undertake to make sense of a complex phenomenon such as postmodern culture is inevitably to tell some kind of story about it, and that story will inevitably be implicated in some metanarrative or other. Rather than letting one's discourse be shaped, or rather deformed, by the desire to evade and deflect accusations of metanarrativity, better to try to tell as good a story as possible, one that makes the richest possible sense of the phenomenon in question and provokes the liveliest possible critical scrutiny, controversy, counter-proposals and (yes, why not?) counter-stories. This, I gather, is something like Fredric Jameson's attitude, when he writes,

> I have proposed a "model" of postmodernism, which is worth what it's worth and must now take its chances independently; but it is the construction of such a model that is ultimately the fascinating matter, and I hope it will not be taken as a knee-jerk affirmation of "pluralism" if I say that alternate constructions are desirable and welcome, since the grasping of the present from within is the most problematical task the mind can face.
>
> (Jameson 1989:383–4)

This was my own approach in *Postmodernist Fiction*, and it is again here, where, acknowledging the inevitability of metanarratives, I have sought only to "demote" them if possible to "little" or "minor" narratives, that is, to endorse them but only provisionally and locally, and otherwise to learn to tolerate the anxiety.

As the father of two young daughters, I am in a sense a professional storyteller – and not just at bedtime, either, but whenever world-knowledge of whatever kind (the day's program, neighborhood gossip, family and personal history, the political situation) needs to be organized and transmitted. No doubt my experience reflects what many thinkers today have come to believe, namely that "one of the ways human beings assess and interpret the events of their life is through the construction of plausible narratives," or even that "narrative is the form of intelligible discourse proper to human life" (Bernstein 1990).[6] Moreover, I have in recent years become increasingly aware of the degree to which I am also a storyteller in my "other" profession, that of university lecturer.[7] A lecture, particularly if it is about literary history (my usual subject), is a story; an entire course of lectures is a long, complicated story with many episodes and sub-plots. Reflecting on the role of narrative in the organiz-ation and transmission of literary-historical knowledge, I have come more and more to emphasize the narrativity, the story-telling character, of my own pedagogical practice. I begin most courses by reminding my students that literary history is, by definition, a narrative discipline, and that we are here to tell cooperatively (in Tyler's sense of "cooperative story making") what we hope will be a "good" story about (say) the relations between the British and American literary systems during a specified period. I often invite my students to reflect on "the story so far" – its intelligibility, its persuasiveness; and I insist on the multiplicity of possible alternative or competing stories, and seek to develop criteria for distin-guishing better literary-historical narratives from less good ones.

Of course, it is also possible to construct literary-historical knowledge in other than narrative forms – for instance, in "spatialized" forms. Thus, instead of a story, one could readily imagine organizing a literary history in the form of a list or anthology of canonical texts (or for that matter, of marginalized or un- or counter-canonical texts). Alternatively, one could organize it in the form of parallel lists of contrasting or opposed features: in the left-hand column, the defining features of period A; in the right-hand column, the contrasting features that define period B. Thus, for example:

Hierarchy	Anarchy
Presence	Absence
Genital	Polymorphous
Narrative	Anti-narrative
Metaphysics	Irony
Determinacy	Indeterminacy

Construction of a   Deconstruction of a
    world-model   world-model
Ontological certainty   Ontological uncertainty

(Lethen 1986:235)

In this particular spatialized representation of history, the left-hand column shows the features of modernism, with the contrasting features of post-modernism on the right.[8]

Yet in a certain sense spatialized forms of representation are only, like written music, notations for a potential performance – in this case, the performance of a narrative. A canon always implies a legitimating story and, vice versa, a literary-historical narrative always implies a canon of texts and authors. Similarly, behind the static oppositions of features organized in parallel columns we readily discern the narrative syntax that absorbs, motivates, and dynamizes them. We read the opposed terms as, respectively, initial state and end state in the story of a transformation, from left to right: from Hierarchy to Anarchy, from Presence to Absence, from Metaphysics to Irony, and so on. If we are disposed to be fanciful, perhaps we even go so far as to "read" the white space between the parallel columns as the sign of postmodernism's "rupture" with the mod-ernist past, a kind of visual icon of the historical fault-line separating the periods. In short, narrative forms of intelligibility are harder to repress than one might have supposed, and even spatialized representations of literary history turn out to be implicitly stories.

THE STORY SO FAR

In terms of E.M. Forster's memorable distinction, the story I told in *Postmodernist Fiction* constituted a plot.[9] That is, it not only arranged events in temporal sequence – first modernist poetics, then postmodernist poetics – but supplied a *causal motivation* for the sequence: first modern-ism, then, *because of* a change of dominant, postmodernism.[10] Of course, causes are always themselves the effects of other, deeper or more ultimate causes. Thus, the shift of dominance from epistemology to ontology, in my narrative the cause of which postmodernism is the effect, could in its turn be motivated as the effect of a further cause. It could, for instance, be seen as symptomatic of the epistemological crisis of the old "bourgeois subject," and the emergence from that crisis of a new, disintegrative postmodern subjectivity and a new sense of the world as restlessly plural. This, of course, is something like Fredric Jameson's story of postmodern-ism as the cultural logic of late capitalism (see Jameson 1991b).[11] I do not see that this higher-level, motivating metanarrative is incompatible with the story I have chosen to tell; but I have preferred to remain at a lower level of narrative motivation, in hopes that any loss in scope and explanatory power will have been compensated for by a closer, finer-grained engagement with the mechanisms of postmodernist texts themselves.

I have by no means abandoned the story of *Postmodernist Fiction* here, and in fact it is retold below not once but several times, in various ways, notably in Chapter 1. However, I have also tried to leave room throughout for alternatives to my own story, in particular for the stories I happen to find (after my own, of course) most persuasive, namely Dick Higgins's (1978 and 1984) and Alan Wilde's (1981). Introduced in Chapter 1, Wilde's story about the "worldliness" or "this-worldliness" of postmodernist fiction returns (somewhat to my own surprise, I confess) at the conclusion of Chapter 7. Other stories featured alongside my own, and serving to complicate the picture, include the one about postmodernism as "double-coding," told in various ways and with differing inflections by Barth, Eco, Hutcheon, and Jencks (Chapters 1 and 6); the one about the effacement of the hierarchical distinction between "high" and "low" culture in the postmodernist period, a story identified especially with Huyssen and Jameson (Chapter 10); and even a story, told by Jameson and by Harvey (1989), according to which modernism and postmodernism are not period styles at all, one of them current and the other outdated, but more like alternative stylistic options between which contemporary writers are free to choose without that choice necessarily identifying them as either "avant-garde" or "arrière-garde" (Chapters 8 and 9).

"Postmodernist" in the title of my first essay, "Telling postmodernist stories," is deliberately ambiguous: on the one hand, these are stories *about* postmodernism; on the other hand, as stories that in some sense do the work of theories, they themselves also *belong to* postmodernism. This essay explicitly addresses the constructed ("as if") character of post-modernism. It endorses Christopher Norris's account of the "narrative turn" of postmodernist thought, and proposes a narrative construction of postmodernism, a story about the "postmodernist breakthrough." Several versions of this story have already been told, and no doubt there are other versions that could be told, so it is important to distinguish among better and less good stories – "better" not in the sense of objectively *truer* (a criterion discredited by the constructivist approach), but in terms of such criteria as rightness of fit, validity of inference, internal consistency, appropriateness of scope, and above all *productivity*. Two versions of the break-through narrative are scrutinized, one John Barth's familiar story about exhaustion and replenishment, the other Dick Higgins's much less familiar one about cognitivism and postcognitivism, and Higgins's is found to satisfy the criteria for a good story better than Barth's. The entire exposition is framed by a close reading of a short fiction/essay by Max Apple, "Post-Modernism," reprinted in an appendix to the chapter.

In *Postmodernist Fiction*, Joyce's *Ulysses* was treated as an exemplary modernist text. Chapter 2, "Constructing (post)modernism: the case of

Ulysses," reopens and problematizes this issue of the modernism of *Ulysses.* In fact, *Ulysses* is (or ought to be) a literary-historical scandal. Split roughly down the middle, its first half has long served as a norm for "High Modernist" poetics, while only recently have we begun to regard its second half as normatively postmodernist. How can the same text both inaugurate "High Modernism" and belong to postmodernism? The awkward case of *Ulysses* makes it clear that any accounts we choose to give of the relations between modernism and postmodernism are only constructs, that there can be no strictly objective criteria for preferring one construct over its competitors, and that, on the contrary, choices among competing constructs can only be made strategically, in the light of the kind of work that the chosen construct might be expected to accomplish.

Pynchon, for me as for many other students of postmodernist literature, is like the episode of the looking-glass house from *Through the Looking-Glass:* try as one might to turn one's back on him and walk away, one always ends up walking right in through his front door again anyway. This is just what has happened, I find, in the essays in this book that are *not* specifically devoted to Pynchon's texts: there he is, time and again, especially *Gravity's Rainbow,* whatever the announced topic might be. The only solution, it seems, is the one Alice finally hit upon, namely, to approach Pynchon head-on (or as nearly head-on as the special difficulties of his texts permit), and then one has some chance of finally reaching the hilltop, from where it is possible to survey the entire countryside. This is the strategy of the three essays, two on *Gravity's Rainbow,* one on *Vineland,* that make up the second part of this book.

Chapters 3 and 4 focus on "the uses of uncertainty" in *Gravity's Rainbow.* The first of these essays, "Modernist Reading, Postmodernist Text: The Case of *Gravity's Rainbow,"* incorporates a tentative first draft of the opposition between the epistemological and ontological dominants later developed more fully in *Postmodernist Fiction.* The second Pynchon essay, " 'You used to know what these words mean': misreading *Gravity's Rainbow,"* focuses on the indeterminacies of the second-person pronoun which effectively undermine overly-confident readings of Pynchon's text. Chapter 5, "Zapping, the art of switching channels," is devoted to *Vineland* (1990), Pynchon's first novel in seventeen years, to date the only successor to *Gravity's Rainbow.* More accurately, this essay uses *Vineland* as the pretext for reflecting on the place of television in postmodernist fiction, in particular its double role as metaphor or model of postmodern culture and as *mise-en-abyme* of the postmodernist text itself.

The first four essays (on postmodernist metanarratives, *Ulysses,* and *Gravity's Rainbow*) are rather intensively preoccupied with the discourse of critical interpretation, and what it tells us about periodization (among other things). To put it differently, these chapters are in part concerned with *institutions of reading*, including the institution of literary criticism. Thereafter this preoccupation subsides somewhat, though it never entirely disappears from the later chapters. In Part 3, the focus shifts to a different level of story-telling: from the story of the historical succession of periods (the preoccupation especially of Part 1) to the story (which may or may not be coordinated with the periodization narrative) of the succession of phases in an author's career or *oeuvre*.[12]

Closest in approach to the essay on *Ulysses* (Chapter 2) is the one on Eco's *The Name of the Rose* (Chapter 6); they are in effect sibling essays, a fact which Eco, himself a Joycean (among many other things), would, I trust, appreciate. This essay examines *The Name of the Rose* in the light both of the literary-historical problematics developed in Part 1, and of Eco's own well-known reflections on modernism and postmodernism. *The Name of Rose* is found to be an "amphibious" text, queasily poised between modernism and postmodernism. Ultimately, the very question "Modernist or postmodernist?" is shown to be misguided, and *The Name of the Rose* comes to be seen not as a puzzle to be solved but rather as a challenge to the entire enterprise of distinguishing period styles, perhaps, indeed, to the entire enterprise of literary historiography.

At the close of Chapter 6, I suggest that whether we found Eco's career and *oeuvre* narratively intelligible or not, and if so in what way, would depend on what he would do next after *The Name of the Rose*. Since that essay was written, of course, Eco has published his second novel, *Foucault's Pendulum* (1988), and so I have devoted a separate chapter to *Foucault's Pendulum* and its implications for the story of Eco's career as a postmodernist.

Chapter 8, "Women and men and angels," turns to the less familiar novels of Joseph McElroy: *A Smuggler's Bible* (1966), *Hind's Kidnap* (1969), *Lookout Cartridge* (1974), *Plus* (1979), and above all his massive (1200–page), synoptic *magnum opus, Women and Men* (1987).[13] *Women and Men* is characterized here (in a Shklovskyan gesture of provocation) as the most typical novel of contemporary literature. This is so, if in no other respect, then at least in the sense that it seems to recapitulate three successive periods in the poetics of fiction, realism, modernism, and (perhaps) postmodernism. This recapitulation is not "horizontal" – realist, modernist and postmodernist segments joined end-to-end, somewhat in the manner of *Ulysses* – but "vertical," in superimposed strata, like a literary-historical layer-cake. In the end, doubt is cast on the postmodernism of the "postmodernist" stratum of *Women and Men*; reasons are given for thinking of *Women and Men* as late-modernist rather than "fully" or "properly" postmodernist.[14]

Like Pynchon, Christine Brooke-Rose had already figured conspicuously, but dispersedly, in *Postmodernist Fiction*. Chapter 9, " 'I draw the line as a rule between one solar system and another': the postmodernism(s) of Christine Brooke-Rose," gives me the opportunity to assemble the dispersed fragments of my treatment of Brooke-Rose into a sustained reading of her fiction from *Out* (1964) through *Verbivore* (1990). The case of Brooke-Rose also gives me the opportunity to correct the misleadingly "progressivist" tenor of my account of literary history in *Postmodernist Fiction*. For, unlike the exemplary authors whose career trajectories I traced at the beginning and end of that book (Beckett, Robbe-Grillet, Fuentes, Coover, Nabokov, Pynchon, and Joyce), Brooke-Rose's career does not follow a smooth course from modernism through a transitional late-modernist phase to postmodernism. Rather, her novels of the sixties and seventies *alternate* between modernist and postmodernist poetics, in a way that is not adequately accounted for in terms of "regression" to a less "advanced" aesthetic. The case of Brooke-Rose's fiction compels us to see modernism and postmodernism as two equally "innovative" or "advanced" alternatives which our historical situation makes available to contemporary writers.[15]

The transition from the "advanced" and "difficult" writers I discuss in Part 3 (the Eco of *Foucault's Pendulum*, McElroy, Brooke-Rose) to the science-fiction writers of Part 4 might at first glance appear abrupt and weakly motivated, as though the SF material had been casually tacked onto a book otherwise very different in orientation. In fact, however, there are many connections linking Part 4 to the rest of the book, most of all to the essay on Brooke-Rose, who several times in her career (in *Out* and *Such*, later on in *Xorandor* and *Verbivore*) has turned to science fiction for motifs, materials, images and language. More generally, I find science fiction to be one of the places where elite (or "art") fiction "interfaces" most actively with popular (or "entertainment") fiction in the postmodern period.

I devoted a chapter to science fiction in *Postmodernist Fiction*, and since then my conviction has grown that SF, far from being marginal to contemporary "advanced" or "state-of-the-art" writing, may actually be *paradigmatic* of it. This is so in at least two respects. First, SF is openly and avowedly ontological in its orientation, i.e., like "mainstream" postmodernist writing it is self-consciously "world-building" fiction, laying bare the process of fictional world-making itself. Secondly, SF constitutes a particularly clear and demonstrable example of an intertextual field, one in which models, materials, images, "ideas," etc. circulate openly from text to text, and are conspicuously cited, analyzed, combined, revised, and reconfigured. In this it differs from "mainstream" postmodernism only in the openness and visibility of the process. It is precisely this relative openness of intertextual circulation in SF that makes it so valuable as a heuristic model of literature in general, and postmodernist literature in particular.

Everything that makes SF a paradigm of contemporary writing at large

is present, if anything even more conspicuously, in the fiction of the latest
SF generation, so-called "cyberpunk" SF. In fact, if cyberpunk did not
exist, postmodernist critics like myself would have had to invent it.

Perhaps we did, in a sense. Certainly, cyberpunk science fiction seems
to be on the postmodernist critical agenda. If it had not been there before,
it has surely made it onto that agenda now with the appearance of Jameson's *Postmodernism, or, the Cultural Logic of Late Capitalism* (1991b).
Here Jameson speaks of cyberpunk as "henceforth, for many of us, the
supreme *literary* expression if not of postmodernism, then of late capitalism itself" (Jameson 1991b:417; emphasis is Jameson's own). If I understand the tenor of this somewhat enigmatic note and the other scattered
allusions to cyberpunk (1991b:28, 286, 321), Jameson seems to be identifying cyberpunk as *the* privileged literary manifestation of postmodernism.
Indeed, he seems even to be implying that cyberpunk is somehow the
direct expression of late capitalism itself, almost as though it were unmediated by inherited literary forms or historical genres. If this is what he
means to imply (but perhaps I have misunderstood him here), then he is
mistaken, for, far from being the "direct" expression of anything, cyberpunk is a complex "layering" of mediating forms and genres, a confluence
of literary-historical streams of diverse provenance. In order to "place"
cyberpunk properly in its cultural-historical context it would be necessary
to take into account, at a minimum, two distinct writing practices, on the
one hand, the poetics of traditional science fiction, on the other the poetics
of postmodernist fiction. This is what I have tried to do in Chapters 10
and 11.

My own interest in the relations between cyberpunk SF and postmodernism might be said to date from the moment I noticed what seemed
to be a duplication of scenes between two novels, one a postmodernist
"surfictional" novel by Raymond Federman (*The Twofold Vibration*,
1982), the other a cyberpunk SF novel, one of the earliest, by Rudy
Rucker (*Software*, also 1982). In each, an aging ex-freak arrives at a
spaceport of the near future, full of trepidation at the prospect of traveling
to an off-world colony where some dubious form of immortality (perhaps
indistinguishable from death) has been promised him. "Why doesn't Cyberpunk Fiction admit that it comes out of Surfiction," Federman complains, "or at least the kind of Surfiction that played around (playgiaristically) with S.F.?" (Federman in McCaffery 1988a:38). Obviously *Software*
couldn't have "come out of" *The Twofold Vibration*, at least not directly,
since their publication dates are the same. Furthermore, each of these two
novels draws independently on its own "tradition" and develops out of
its own intertextual field: Federman, out of the exitless spaces of Beckett's
fiction (e.g. "The Lost Ones") and his own autobiographical myth,
repeated in novel after novel, of having survived his own death in the
Holocaust; Rucker, out of what he calls the "beat old clichés" of the SF

genre – "the robots and the brain eaters and the starships" – transformed, under the pressure of cyberpunk's generic self-reflexiveness, into something if not absolutely new, then at least qualitatively different from anything that has come before in the genre (Rucker in McCaffery 1988b:56–7). Nevertheless, Federman does have a point: these two novels do seem to share some common intertextual field, and there does seem to have been some kind of convergence or interaction between cyberpunk and postmodernist fiction. Moreover, Federman is also right when he observes that cyberpunk draws specifically on the kind of postmodernist writing "that played around (playgiaristically) with S.F.," that is, postmodernism that has itself already drawn on the stock of SF motifs and materials. In other words, the traffic between cyberpunk and postmodernism is two-way; and it is to this two-way traffic that the essays on cyberpunk in Chapters 10 and 11 are devoted.

ESSAYING

If I have chosen to refer to the chapters that follow as "essays," this is not because they are particularly "essayistic" in the *belles-lettres* sense, but in order to emphasize their provisional and exploratory nature. They are to be regarded as test borings or samplings, forays into new terrains for purposes of reconnaissance and mapping. Moreover, they are "occasional" essays, in the sense that most, at least in their early versions, were tailored to fit specific occasions, for which they had originally been commissioned. Some began as conference papers ("Modernist Reading" and the essays on Joyce, *The Name of the Rose*, and cyberpunk); other as book reviews (the essays on *Vineland* and Joseph McElroy); one, the essay on Brooke-Rose, was originally commissioned for a book project that sadly failed to materialize. I have sought to preserve the "occasional" quality of these essays as appropriate to the book's theme of provisionality.

The present book differs most markedly from *Postmodernist Fiction* in undertaking full-dress readings of specific works and *oeuvres*. Some reviewers complained of the earlier book that it nowhere demonstrated the adequacy of its model of postmodernism through a sustained reading of a single text. Now such a complaint rests, it seems to me, on a dubious assumption about what poetics is for, namely, that its purpose is to generate new interpretations of texts. Nevertheless, one way to answer such complaints is obviously to undertake readings, such as the ones to be found here, which demonstrate, among other things, the dialectical relationship between "readings" and "poetics." The categories of poetics, including historical poetics – such as, say, the period category "postmodernism" – cannot be "applied" to texts, as tools to raw materials; rather, in the process of reading, the texts' resistances inevitably modify the categories brought to bear on them, re-tooling the tools.

The texts and authors I have chosen to discuss here do not necessarily represent my judgment of the "best" (whatever that could mean) of the postmodernists, or those with the greatest potential staying-power ("able to withstand the test of time"); nor are they even necessarily my personal favorites. Rather, they seem to me in some sense (a sense I have tried to clarify at the beginning of my essay on Joseph McElroy in Chapter 8) the *most typical* texts of postmodernism, or the most *typically postmodernist*; the ones through which, as through a selection of differently-shaped lenses, we get the sharpest, clearest "fix" on postmodernist poetics. Further, each of the texts I discuss seems to generate a kind of magnetic or, better, gravitational field around itself, attracting other texts into orbit around it, some nearer, some farther out. Part of what interests me in these texts is precisely this capacity they have to create their own intertextual fields, and I have sought, typically in the middle sections of these essays, to map selected regions of their fields.

Rereading these essays, I have been struck by the oddly discontinuous and suspensive organization that many of them share. That is, the main line of argument tends to break off at a certain point, and to remain suspended, not resuming again until certain more or less lengthy "blocks" of supporting argumentation or evidence have been maneuvered into place. I call them "blocks" advisedly, for this mode of organizing material might well be an artifact of electronic word-processing, which makes it possible, for instance, to shift blocks of text around freely, to open windows onto other documents, to merge files, etc. In other words, the characteristic organization of these essays might itself be a further example of the "interface" between writing and computer word-processing technology that I discuss below (in Chapter 9 and again in Chapter 10) in the case of postmodernist "interface fiction" (e.g. Hoban's *The Medusa Frequency*, Vollmann's *You Bright and Risen Angels*, Brooke-Rose's "computer tetralogy").

Or, if my metaphors of "blocks" and "suspension" do not quite capture what I imagine to be the oddity of these essays' organization, then perhaps I could speak of them as "spiral" in form. Beginning with a specific, nodal text, they tend to spiral outward, collecting ever-widening sweeps of "incidental" material until, just before the end, they collapse back again into the text from which they set out initially. Among the incidental topics (perhaps not so incidental after all) that have been "swept up" into the essays in this way are television and TV-viewing (Chapter 5), nuclear apocalypse (Chapter 6), paranoia and conspiracy (Chapter 7), angels and angelology (Chapter 8), and everywhere, obsessively I fear, death.

Some of these topics – television, nuclear war, paranoia – have the status of postmodernist topoi, in the sense that they first enter the literary repertoire in the postmodernist period; in this respect, *Constructing Postmodernism* attempts a kind of census, however preliminary and partial, of the specifically postmodernist topic repertoire. Other topics, far from being specific to the postmodernist repertoire, belong to the perennial repertoire of literary topoi, and in this case I have sought to demonstrate why and how postmodernist poetics has appropriated these traditional topoi to its own repertoire. Preeminent among these perennial topics is, of course, death. How postmodernists appropriate death, and to what end, is especially evident in the coupling of death with television, a traditional topos with a specifically postmodernist one, in texts such as Pynchon's *Vineland* (1990), described below in Chapter 5. Postmodernist modelings of death, I conclude, serve us, in lieu of traditional religious models, as imaginative rehearsals for our own personal extinctions, dry runs for what we can each really do once and once only. Thus, my conclusion echoes the poet Joseph Brodsky's in his jacket blurb for Danilo Kiš's death-obsessed *Encyclopedia of the Dead* (Kiš 1989): "Having read this book," Brodsky writes, "one stands a chance of deriving from one's own extinction the comfort of knowing that one has already been here with this Kilroy" – or, if Kilroy seems a bit dated, then let's say with these postmodernist graffiti artists, spray-painting their logos all over death's walls.

Part I

Narrating literary histories

Chapter 1

Telling postmodernist stories

THE FIRST STORY: "POST-MODERNISM"

In quest of a theory of postmodernism, we might turn to a short text by Max Apple with the likely-sounding title of "Post-Modernism" (from *Free Agents*, 1984; see Appendix 1.1). We would be disappointed, for instead of a theory – or at least a manifesto or polemic from which an implicit theory might be inferred – we get a story. Not *much* of a story, granted, and one that starts out rather like an essay ("It's always safe to mention Aristotle in literate company") before settling down into the narrative mode: "having no theory to tell, I will show you a little post-modernism" (Apple 1984:135). This is only the first of a series of disorienting reversals in the relative roles of theory (or "analysis," Apple's other term for it, 137) and story in the course of this text. Indeed, this opening reversal already contains another reversal in it: Apple will not "tell" a theory but will "show" a little postmodernism; but surely one "tells" a story, not a theory, and in any case the sample of postmodernism he "shows" us takes the form of a little story.

Incredulity toward metanarratives

In this disorienting reversibility of story and analysis, as well as its manifest dissatisfaction with theorizing, Apple's text justifies its title after all. For Apple's "Post-Modernism" shares these features with the "postmodernism" of J.-F. Lyotard's influential account (1979; English trans. 1984b). Lyotard, of course, has defined postmodernism as "incredulity toward metanarratives" (1984b:xxiv). Scientific (analytical, theoretical) knowledge, he argues, arose in opposition to "traditional" narrative knowledge. Yet because scientific knowledge is incapable of legitimating itself, of lifting itself up by its own epistemological bootstraps, it has always had to resort for legitimation to certain "grand narratives" *about* knowledge – the Enlightenment narrative of human liberation through knowledge, the Hegelian narrative of the dialectical self-realization of Spirit, the Marxist narrative of revolution and the founding of a classless society, and so on. In our time, according to Lyotard, faith in these and other grand or metanarratives has ebbed, so that knowledge has had to seek its legitimation *locally* rather than universally, in terms of limited language-games and institutions, through what Lyotard calls "little narratives" (1984b:60). Unlike scientific knowledge, "little" or first-order narratives are self-legitimating. They construct their own pragmatics: they assign the participant roles in the circulation of knowledge (addressor, addressee, narrative protagonist), and found the social bond among these participants. They "define what has the right to be said and done in the culture in question, and since they are themselves a part of that culture, they are legitimated by the simple fact that they do what they do" (1984b:23).[1]

Lyotard is not alone in discrediting metanarratives and endorsing self-legitimating "little narratives." For example, we also find Richard Rorty distinguishing in analogous terms between the two ways in which "reflective human beings" give sense to their lives. One is "to describe themselves in immediate relation to a nonhuman reality," i.e., to aspire to objectivity, or scientific knowledge in Lyotard's sense; while the other involves "telling the story of their contribution to a community," i.e. solidarity, or Lyotard's narrative knowledge (Rorty 1985:3).[2] Similarly, Hayden White has recently undertaken the "redemption of narrative" in historiography (White 1987). White vindicates narrative history on the grounds that it serves to test our culture's "systems of meaning production" – systems which, to the embarrassment of "scientific" historians, narrative history shares with myth and literature – against real-world events:

> The historical narrative does not, as narrative, dispel false beliefs about the past, human life, the nature of the community, and so on; what it does is test the capacity of a culture's fictions to endow real events with the kinds of meaning that literature displays to consciousness through its fashioning of patterns of "imaginary" events.
>
> (White 1987:45)

In other words, where Lyotard sees narrative as self-legitimating because of its deep complicity with our culture's social construction of reality, White sees it, for precisely the same reason, as critical and self-critical. Finally, Jerome Bruner has recently sought to confer legitimacy on narrative as a "mode of thought" on a par, epistemologically and ontologically, with the empirico-logical mode of science (Bruner 1986). It is with these and similar developments in mind that Christopher Norris (1985), surveying the intellectual landscape, has claimed to discern a general "narrative turn" of postmodern thought analogous to, but also in some ways undoing, the "linguistic turn" of modern thought earlier in this century. "As the idea gains ground that *all* theory is a species of sublimated narrative, so doubts emerge about the very possibility of *knowledge* as distinct from the various forms of narrative gratification" (Norris 1985:23). This is where Max Apple comes in. Sharing the postmodernist incredulity toward analysis and its legitimating metanarratives which also characterizes Lyotard, Rorty, White, Bruner and others, Apple conspicuously opts for the gratifications of "little narratives" *about* postmodernism in lieu of theories of it.

This is not yet the whole story of Apple's "Post-Modernism," however. There is, after all, "a bit of analysis" (1984:137) in Apple's text, some theorizing amid the storytelling. Despite his suspicion of theorizing, Apple actually does undertake to define the " 'post-modern' attitude" which his little story, he says, demonstrates: "Maybe you would characterize this attitude as a mixture of world weariness and cleverness, an attempt to make you think that I'm half kidding, though you're not quite sure about what" (1984:137). In other words, Apple defines the "postmodern attitude" in terms of what Alan Wilde (1981) has called "suspensive irony." Where the characteristic "disjunctive irony" of modernism sought to master the world's messy contingency from a position above and outside it, postmodernist suspensive irony takes for granted "the ironist's immanence in the world he describes" (Wilde 1981:166) and, far from aspiring to master disorder, simply accepts it. When the writer in Apple's little exemplary story, pondering the likelihood of error in an ad for a $6.97 pocket calculator (battery included), observes that the situation leaves "plenty of room for paranoia and ambiguity, always among the top ten in literary circles" (1984:136), he is naming characteristically *modernist* forms of closure; paranoia and ambiguity are forms of disjunctive irony. But in *making* this remark about paranoia and ambiguity ranking among the literary top ten, the attitude which Apple's narrator displays is characteristically *postmodernist* and suspensive – the attitude of someone who is half kidding, though we are not quite sure about what.

Apple's postmodernist suspensiveness is also evident in the flood of inconsequential detail which all but overwhelms his little story: Target Stores and Woolco and K-Mart and Sears and Penney's and Ward's; a calculator originally priced $49.95, then $9.97, now $6.97; Col. Qaddafi and weight-lifting accidents and Vietnamese wet-nurses and the *National Enquirer*; and so on and so on. Wilde writes, about another postmodernist writer,

> Like the pop artists, [he] puts aside the central modernist preoccupation with epistemology, and it may be the absence of questions about how we know that has operated most strongly to "defamiliarize" his (and their) work. [His] concerns are, rather, ontological in their acceptance of a world that is, willy-nilly, a given of experience.
>
> (Wilde 1981:173)

Or, as Max Apple succinctly puts it in the final sentence of "Post-

Modernism": "Everything is the way it is" (1984:139). Wilde is actually talking about Donald Barthelme in the passage I have quoted, but he might as well be talking about Max Apple, and in fact does talk about Apple in strikingly similar terms elsewhere in the same book (Wilde 1981:132–3, 161–7).

The postmodern breakthrough

But if, as appears to be the case, Wilde and Apple are theorizing and/or telling stories about the same postmodernism, then after all there *is* a metanarrative lurking behind Apple's little story. For Wilde's theory of postmodernism is explicitly inscribed within a metanarrative of change and innovation, the story which Gerald Graff has called "the myth of the postmodern breakthrough" (1979). Once upon a time, so Wilde's story runs, there was modernism, a period style characterized by disjunctive irony and reflecting a crisis of consciousness, the modernists' painful sense of the irreducible gap between their need for order and the disorderliness of reality. Then came "a space of transition" (Wilde 1981:120) – rather less abrupt in Wilde's account than in other versions of the breakthrough myth – which Wilde calls late-modernism, and which he associates with the writing of Christopher Isherwood and Ivy Compton-Burnett. Beyond this threshold lies a strange new world of suspensive irony, in which the pathos of the modernist hunger for order has been attenuated, "turned down" to a less anxious acceptance of the world as "manageably chaotic" (1981:44), and where the new literary emotions are low-key, understated ones. What especially characterizes Donald Barthelme's postmodernist writing, Wilde tells us, is

> the articulation not of the larger, more dramatic emotions to which modernist fiction is keyed but of an extraordinary range of minor, banal dissatisfactions ... Barthelme's stories express not anomie or accidie or dread but a muted series of irritations, frustrations, and bafflements.
>
> (Wilde 1981:170)

This is precisely the emotional tone of Apple's "Post-Modernism":

> In her own life Joyce Carol is undeluded by romantic conventions. Her stories may be formulaic but she knows that the shortness of life, the quirks of fate, the vagaries of love are always the subjects of literature.
> Sometimes her word processor seems less useful than a 19-cent pen. Sometimes she feels like drowning herself in a mud puddle.
> Still she is neither depressed nor morose.
>
> (Apple 1984:138–9)

Wilde's (and presumably Apple's) version of this story differs from other versions of the breakthrough myth in the strangely muted, minor-key character of its brave new world, neither heroically utopian nor tragically dystopian,[3] and, as I have already noted, in the relative gradualness of the transition. Nevertheless, it has much in common with the other versions of this metanarrative, all of which in turn have something in common, as Dominick LaCapra has observed, with the "traditional apocalyptic paradigm." In LaCapra's retelling of it, that metanarrative runs something like this:

> an all but inscrutable (magical, hermetic, religious, archaic, pre-Socratic, savage, medieval, pre-Renaissance – in any event, totally "other") discourse of the past was disrupted at some time by the rise of a scientific, secular, analytic, reductive, referential, logicist . . . discourse that dominates modernity; all we have at present are faint glimmerings of another global turning point in the history of discourse that will give content and meaning to what must be for us a blankly utopian future.
>
> (LaCapra 1985:104)

Versions of this metanarrative have been told, for instance, by T.S. Eliot, where it takes the form of a story about the dissociation of sensibility and its imminent re-association; by Michel Foucault, where it occurs as the story of the emergence and disappearance of the category "Man"; and more recently by Timothy Reiss (1982) and Francis Barker (1984), who in their different ways tell a similar story of the emergence in the seventeenth century of the entire complex of bourgeois subjectivity, textuality, representation, and the Cartesian "mind." Barker's version of the story differs from the others in its *literal* apocalypticism: threatened with annihilation, bourgeois discourse will, Barker fears, contrive to bring the whole world down with it in a real, not discursive, nuclear apocalypse.[4]

So pervasive is this apocalyptic metanarrative of the postmodernist breakthrough that few who address the issue of postmodernism have wholly escaped its influence, including those who are skeptical of it or indifferent to it.[5] Gerald Graff, who gave currency to the phrase "myth of the postmodern breakthrough," is of course one of the skeptics; by calling it a "myth" he implies that it is a delusion, so much mystification. But by attacking the breakthrough story he testifies to its existence *as a myth* in our culture – in other words, as a legitimating metanarrative.

Both David Lodge (1977, 1981) and Christine Brooke-Rose (1981) have proposed accounts of postmodernist writing radically at odds with the breakthrough narrative, construing postmodernism as essentially *parasitic* on earlier modes; nevertheless, the breakthrough scenario seems to insinuate itself into their discourses anyway, as if against their wills. For Lodge, postmodernism is essentially rule-breaking art, and thus ultimately dependent on the persistence of the rules that it sets out to break, as a figure depends upon the ground against which it defines itself. But postmodernist writing breaks the rules of metaphoric and metonymic writing alike, and thus stands outside and apart from the pendulum-like alternation of metaphoric and metonymic modes which, according to Lodge, constitutes the history of twentieth-century writing. Lodge's discourse thus conforms to the postmodernist breakthrough narrative without apparently meaning to.

Similarly, Brooke-Rose seems unable to accommodate postmodernism to her narrative about the varieties of fantastic and quasi-fantastic fiction in the nineteenth and twentieth centuries. Pursuing her story as far as the *nouveau roman* and contemporary science fiction and fantasy, she abandons it abruptly when she comes to (American) postmodernism. Postmodernist fiction, it would appear, does not continue the historical sequence of fictional modes, but rather is parasitic on earlier modes, and so requires a new model for its description, one based not on the principle of hesitation (the underlying principle of fantastic fiction and kindred modes) but on principles of parody and stylization. Ironically, by substituting one model for another in this way and changing her story just at the denouement, Brooke-Rose testifies, if only inadvertently, to postmodernism's radical discontinuity with earlier modes – the breakthrough narrative once again (see McHale 1982.)

In the key of "as if"

Do not suppose, however, that by associating Wilde's and (by implication) Apple's postmodernist stories with this pervasive breakthrough metanarrative I am seeking in some sense to unmask or denounce or deconstruct their discourses. Far from it. I would insist that there is nothing wrong with the so-called myth of the postmodernist breakthrough, including Wilde's and Apple's versions – it makes quite a satisfying story, in fact – but just so long as we divest it of its *authority as* metanarrative. To escape the general postmodernist incredulity toward metanarratives it is only necessary that we regard our *own* metanarrative incredulously, in a certain sense, proffering it tentatively or provisionally, as no more (but no less) than a strategically useful and satisfying fiction, in the key of "as if" (see Vaihinger 1965 (1935)). I am recommending, in other words, that we need not abandon metanarratives – which may, after all, do useful work for us – so long as we "turn them down" from metanarratives to "little narratives," lowering the stakes, much as the postmodernists themselves (in Wilde's and Apple's account of them) turn down modernism and lower its stakes.

This "turning down" or attenuation of metanarrative is undertaken very much in the spirit of Barthelme's program for undoing patriarchy:

Your true task, as a son, is to reproduce every one of the enormities [committed by your father], but in attenuated form. You must become your father, but a paler, weaker version of him. The enormities go with the job, but close study will allow you to perform the job less well than it has previously been done, thus moving toward a golden age of decency, quiet, and calmed fevers. Your contribution will not be a small one, but "small" is one of the concepts you should shoot for . . . Begin by whispering, in front of a mirror, for thirty minutes a day. Then tie your hands behind your back for thirty minutes a day, or get someone else to do this for you. Then, choose one of your most deeply held beliefs, such as the belief that your honors and awards have something to do with you, and abjure it. Friends will help you abjure it, and can be telephoned if you begin to backslide. You see the pattern, put it into practice. *Fatherhood can be, if not conquered, at least "turned down" in this generation* – by the combined efforts of all of us together. Rejoice.

(Barthelme 1982b (1975): 270–1)

I take it that a similar program of deliberate attenuation of the "strong" claims of metaphysical foundationalism characterizes recent developments in Italian philosophy, so-called *pensiero debole*, "weak thought" (see Rosso 1987; Borradori 1987/8).

Instead of taking metanarratives at their own valuation, I am advocating "trivializing" them, in a certain sense, so that instead of a Hegelian metanarrative we have a "little" or minor Hegelianism, instead of a Marxist metanarrative we have a minor Marxism – and instead of postmodernist apocalypticism we have a minor apocalypticism.[6]

We are justified in telling or entertaining the metanarrative of the post-modernist breakthrough just so long as we do so not in the mode of objectivity (to revert to Rorty's opposition) but in the mode of solidarity; in other words, so long as we do not claim that our story is "true," a faithful representation of things as we find them "out there" in the world (but what "things" correspond to a literary-historical construct such as "postmodernism" anyway? and where, in such a case, is "out there"?), but only that our story is *interesting to our audience* and *strategically useful.* "Period terms," writes Matei Calinescu,

> function best when they are used heuristically, as strategic constructs or means by which we inventively articulate the continuum of history for purposes of focused analysis and understanding. Strategic is the key word here . . . It suggests goal-directed action, permanent readiness to weigh possible scenarios against each other, and ingenuity in the selection of those scenarios that are at the same time most promising and unpredictable. (The right degree of unexpectedness is a major strategic value.)

(Calinescu 1987b:7)

But if all our stories about postmodernism, big or little, are strategic fictions, if all our categories are constructions, this does not mean that they are all equally *good* stories, equally *sound* constructions. It makes a difference which story or variant we choose to tell, and there are criteria for preferring certain stories or variants over others. Now our criteria of choice can hardly be criteria of objective *truth*, given that the "object" about which the discourse may be said to be true (or false) has been *constructed by* that discourse itself (cf. Guillén 1971:433). Rather, we must choose among competing constructions of postmodernism on the basis of various kinds of *rightness* or *fit* such as, for instance, validity of inference; internal consistency or coherence; representativeness of sample; appropriateness of scope; richness of interconnections; fineness of detail; and productivity, a story's capacity to generate *other* stories, to stimulate lively conversation, to keep the discursive ball rolling (see Goodman 1978:129; Calinescu 1983:279–84). In the case of categorizing systems, which of course would include systems of period categories such as modernism vs postmodernism, we need to be able to show that the categories can do useful *work*: "For a categorial system, what needs to be shown is not that it is true but what it can do. Put crassly, what is called for in such cases is less like arguing than selling" (Goodman 1978:129). Above all, we choose one story or variant over another for its superior *interest*. Minimally, we strive to tell stories that are at least *relevant* to our audience; optimally, we hope to make our stories compelling, if possible even gripping.

ANOTHER STORY: EXHAUSTION, REPLENISHMENT

Once upon a time – so John Barth ought to have begun his story but (as we shall see) unfortunately didn't – once upon a time modernist literature reached the point of exhaustion; then came the postmodernist breakthrough, and literature replenished itself. Perhaps the most celebrated version of the breakthrough myth, Barth's story has recently received the imprimatur of Charles Jencks, self-appointed custodian of the term "postmodernism" (Jencks 1986:7). But just how good a story is it? How well does it fit?

Originally published in 1967, when Barth was teaching at SUNY, Buffalo, his essay "The Literature of Exhaustion" retains some of the apocalyptic tone of that "somewhat apocalyptic place and time" (Barth 1984b:205). Nevertheless, looking back on the 1967 essay from the perspective of 1979, Barth insists that it did not after all emphasize the "used-upness" of literature to the degree that many readers (to his dismay) have supposed it did. The emphasis fell, rather, on the possibility of artistic conventions being "deployed against themselves to generate new and lively work." "In homelier terms," wrote Barth in 1967, "it's a matter of every moment throwing out the bath water without for a moment losing the baby" (1984b:70).

A neat trick, but how is it actually done? Barth exemplifies the literature of exhaustion by Borges's strategy in one of his more familiar fables, "Tlön, Uqbar, Orbis Tertius" (from *The Garden of Forking Paths*, 1941). This is one of those texts in which Borges, presumably aware of the impossibility of writing with "originality" in a tradition as long and crowded as our own, conspicuously *refuses* to write an "original" text, instead producing a meta-text, a pseudo-learned commentary on *other* texts — texts which exist, however, only in his own imagination. The paradox, of course, is that by writing a metatextual commentary on an unwritten "original" text, instead of the original itself, Borges has actually created the fiction he is ostensibly refusing to create.

The "new and lively work" which Barth promises arises from the play of ontological levels, the way in which the story's fictional world is reflected by its actual mode of existence in the real world. "Tlön" is *about* a text which calls into being an imaginary world; but of course it also *is* a text which in some sense calls into being an imaginary world. Moreover, the imaginary world of Tlön (*within* the imaginary world of "Tlön") contains objects – *hrönir*, Borges calls them – which have been generated by pure acts of imagination, as the world of Tlön itself has; as the story "Tlön" has. "In short," says Barth, "it's a paradigm of or metaphor for itself; not just the *form* of the story but the *fact* of the story is symbolic; 'the medium is the message' " (1984b:71). By using the strategy of the fictional meta-text to produce a kind of short-circuit in the hierarchy of ontological levels, the story turns its disadvantageous situation at the the tail-end of a long literary tradition, when "original" stories apparently can no longer be written, into a positive advantage, thereby contributing something genuinely "new and lively" after all.

If Borges's "late-modernism" (a term Barth adopts in 1979) is the literature of exhaustion, then, Barth tells us, postmodernism is, or ought to be, the literature of replenishment. Exhausted literature can be replenished by reviving the traditional ("premodernist," says Barth) values of fiction. But, to be valid, such resurrection cannot be mere retrogression to the poetics of Balzac, Flaubert, Dostoevsky, Tolstoy. No more than anything else can fiction go home again; the old values must be revived in a way which takes the twentieth century into account. Postmodernist fiction must transcend the antitheses of modernist and premodernist writing, keeping "one foot always in the narrative past . . . and one foot in, one might say, the Parisian structuralist present" (Barth 1984c:204). This straddling of modes Barth finds in the work of Italo Calvino and Gabriel García Márquez, who epitomize for him the replenishment he has in mind.

Art in a closed field

We need to look more skeptically at Barth's choices of representative writers of exhaustion and replenishment. Apart from Borges, the exemplary writers of exhaustion in the 1967 essay are Beckett and Nabokov. It is easy enough to see why Beckett might qualify, though Barth himself says little about it. Think only of those passages, for instance in *Molloy* or *Watt* or "The Lost Ones," where Beckett has his protagonist(s) literally exhaust, in a systematic way, all the possibilities of action calculable given a certain restricted set of objects and states:

> Here he moved, to and fro, from the door to the window, from the window to the door; from the window to the door, from the door to the window; from the fire to the bed, from the bed to the fire; from the bed to the fire, from the fire to the bed . . . from the door to the window, from the window to the fire; from the fire to the window, from the window to the door; from the window to the door, from the door to the bed; from the bed to the door, from the door to the window. . . .

and so on and on for a further twenty-odd lines (Beckett 1970 (1953):203–4). "Art in a closed field," Hugh Kenner has called this typical Beckett strategy (Kenner 1964). A strategy of exhaustion in more ways than one, it exhausts (in Barth's sense) certain basic conventions of fiction at the same time that it literally exhausts the possibilities of a closed field. No doubt it also tends to exhaust the reader's patience; no doubt it was designed to do so.

But if Beckett qualifies for membership in the late-modernist category, on the grounds of his practice of art in a closed field, then so too must Italo Calvino, on the same grounds. Calvino's fascination with the systematic exhaustion of narrative possibilities is reflected in his membership, from 1973, in the Ouvroir de Littérature Potentielle, or OuLiPo. This group, whose members included Raymond Queneau, Georges Perec, and Harry Mathews, speculated about and practiced combinatorial methods for generating texts from the systematic combinations of a limited number of elements.[7] Calvino not only speculated about combinatorial narrative, but also practiced it in texts such as "The Count of Monte Cristo" (from *t zero*, 1967) and, above all, in *The Castle of Crossed Destinies* (1973).

This text, it will be recalled, involves a set of characters, strangers to one another, who, deprived mysteriously of the power of speech, must "tell" their life-stories visually, by selecting and arranging images from a deck of tarot fortune-telling cards. Now, according to an appended "Note," this fictional situation actually reproduces the method by which the text itself was generated. The author, manipulating a tarot deck, "discovered" in the lay-out of the cards the tales of his fictional characters, and even various "archetypal" narratives from world literature: tales from *Orlando Furioso*, the stories of Oedipus, Parsifal, Faust, Hamlet, Macbeth, Lear . . . "I was tempted," this Note continues, "by the diabolical idea of conjuring up all the stories that could be contained in a tarot deck" – in short, an exercise in exhausting all the narrative possibilities within a closed field. Admittedly, Calvino, unlike Beckett, fails to carry out his program to the bitter end, limiting himself to the recognition of how it *might* be done: "It was absurd to waste any more time on an operation whose implicit possibilities I had by now explored completely, an operation that made sense only as a theoretical hypothesis" (Calvino 1978:120). Yet this is precisely what Barth had commended Borges for: his ability to *recognize* the possibilities of exhaustion without feeling compelled tediously to *execute* them (1984b:75–6). And as we know, Borges is for Barth the exhaustive late-modernist *par excellence*. The conclusion seems unavoidable: Calvino's *Castle of Crossed Destinies* is in important respects more like the literature of exhaustion, as Barth defines it, than it is like the literature of replenishment that Barth envisages.

World-games

If Calvino's role in John Barth's postmodernist breakthrough story is problematic because he too closely resembles the literature of exhaustion, Nabokov's role is problematic because he does not always resemble it closely enough. Barth calls Nabokov a late-modernist, and he is right, as long as what he has in mind is texts such as *Pale Fire* (1962), which uses the same strategy of the fictonal metatext as Borges's "Tlön," Barth's exemplary text of exhaustion. What is exhausted in *Pale Fire*, of course, is not, as in Beckett's *Watt* or *Molloy*, the possibilities of narrative action in a closed field of objects, but instead the possibilities of narratorial reliability – or, rather, of narratorial *un*reliability (see Rabinowitz 1977; McHale 1987:18–19). We suspect that the first-person narrator of *Pale Fire*, one Kinbote or Botkin (we are not even sure of his name), author of a pseudo-scholarly line-by-line commentary on John Shade's long poem "Pale Fire," has distorted various (fictional) facts, but we cannot determine which facts these might be or in what way they might have been distorted. Having exhausted all the interpretive possibilities, we are left in the end with nothing certain.[8]

Nabokov's next novel, *Ada* (1969), is quite a different matter, however. On the face of it, *Ada* and *Pale Fire* are much alike, sharing, for example, the linguistic playfulness for which Nabokov is notorious. *Pale Fire* has its "word golf," its "mirror words," its invented Zemblan language and comically corrupt translations. *Ada* is similarly full of anagrams, secret codes, multilingual puns, and slyly altered names and book titles. The difference is that in *Ada* this play of language has ontological consequences that it cannot have in the elusive world of *Pale Fire*. The word-games generate a *world*: "An American governor, my friend Bessborodko, is to be installed in Bessarabia, and a British one, Armborough, will rule Armenia" (Nabokov 1970:252). Here the witty scrambling and recombination of the syllables *arm*, *bess*, *boro*, drags a world in its wake: American and British governors are being posted to Bessarabia and Armenia because these Near-Eastern lands have just been captured, in the twentieth-century present of *Ada*, from the Tartars of the Golden Horde in the Crimean War. As for the American governor's distinctly un-American name, this is explained by the fact that in this world North America is inhabited by people of Russian-speaking, not English-speaking, descent. In short, much of the linguistic playfulness of *Ada* is elaborately motivated by the fiction of a parallel world, an Antiterra whose history and geography are uncannily both like and unlike that of our own Earth.[9]

We will never know for certain whether Zembla, the kingdom of *Pale Fire*, "really" exists or not. According to some hypotheses which may be entertained about *Pale Fire*, it does exist, and Kinbote/Botkin, the narrator-commentator, is its exiled king; according to other hypotheses, it exists but Kinbote was never its king; according to still others, it does not exist at all. By contrast, we can be quite sure that Antiterra exists – fictionally exists, that is, as the projected world of *Ada*. Whereas in *Pale Fire* we are left in a state of anxious uncertainty about how much of the story "really happened," how much was hallucination or self-aggrandizing lie, in *Ada* we are simply called upon to suspend disbelief and accept the anti-world of Antiterra as a matter of (fictional) fact. This suggests that *Ada* is different from *Pale Fire* in ways that Barth fails to take into account when he groups Nabokov with the late-modernists.[10] To the degree that Nabokov is not like himself (i.e. to the degree that *Ada* is not like *Pale Fire*), he is not like the literature of exhaustion.

Moreover, he not only is *not* like the literature of exhaustion, he *is* like the literature of replenishment. In the parallel Earth of *Ada*, alternative technologies replace those with which we are familiar, among them the alternative technology (or pseudo-technology) implied by the following passage:

> Rolled up in its case was an old "jikker" or skimmer, a blue magic rug with Arabian designs, faded but still enchanting, which Uncle Daniel's father had used in his boyhood and later flown when drunk. Because of the many collisions, collapses and other accidents, especially numerous in sunset skies over idyllic fields, jikkers were banned by the air patrol; but four years later Van who loved that sport bribed a local mechanic to clean the thing, reload its hawking-tubes, and generally bring it back into magic order and many a summer day would they

spend, his Ada and he, hanging over grove and river or gliding at a safe ten-foot altitude above surfaces of roads or roofs.

(Nabokov 1970:43–4)

A characteristically exhausted gesture, one might be tempted to say of this: the ironic "re-invention" of a stage property out of the *Arabian Nights*, in the context of a science-fiction parallel world. But it also brings irresistibly to mind another contemporary re-inventor of the fantastic:

> the gypsies returned. They were the same acrobats and jugglers that had brought the ice . . . This time, along with many other artifices, they brought a flying carpet. But they did not offer it as a fundamental contribution to the development of transport, rather as an object of recreation. The people at once dug up their last gold pieces to take advantage of a quick flight over the houses of the village . . . the boys grew enthusiastic over the flying carpet that went swiftly by the laboratory at window level carrying the gypsy who was driving it and several children from the village who were merrily waving their hands.

This comes, of course, from *One Hundred Years of Solitude* by Gabriel García Márquez (1977 (1967):34–5), and the resemblance is more than coincidental. For García Márquez, like the Nabokov of *Ada*, reclaims the fantastic for "advanced" writing by reintegrating it in a context of conventional novelistic realism. His world, like Nabokov's, is a composite of fantastic elements and the familiar elements of verisimilar fiction: the gypsies bring flying carpets, but they also introduce telescopes, magnifying glasses, and ice to tropical Macondo; some of Macondo's citizens ascend bodily into heaven, while others are massacred, with all too credible historical realism, by troops in the service of the banana company. No doubt this is what Barth means by postmodernism keeping one foot in the narrative past and one foot in the present – one foot, let's say, in the *Arabian Nights*, and one foot in the grim real-world history of Latin America. But if this is what makes García Márquez a postmodernist writer, then by the same token it must make a postmodernist of Nabokov, at least the Nabokov of *Ada*. García Márquez's Macondo is an alternative or parallel world in much the same way that Nabokov's Antiterra is, merely lacking the pseudo-scientific "explanation" – an anti-Colombia to match Nabokov's Antiterra. Conversely, Nabokov, at least in *Ada*, is as much a practitioner of so-called "magic realism" as García Márquez.

"It goes without saying," John Barth writes, "that critical categories are more or less fishy as they are less or more useful" (1984c:200). By Barth's own criterion, then, we can only conclude that his categories of exhaustion and replenishment, or late-modernism and postmodernism, are pretty fishy. Far from helping us to group like with like and to distinguish same from different, his categories create groupings of texts which are in important ways less like others in the same group than they are like texts in the other group. Family resemblances have been obscured rather than enhanced. There would seem to be something askew in Barth's version of the story. Surely there must be better ways to tell it.

A THIRD STORY: COGNITIVE, POSTCOGNITIVE

"Long ago," writes Dick Higgins, poet, composer, performance artist, and sometime small-press publisher,[11]

> Long ago, back when the world was young – that is, sometime around the year 1958 – a lot of artists and composers and other people who wanted to do beautiful things began to look at the world around them in a new way (for them).

This is Higgins's version of the myth of the postmodernist breakthrough (although in fact he avoids the term "postmodernist" or "postmodernism"). According to this version of the story, for the half-century or so preceding this watershed of 1958, innovative artists and thinkers had typically been preoccupied with the process of cognition: with, on the one hand, the *object* of cognition, in the tradition of imagism, objectivism, Bauhaus aesthetics, and so on; and, on the other hand, with the *subject* of cognition, thus focusing on issues of self and identity in the tradition of expressionism, cubism, Freudian psychology, abstract expressionism and Beat poetry and, at the extreme limit, existentialism. Long in emerging – Higgins suggests that it actually characterizes most pre-twentieth-century Western art, though it only becomes central beginning with the Romantics – cognitivism reaches its climax and crisis in the late 1950s, when a "rupture" occurs. With the emergence during those years of such phenomena as Pop Art, happenings, concrete poetry, various forms of aleatory and "modular" music, and so on, cognitivism is shifted to the sidelines of innovatory art, displaced by what Higgins is forced to call "postcognitive" art. If he is unwilling to define too narrowly the characteristics of postcognitivism – it is, after all, an art still in the making, still emergent – Higgins at least specifies that in it, by contrast with cognitive art, issues of identity and the subject of cognition dwindle in importance. The persona of the artist is submerged in the *gestalt* of the artwork, and the mythic image of the artist, so strong in modernism, is weakened nearly to the point of obliteration.[12]

Higgins summarizes his story about cognitivism and postcognitivism in the following way:

The Cognitive Questions
(asked by most artists of the 20th century, Platonic or Aristotelian, till around 1958):

"How can I interpret this world of which I am part? And what am I in it?"

The Postcognitive Questions
(asked by most artists since then):
"Which world is this? What is to be done in it? Which of my selves is to do it?"

(Higgins 1978:101)[13]

I find Dick Higgins's story about the breakthrough to postcognitivism a good deal more attractive than John Barth's story about literature's exhaustion and replenishment. This is partly because of its more overt fictionality. To begin a historical narrative (entitled, incidentally, "A Child's History of Fluxus") "Long ago, back when the world was young," is obviously to evoke the generic conventions of the fairy tale; to continue by specifying the date 1958 – instead of a more conventional "round number" such as 1960 – is to confirm that this is fictionalized history. This is the same sort of gesture as Virginia Woolf's specification of December 1910 as the moment on or about which human nature changed. In both cases what is explicitly offered us is a useful fiction, an "as if" proposition, not the "truth."

Apart from its more transparently strategic and fictional character, we might want to see whether Higgins's story has any other advantages over Barth's story, whether it "fits" better. Comparison is tricky, however, because the two stories bear on quite different corpuses: where Barth is exclusively concerned with literary fiction, Higgins seems interested in everything *but* literary fiction, and even seems disposed to dismiss fiction as by definition cognitivist and "passéist" (1978:158). I shall take the liberty of extrapolating Higgins's story of the postcognitive breakthrough to the kinds of texts Barth discusses, to see what kind of work his version of the story might be capable of, by comparison with Barth's.

Begin, for example, with Barth's exemplary fiction of exhaustion, the Borges fable of "Tlön, Uqbar, Orbis Tertius." Where Barth sees a late-modernist jiu-jitsu strategy, by which the story's awareness of its own belatedness is turned to creative advantage, Higgins might see a text which stages or enacts the first of his "Postcognitive Questions": "Which world is this?" Granted, the artist-persona so typical of cognitive art is conspicuous here, but his importance dwindles before our eyes as the ontological issues raised by the projection of the world of Tlön, and its "disintegration" of our world (Borges 1962c:34), come to dominate the text. Gradually, through parallelisms and mirrorings among its various ontological levels (objects imagined into being *within* the world of Tlön, the world of Tlön itself, the fictional world of the story "Tlön," the real world in which Borges once wrote and we now read the story), a whole series of postcognitive ontological questions come into focus: how many worlds?

how many kinds of world? what relationships hold among them? according to what criteria are they to be assessed? and so on (see Calinescu 1983:267). Thus, according to the account that Higgins might give, the divide separating late-modernism from postmodernism ought to fall, not where Barth located it, *between* Borges's "Tlön" and writers of replenishment such as Calvino and García Márquez, but in such a way as to include Borges along with Calvino and García Márquez on the postcognitive, postmodernist side of the line.

If we do redraw the map in this way, we find that the cognitive/ postcognitive divide very often runs through the middle of careers and *oeuvres* that Barth tends to treat monolithically as *either* modernist or postmodernist, exhausted or replenishing. Thus, Barth's account of Samuel Beckett's career is a story of progressive exhaustion, of writing that approaches ever nearer to the silence which is its logical ultimate conclusion (Barth 1984b:67–8). This effaces the differences between earlier and later Beckett: between the Beckett who is still preoccupied with modernist issues of reliability and unreliability of narrators, radical subjectivity, and multiplicity of perspectives, as in *Watt* and *Molloy*, and the Beckett who focuses instead on the status of fictional worlds, the power (and impotence) of language to make and unmake worlds, and the relationship between fictional being and elusive "real" being, as in *Malone Dies*, *The Unnamable*, and many of the later short texts (see McHale 1987:12–13). Barth effaces, in short, the distinction between the cognitivist and the postcognitivist Beckett.[14] Similarly with Nabokov: by treating him as a representative master of exhaustion, Barth, as we have already seen, flattens out the salient differences between the radically skeptical epistemologist of *Pale Fire* and the playful ontological improviser of *Ada*. Again, just such a distinction between the cognitivist earlier Nabokov, author of *Lolita* and *Pale Fire*, and the postcognitivist later Nabokov, author of *Ada* and *Look at the Harlequins*, could be extrapolated from Higgins's version of the story.

On the other hand, when Barth *does* recognize a shift of orientation in a writer's career, Higgins's narrative might serve to corroborate rather than contradict Barth's. Thus, for example, Barth, in the "Replenishment" essay of 1979, briefly traces the stages of Calvino's development from the neorealism of *The Path to the Nest of Spiders* (1947) to the full-fledged postmodernism of *Cosmicomics* (1965) and *Castle of Crossed Destinies* (1969) (Barth 1984c:196). In this case, Higgins's narrative would be likely to parallel Barth's, mapping out parallel stages from cognitivism to postcognitivism in Calvino's *oeuvre*. But even where, as here, Barth's and Higgins's stories appear to unfold in parallel, the two stories prove to be differently motivated. For Barth, Calvino qualifies as a postmodernist writer of replenishment because he synthesizes the premodernist gratifications of storytelling with modernist self-consciousness and high artistry.

For Higgins, on the other hand, Calvino might be thought of as a postcognitivist in *Castle of Crossed Destinies* because he relinquishes control of "his" narrative to chance configurations of the tarot cards, thereby submerging his artistic persona in the *gestalt* of the aleatory (or quasi-aleatory) work (see Higgins 1984:75).

Higgins's story, then, is in my view preferable to Barth's for strategic reasons. It makes only the claims on our belief that fiction does – no more, but no less. It has "the right degree of unexpectedness" (Matei Calinescu's phrase, Calinescu 1987b:7). It "fits" better than Barth's: internally better-organized, more coherent, more "compact," it brings together better than Barth's does texts, writers and phenomena which seem properly to "go together," while keeping separate, again better than Barth's, things which seem properly kept apart. It seems likely to be a highly productive story, enabling us to tell many exciting sub-narratives about the manifold adventures of cognitivism through the centuries, its crisis in the middle decades of the twentieth century, and the strange birth of new, postcognitive forms. For instance, Higgins suggests in several places how we might begin to disinter early, precursor postcognitivists such as Satie, Duchamp, Joyce, Gertrude Stein, and the Dadaists from the mass of dominant cognitive art which surrounded them and tends to obscure their true outlines from us (Higgins 1978:101, 1984:5–6; cf. Lethen 1986). Finally, Higgins's story seems to me – and to others too, I would hope – intrinsically a more interesting story than the one Barth tells.

As a test of the usefulness of Higgins's account, perhaps we might return to the text with which we started, Max Apple's "Post-Modernism," and try rereading it in the light of Higgins's "little narrative" of the postcognitive breakthrough.

THE FIRST STORY AGAIN: UNLICENSED METAPHYSICS

"As an exercise," Apple begins, "let's imagine a character" (1984:136). With this metafictional gesture, he invites us into the fiction-writer's workshop to demonstrate for us how a fictional person, and with him a world, is made. Stroke by stroke, detail by detail, Apple builds up his character: a contemporary writer, student of the modernists, who uses a word processor; who lives in a world which also contains morning newspapers, Colonel Qaddafi, Target Stores and Woolco and K-Mart and other retail chains, Texas Instruments pocket calculators, and so on; but nameless as yet. We are shown, in effect, what Borges also shows us in his equally brief but ontologically more spacious story of Tlön: the construction or projection of a world by a fictional text, with the reader's collaboration. All fictions do this, of course, but this one does it in full view and in slow motion, as it were. Then, abruptly, the world-making operation is suspended. The author withdraws his authority from the collaborative project, leaving us holding the bag: "You were wrong" (137). At a stroke, the character-in-the-making vanishes into a kind of limbo; still legible, he has nevertheless been canceled, placed *sous rature*.

Having erased his character, however, Apple next proceeds to construct, again in full view and slow motion, a new one, female this time where the first was male; this time bearing a name, Joyce Carol, where the first one was nameless; also a writer, but of women's Gothic romances, not avant-garde postmodernist fiction; a widow with quintuplets to support; living in a world which also contains the *National Enquirer*, fertility drugs, weight-lifting, and so on. Thus Apple leads us through an entire cycle of fictional creation, de-creation, and re-creation, laying bare in the process the fiction-writer's ways of world-making, and asserting his freedom to project a world (*"Shall I project a world?"* Pynchon's heroine agonized in *The Crying of Lot 49*).

In the process he also lays bare some of the essential characteristics of the ontological structure of fictional works and their worlds. He draws our attention, for instance, to the partial indeterminacy, the "gappiness," of fictional objects, including fictional characters. No description of a fictional character could ever be complete in the way that we suppose real people (at least *ourselves*) are complete:

> No doubt I've made some mistakes. In my descriptions I forgot to tell you how she looked, the color of her hair or skin or eyes. I neglected to mention her bearing and/or carriage and said nothing at all about her interpersonal relations.
>
> (Apple 1984:138)

"In the case of fictional worlds," writes Roman Ingarden, "it is always as if a beam of light were illuminating a part of a region, the remainder of which disappears in an indeterminate cloud but is still there in its indeterminacy" (1973 (1931):218). Some of the indeterminacy of fictional worlds and the objects in them is permanent: we will never be able to close the gap. Other gaps, however, are temporary, designed to be filled in by the reader in the process of realizing or concretizing the text. Thus, it is entirely appropriate for Apple to solicit our collaboration in fleshing out his skeletal character: "Wallace Stevens once said, 'Description is revelation,' and you know, I fell for it. If you want to know any of the nonrevelations you'll have to help me out; after all, readers and listeners are always friends" (1984:138).

But just because "Post-Modernism" foregrounds and lays bare the process of world-making (and -unmaking) and the ontological structure of the fictional world, does this necessarily mean it qualifies as "postcognitive" in Dick Higgins's sense? After all, for all its emphasis on the ontological instead of the epistemological, this text does still submit in a conspicuous way to the authority of the artist-persona; the subject of cognition is firmly in place, as by rights he should *not* be in what Higgins would call postcognitive art.

Or is he so firmly in place? Throughout the first half of "Post-Modernism," Apple seems to be inscribing himself into his text in the persona of its writer-hero, building up a portrait of the artist as a postmodernist; but then abruptly, even aggressively, he denies his autobiographical presence here, in effect erasing his self-inscription:

> you assumed, no doubt, that it was me.
>
> You were wrong. I don't even know how to type and am allergic to word processors. Furthermore, I have never read a thesaurus and I do my work standing at a Formica-topped counter.
>
> (Apple 1984:137)

But if *that* inscribed author, the postmodernist writer-hero, turns out not to have been the "real" Max Apple, then perhaps *this* one is, the one who intervenes in his own text to set things straight. He isn't, of course, any more than the other one was. This inscribed author is every bit as fictional as the earlier inscribed author had been; the ontological barrier between inscribed characters and real-world persons is unbreachable. We have, in short, a situation analogous to the one in Borges's astonishing two-page *tour de force*, "Borges y yo" (1957), in which the real author and the inscribed fictional author displace one another turn and turn-about, until the "real" author is lost in the shuffle of selves: "I don't know which one of the two of us is writing this page" (1968:201). In short, "Post-Modernism" constructs a subject of cognition only to deconstruct it, dispersing it among the various authorial inscriptions. Thus Apple's story passes beyond modernist cognitivism to what Higgins would call postcognitivism.[15]

Apple's opening gambit in "Post-Modernism" is to assert his own and other storytellers' "right to stop being philosophers when it suits us, which is most of the time" (1984:135). This assertion proves to be as paradoxical as everything else in Apple's story/theory. For by exploring and exposing the postcognitive, ontological aspects of fictional world-making, the structure of fictional worlds and their contents, and the problematic presence of the author in his text, Apple turns out to be doing what Annie Dillard calls "unlicensed metaphysics in a teacup" (1982:11).

But of course *it's only a story*.

APPENDIX 1.1

Post-Modernism

Max Apple

It's always safe to mention Aristotle in literate company. I have known this since my freshman year in college. Furthermore, that esteemed philosopher by praising Homer for showing rather than telling gave all storytellers forever after the right to stop being philosophers whenever it suits us, which is most of the time.

So, invoking sacred Aristotle and having no theory to tell, I will show you a little post-modernism. Alas, I have to do this with words, a medium so slow that it took two hundred years to clean up Chaucer enough to make Shakespeare, and has taken three hundred years since then to produce the clarity of Gertrude Stein. Anyway, I confess that we writers are as bored as any other artists. We get sick of imitating the old masters, the recent masters, and the best sellers. We are openly jealous of composers who can use atonal sounds, painters who experiment with xerography and sculptors with Silly Putty and polyester. Other makers of artistic objects have all this new technology, not to speak of color, and here we are stuck with the rules of grammar, bogged down with beginnings, middles, and ends, and constantly praying that the muse will send us a well-rounded lifelike character.

As an exercise, let's imagine a character who is a contemporary writer. He has read Eliot and Proust and Yeats and even had a stab at *Finnegans Wake*. He is well acquainted with the Oxford English Dictionary and Roget's Thesaurus. There he is sitting before his word processor thinking, What will it be today, some of the same old modernist stuff, a little stream-of-consciousness perhaps with a smattering of French and German? Or maybe he looks out the window, notices the menacing weather, and thinks, This will be a day of stark realism. Lots of he saids and she saids punctuated by brutal silences.

As he considers epiphanies, those commonplace events that Joyce put at the heart of his aesthetic, our writer scans the morning paper. This is a research activity. In the trivial he will find the significant, isn't that what art is all about?

So the writer looks, and it is astonishingly easy. There it is, the first gift of the muse. One column quotes Colonel Muammar Qaddafi of Libya stating that his nation is ready to go to war against the United States. Directly across the page an ad for Target Stores pictures a Texas Instruments pocket calculator, regularly $9.97: "today only" $6.97, battery *included*.

The writer is stunned. He has followed this particular calculator since its days as a $49.95 luxury. He has seen it bandied about by Woolco and

K-Mart and, under various aliases, by Sears, Penney's, and Ward's. Never
has it been offered with the battery included. This is something altogether
new. He remembers Ezra Pound's dictum, "Make it new." Still there is
the possibility of an error, a misprint, a lazy proofreader, a goof by the
advertising agency – plenty of room for paranoia and ambiguity, always
among the top ten in literary circles. And the sad thing is, this particular
ad will never appear again. Qaddafi will be quoted endlessly, but the sale
was "today only". This is one of the ambiguities the writer has to live
with.

Of course our writer doesn't equate Target and the battery to war and
peace, not even to the United States and Libya. He hardly considers the
nuance of the language that uses the same terms for commerce and war:
"Target," "battery," "calculate" – he can't help it if the language is a kind
of garbage collector of meanings. All he wants to do is know for sure if
that nine-volt battery is really included. He can, if he has to, imagine a
host of happy Libyans clutching their $6.97 calculators and engaged in a
gigantic calculating bee against the U.S., a contest that we might consider
the moral equivalent of war and save everyone a lot of trouble.

His imagination roams the Mediterranean, but the writer will suppress
all his political and moral feelings. He will focus absolutely on that calculator and its quizzical battery. He will scarcely notice the webbed beach
chair peeking out of the next box or the sheer panty hose or any of the
other targeted bargains.

Let's leave our writer for a moment with apologies to Aristotle and begin
to do a bit of analysis. Of course you have known all along that I have
been trying to demonstrate a "post-modern" attitude. Maybe you would
characterize this attitude as a mixture of world weariness and cleverness,
an attempt to make you think that I'm half kidding, though you're not
quite sure about what.

But even in this insignificant example nothing quite fits. It should be
easy. We have only one character, the writer. He was sitting before his
word processor and reading the paper. He was not described, so you
assumed, no doubt, that it was me.

You were wrong. I don't even know how to type and am allergic to
word processors. Furthermore, I have never read a thesaurus and I do my
work standing at a Formica-topped counter.

The writer I was talking about was Joyce Carol, a young widow supporting quintuplets by reviewing books for regional little magazines. Her
husband died in a weight-lifting accident. Her quints were, you have
already guessed, the chemical outcome of what for years had seemed a
God-given infertility. Joyce Carol struggles to understand all the books
she reviews though she could earn a better wage as a receptionist for

Exxon or even selling industrial cleaners and have a company car to boot; but then who would stay home with the quints?

Poor Joyce Carol is stuck with being a book reviewer as women have been stuck at home with books and children for at least two hundred years.

She is also about to begin composing her thirty-ninth gothic romance. Ladies in fifteenth-century costume will waste away for love while men in iron garments carry fragrant mementoes of their ladies and worry about the blade of their enemy penetrating the few uncovered spots of flesh.

Joyce Carol's quints lie in a huge brass carriage. They are attended by five Vietnamese wet nurses and a group therapist.

There is a photographer from the *National Enquirer* doing an in-depth story on the drug that gave Joyce Carol her quints. He is blacking out fingers and toes on the babes and asking the wet nurses to look forlorn.

Joyce Carol used to write exquisite stories of girls who couldn't decide whether they truly loved their lovers enough to love them. Her stories ended in wistfulness with the characters almost holding hands. Two were sold to the movies but never produced.

It occurs to me that you're probably not very interested in Miss Carol. No doubt I've made some mistakes. In my descriptions I forgot to tell you how she looked, the color of her hair or skin or eyes. I neglected to mention her bearing and/or carriage and said nothing at all about her interpersonal relations.

Wallace Stevens once said, "Description is revelation," and you know, I fell for it. If you want to know any of the nonrevelations you'll have to help me out; after all, readers and listeners are always friends.

I can only tell you that Joyce Carol is modest and desperate. She has a peasant's cunning, and you would not want to be her sister or roommate. She spends a lot of time missing her weight-lifter husband. The five offspring and the thirty-nine novels do not make her miss him any less. She sits at the word processor and imagines his strained biceps. When he pushed the bar over his head he grunted like an earthquake and won her heart.

In her own life Joyce Carol is undeluded by romantic conventions. Her stories may be formulaic but she knows that the shortness of life, the quirks of fate, the vagaries of love are always the subjects of literature.

Sometimes her word processor seems less useful than a 19-cent pen. Sometimes she feels like drowning herself in a mud puddle.

Still she is neither depressed nor morose. She is sitting there before you virtually undescribed, a schematic past, a vague future, possibly a bad credit risk as well.

Lots of times the strings of words she composes make all the difference to her. In the paragraph she had just written, a knight has survived the plague though everyone with him has perished. He carries a bag of infidel teeth as a souvenir for his lady. His horse slouches away from Bethlehem.

Joyce Carol looks up from her labor. The wet nurses are cuddling the babes. She is glad that she did not choose to bottle-feed. The *Enquirer* photographer snaps his pictures. In the photographs the fingers of the infants almost touch. Everything is the way it is.

From *Free Agents* (1984)

Chapter 2

Constructing (post)modernism: the case of *Ulysses*

"Postmodernism," says Lyotard, "is not modernism at its end but in the nascent state, and this state is constant" (1984a:79). There are those who regard this as a fatuous remark (e.g. Mepham 1991:145); certainly it is paradoxical. If we are sufficiently impatient with paradox we may try to smooth out the logical kink in this one by supposing that Lyotard has perversely used a *post* where he ought to have used a *pre*: for "*post*modernism" read "*pre*modernism" and the kink unkinks. But no, we are not to be let off the hook so easily: "this state is constant," Lyotard tells us. How can any state which is identified as either *pre* or *post* some other state also be "constant"? The kink returns.

If we can even entertain such a paradox, then something must be wrong with the opposition between modernism and postmodernism, and perhaps even with periodization in general. We *can* entertain it, I think (and I shall show how later); and indeed, in a certain sense, something *is* wrong with the modernism vs postmodernism opposition, and periodization in general is *all* wrong. But only in a certain sense, in terms of a certain conception of periodization. Shift the ground of our conception a little, and it turns out that there's nothing wrong with the opposition modernism vs postmodernism after all, and periodization is quite all right.

My text is James Joyce's *Ulysses*. *Ulysses*, literary historians agree, is one of the founding texts of the "High Modernist" phase of literary modernism, a text in which modernist poetics is simultaneously elaborated, consolidated, and made conspicuous, available for appropriation and imitation. "*Ulysses*," wrote Maurice Beebe over fifteen years ago, "can be seen as a demonstration and summation of the major features of the entire [modernist] movement" (1974:176). It "relies on the Modernist code, and contributed to its definition and recognition," write Fokkema and Ibsch more recently: "With *Ulysses* Modernism was accepted *in ultima forma*" (1987:66, 73). Yet, like other founding texts of High Modernism, in particular *The Waste Land* (see Nevo 1982; Fokkema and Ibsch 1987:83, 89), *Ulysses* has lately entered upon a strange second career as a *post*modernist text. In the case of *Ulysses*, however, the potential for a second career was always there. For, as readers recognized almost from the beginning, *Ulysses* is *double*, two differentiable texts placed side by side, one of them a landmark of High Modernism, the other something else. Only lately have we learned to call this "something else" postmodernism.

To date, the most fully elaborated account of the "doubleness" of *Ulysses* has been Karen Lawrence's (1981). In her account, *Ulysses* splits roughly down the middle. A single "narrative norm" (what Joyce called his "initial style") prevails in the first half, through "Scylla and Charybdis"; beginning with "Wandering Rocks" and "Sirens," this normative style is abandoned for a diverse series of extravagant stylistic performances. There are exceptions to this distribution: "Aeolus," in particular, anticipates the extravagances of the second half, while "Nausicaa" and especially "Penelope" regress to the narrative norm of the first half. This bisection of *Ulysses* has been corroborated by many other commentators (e.g. Kenner 1978; MacCabe 1978; Bašić 1986–7; Hayman 1987:155–64), with certain variations (e.g. MacCabe locates the divide earlier, at the end of "Hades"; Kenner places it later, between "Wandering Rocks" and "Sirens"; etc.). Nor does this perception of *Ulysses* as double belong only to recent revisionist or iconoclastic readings: it is already to be found in such canonical earlier commentaries as those of Edmund Wilson (1931) or S.L. Goldberg (1963).

If there is consensus between earlier and later commentators on *Ulysses* about the *fact* of its doubleness, there is no such agreement about the relative importance or value of the two halves. Indeed, when we compare earlier critics such as Wilson and Goldberg with more recent ones we find an almost exactly complementary distribution of emphases: where the emphasis for the earlier critics falls on the first half of the text, for more recent critics its falls on the second half. For Wilson and Goldberg, the chapters in the so-called initial style constitute the "authentic" *Ulysses*, and they are full of reservations and misgivings about the chapters from "Sirens" through "Ithaca." By contrast, more recent commentators such as Lawrence and MacCabe have tended to generalize about the early chapters from "Telemachus" through "Hades" (and including "Lestrygonians" and "Scylla and Charybdis") but to focus their attentions more specifically on one or more of the later chapters. MacCabe, for instance, devotes special attention to "Sirens" and "Cyclops," Iser (1974) to "Oxen of the Sun," and Attridge (1988) to "Sirens" and "Eumaeus." That critics would one day come to regard "Oxen of the Sun" as epitomizing *Ulysses* (as Iser does, for instance, 1974:194; and cf. Lawrence 1981:137) would no doubt have struck Wilson and Goldberg as incomprehensible, or merely perverse.[1]

In short, earlier critics sought in *Ulysses* a "normal" modernist poetics, a poetics that could be seen to have evolved from the early-modernist phase represented by *Dubliners* and *A Portrait of the Artist as a Young*

Man, and they found it in the chapters of the first half. They had less use for the second half of the text, and it was left to later critics to undertake the recuperation of the chapters from roughly "Wandering Rocks" and "Sirens" on (perhaps including "Aeolus," perhaps excluding "Nausicaa" and "Penelope"). This recuperation has been undertaken in terms of a poetics closer to that of *Finnegans Wake* than that of *A Portrait*:[2] call it postmodernist poetics.

So *Ulysses* is a text fissured and double, like a landscape made up of two adjacent but disparate geophysical terrains, brought together by the massive displacements of tectonic plates. To map *Ulysses* literary-historically is to describe the relation between these terrains, and between the plates on which they ride – between, in other words, the modernist poetics of its "normal" half and the postmodernist poetics of its "other" half. This relation, I shall argue, is one of *excess* and *parody*: the poetics of the postmodernist chapters *exceed* the modernist poetics of the "normal" chapters, and the postmodernist chapters *parody* modernist poetics.[3]

MODERNIST *ULYSSES*

What exactly *have* critics and readers found in the "normal" chapters of *Ulysses* which leads them to regard it as the "demonstration and summation" of modernism, the definitively modernist novel? They have found a repertoire of strategies that *Ulysses* shares with other modernist texts, both earlier and later. Many of these characteristically modernist strategies were, if not actually innovated by Joyce, at least perfected by him, and made conspicuous in *Ulysses*. This is not the place to attempt to elaborate the full modernist repertoire (or "code") of *Ulysses*; in any case, Beebe (1974) already proposed an outline of it some years ago, and Fokkema and Ibsch (1987) have recently filled in the outline in considerable detail. Here I shall restrict myself to reviewing very briefly two familiar sub-repertoires of the full modernist repertoire: strategies of *mobile consciousness* and the related strategies of *parallax* (perspectivism, counterpoint).

Mobile consciousness

"The most influential formal impulses of canonical modernism have been strategies of inwardness," according to Jameson (1979:2). This is certainly true, but not the whole truth, for, as Quinones (1985:91–119) argues, modernism's centripetal strategies of inwardness simultaneously function as centrifugal strategies of "openness" to the world outside and beyond consciousness. It is in the light of these complementary functions of inwardness and openness, centripetal movement and centrifugal movement, that we must view modernist innovations in the presentation of consciousness.

The varieties of interior discourse perfected by Joyce – direct interior monologue (both integrated in the third-person matrix and "autonomous"), free indirect discourse (see Cohn 1978; Bašić 1986–7:34–5) – do not so much heighten the realism of presented consciousness (though they have that effect as well) as secure a finer-grained interaction between consciousness and the world outside consciousness. Mind is rendered more *mobile* by these strategies, quicker to seize on objects of external reality and then to abandon them for others, freer to digress along associative pathways and to project "subworlds" of its own making (see Eco 1979; Pavel 1980). The corollary of mobility of consciousness is stability of presented world: if the presented world outside consciousness is not presumed to be stable, we have no background against which to gauge the relative motion of consciousness, and our sense of its mobility is dissipated. It follows, then, that if consciousness is the mobile partner in this interaction – shifty, unreliable, digressive – it is the world that must be the correspondingly stable partner, really (that is, fictionally), reliably "out there" – though not, of course, necessarily easy of access, precisely because the consciousness on which it registers is so mobile.

This fine-grained interaction between mobile mind and stable world is most conspicuous in the direct interior monologue which is the staple variety (the "narrative norm") of the three chapters of the "Telemachia" and the first eight chapters of part two of *Ulysses*,[4] as well as the second half of "Nausicaa" (see Cohn 1978:58–76). Here the reader is shuttled between, on the one hand, sentences directly presenting what passes in the character's mind, and indirectly presenting (or refracting) the outside world; and, on the other hand, authorial (and authoritative) sentences directly projecting that world. We engage in a constant, microscopic collation of the two world-versions, the authoritative one and the one constructed by the character's consciousness, finding that they sometimes corroborate one another, sometimes diverge, in the process developing a sense of how this particular mind "filters" the world, the precise angle of its perspective, the kind and degree of distortion it introduces (see, e.g., Goldberg's account of this interaction in "Hades," 1963:271–5).

When the proportion of authorial sentences to "mind-sentences" decreases, as in "Proteus" or the second half of "Nausicaa," or authorial sentences disappear entirely, as in the "autonomous" monologue of "Penelope" (see Cohn 1978:217–32; Spinalbelli 1986), it is not so much the interaction between mind and world that changes as our processing of these passages. Since we can no longer measure Molly's construction of her world against adjacent authoritative sentences, we must measure it against the fragments of world which we have reconstructed from all the chapters which precede her monologue. Absence of direct authorial world-projections in "Penelope" does not mean absence of world: Molly's consciousness is still deployed against the background of a stable world, but here that world is relatively more difficult of access than in the "integrated" chapters. Similarly with the sentences of free indirect discourse (see Cohn 1978:99–114) scattered throughout the "normal" half of *Ulysses* and appearing in concentration in the first part of "Nausicaa" (and, more problematically, in "Eumaeus"):[5] here our processing of sentences is complicated, but the interaction of mobile mind and stable world persists. The complication arises from the conflation of authorial world-projecting function and (indirect) quotation of character's consciousness in the same sentence. If we are not always able to disengage the world "out there" from the character's construction of it with the sharpness that we can in direct interior discourse passages, we nevertheless do succeed in distinguishing a generally stable background world from foreground consciousness even in free indirect discourse.

These strategies of mobile consciousness have, of course, occupied a conspicuous and central place in "normal" modernist (and late-modernist) poetics from 1922 to the present. Examples of "integrated" direct interior monologue include Dos Passos's *Manhattan Transfer*, Doblin's *Berlin Alexanderplatz*, Malcolm Lowry's *Under the Volcano*, and Donleavy's *The Ginger Man*; of "autonomous" monologue, Faulkner's *As I Lay Dying* and *The Sound and the Fury* and Puig's *Betrayed by Rita Hayworth*; of free indirect discourse, Dos Passos's *U.S.A.*, Woolf's *Mrs. Dalloway* and *To the Lighthouse*, and Pynchon's *The Crying of Lot 49*.

Parallax

Interior discourse, whether direct or free indirect, already involves a form of perspectivism or *parallax*. A character's interior construction of the world diverges from the authorial projection of it, and the "angle" of this divergence serves to inform us about the structure of this character's consciousness. The obvious extension of this principle of parallax is to juxtapose two or more characters' different constructions of the same world, or same part of a world. "Two different versions at least," writes Kenner, "that is Joyce's normal way" (1980:63). This multiplication of versions has two simultaneous functions: it both serves to confirm the stability of the world outside consciousness (on the assumption that one version may be mistaken, but two mutually corroborative versions must be reliable (see Kenner 1980:63); and at the same time exposes the similarities and differences between different minds.

Thus, for example, in "Ithaca" our attention is drawn to the coincidence of Stephen and Bloom both having experienced, early in the morning, the same cloud, "perceived by both from different points of observation, Sandycove and Dublin" (Joyce 1986:17.41–2).[6] Searching "Telemachus" (1.248–53) and "Calypso" (4.218–29) we confirm that this is indeed the case, which yields a satisfying (Kenner says "uncanny") sense of a world fully substantial, independent of any one perceiver's construction of it. We note, too, that the sudden overcast has a similar effect on both perceivers, plunging Stephen and Bloom alike into a mood of "desolation" (the word is Bloom's own, part of his interior discourse at this point). But the chain of associations triggered by this overcast is instructively different in each case: Stephen remembers his mother on her death-bed, Bloom thinks of the Jewish diaspora; Stephen withdraws from the immediate scene, Bloom incorporates details from it; Stephen's interior discourse is a fabric of quotations and allusions (to Yeats's "Who Goes with Fergus?" and Numbers 5; see Gifford and Seidman 1974:10); while Bloom resorts to a four-letter obscenity unique in his interior or spoken discourse. From this minor effect of parallax, then, we learn not only some of the qualities Stephen and Bloom share – a susceptibility to melancholy, for instance – but also some of the ways their mental processes and the experiences which fuel them differ.

This is a local example of parallax. On a larger scale, parallax or counterpoint of perspectives organizes the "Nausicaa" chapter and, much more elaborately, "Wandering Rocks," where the separate itineraries of Father Conmee and the viceregal cavalcade through Dublin are monitored by a variety of onlookers.[7] In both cases, the counterpoint of different characters' constructions of the same external objects and events (Bloom's masturbation and the fireworks in "Nausicaa," Conmee and the viceroy's carriage in "Wandering Rocks") not only buttresses the stability of the projected world but allows us to infer the perceivers' respective positions, ideological as well as physical. On the largest scale of all, it might well be said that the city of Dublin itself, on a particular day in June 1904, is the composite object of a global parallax based on two major perspectives (Bloom's and Stephen's) and a host of subsidiary ones.

Strategies of parallax, like the varieties of interior discourse, also persist in the repertoire of the modernist canon, occupying a conspicuous place in, for instance, Huxley's *Point Counter Point*, Gide's *Faux-monnayeurs*, Faulkner's *As I Lay Dying* and *Light in August*, Woolf's *Mrs. Dalloway* and *To the Lighthouse*, Dos Passos's *Manhattan Transfer*, Pynchon's *V.*, and B.S. Johnson's *House Mother Normal*; and, on an even larger scale, in multi-volume perspectivist or contrapuntal novels such as Dos Passos's *U.S.A.* trilogy, Musil's *Der Mann ohne Eigenschaften*, and Durrell's *Alexandria Quartet*.

POSTMODERNIST *ULYSSES*

The "other" *Ulysses*, the *Ulysses* that runs roughly from "Sirens" to the end, excluding "Nausicaa" and "Penelope" but including "Aeolus," has eluded modernist codifiers (see Attridge and Ferrer 1984a:4–5).[8] It both pushes the modernist poetics of mobile consciousness and parallax to a point of excess where it topples over into something else (see McHale 1987:11), and parodically undermines that modernist poetics. In this sense, the second half of *Ulysses* is avant-garde where the first half is modernist, for, as Calinescu observes, the avant-garde can be seen as "a deliberate and self-conscious *parody* of modernity itself" (1987a:141). This avant-garde parody is quite specific: to each of the sub-repertoires of modernist strategies in the first half corresponds a parodic sub-repertoire in the second, a mobility of worlds to answer the first half's mobility of consciousness, a parallax of discourses to match its parallax of subjectivities.

Mobile world

When the mobility which Joyce's strategies secured for consciousness comes to contaminate the world outside consciousness, then consciousness itself threatens to vanish from sight in a general fluidity of world and mind alike. Where there are no stable landmarks "out there" to measure consciousness against, its movements cannot readily be gauged. This is precisely what tends to happen in certain chapters of the "other" *Ulysses*. In chapters such as "Oxen of the Sun" or "Circe," the world of *Ulysses*, (fictional) reality itself, has become fluid, metamorphic, not merely as a function of the consciousnesses impinging upon it – though anxious readers and critics have often tried to recuperate these chapters by reading them as functions of consciousness – but *in its own right*. Thus, where the modernist *Ulysses* deploys a mobile consciousness against the background of a stable world, the "other" *Ulysses* parodically substitutes a *mobile world* (see Topia 1984:123–4).

"By 'Oxen of the Sun,'" writes Kenner (looking back on that chapter from the perspective of "Circe"),

> the "real" events were growing difficult to recover from the text, but we were encouraged to feel sure they were going on, and that their substance remained accessible . . . . We persuaded ourselves (with considerable effort) that we could "read through" each style.
>
> (Kenner 1980:121)

Kenner's extraordinary hedging here is perfectly justified. Consider only this passage:

> But Malachias' tale began to freeze them with horror. He conjured up the scene before them. The secret panel beside the chimney slid back and in the recess appeared . . . Haines! Which of us did not feel his flesh creep? He had a portfolio full of Celtic literature in one hand, in the other a phial marked *Poison*. Surprise, horror, loathing were depicted on all faces while he eyed them with a ghostly grin. I anticipated some such reception, he began with an eldritch laugh, for which,

it seems, history is to blame. Yes, it is true. I am the murderer of
Samuel Childs. And how I am punished! . . . With a cry he suddenly
vanished and the panel slid back. An instant later his head appeared in
the door opposite and said: Meet me at Westland row station at ten
past eleven. He was gone! . . . Malachias, overcome by emotion, ceased.

> (14.1010–32; first ellipsis Joyce's; the others, mine)

What "really" happens here? Is Haines "really" present in the Holles
Street maternity hospital? What is he "really" carrying? Perhaps, as Kenner
says, we do "persuade ourselves" that we are able to "read through" the
screen of style to the "real" events, but it seems that different readers are
differently persuaded about what those "real" events might be.[9] Janusko
(1983:28, 80), in common with many other readers, assumes that Haines
really makes an appearance at the hospital; but Kenner (1980:121–3, 115)
insists that this is a retrospective narrative, and that Haines had really
appeared earlier in the evening at George Moore's house, causing a scene
which Mulligan is here recounting in the narrative present to his audience
of medical students. I am disposed to think that Kenner is probably right;
but how would one go about proving it?

The source of the uncertainty, of course, is the pastiche style which
interposes here between us and (fictional) reality, a style (in this case that
of Gothic fiction, specifically Walpole's *Castle of Otranto*, but with echoes
of Sheridan LeFanu as well; see Gifford and Seidman 1974:354) which
brings with it its own complement of realia (or "realemes"; see Even-
Zohar 1990b). The phial of poison, the secret panel, the language of
Haines's "confession": all these elements clearly belong to the repertoire
of Gothic fiction and have been "illicitly" imposed on the "real" events.
But what about the "portfolio of Celtic literature"? This is evidently to
be identified with the volume of Irish poetry which we know Haines had
bought earlier in the day (as reported in "Scylla and Charybdis," 9.154),
and thus belongs as much to the "real" scene as it does to the Gothic
repertoire. Finally, what about the framing of this episode within Malachias' (Mulligan's) spine-tingling narrative? If the frame-tale structure is just
another artifact of the Gothic pastiche, imposed on "reality" like the phial
or the secret panel, then we are free to "edit it out" of the scene in the
hospital, and to assume with Janusko that Haines's intrusion occurs in the
narrative present after all. But if the frame-tale structure really belongs to
the *Ulysses* world rather than to the Gothic repertoire, if Mulligan "really"
is telling this story in the narrative present, then we should certainly
follow Kenner in locating the narrated event earlier in the evening.[10] Thus
we are left with a doubled or hybrid world, part "really real," part merely
a side-effect of the Gothic style, a selection from the Gothic repertoire,
and we lack criteria for distinguishing conclusively between the two.

By "Circe" the situation has further deteriorated. "Nothing, in 'Circe,' distinguishes 'real' from 'hallucination,' " writes Kenner (1980:123). "Deprived of reliable criteria for 'reality,' we have no recourse save to read the text as though everything in it were equally real" (1980:126; cf. Kenner 1978:91–2; Ferrer 1984). Corroborative evidence from other, less unstable chapters, Kenner continues, confirms the (fictional) reality of certain events; for instance, there is Bloom's close encounter with the sand-strewer (15.180–97), which is subsequently corroborated in "Ithaca" (16.342–5). And common sense assists us in "editing out" certain events which could not plausibly have happened. For instance, of all the large cast of characters who might or might not "really" be present in Nighttown, we can say with some confidence that Paddy Dignam, Stephen's mother, and Bloom's son Rudy certainly are not, for all three are dead. But common sense is a tricky thing. Kenner himself (1980:9, 81), for instance, assumes that the girls from the beach, Cissy Caffery and Edy Boardman, are "really" there. Now, this does not strike me as particularly plausible, but I do not see how anyone could adjudicate between Kenner's view and my own: there simply is not enough "solid" reality to go on.

And what about Blazes Boylan: is he "really there" in Nighttown or not (15.3726–810)? Here is a genuine difficulty. For a man of Boylan's character to be found in the red-light district at such an hour is plausible enough – a good deal more plausible than for the girls from the beach to be found there. Less plausible, however, is his appearing in the same hackney car (number 324), driven by the same driver (James Barton, or Barton James, of Donnybrook), that he had taken much earlier in the day to his rendezvous with Molly. Yet if Boylan's presence is not real, but hallucinated, to whose hallucination does he belong? Not that of Bloom, the likeliest candidate: for how could Bloom know such details as the number of the car and the name and residence of the driver? So the hallucination hypothesis breaks down; but the "real presence" hypothesis is no sounder.

The disorienting mobility of the world in "Circe" is the more readily seen if we contrast it with the pseudo-mobility of the world, which is actually the mobility of consciousness, and not of the world at all, in "Proteus." The dog which Stephen observes on Sandymount strand metamorphoses from hare to buck to bear to wolf to calf and back to dog again – but all in metaphor: *like a bounding hare, bearish fawning, at a calf's gallop*, and so on (3.334–49; see Kenner 1980:39; Perl 1984:194). These metaphors presumably reflect Stephen's projections, though not all of them are explicitly framed as his interior discourse. The dog which Bloom encounters in Nighttown also metamorphoses, changing breed from retriever to wolfdog to setter to mastiff to spaniel to bulldog to boarhound (15.634–706; see Perl 1984:198, 304 n. 21) – not in metaphor, however, but evidently in "reality." Unless, of course, it is all a hallucination; but if so, we are left in the position of not being able to say conclusively what breed of dog Bloom "really" encounters (if any), while in Stephen's case we're able to say with confidence that the dog he encounters "really" is . . . a dog.[11]

Such mobility and instability of the world, displacing as they do the "normal" modernist preoccupation with mobility of consciousness, and even parodying it, play no very salient role in the subsequent development of modernist poetics. Not until postmodernism, from the French *nouveau nouveau roman* (e.g. Robbe-Grillet's *Dans le labyrinthe* and *Maison de rendez-vous*) through American "surfiction" (e.g. Katz's *The Exagggerations of Peter Prince*, Sukenick's *Out*, Federman's *Take It or Leave It*, Major's *Reflex and Bone Structure*) and beyond, have the destabilizing strategies of "Oxen of the Sun" and "Circe" come belatedly into their own (see McHale 1987:99–111).

Parallax of discourses

The parallax of subjectivities, as we have seen, helps to confer solidity and stability on the world outside of consciousness. But there is another form of parallax, occurring in the "other" *Ulysses*, especially in "Cyclops" and "Oxen of the Sun," but also in "Aeolus," "Sirens," "Eumaeus," and "Ithaca," which has the opposite effect, that of dissolving the *Ulysses* world into a plurality of incommensurable worlds. This is the *parallax of discourses* ("parallax of styles," Kenner calls it, 1980:106, 107).

If, in the "normal" chapters of *Ulysses*, there is an effect of parallax between adjacent sentences of a character's interior discourse and authorial discourse, there is an even finer-grained parallax *within* a character's discourse, a kind of micro-parallax.[12] For, far from constituting a homogeneous bloc of verbal material, each character's discourse proves, on closer examination, to be more like a mosaic of heterogeneous discourse fragments (see Topia 1984:106–16) – quotations, allusions, echoes of other characters, bits of anonymous social wisdom or prejudice, words from specialized registers (such as "parallax" itself in Bloom's interior monologue, 8.110, 111), and so on. In reading, of course, we readily naturalize this verbal heterogeneity by constructing an image of each character which will accommodate his or her particular linguistic resources (Stephen's literary and philosophical training, Bloom's indiscriminate curiosity and imperfect memory, etc.). In short, we resolve the parallax into a single view; we smooth it out.

This micro-parallax of the first half of *Ulysses* is in effect blown up to monstrous proportions in its second half (see Kenner 1980:100). Here discourses are introduced and played off against each other which have no personified verbal source within the *Ulysses* world. These are free-standing specimens of discourse for which no character can be made directly or indirectly responsible, discourse which cannot be "naturalized" at the level of the fictional world. The characterological frames which bounded the micro-parallax are overrun, characters are submerged in discourses, and a discursive parallax, a counterpoint of discourses, is parodically substituted for the first half's parallax of subjectivities (see Topia 1984:120).

Just how discourse overwhelms and submerges character in the "other" *Ulysses* can be seen if we contrast the first half of "Nausicaa," which still belongs to the "narrative norm," with "Eumaeus." Gerty MacDowell's interior monologue, rendered here in free indirect discourse, is contaminated through and through with verbal material from women's magazines and sentimental fiction, with occasional lapses into what we assume must be a more "natural" idiom for her, that of her own lower-middle-class Dublin milieu. Nevertheless, although the ultimate stylistic source for much of this material lies outside of Gerty, in her reading and her milieu, its immediate, personified source is Gerty herself.[13] The source for the verbal material in "Eumaeus," also transmitted in what appears to be free indirect discourse (see note 5 above), is a good deal harder to trace. Who is responsible for this cliché-ridden, periphrastic, incompetently "elegant" style?

The likeliest candidate would seem to be Bloom, through whom most of this chapter is focalized (i.e. he occupies its "point of view"). Yet few commentators have ever been completely comfortable with this attribution of "Eumaeus" to Bloom. Goldberg, for instance, assumes that the chapter captures "the cliches jibbering in Bloom's mind," but goes on to complain about Joyce's unfairness toward Bloom in representing him this way (1963:140, 257–8). Ellmann (1972:151) sees "Eumaeus" as a fabric of "bloomisms" (i.e., Bloom's characteristic verbal near-misses; see Ellmann 1972:36); but Lawrence (1981:170) rejoins that "this is not the sound of Bloom's mind." For Kenner, "Eumaeus" reflects neither Bloom's spoken style nor the style of his thoughts, but rather the *writing* style Bloom would have used if he had written this chapter himself (Kenner 1978:35, 38; 1980:130), and even so circumspect a reader of Joyce as Bersani concurs: "Eumaeus" is "written in the manner of Bloom, that is, in the style he would presumably use were he to try his hand at writing" (Bersani 1990:157).[14]

There is another difficulty here. The perspective (focalization) in this chapter is predominantly Bloom's, but not *entirely* his. There are passages here, stylistically homogeneous with the rest, which nevertheless cannot plausibly be attributed to Bloom's consciousness, reporting as they do what passes through Stephen's mind (inaccessible to Bloom), or viewing Bloom and Stephen from outside and at a distance:

Stephen of his own accord stopped for no special reason to look at the heap of barren cobblestones and by the light emanating from the brazier he could just make out the darker figure of the corporation watchman inside the gloom of the sentrybox. He began to remember that this had happened or had been mentioned as having happened before but it cost him no small effort before he remembered that he recognised in the sentry a *quondam* friend of his father's, Gumley.

(16.103–110)

The driver never said a word, good, bad or indifferent. He merely watched the two figures, *as he sat on his lowbacked car*, both black, one full, one lean, walk toward the railway bridge . . . As they walked they at times stopped and walked again continuing their *tête-á-tête* (which of course he was utterly out of) . . . while the man in the sweeper car or you might as well call it in the sleeper car who in any case couldn't possibly hear because they were too far simply sat in his seat near the end of lower Gardiner street.

(16.1885–94; my ellipses; emphasis in the original)

In passages like these, the perspective lifts right away from Bloom, and the "Eumaeus" style (improperly, if its source is Bloom himself) goes with it.[15]

Other naturalizations have been proposed. There is, for instance, the old chestnut about the "Eumaeus" style reflecting in its clichés, *non sequiturs*, and general syntactical bagginess the physical exhaustion of the characters at the fag-end of their long day: "[Bloom] is fagged out, and so is the language which describes him" (Ellmann 1972:151); "the narration is affected not only by the sort of style with which Bloom is familiar, it is also tired, as is Bloom" (Adams 1990:104). It has even been thought a plausible naturalization to attribute the tiredness of this style to "Joyce himself at a moment of exhaustion in his artistic labors" (Attridge 1988:174; cf. Stanzel 1971:142–4). Even Joyce sometimes nods?

But surely Attridge is right in rejecting all these naturalizing interpretations as premature and coercive. "The initial impression that 'Eumaeus' represents . . . the unfolding of a single consciousness's experiences and formulations, cannot survive close attention to Joyce's text," he writes.

[The] achievement [of "Eumaeus"] is not primarily the representation of a fictional character's mental world (the interior monologue style would be more justly described in these terms) or of a particular cultural moment; its peculiar language cannot be recuperated within some notion of "state of mind" or "state of civilization" . . . the ways in which the language of this episode permits slippage and uncertainty, deception and detour . . . go beyond a particular character's mental condition and spring from the propensities and liabilities of language itself.

(Attridge 1988:184)

In other words, what is primarily on display in "Eumaeus" is neither

Bloom's consciousness (nor any other character's, for that matter), nor some kind of stylistic correlative for the fictional situation of the characters, nor Joyce himself on the brink of creative exhaustion, but *discourse* – or rather, a whole range of discourses echoing in the English language of Bloom's (and Joyce's) time and place. " 'Eumaeus,' " Attridge concludes, "dethrones the controlling subject, whose language is seen to be a tissue of slightly soiled phrases, all too available to the first-comer" (1988:187).

A discourse (style, register) implies a world – so we have been told, in different ways and with various inflections, by some of those who have thought most profoundly about language in our century, from Wittgenstein and Whorf to Baxtin and Foucault. The categories a discourse carves out, the relations it establishes among them, its characteristic patterns of linking elements, and so on – all these encode a particular version of reality, and the different versions of reality encoded by different discourses must inevitably be, to some larger or smaller degree, mutually incompatible, incommensurable. Consequently, discursive parallax, in cases where discourses cannot be attributed to personified sources within the fictional world, implies an *ontological* parallax, a parallax of worlds. In effect, to juxtapose two or more free-standing discourses is to juxtapose disparate worlds, different reality templates. Each discourse is governed by its own set of constraints on which realemes are "licit" candidates for presentation and which are not (Even-Zohar 1990b; cf. Iser 1974:191–3). States of affairs which may be possible in one discourse-world need not be possible in the adjacent world; characters who are "at home" in one world need not be so in the world next door.

Thus, for example, the characters from the first-person narrative of "Cyclops," who are so fully integrated in the naturalistic Dublin of *Ulysses*, could not easily be transferred to the flagrantly unnaturalistic, cartoonish worlds of the adjacent parodies – the grandiose public excecution (12.525–678), the high-society wedding attended by trees (12.1266–95), and so on. We need only reflect on the characters' names to see that this is so: names such as *Joe Hynes, Alf Bergan, Bob Doran, J.J. O'Molloy, John Wyse Nolan*, and so on, belonging to the conventions of novelistic realism and richly endowed with social identity, could only with considerable strain and incongruity be made to coexist with such jokey, ontologically "shallow" names as *Commendatore Bacibaci Beninobenone, Monsieur Pierrepaul Peititepatant, the Grandjoker Vladinmire Pokethankerscheff*, or *Miss Fir Conifer of Pine Valley, Lady Sylvester Elmshade, Miss Daphne Bays*, or *Miss Virginia Creeper*; nor is it clear that these last two sets of names could easily mingle with each other in the same world, either.[16]

Thus, where the "normal" modernist chapters of *Ulysses* juxtapose different characters' perspectives on the same world, the "other" chapters juxtapose disparate discourse-worlds; where modernist *Ulysses* explores the incommensurability of subjectivities, the "other" *Ulysses* explores the incommensurability of worlds. Ontological perspectivism, the parallax of discourses and the worlds they encode, is not a characteristic structure of modernist poetics; but it *is* characteristic of postmodernism, where it may be traced through a whole sequence of carnivalesque, collage, and cut-up or fold-in texts, from Queneau and Burroughs to Barthelme, Puig, Goytisolo, Sorrentino, Acker and others (see McHale 1987:162–75).

MODERNISM-CUT-IN-HALF

Gob he's like Lanty MacHale's goat that'd go a piece of the road with every one.

(Joyce 1986:12.1584–5)

Joyce's *Ulysses* is a literary-historical scandal. It is at one and the same time a founding text of "High Modernism" and a postmodernist text, a "demonstration and summation" of modernist poetics and a parody of modernist poetics; it defines and consolidates modernism yet at the same time exceeds and explodes it. Fokkema and Ibsch (1987) plausibly display *Ulysses* as one of their prize exhibits of a modernist code which foregrounds the epistemological,[17] while Perl (1984:210) equally plausibly describes it as "post-epistemological."[18] How can this paradox be resolved?

Not easily; not, for instance, by construing *Ulysses* as a "transitional" text which begins in modernism (the first half) and ends in postmodernism (the "other" half). This is the sort of solution which seems to be implicit in Lawrence's account of the "sequence of styles" in *Ulysses* (and see Scholes 1974:184–5). If we insist on reading the sequence of styles as a transition, we will have to confront the awkward fact that the sequence ends not with its most radically avant-garde (or postmodernist) chapter but with a chapter which regresses to the modernist "narrative norm" of the first half. This suggests that the transition in *Ulysses* is not from modernism to postmodernism at all, but rather from the early phase of modernism reflected in Joyce's preceding works, *Dubliners* and *A Portrait of the Artist as a Young Man*, to the full-fledged "High Modernism" of the "narrative norm" (including "Penelope").[19] But where does such a transitional sequence leave the postmodernist text which seems to be folded within this modernist one? Out of sequence; out of place, literary-historically speaking; out of time. *Ulysses*, as Colin MacCabe remarks (1978:109), is one of those "untimely works" that anticipates the end of an era even before that era has properly gotten under way.

Something, as I observed at the outset, must be wrong with our conceptions of modernism and postmodernism, or with our conception of periodization in general, or both, if we are led to entertain the paradox of a text which initiates the "High Modernist" phase yet somehow also belongs to the postmodernist phase which lies *beyond* "High Modernism," on the *far side* of it (this is what the *post* of postmodernism means, after all). So, what *is* wrong here, exactly? How are we to make sense of the "untimeliness" of *Ulysses*?

Helmut Lethen, in a provocative article entitled "Modernism Cut in Half" (1986), argues that such paradoxes of periodization as the one I have outlined in the case of *Ulysses* arise from literary-historians' retrospective revisions, or indeed *constructions*, of modernism. The historical phenomenon of modernism, he says, is typically reduced in retrospective accounts to its conservative half, to the modernism of, say, Thomas Mann – or, in my account, to the "normal" modernism of the first half of *Ulysses*. Excluded from modernism by this bifurcation is its radical, avant-garde half, the modernism of Dada or of the "other" *Ulysses*.[20] The expulsion of the modernist avant-garde leaves a more homogeneous modernism, one from which a postmodernism can be more sharply and dramatically distinguished: "The concept [of modernism] was constructed so as to form a dark background for the brilliant claims of Postmodernism" (Lethen 1986:233). The irony, of course, is that the postmodernism which so dramatically detaches itself from the modernist background largely repeats or extends the innovations of the excluded modernist avant-garde. Cutting modernism in half allows us at one and the same time to consolidate and monumentalize (in a negative sense) modernism, and to project modernism's "lost" avant-garde onto postmodernism.

No doubt Lethen is right, and this really is the operation by which the modernism vs postmodernism opposition has been constructed. Indeed, this is one interpretation of Lyotard's enigmatic formula, with which I began: "A work can become modern only if it is first postmodern. Postmodernism thus understood is not modernism at its end but in the nascent state, and this state is constant" (1984a:79). To paraphrase: postmodernism is precisely what is "left over" after we have crystallized out a coherent, tidily compact, homogeneous modernism (cf. Jameson 1991b:73, 302). Postmodernism, in this sense of the term, thus precedes the consolidation of modernism – it is modernism with the anomalous avant-garde still left in – and makes itself available for a later consolidation of the *next* phase. And this process, as Lyotard remarks, is constant: he has described, in effect, not the particular history of the phases of twentieth-century culture, but a general historical principle whereby each successive cultural phase recuperates what has been excluded and "left over" from the preceding phase and bases its "new" poetics on that leftover.

But this operation of constructing modernism by cutting it in half is not the only tendency in the recent literary historiography of modernism. There is also an opposite tendency toward the assimilation of the whole of modernism to its avant-garde half, and thus toward assimilating modernism to postmodernism. A representative of this tendency is John Frow. Here is his working definition of modernism:

> The modernist aesthetic . . . is characterized above all by (1) its attention to the status of the utterances it produces . . .; (2) consequently an antimimetic impulse: the realities it constructs have a discursive rather than an onotological foundation; and (3) an antiorganicist impulse, working typically through the fragmentation of textual unity, through the play of contradictory genres of discourse, and through a splitting of the subjects of utterance.
>
> (Frow 1986:117)

Frow's list of modernist features has strikingly little in common with comparable lists by Beebe or Fokkema and Ibsch, presumably because their codifications reflect the practice of the "mainstream" or "core" modernists while his is based on the avant-garde.[21] In any case, Frow's definition does not seem very adequate to the conservative, by and large mimeticist and organicist modernist poetics of, say, Woolf, Proust, Larbaud, Gide, Svevo, Musil, or Mann (Fokkema and Ibsch's "core" canon) or the Joyce of *Portrait of the Artist* and the "normal" modernist chapters of *Ulysses*; but it is easy to see how it would apply to the more radical modernists – to Gertrude Stein, the Dadaists, or the Joyce of the "other" *Ulysses* and *Finnegans Wake*. "The complexity of the organization of the modernist paradigm," Frow frankly admits, "seems to me to anticipate those forms of radical difference proposed as postmodern" (1986:117). In short, his is, by contrast with the reduced modernism described by Helmut Lethen, a "postmodernized" modernism.

Embarrassingly enough (if you happen to find this sort of thing embarrassing, which I do not), there is no way of deciding *objectively* between these two constructions of modernism, that is, between modernism-cut-in-half and postmodernized modernism. Insofar as both constructs address the same givens – the same canonical writers and texts, the same practices of writing, and so on – they each deal adequately enough with them in their own respective ways, but their respective ways of dealing with them are mutually incompatible. On the other hand, each construct also "creates" certain "givens" which the other construct does not even recognize *as* "givens," and so does not bother to address at all.[22] Thus, for example, from the point of view of a postmodernized modernism, Gertrude Stein appears as a major modernist writer, and her poetics must accordingly figure conspicuously in any account of modernism; while from the point of view of modernism-cut-in-half she is at best a marginal, anomalous figure and need not be taken into account at all.[23]

But, if there are no objective criteria for choosing between these constructions of modernism, then how *does* one choose? The choice of one construct over the other (or between either of these two and any others that might be proposed) can only be made *strategically*, that is, in the light of the kind of work which, it is hoped, the construct could accomplish. By "work" here I mean the generation of new insights, new connections and groupings, interesting problems and hypotheses, and so on. And this is the main criterion not only in the case of the competing constructions of modernism, but in literary periodization generally. "Period terms," writes Calinescu,

> function best when they are used heuristically, as strategic constructs or means by which we inventively articulate the continuum of history for purposes of focused analysis and understanding. Strategic is the key word here . . . It suggests goal-directed action, permanent readiness to weigh possible scenarios against each other, and ingenuity in the selection of those scenarios that are at the same time most promising and unpredictable. (The right degree of unexpectedness is a major strategic value.)
>
> (Calinescu 1987b:7)

My own preference (as must have been evident from my account of *Ulysses* above) is for the modernism-cut-in-half scenario, the construct which excludes the most radical wing of modernism, enabling us to consolidate a "normal" modernism and to place in opposition to it a sharply-distinguished postmodernism. Recognizing the cogency of Lethen's critique of this construct, I nevertheless choose it for *strategic* reasons. It seems to me the construct likeliest to shed light on the regularities of modernism and the specific "otherness" of postmodernism – sufficiently interesting objects of inquiry, in my judgment. And if this construct should happen to lead me to draw paradoxical conclusions, such as the paradox of the precocious postmodernism of *Ulysses*, then at least I can hope that these will prove to be productive paradoxes, useful stimulants to further thought, and charged with an appropriate degree of unexpectedness.

Part II

(Mis)reading Pynchon

Modernist reading, postmodernist text: the case of *Gravity's Rainbow* (1979)

MODERNIST (MIS)READINGS

> Welcome Mister Slothrop Welcome to Our Structure We Hope You
> Will Enjoy Your Visit Here.
>
> (Pynchon 1973:194)

Thomas Pynchon's novel *Gravity's Rainbow* (1973) opens, apparently, *in medias res*:

> A screaming comes across the sky. It has happened before, but there
> is nothing to compare it to now.
> It is too late. The Evacuation still proceeds, but it's all theater. There
> are no lights inside the cars. No light anywhere. Above him lift girders
> old as an iron queen, and glass somewhere far above that would let the
> light of day through. But it's night. He's afraid of the way the glass
> will fall – soon – it will be a spectacle: the fall of a crystal palace. But
> coming down in total blackout, without one glint of light, only great
> invisible crashing.[1]

This opening passage abounds in the sort of provocatively matter-of-fact
references with which one is familiar from other fictional beginnings. The
reader's need to know is immediately aroused: who is this "he" whom
the narrative does not find it necessary to identify? where and when is
this Evacuation taking place? what screams across the sky? The reader's
queries are directed toward reconstructing, among other patterns, the
fictive world in which the events of the novel unfold. No doubt he or
she takes it for granted that this opening passage gives one access to that
world.[2] Hence the disorientation when one learns that one has begun not
"in the midst of things," as might have been assumed, but in the midst
of a dream: on the next page "Pirate" Prentice awakens from his nightmare
of Evacuation to the real (that is, fictive) morning of wartime London.
With this reversal begins the reader's re-education – or, to borrow a
metaphor from the Pavlovian discourse which this novel sometimes appropriates, the reader's de-conditioning. For this passage is a paradigm of

problematic passages throughout *Gravity's Rainbow*: the reader, invited
to reconstruct a "real" scene or action in the novel's fictive world, is
forced in retrospect – sometimes in long retrospect – to "cancel" the
reconstruction he or she has made, and to relocate it within a character's
dream, hallucination, or fantasy.

After such an embarrassment, the reader, in order to reassert mastery
over the text, may evoke the model of a genre or period which will
"explain" what has happened. In this case, he or she may evoke the model
of so-called postmodernist fiction. In doing so the reader will presumably
have in mind certain contemporary (post-war) fictional texts which are
strongly self-conscious, self-reflective, self-critical; which, by laying bare
their own devices, continually raise the problem of the relation between
the game-like artifices of fiction and the problematic imitation of reality;
which actively resist and subvert the reader's efforts to make sense of
them in the familiar novelistic ways; "writerly" texts, in short.[3] But such
a model, particularly when used in this defensive or naturalizing way, is
apt to draw less on the full range of phenomena it ought to capture than
on certain extreme cases: Borges, late Beckett, Burroughs, North American
surfiction, the French *nouveau nouveau roman*. The example of such limit-
cases is not, however, all that helpful in dealing with the intractabilities
of *Gravity's Rainbow*, which falls somewhat short of these limits. Roland
Barthes might have said of *Gravity's Rainbow* that it is a text of the kind
that still casts a "shadow": it still contains "a *bit* of ideology, a *bit* of
representation, a *bit* of subject" (1975:32). It has, at least at the outset,
characters who can actually be " 'found' [. . .] in the conventional sense
of 'positively identified and detained' " (*GR*:712). It has plot, or rather a
proliferation of plots, to the point that "plot" here acquires the punning
sense of "conspiracy" as well as "intelligible sequence of actions." And it
has an openness to real-world facts – historical, socio-economic, linguistic,
scientific, esoteric – perhaps unequalled even by the great nineteenth-
century realist and naturalist novelists.[4]

Is there, then, any sense in which evoking postmodernism is more than
merely a defensive gesture, a fending-off of the embarrassments of intractable fiction by relating it to certain extreme examples of intractability? Is
there any way in which this period- and genre-label can be made to do
useful descriptive work? There is, if one takes the label "postmodernist"
sufficiently at face value: "post," coming after, the "modern*ist*" movement
in literature and the other arts. To take the label at face value is to orient
oneself toward the relation between Pynchon's text and modernist textual
models. Thus, in this paper I propose to inquire into the modernism of
Pynchon's postmodernism in *Gravity's Rainbow*.

There is perhaps a mandate for this sort of inquiry in Pynchon's obvious
debt to modernist theory and practice in his earlier fiction. *The Crying
of Lot 49* (1966) is in many ways a classic example of the Jamesian

novel with a single consistent point of view and restrained narratorial
intervention: *What Mrs. Maas Knew*, perhaps? [5] What disqualifies *Lot 49*
as a proper Jamesian novel is the fact that the "central consciousness" or
"reflector" is not well-developed, not very interesting, indeed not the
point at all (Mendelson 1978a:2–5). The novel *V.* (1963) incorporates
elaborate parodies, or at least self-conscious exploitation, of characteristic
modernist techniques.[6] It includes a Conrad-like unreliable narration at
two removes, bearing on events in German Southwest Africa which recall
Marlow's and Kurtz's Belgian Congo; a Proustian first-person "confession" displaying the successive selves of the character-narrator (Patteson
1974:37–8; Siegel 1976:41); a baring of the characteristic modernist device
of *style indirect libre* through a character who practices "forcible dislo-
cation of personality" by referring to himself exclusively in the third
person;[7] and above all, a tour-de-force use of eight distinct points of view
to render an espionage melodrama, reminiscent perhaps of the perspectivism of Durrell's *Alexandria Quartet* (Hite 1983a:60), and climaxing in a
rare instance of the limit-case of point of view, the so-called "camera eye"
perspective.[8]

Thus, the modernism (even if it is only mock-modernism) of Pynchon's
earlier fiction gives one a priori some reason to think that the investigation
of modernist aspects of the poetics of *Gravity's Rainbow* should be fruit-
ful. But how are we to formulate the modernist model of fiction so as to
bring into sharpest focus the relation between this model and our allegedly
postmodernist text? This relation emerges most clearly when we concen-
trate not on formal textual organization as such but on text-processing, the
pattern-making and pattern-interpreting behavior which the text's formal
organization elicits from the reader. Concentration on text-processing is
particularly appropriate where modernist fiction is concerned, for one of
modernism's fundamental characteristics is the relatively expanded function
of the reader; or, shall we say, the apparently new and expanded repertoire
of operations which the reader is expected to undertake. For we can
conceive of period-models in literary history as specific sets or repertoires
of pattern-making and pattern-interpreting operations which readers must
undertake in order to render texts intelligible.[9] It would obviously be
impossible to attempt a full inventory of the modernist repertoire here.
Let it suffice to observe that the modernist repertoire certainly includes
operations through which readers reconstruct the chronology of the *fabula*
from the sometimes drastically displaced order of the *syuzhet*; impart
intelligible motivation to enigmatic sequences and abrupt transitions;
motivate large-scale parallelisms, doublings, and analogies (Perry 1968;
Sternberg 1970); discover narrators, and evaluate their knowledgeability
and reliability; reconstruct psychological processes, and the external reality
which they mediate, from such conventions as interior monologue and
style indirect libre; and so on.[10] Clearly, none of these operations is strictly

"new" in the modernist repertoire; what *is* new, however, is how frequently one is called upon to apply them, the sophistication with which
they must be applied, and their relative prominence in the repertoire.

For our present purposes, we can best proceed by restricting ourselves
to two groups of operations from the modernist repertoire. First, we shall
consider the process of reconstructing elements of external (fictive) reality
from the evidence of a character's mediating consciousness. Aferwards, we
shall look into a characteristic modernist process of motivating transitions
between characters' minds in a sequence.

WORLD UNDER ERASURE

> Those like Slothrop, with the greatest interest in discovering the truth,
> were thrown back on dreams, psychic flashes, omens, cryptographies,
> drug-epistemologies, all dancing on a ground of terror, contradiction,
> absurdity.
>
> (*GR*:583)

Criticism of modernist fiction has tended, quite properly, to dwell on the
unreliability of characters' visions or accounts of the external world, compared to the quasi-divine reliability of the narrators and implied authors
of earlier fiction. This is undoubtedly a crucial factor when the narrative
has been entrusted, totally or in part, to the mediating consciousness or
mediating language of a fictional character. But equally crucial in this sort
of narrative is the somewhat neglected broad zone of reliability. In texts
like *Ulysses*, *To the Lighthouse*, or *The Sound and the Fury*, the reader
has no choice but to rely for much of the material from which he or she
reconstructs a fictive world on the mediating consciousness of fictional
characters; that one can do so with considerable confidence is a measure
of the reliability of the "reflectors." Unreliability and reliability can coexist
in this way because they are found at different levels. A character's unreliability normally manifests itself in his or her interpretations or evaluations
of the fictive world; unreliability can also be epistemological, involving
the character's knowledge or ignorance of that world; but it is seldom
ontological. What the character definitely knows to be there normally *is*
there in the fictive world, and the reader can confidently incorporate it in
his or her reconstruction; as indeed one must, if one is to reconstruct at
all.

From the evidence of a character's mediating consciousness, the reader
will often be able to reconstruct, first, the immediate "reality" – objects
and persons in the character's field of perception, his actions and those
of others, etc.; secondly, absent "reality" – objects, persons and events
present in the character's memory or, more dubiously, in his speculative
projections or imaginings; and thirdly, by extrapolation, the general

material culture, mores and norms, etc. These reconstructions are not, of course, relevant only for visualizing the scene directly at hand. They may function as the basis for further reconstructions, whether of another such scene or of the fictive world in general; or they may participate in other types of patterning, formal or thematic.

The reliability of evidence obtained from a character's consciousness may be guaranteed in several ways. The narrative may shuttle back and forth between the character's consciousness and external reality directly presented by the narrator, thereby confirming the character's perceptions. This is the strategy used, for instance, with Bloom and Stephen in *Ulysses* (1922), where continual microscopic shifts between interior monologue and narratorial segments produce a composite picture, part contributed by the perceiving characters, part directly presented. But the same strategy is not employed in Molly's interior monologue, from which all narratorial segments have been excluded. Nevertheless, we confidently undertake to reconstruct large sectors of fictive reality from Molly's monologue: her immediate experience (train-whistles and church-bells, the unexpected onset of her period, her noisy recourse to the chamber-pot), her recent past (what the cards foretold that morning, her sexual interlude with Boylan that afternoon, Bloom's order of eggs), her more distant past (her first lover "under the Moorish wall," Bloom's courtship and proposal, successive homes), and a fairly thick slice of Dublin life at the beginning of the century.

Thus, reliability may be guaranteed by other means than direct narratorial intervention. Principally, of course, reconstructions based on the content of characters' consciousness are tested against the reader's extra-textual knowledge, the models of physical phenomena, norms of verisimilar behavior, and real-world information which one brings to bear on the text. But reconstructions may also be confirmed internally at a distance, so to speak, rather than immediately as in Bloom's and Stephen's interior monologues. This is classically the case with *The Sound and the Fury* (1931). Here, increasingly intelligible mediators – Jason, and the completely authoritative voice of the Dilsey section – retroactively substantiate the reconstructions which the reader has made on the basis of less intelligible mediators – the suicidally disturbed Quentin, and, most radically, the idiot Benjy.

When ontological doubt, uncertainty about what is (fictively) real and what fantastic, insinuates itself into a modernist text, we might well prefer to consider this the leading edge of a new mode of fiction, an anticipation of postmodernism. For the ontological stability of external reality seems basic to modernist fiction. Even where, as in the "Circe" section of *Ulysses*, we are unsure of the exact boundary between the real and the hallucinatory, we can nevertheless be fairly confident of the underlying reality upon which the hallucinations rest. The underlying reality of Nighttown reasserts itself, for instance, in certain "real" conversations between the whores and their clients, in Stephen's frenzy in the whore-house parlor, in the fist-fight with the soldiers, in Corny Kelleher's intervention, etc.[11] Only in such cases as the joint imaginative projection of the Sutpen story by Quentin and Shreve in Faulkner's *Absalom, Absalom!* (1936) must the reader fully relinquish ontological certainty.

But if one seeks a stable reality among the minds of *Gravity's Rainbow* – and the novel anticipates that one will – one will be checked and frustrated. Reconstructing a fictive world is a hazardous undertaking here, as more than one critic has observed; "it is not always clear", writes Tony Tanner, "whether we are in a bombed-out building or a bombed-out mind" (Tanner 1974:51; cf. Wolfley 1977:885). While the minds of James's child and Faulkner's idiot give us reliable access to the worlds of their novels – although not without some interpretive effort on our parts – the minds of *Gravity's Rainbow* give us access only to provisional "realities" which are always liable to be contradicted and canceled out. For most of Pynchon's central characters are either paranoiacs "who may possibly be suffering systematized delusions and projecting hostile forces" (Siegel 1976:50), or are otherwise hallucination-prone. Tyrone Slothrop, the "hero" insofar as this novel has one, is described as "psychopathically deviant, obsessive, a latent paranoiac" given to "falsification, distorted thought processes" (*GR*:90). Pirate Prentice's "talent" for "getting inside the fantasies of others" (*GR*:12), Franz Pökler's cinema-oriented dreaminess, Mr. Pointsman's burgeoning megalomania, Tchitcherine's and Enzian's predilections for powerful drugs – all these belong to the same general tendency. Motivation here is reciprocal: hallucination-prone characters motivate the presence of hallucinatory structure and content, while hallucinatory structure and content motivate the presence of hallucination-prone characters (see Hite 1983a:142).

The shape of the reader's experience in *Gravity's Rainbow* is repeatedly that of the opening encounter with the Evacuation nightmare.[12] Having reconstructed a partial picture of the novel's fictive world, the reader learns that the episode on which he or she has based that reconstruction never "really" occurred after all. The episode must now be remotivated as "dream, psychic flash, omen, cryptography, drug-epistemology," and the supposed realia must be edited out of the reconstructed picture. These unreal realia are now available for integration into other patterns: characterological patterns, thematic patterns, or perhaps the supernatural reality "beyond the Zero" which is a feature of this novel's "world" (see below) – but in any case not the reconstructed external "this-worldly" reality.

Reconstructing, deconstructing

There are three variants of this recurrent concretization-deconcretization structure, depending upon the nature and location of the indicators of unreality. In the least problematic variant, the reader is given advance warning that what follows does not belong to the reconstructed "real" world, that it is only a hashish hallucination (*GR*:367–8) or a "Leunahalluziationen" (produced by "Leunagasolin," *GR*:523–4). In another variant, the most common one, the marker is not prospective but retrospective. Prentice's nightmare is a good example; so is an episode from the history of Franz Pökler's relationship with his supposed daughter Ilse. Pökler is beginning to suspect that the girl who is allowed to visit him once annually may not be his long-lost daughter but a surrogate supplied by the Nazi brass to keep him pacified in his job at Peenemünde, and that through her "They" might also be catering to certain unspoken desires:

> "Papi," gravely unlacing, "may I sleep next to you tonight?" One of her hands had come lightly to rest on the beginning of his bare calf. Their eyes met for a half second. A number of uncertainties shifted then for Pökler and locked into sense. To his shame, his first feeling was pride. He hadn't known he was so vital to the program [. . . .]
> He hit her upside the head with his open hand, a loud and terrible blow. That took care of his anger. Then, before she could cry or speak, he had dragged her up on the bed next to him, her dazed little hands already at the buttons of his trousers, her white frock already pulled above her waist. She had been wearing nothing at all underneath, nothing all day . . . *how I've wanted you*, she whispered as paternal plow found its way into filial furrow . . . and after hours of amazing incest they dressed in silence, and crept out into the leading edge of faintest flesh dawn, everything they would ever need packed inside her flowered bag, past sleeping children doomed to the end of summer, past monitors and railway guards, down at last to the water and the fishing boats, to a fatherly old sea-dog in a braided captain's hat, who welcomed them aboard and stashed them below decks, where she snuggled down in the bunk as they got under way and sucked him for hours while the engine pounded, till the Captain called, "Come on up, and take a look at your new home!" Gray and green, through the mist, it was Denmark. "Yes, they're a free people here. Good luck to both of you!" The three of them, there on deck, stood hugging . . .
> No. What Pökler did was choose to believe she wanted comfort that night, wanted not to be alone. Despite their game, Their palpable evil, though he had no more reason to trust "Ilse" than he trusted Them, by an act not of faith, not of courage but of conservatism, he chose to believe that.
>   (*GR*:420–1)

Pökler's incestuous fantasy is identified as such almost immediately, and "edited out" of the real-world sequence of events: "No. What Pökler did was [. . .]." Moreover, should one still be in any doubt about the unreality of this incest (since there is some ambiguity here about exactly how much of this episode *did not* happen), confirmation is to be found (1) in the fact that Franz and Ilse do not defect to Denmark, and (2) in a later moment when "Pökler got hysterical and did slap her" (*GR*:430) – the "did" here indicating that the first time he had not actually slapped her after all. If he did not slap her, and if they did not defect, then the intervening events (the "hours of amazing incest") seem unlikely to have "really" occurred. The problem here is not that the incest scene remains ambiguous between fantasy and reality for very long, but rather that, in the face of such concretely, not to say shockingly, realized actions, the retraction is apt to go overlooked. Indeed, it *has* been overlooked by a number of critics, who retain the incest episode among the "real" events of the *Gravity's Rainbow* world (see, e.g., Lippman 1977:33; Levine 1978:186; Weisenburger 1981:145; Seed 1988:170).[13] Having been called upon to concretize an arresting and no doubt disturbing scene, the reader is all the more unwilling to deconcretize it again, perhaps even misreading in order to avoid having to do so.

Often, however, the unreality of an episode is not indicated by any explicit marker, prospective or retrospective, but only by some internal contradiction, or incompatibility with the frame of "reality" within which the episode has been placed, or by some gross violation of extra-textual norms of verisimilitude. Tchitcherine, describing the peculiar hallucinogenic effect of the drug Oneirine, calls this the "radical-though-plausible-violation-of-reality" (*GR*:703–4). In a modernist text like, e.g., Conrad's *Under Western Eyes* (1911), such a criterion for determining what is "real," what fantastic, might be adequate. When, say, Razumov strides through the supine body of Haldin on the snowy pavement of St. Petersburg, we have no difficulty in bracketing this apparition, however "solid, distinct, real" (Conrad 1971:38), as hallucinatory. But identifying a "radical-though-plausible-violation-of-reality" in *Gravity's Rainbow* is a rather more daunting task, as Tchitcherine himself discovers when trying to determine whether Nikolai Ripov of the Commissariat for Intelligence Activities is really, threateningly there, or only an Oneirine hallucination (*GR*:703–5). However, there are passages in which unmistakable "radical-though-plausible-violations-of-reality" reliably indicate unreality. Several of Slothrop's many fantasies and dreams fall under this category (*GR*:251, 255–6, 266, 293). So does the following passage, in which Seaman Bodine and Roger Mexico experience a joint fantasy or imaginative projection of what is about to happen to them at a banquet given by their direst enemies:

At the edge of the pit, with Justus about to light the taper, as Gretchen daintily laces the fuel with GI xylene from down in the dockyards, Seaman Bodine observes Roger's head, being held by four or six hands upside down, the lips being torn away from the teeth and the high gums already draining white as a skull, while one of the maids, a classic satin-and-lace, impish, torturable young maid, brushes the teeth with American toothpaste, carefully scrubbing away the nicotine stains and tartar. *Roger's eyes are so hurt and pleading* . . . All around, guests are whispering. "How quaint, Stefan's even thought of head cheese!" "Oh, no, it's *another* part I'm waiting to get my teeth in . . ." giggles, heavy breathing, and what's that pair of very blue peg pants all ripped . . . and what's this staining the jacket, and what, up on the spit, reddening to a fat-glazed crust, is turning, whose face is about to come rotating around, why it's –

"No ketchup, no ketchup," the hirsute bluejacket searching agitatedly among the cruets and salvers, "seems to be no . . . what th'fuck kind of a place is this, *Rog*," yelling down slant-wise across seven enemy faces, "hey, budd*ih* you find any *ketch*up down there?"

Ketchup's a code word, okay –

"Odd," replies Roger, who clearly has seen exactly the same thing down at the pit, "I was just about to ask you the same question!"

(GR:714)

What signals unreality here is the incompatibility between the framed passage, in which Roger and Bodine are already prepared and spitted, and the framing "reality," in which they are still intact.

Retroactive world-making -unmaking

If the reader experiences disorientation even when markers of unreality come before, within, or immediately after an episode, the disorientation only increases when there is a lag between concretization and deconcretization. Recall that in, e.g., *The Sound and the Fury*, reality as it appears in later, more intelligible sections only confirms and substantiates, never repudiates, the reality reflected in Benjy's mind at the beginning. In *Gravity's Rainbow*, the reverse is apt to be true: reconstructed realities are liable to be undermined by passages appearing literally hundreds of pages later in the book. This is particularly demoralizing when the elements involved participate in crucial patterns in the text. Slothrop's sexual conquests in London are crucial to the plot of *Gravity's Rainbow*, since they provide the first evidence of that affinity for the V-2 blitz which will determine Slothrop's subsequent career in the novel. So it is with some dismay that we later learn from Slothrop himself that at least some of these conquests were simply erotic fantasies, not real girls (*GR*:302).[14] Mr.

Pointsman, who is vitally interested in Slothrop's sexual activity, can console himself with the thought that Freud's hysterics, too, reported sexual experiences which "might have been lies evidentially, but were certainly the truth clinically" (*GR*:272). This sort of consolation may do for Mr. Pointsman, but it will hardly do for the reader, who, unlike Pointsman, has "witnessed" some of the scenes which are now in jeopardy of disappearing into Slothrop's fantasy-life. In particular, the reader's reconstructed picture incorporates the scene in which Slothrop returns with a girl named Darlene to her East End flat, where her landlady, Mrs. Quoad, subjects him to the "Disgusting English Candy Drill" (*GR*:114–20). Mrs. Quoad is minutely particularized: she is a widow, suffers from "a series of antiquated diseases" – currently scurvy – and dreams of her meeting with a royal pretender in the gardens of Bournemouth. But when Pointsman's agents, Speed and Perdoo, seek to verify this episode from Slothrop's erotic history, they find no Darlene at all, and as for Mrs. Quoad, the woman they find by that name is a "flashy divorcée," not a widow with scurvy, living at "a rather pedicured Mayfair address," not in the East End (*GR*:271). Mrs. Quoad, with all her minute particulars, evidently must be edited out of our reconstructed world, and along with her the "Disgusting English Candy Drill" itself, a memorable slapstick scene. As with Pökler's "amazing incest," the reader is reluctant to surrender the reality of Mrs. Quoad and the Candy Drill, and at least one critic has instructively misread the later passage, assimilating the "new" Mrs. Quoad to the Mrs. Quoad of the Candy Drill (Kaufman 1976:204).

But there are additional dimensions of uncertainty in the case of Mrs. Quoad. For the interview with the contradictory Mayfair divorcée is conducted in a context of hallucination. Speed and Perdoo themselves seem to be given to joint fantasies (*GR*:270–1), and we approach the Speed-Perdoo episode by way of the consciousness of Mr. Pointsman, who is "feeling a bit megalo these days" (*GR*:269), and who shortly thereafter will suffer hallucinations. Is this "new" Mrs. Quoad another of Speed's and Perdoo's joint fantasies, or do all three, Speed, Perdoo, and Quoad, perhaps belong to Mr. Pointman's hallucination? Is Slothrop's version, then, the "real" Mrs. Quoad after all? There is simply no way to decide, so that we are left not with a "real" Mrs. Quoad, but not quite with a figment of Slothrop's imagination, either; rather, we are left with elements whose ontological status is unstable, flickering, indeterminable.[15]

Mrs. Quoad, Darlene, and Slothrop's other girls are victims of a process of retroactive deconcretization. The opposite possibility is also exemplified in *Gravity's Rainbow*: retroactive concretization of what was originally presented as not real. Again, this effect is especially pronounced when it bears upon crucial patterns in the text. The Schwartzkommando, displaced black Africans who man German V-2 installations, play an increasingly major role at all levels of the text in the latter part of the novel. They first appear as a fiction devised by an Allied psychological-warfare unit (*GR*:74–5, 112–13), so that the discovery of real black rocket troops in Germany is understandably traumatic for all concerned, not least of all the reader (*GR*:275–6; see Smith 1982:17–28). Certain "experts" theorize that the Schwartzkommando were actually called into being by Operation Black Wing's phoney evidence of their existence.[16]

This and similar instances of the concretization of fantasy, of the "return of the repressed" (Wolfley 1977:879–80), lack the impact that the flickering reality-unreality of Mrs. Quoad has, for they are narrated summarily rather than presented to the reader through fully particularized scenes.[17] More concrete, and therefore more disorienting, is the problematical reality of Tchitcherine's rumored interviews with Wimpe, the head salesman for an IG Farben subsidiary. These scenes are said to be at best highly improbable, for political reasons: "If it were literally true, Tchitcherine wouldn't be here – there's no possible way his life could have been spared [. . .]" (*GR*:344). Nevertheless, the narrator presents a sample or composite conversation between Wimpe and Tchitcherine, hedging it round with conditionals: "Certainly he could have known Wimpe" (*GR*:344); "Tchitcherine would have stayed" (*GR*:344); "Surprising they could have got this far, if indeed they did" (*GR*:345).[18] Occasionally the narrator will sharply remind us of the doubtfulness of the whole episode: "Was Tchitcherine there at all?" (*GR*:345); "But these are rumors. Their chronology can't be trusted. Contradictions creep in" (*GR*:349). The reality of the scene is further undermined by the interpolation of an unrelated opium hallucination of one Chu Piang, an associate of Tchitcherine's, and by our knowledge that Tchitcherine is himself a habitual drug-user. All of this raises the suspicion that the interviews with Wimpe might be no more than drug-induced hallucinations of Tchitcherine's.

But the doubts so deliberately fostered throughout this episode are abruptly dispelled by a reprise that comes some three hundred and fifty pages later (*GR*:701–2). Tchitcherine's memories of one of his conversations with Wimpe are here presented in a context free from grammatical hedging and the possibility of hallucination (despite the presence of the ubiquitous Oneirine). Thus, the reality of Tchitcherine's interviews with Wimpe is retroactively confirmed.

Naturalizing

We can get some insight into the interpretive operations which are responsible for the ontological instability of *Gravity's Rainbow* if we consider the case of Pirate Prentice and his "strange talent." Prentice is a "fantasist-surrogate" (*GR*:12): he "liv[es] the fantasies of others" (*GR*:620), he is able "to take over the burden of managing them [. . .]" (*GR*:12). Early in the novel we observe Prentice in the act of managing a monstrous Adenoid which is absorbing London, the fantasy of a certain Lord Osmo of the Foreign Office (*GR*:14–16). Another early episode, Frans van der Groov's extermination of the dodoes of Mauritius (*GR*:107–11), is only revealed many hundreds of pages later to have been a fantasy in Prentice's management, one he had taken over from Katje Borgesius (*GR*:545, 620–1). And this is precisely the unsettling thing about Prentice's talent, so far as our reconstruction of the novel's world is concerned: any passage whatsoever may be a candidate for the internal world of Prentice's managed fantasies. The reader has no real right to be surprised – although we always are – when an episode is retroactively revealed to have been lifted from Prentice's mind, for that possibility is always open. Presumably, to qualify as one of Prentice's second-hand fantasies a passage should display some "radical-though-plausible-violation-of-reality," and should stand in some relation, even if only of textual continuity, to Prentice himself, but it is not clear that these conditions must invariably be met. In short, Pynchon's invention of the man who manages other people's fantasies places in our hands an immensely powerful naturalization, a ready-made strategy for accounting for anomalous passages. Critics of *Gravity's Rainbow* have not been slow to appreciate the uses to which such an all-purpose naturalization could be put.[19] For instance, one of them has suggested that we should attempt to read the dream-passage which opens the novel as somebody else's nightmare, taken over by Prentice. Perhaps, suggests this critic, it is none other than Thomas Pynchon's own personal nightmare! (Siegel 1976:52).

Now this may be whimsical, but it does at least hint at the potential comprehensiveness of this naturalization, and the quality of the intelligibility it produces. Like any powerful naturalization of a more general type – e.g. psychoanalytic, archetypal – this one is also powerfully reductive. Ultimately, it is capable of the *reductio ad absurdum* of locating the whole of the novel within the capacious mind of Pirate Prentice, converting *Gravity's Rainbow* into a peculiar psychological novel: *A Portrait of the Artist as a Fantasist-Surrogate*.[20] However, Prentice's is not the only mind capacious enough and pliant enough to absorb otherwise unmotivated material. He is not even the only fantasist-surrogate; much later, a minor character named Miklos Thanatz also shows signs of possessing Prentice's talent (*GR*:672). But with so many hallucination- and fantasy-prone characters to choose from – Slothrop, Pökler, Tchitcherine, Enzian, Pointsman, and others – there is no reason to center exclusively on Prentice the naturalizing operation that might equally well be centered on any of them.

The temptation to apply this type of naturalization on a large scale is especially strong when we reach the later parts of the novel, where fragmentation, discontinuity, lack of motivation, and unintelligibility increase drastically. The textual evidence which might justify our naturalizing these fragments as characters' dreams or fantasies is there for us to discover if we choose. For instance, the "disquieting structure" in which Prentice and others inexplicably find themselves (*GR*:537–48), and which a cryptic epigraph suggests might be Hell, seems eminently suitable for naturalization as Pirate's fantasy, perhaps a joint fantasy shared with Katje Borgesius (see Schaub 1981: 50). The clue is there: at one point, it passes through Pirate's mind that "This is one of his own in progress. Nobody else's" (*GR*:543). The even more bizarre story of Byron, the sentient and immortal light-bulb (*GR*:647–55), is explicitly connected with dream-dialogues Franz Pökler once held with a light-bulb in the underground rocket factory at Nordhausen (*GR*:647; cf. *GR*:426–7): an unmistakable invitation to naturalize.[21] The comic-book-style adventures of the Floundering Four (*GR*:647–81, 688–90) and of Takeshi and Ichizo, the "Komical Kamikazes" (*GR*:690–2, 697–9), might be read as emanating from Slothrop's mind. Here the textual evidence is more plentiful than in the case of Prentice's "disquieting structure" or Pökler's sentient bulb, but less straightforward.[22] The contents of these fragments are of a kind with which we already know Slothrop's mind to be stocked; moreover, they are all more or less contiguous with plausibly "real" episodes involving Slothrop. That is, Slothrop is "on the scene," available should one require a likely mind to which to attribute an unattached fantasy. Accordingly, more than one critic has attached these fantasies to Slothrop (Mendelson 1976:183–4; Sanders 1976:143; Slade 1983.185, 193).

If we concur in this, we will have succeeded in imposing a high degree of order on a violently disorderly section of the text. This may be a satisfying outcome, but our satisfaction will have been purchased at the price of too much of the text's interest. The text is more intelligible now, true, but less interestingly so than if we had allowed ourselves to entertain less total naturalizations, to build, if only provisionally, other possible worlds, to give full play to sheerly formal patterning, to dwell on the very tension between modes of intelligibility and the apparently unintelligible. The naturalization we have been tracing, which absorbs otherwise unmotivated passages into the minds of characters, is too powerful: it drastically curtails the process of reconstructing a world, ultimately leaving too little unresolved.

MEDIUMS AND MAPPINGS

"[. . .] not cause. It all goes along together. Parallel, not series. Metaphor. Signs and symptoms. Mapping onto different coordinate systems, I don't know . . ." [. . .] But he said: "Try to design anything that may and have it work"

(*GR*:159)

If one long-recognized trademark of Modernist fiction is the interposing of a character's mind between the reader and the external (fictive) world, with all that that implies for the reader's reconstruction of reality, then another is certainly the use of more than one mediating consciousness. The presentation of multiple minds is likely to entail the use of some device for effecting transitions from one mind to another, some device, that is, for motivating the sequence of minds. Where, as in earlier fiction, a narrator is present who is able to enter any character's mind more or less at will, mind-to-mind transitions pose relatively little difficulty.[23] But where, as typically in modernist fiction, the narrator voluntarily renounces some of his powers or even absents himself entirely, some device must be developed for motivating mind-to-mind transitions. This new device – new at least in its frequency and prominence, if not an absolute innovation – involves the use of coordinates in the "real" world external to all the minds in question. The transition from the third to the fourth chapters of the final section of Virginia Woolf's *To the Lighthouse* (1927) makes use of external coordinates in this way:

> Down there among the little boats which floated, some with their sails furled, some slowly, for it was very calm, moving away, there was one rather apart from the others. The sail was even now being hoisted. She decided that there in that very distant and entirely silent little boat Mr. Ramsay was sitting with Cam and James. Now they had got the sail up; now after a little flagging and hesitation the sails filled and, shrouded in profound silence, she watched the boat take its way with deliberation past the other boats out to sea.

4

> The sails flapped over their heads. The water chuckled and slapped the sides of the boat, which drowsed motionless in the sun. Now and then the sails rippled with a little breeze in them, but the ripple ran over them and ceased. The boat made no motion at all. Mr. Ramsay sat in the middle of the boat. He would be impatient in a moment, James thought, and Cam thought, looking at their father, who sat in the middle of the boat between them (James steered; Cam sat alone in the bow) with his legs tightly curled. He hated hanging about.
>
> (Woolf 1974:184)

The narrative moves from the mind of Lily Briscoe, watching from the shore, to the minds of those in the boat – James's, Cam's, and, at one remove, Mr. Ramsay's – by way of the sail. The sequence is evidently to be motivated in terms of some notion of "triangulation": two perceivers having focused on the same object of perception, the sail in this case, a channel is opened through which we pass from one perceiver to the other. Examples include not only the various transitions back and forth between shore and boat in the final section of *To the Lighthouse*, but also the intriguing motor-car and the skywriting airplane which motivate transitions among whole series of minds in *Mrs. Dalloway* (1925; cf. Sternberg 1970). But *Mrs. Dalloway* also features several less spectacular, more routine, but equally functional transitions of this kind: between Peter Walsh and Rezia, once by way of the little girl in Regent's Park and once by way of the vagrant woman who sings opposite the tube station; between Rezia and Hugh Whitbread, by way of the clock on Harley Street; between Elizabeth and Septimus, by way of the alternating shadow and light of an afternoon in the Strand; between various minds gathered at Clarissa Dalloway's party, first by way of the billowing yellow curtains, then later by way of the Prime Minister, who functions here much as the royal motor-car did earlier; and finally, pervasively, by way of the chimes of Big Ben.[24] There are other good modernist examples of transition by triangulation in, for instance, the "Wandering Rocks" section of *Ulysses*.

As with all types of sequence in fiction, the temporal dimension of the sequence of minds is crucial. What is the relation between the order of the formal sequence mind-object-mind and the temporality of the reconstructed fictive episode? Evidently there are two possibilities. Either the order at the formal level represents, by its own sequentiality, consecutiveness at the reconstructed level – one person perceives an object, then another person does, as is predominantly the case with the motor-car and skywriter of *Mrs. Dalloway*; or sequential order at the formal level represents simultaneity at the reconstructed level, as is the case with the transition from Lily Briscoe to those in the boat or, even more markedly, with the following transition from Mrs. Dalloway's mind to Miss Kilman's. (The preceding paragraphs had been devoted to Mrs. Dalloway's interior monologue.)

but here the other clock, the clock which always struck two minutes after Big Ben, came shuffling in with its lap full of odds and ends, which it dumped down as if Big Ben were all very well with his majesty laying down the law, so solemn, so just, but she must remember all sorts of little things besides – Mrs. Marsham, Ellie Henderson, glasses for ices – all sorts of little things came flooding and lapping and dancing in on the wake of that solemn stroke which lay flat like a bar of gold on the sea. Mrs. Marsham, Ellie Henderson, glasses for ices. She must telephone now at once.

Volubly, troublously, the late clock sounded, coming in on the wake of Big Ben, with its lap full of trifles. Beaten up, broken up by the assault of carriages, the brutality of vans, the eager advance of myriads of angular men, of flaunting women, the domes and spires of offices and hospitals, the last relics of this lap full of odds and ends seemed to break, like the spray of an exhausted wave, upon the body of Miss

Kilman standing still in the street for a moment to mutter, "It is the flesh."

(Woolf 1971:141–2)

In the "real" world, Clarissa's and Miss Kilman's experiences are simultaneous, in parallel, as the presence of the late clock's chimes in both their fields of perception emphasizes. But narrative, by its very nature incapable of representing simultaneity except by sequence, must deploy this moment of parallel experience as a transition from one perceiving mind to another by way of a mutually-perceived sound.

Is the real-world temporal order ever reversed in this kind of sequence? Do we ever pass from a mind in the present to a mind in the past by way of external coordinates? Evidently not, unless we extend our description of this device to cover certain related phenomena: the use of external objects to effect a transition between different moments of consciousness of a single individual, or between present experience and memorial experience. The *locus classicus* is of course Proust (the madeleine, the uneven paving-stones, etc.), although in *A la recherche du temps perdu* (1913–27) such transitions, instead of being left to the reader to motivate, are explicitly motivated by the narrator's elaborate discurses on the mechanism of "involuntary memory." However, motivation is left to the reader to supply in the idiot's monologue of *The Sound and the Fury* – of necessity, since Benjy lacks Marcel's powers of introspection and articulation. Not only do objects or phenomena in Benjy's immediate field of perception (snagging himself on a nail, wading in the branch, the carriage, the gate, the fire) give him access to past moments of consciousness, allowing him to relive them, but certain remembered objects or phenomena (cold weather, the smell of Versh's house, a phrase uttered by Roskus, rounding a corner) allow him to pass from one past experience to another within his memory.

Mediums of transition

Several crucial transitions in *Gravity's Rainbow* similarly reverse real-world temporal order; yet these are not transitions among moments of consciousness of a single self, as in Proust and Faulkner, but genuine transitions among separate minds. In order to motivate these mind-to-mind transitions, one must shift one's sights from coordinates in the characters' "real" phenomenal world to coordinates in the Other World, the world "beyond the Zero."

A passage early in the novel establishes the paradigm for all subsequent occurrences of this "mediumistic" transition. Carroll Eventyr has been serving as the principal "reflector" of life at a wartime parapsychology-research unit in Kent. Although the narrative shifts fairly freely from his mind to other, contiguous minds, or to the narrator's perspective, Eventyr's consciousness is nevertheless the touchstone throughout the passage

(*GR*:145–54). Now, Carroll Eventyr is a spiritualist medium. His "control," the spirit who speaks through him, and through whom he contacts others in the spirit-world, is one Peter Sachsa, himself once a successful medium in Weimar Germany. Thus, it is by way of Sachsa that a transition is made between Eventyr in Kent, 1945, and the Weimar Republic sometime in the late twenties:

> On his side, Eventyr [the medium] tends to feel wholly victimized, even a bit resentful. Peter Sachsa [the control], on his, falls amazingly out of character and into nostalgia for life, the old peace, the Weimar decadence that kept him fed and moving. Taken forcibly over in 1930 by a blow from a police truncheon during a street action in Neukölln, he recalls now, sentimentally, evenings of rubbed darkwood, cigar smoke, ladies in chiseled jade, panne, attar of damask roses, the latest angular pastel paintings on the walls, the latest drugs inside the many little table drawers. More than any mere "Kreis," on most nights full mandalas come to bloom: all degrees of society, all quarters of the capital, palms down on that famous blood veneer, touching only at little fingers. Sachsa's table was like a deep pool in the forest. Beneath the surface things were rolling, slipping, beginning to rise . . . . Walter Asch ("Taurus") was visited one night by something so unusual it took three "Hieropons" (250 mg.) to bring him back, and even so he seemed reluctant to sleep. They all stood watching him, in ragged rows resembling athletic formations, Wimpe the IG-man who happened to be holding the Hieropon keying on Sargner, a civilian attached to General Staff, flanked by Lieutenant Weissman, recently back from South-West Africa, and the Herero aide he'd brought with him, staring, staring at them all, at everything.
>
> (*GR*: 152)

Having accomplished the passage from present to past, from Eventyr's world to Sachsa's, the narrative is now able to circulate among the minds of Sachsa's circle as it had among those of Eventyr's:

> Each face that watched Walter Asch was a puppet stage: each a separate routine.
> . . . shows good hands yes droop and wrists as far us as muscle relaxant respiratory depression . . .
> . . . same . . . same . . . my own face white in mirror three threethirty four march of the Hours clock ticking room no can't go in no not enough light not enough no *aaahhh* –
> . . . theatre nothing but Walter really look at head phony angle wants to catch light good fill-light throw a yellow gel . . .
> (A pneumatic toy frog jumps up onto a lily pad trembling: beneath

the surface lies a terror . . . a late captivity . . . but he floats now over
the head of what would take him back . . . his eyes cannot be read . . .)
    . . . mba rara m'eroto ondyoze . . . mbe mu munine m'oruroto ayo
u n'omuinyo . . .

(*GR*:152)

We are plunged successively into the streams-of-consciousness of the spec-
tators of Walter Asch's memorable seance, although we can only identify
a few of them specifically: Wimpe ("shows good hands," etc.), the Herero
aide ("mba rara m'eroto," etc.), perhaps others who have not even been
named here (does the passage beginning "theatre nothing but" indicate
that the film-director Gerhard von Göll was present?).

The structural parallelism between this mode of transition and modernist
transition by triangulation is striking. However, where the modernist
device involves the use of coordinates in the "real" visible, audible, tan-
gible, etc. world shared by the characters, Pynchon's device involves the
invisible, extra-sensory world, accessible only to the likes of Eventyr.
Where the modernist sequence represents either simultaneity or consecutiveness at the level of the reconstructed world, Pynchon's sequence carries
the narrative by mind-to-mind transition backwards into the past.

The mode of transition worked out in little in this passage is almost
immediately afterwards applied on a much larger scale (*GR*:154–67). Again
the narrative moves from Eventyr the medium, through Sachsa, his control,
to Sachsa's Weimar milieu; but this time it lingers within the various
minds it finds there – that of Sachsa's lover Leni, that of her husband
Franz – rather than hurrying on from one to the next as in the earlier
passage. Note that Sachsa's mind is not in any sense embedded in Carroll
Eventyr's, as one narrator may be embedded within another's narration
Chinese-box fashion in, e.g., Conrad or Faulkner. Nor is Leni's consciousness embedded in Sachsa's; and certainly Franz's is not. Mediumistic contact
only allows us to motivate, in terms of norms of verisimilitude presupposed
by this novel (mediums, controls, a spirit-world, etc.), transitions on the
formal level; it does not authorize our reconstructing a "real" situation
in which the contents of one mind are accessible to another.

Mapping

When the narrative next makes the transition from Eventyr's world to
Sachsa's by way of the "Other Side," a new element will be introduced,
one which also recalls typical modernist structures, but again with a
difference. Eventyr has been given to understand, by oblique and sinister
hints, that he is in some sense Peter Sachsa's double. He speculates that
the parallelism might extend to his lover, Nora Dodson-Truck: "If there
are analogies here, if Eventyr does, somehow, map on to Peter Sachsa,

then does Nora Dodson-Truck become the woman Sachsa loved, Leni Pökler?" (*GR*:218). The passage which immediately follows serves to answer this question in the affirmative, for here we pass imperceptibly – ambiguous pronoun references help smooth the transition – from Eventyr's relationship with Nora, to Sachsa's with Leni (*GR*:218–20). Clearly this transition is motivated at least in part by the mediumistic contact which we already know to exist between Eventyr and Sachsa. But just as clearly it also relates to the characteristically modernist structure of analogical integration. As Sternberg has demonstrated with respect to Faulkner's *Light in August*, the modernist novel often resists attempts to unify it according to mimetic models, forcing the reader to discover non mimetic unifying patterns: analogies between events, strands of action, characters, themes (Sternberg 1970; cf. Perry 1968). Pynchon's metaphor of "mapping" is a good one for this process; nevertheless, the transition in this passage is significantly unlike modernist analogical integration. In novels like *Light in August*, analogical integration cannot be related to norms of verisimilitude; it is expressly anti-mimetic. That is, analogical patterns lie at a level above that of the fictive world in which the characters move. By contrast, in *Gravity's Rainbow* "mapping" is mimetically motivated. The correspondence between Eventyr and Nora on the one hand, and Sachsa and Leni on the other, is, in the terms of the model of reality presupposed by this novel, "real" – parapsychological or supernatural, but "real."

This transition by "mapping," if dependent upon bizarre norms of verisimilitude, is, at least, readily intelligible in one respect: the analogical pattern upon which it is based is known in advance. Indeed, Eventyr's troubled ruminations have no other function than to inform the reader that Eventyr maps onto Sachsa, Nora onto Leni, thereby explicitly motivating the transition from Eventyr, 1945, to Sachsa, 1930, which follows. The text is less attentive to the reader's comfort in other instances of transition by "mapping." Consider the bizarre transition between Slothrop's sado-masochistic episode with Margerita Erdmann and Franz Pökler's memories of the begetting of his daughter Ilse (*GR*:395–8). In a derelict film studio, 1945, Slothrop and Greta recreate a scene of bondage and copulation from a film in which Greta once played, Slothrop doubling as Greta's one-time co-star, Max Schlepzig, whose passport he happens by an absurd coincidence to be carrying. Sometime in the thirties, Franz Pökler, sexually aroused by this same film, had come home to father a child on his wife Leni. This daughter, Ilse, is thus the double on this side of the cinema-screen, so to speak, of the daughter that Greta conceived during the filming of the scene. A whole system of analogies among characters and events arises from these episodes: both Slothrop and Franz Pökler map onto Max Schlepzig; Leni maps onto Greta, Ilse onto Greta's daughter Bianca, and Greta onto her own earlier self. But one could not say that this paradigm of doublings allows us to motivate the transition from Slothrop's consciousness to Pökler's. If anything, the reverse is true: it is, rather, the sequence which allows us to reconstruct the analogical pattern.

Or, finally, consider the even more bizarre transition from Geli Tripping, the witch, to Gottfied, Captain Blicero's catamite, very late in the novel (*GR*:720–1). One critic (Wolfley 1977:883–4) has rightly observed that there is no justification for this transition in terms of plot or chronology: Geli and Gottfried have never had even indirect dealings, and Geli's moment of consciousness is located in spring 1946, Gottfried's the year before. This critic is equally correct in finding the motivation for this conjunction at the level of thematic analogy: Geli meditates upon man's role as promoter of death in Creation, while Gottfried is harangued by Blicero on the "American Death" about to be visited on Europe. But there are, in addition, other analogies which make this another example of the mediumistic "mapping" transition. Blicero reminds Gottfried of a time when "you used to whisper me to sleep with stories of us one day living on the Moon" (*GR*:723). Now, we have heard of such stories before, but in connection with Franz Pökler's daughter Ilse (*GR*:410, 420), never in connection with Gottfied. So Gottfried, it seems, maps onto Ilse; and Ilse, as we know, maps onto Greta Erdmann's daughter Bianca. Geli Tripping, in turn, is a sort of Bianca-surrogate, both having been Slothrop's lovers at one time or another. This might seem an extraordinarily devious way to establish an analogy between Geli and Gottfried, but it should be borne in mind, first, that by this point in the novel all the young female characters have begun to merge in Slothrop's mind, but more so in the reader's, so that to equate Gottfried with any one of them is tantamount to equating him with the whole series; and, secondly, that the deviousness and implausibility of the connection may very well be the point. This transition may have been introduced, among other reasons, to focus sharply for us our growing suspicion that almost any character in this novel can be analogically related to almost any other character – to raise for us the demoralizing prospect of free and all but unmanageable analogical patterning (see Bersani 1990:189–96).

Last but not least, it should be recalled that Geli Tripping, as a practicing witch, is qualified to effect "mediumistic" transitions from mind to mind by way of the "Other Side" in the same way that the spiritualist medium Carroll Eventyr was. Viewed in one light, then, the transition from Geli to Gottfried, just as the earlier transition from Slothrop to Franz Pökler, appears as an instance of Pynchon's outrageous and subversive manipulation of analogies. But it is also strictly mimetic in a world in which, as we already know, occult "mappings" are possible.

DE-CONDITIONING THE READER

> If there is something comforting – religious, if you want – about paranoia, there is still also anti-paranoia, where nothing is connected to anything, a condition not many of us can bear for long.
>
> (*GR*:343)

Pynchon's readers have every right to feel conned, bullied, betrayed. Indeed, these responses are the essence of the aesthetic effect of *Gravity's Rainbow*. We have been invited to undertake the kinds of pattern-making and pattern-interpreting operations which, in the modernist texts with which we have all become familiar, would produce intelligible meaning; here, they produce at best a parody of intelligibility. We have been confronted with representations of mental processes of the kind which, in modernist texts, we could have relied upon in reconstructing external (fictive) reality. In *Gravity's Rainbow*, such representations are always liable to be qualified retroactively as dream, fantasy, or hallucination, while the reconstructions based upon them are always subject to contradiction or cancellation. The ultimate effect is radically to destabilize novelistic ontology. Similarly, we have been invited to motivate transitions among sequences of minds in a way which obviously relates to the modernist device of transition by "triangulation," only to find ourselves led into increasingly bizarre and increasingly unstable "occult" transitions. Elusive modes of intelligibility and, if that weren't enough, unacceptable or distressing types of content – pornography, broad slapstick comedy, technical scientific material, etc. – one might well wonder, along with the Pulitzer committee that rejected *Gravity's Rainbow*, what to make of it all.

Or perhaps the question should be not so much what to make of it, as what it makes of one. For the effect of this troublesome novel is, finally, the salutary one of disrupting the conditioned responses of the modernist reader (and we are all, still, modernist readers), of de-conditioning the reader. It is the same effect, no doubt, as *Ulysses*, *Mrs. Dalloway*, and *The Sound and the Fury* had on their first readers. Pynchon at one point quotes Pavlov's remarks about the extinction of a conditioned reflex "beyond the point of reducing a reflex to zero," "a silent extinction beyond the zero" (*GR*:84–5). The readerly equivalent of this de-conditioning "beyond the zero" is that state in which "nothing is connected to anything" which Pynchon calls anti-paranoia. It is an instructive, perhaps even hygienic, state to be in for a time, even though it is, as Pynchon goes on to say, "a condition not many of us can bear for long" (*GR*:434). My use of the metaphors of paranoia and anti-paranoia for our habits of reading and the damage which *Gravity's Rainbow* does them may seem extravagant, but it is not wholly unadvised. As one of Pynchon's critics has penetratingly remarked, the frame of mind in which one is required to read modernist fiction, the mind-set of *tout se tient*, might aptly be characterized as paranoiac. Paranoia, it seems,

> is the condition under which most of modern literature comes to life: the author relies on the reader to find correspondences between names, colors, or the physical attributes of characters and other invisible qualities of those characters, places, and actions, while to do so in "real life" would clearly be an indication of paranoid behavior.
>
> (Siegel 1976:50)

Pynchon's text sets itself against this modernist mind-set, chiefly by luring paranoid readers – modernist readers – into interpretive dark alleys, culs-de-sac, impossible situations, and requiring them to find their way out by some other path than the one they came in by.

We could make a different approach to the effect of *Gravity's Rainbow* by way of Tsur's (1975) illuminating distinction between certitude and "negative capability" in literary interpretation. This distinction derives, of course, from the famous and much-debated remark in John Keats's letter to his brothers (21/7 December 1817): "I mean Negative Capability, that is when a man is capable of being in uncertainties, Mysteries, doubts, without any irritable reaching after fact & reason" (quoted in Tsur 1975:776). It is certainly the case, as Tsur observes, that too much literary criticism is characterized by a "reaching after fact & reason" and an incapability of "being in uncertainties, Mysteries, doubts"; and scarcely any criticism has been more "irritable" in its "reaching" than the criticism written on *Gravity's Rainbow*. It has become commonplace among Pynchon's critics to complain about the way Pynchon criticism has tended to translate the disturbing experience of reading *Gravity's Rainbow* directly into tractable, coherent statements of theme (see, e.g., Poirier 1973:167, 1975:19; Levine 1976:113; Levine and Leverenz 1976a:11; Rosenbaum 1976:67–8); needless to say, nearly everything is lost in the translation. From first to last, the reader's experience proves that *Gravity's Rainbow* will not boil down quite so readily to intelligible patterns of theme, or indeed to any of the patterns which we have learned to expect from modernist texts. Reading *Gravity's Rainbow* is good, if strenuous, training in negative capability.

I would, finally, like to venture some hypotheses about the general relation between postmodernist writing and literary history. These are not in the nature of considered conclusions, but strictly of hypotheses to be verified only by further empirical study.

The received verdict on postmodernist fiction has tended to be that it constitutes an affront to the whole prior history of literature, that it is directed against representation and intelligibility in general. This view of the universal subversiveness of postmodernism can be traced, I suspect, to the French criticism of the 1950s and 1960s which sprang up around the *nouveau* (and later *nouveau nouveau*) *roman*, on both sides, pro and con of the question (see, e.g., Barthes 1964:29–40, 63–70, 101–5, 198–205). I would like to suggest that this view is an effect of the perspective of these particular critics and apologists at their particular historical moment. Postmodernism, I would like to suggest, is less an indiscriminate shotgun-blast than a kind of sharpshooting directed at specific targets.

For the postmodernism which those seminal critics defined (without, indeed, ever using the term, which did not enter French critical discourse until Lyotard) was a particular postmodernism – that of the *nouveau* and *nouveau nouveau roman* – and the literary past which it spurned and subverted was equally specific: not representation or intelligibility in general, but the particular historical phenomenon which might be called Balzacian realism. By the same token, I have been arguing that the variety of postmodernist writing exemplified by *Gravity's Rainbow* – the variety of which Pynchon is perhaps the preeminent practitioner[25] – is specifically directed against a particular norm of modernist reading.[26] Other varieties may well be related to other specific historical phenomena; in any case, it is clear that it will not do simply to set postmodernism in opposition to the whole prior development of narrative fiction. Any respectable description of a postmodernist text should include some account of the specific repertoire of interpretive operations – whether that of Balzacian realism, that of some particular variety of modernism, or any other – against which it is directed; the repertoire, in other words, which the text in question "keys on." This way we will eliminate the "apocalyptic" view of literary history (see, e.g., Barthes 1977:155 64), whereby serious fiction is supposed to have become at one moment, and across the board, irrevocably and monolithically postmodernist.[27]

APPENDIX 3.1: WRITING PYNCHON

The present essay has provoked interesting responses both from the conservative wing of Pynchon criticism (e.g. Hume 1987) and from its radical wing, but it is in particular to the radical poststructualist critique by Alex McHoul and David Wills in *Writing Pynchon* (1990:45–50) that I would like to reply here.

McHoul and Wills treat my paper as parallel to their own frustrated attempt at analyzing *Gravity's Rainbow* in terms of a distinction between the cinematic and the real. Their cinematic analysis fails, they conclude, because the fluidity and indeterminacy of representation in *Gravity's Rainbow* makes distinguishing between representations of movies and the "real world" virtually impossible. McHoul and Wills rightly see this failure as bearing on my analysis of the unstable relationship between the hallucinated and the real in the case of the two (or one? or non-existent?) Mrs. Quoads. That is, just as in the one case it is finally impossible to sort out segments "belonging" to movies from those lying "outside" the cinematic sphere in the "real" world, so in the case of Mrs. Quoad (and the other ontological cruxes I describe) it is finally impossible to distinguish reality from hallucination, or to use the "reality" segments as norms for determining which segments are "hallucinated." In the final analysis, the distinction between real and hallucinated is indeterminable – and my attempt to use these categories in describing the text misguided – because of the leveling effect of ontological instability in *Gravity's Rainbow*, so that in the end what remains is not segments possessing identifiably different ontological statuses (real, hallucinated, filmic, etc.), but only "text" and "more-text": "Bits of *Gravity's Rainbow* ... should be treated as bits of other text rather than as privileged 'quotations' or points of determinate verification of the reading" (McHoul and Wills 1990:49).

Furthermore, according to McHoul and Wills it is misguided to try to speak of isolable consciousnesses in the text, at least if by "consciousness" one means some kind of "sovereign" or "transcendent" consciousness distinguishable from other consciousnesses and from its own contents (thoughts). This leaves us with no way of talking about transitions from consciousness to consciousness, given that neither consciousnesses nor their contents can be isolated in the flux of textuality. Here, I think, I have been slightly misread, for McHoul and Wills seem to imply (1990: 49–50) that the mind-to-mind contact I describe in "Mediums and mappings" above involves transfer of the *contents* of these minds (thoughts), while, if they had read more carefully, they would have seen that this possibility has been explicitly ruled out: "Mediumistic contact," I wrote, "only allows us to motivate ... transitions on the formal level; it does not authorize our reconstructing a 'real' situation in which the contents of one mind are accessible to another." That is, mind-to-mind contact in *Gravity's Rainbow* only serves as a formal alibi for shifts of focus from one time and space to another, not for the circulation of "thoughts" among different minds.

This last incidental misreading apart, I find I can agree with everything McHoul and Wills say; in fact, I believe I *have already said it myself*, if not outright then in effect and by implication, in the present essay. Nevertheless, when they describe me as having a "hang-up with readers having to reconstruct what 'really' happened from what a character dreamed, hallucinated, etc." (1990:49), I do not recognize in this a description of my practice. Why not? Obviously, there has been some talking at cross-purposes somewhere, but where?

The "where" emerges when McHoul and Wills quote my phrase about the "demoralizing prospect of free and all-but-unmanageable analogical patterning," and suggest that, unlike themselves, I am "aghast" at this prospect (1990:50). In fact, of course, "demoralizing" is ironic here, as even a cursory reading of the larger context would show (and McHoul and Wills have given this paper a good deal more than a cursory reading). This "free and all-but-unmanageable" patterning I regard as one of the pedagogical tools employed by *Gravity's Rainbow* in its de-conditioning and re-education of the modernist reader. The "demoralizing prospect" is not mine, but the modernist reader's, facing this challenge to his or her codes of reading; or rather it is that of the modernist reader *in myself*, that part of my reading self that persists in trying to read according to the codes of my modernist education, despite my already knowing that these codes are inappropriate and bound to fail. Similarly with my alleged "hang-up" with having to reconstruct what really happened: this "hang-up," I would maintain, is the modernist reader's, and *Gravity's Rainbow* has been designed so as to provoke it in us and to demonstrate to us its futility.

McHoul and Wills begin by saying that "it's possible to argue that all critical readings are based on assumptions about what constitutes the 'real' (as opposed to, say, the dreamed, the fantasised, the cinematic, the fictive and so on)" (1990:45); and that "we know of no critical reading . . . (present company included)" that can do without either "explicit decisions" or "implicit assumptions" concerning "what is veridical in *Gravity's Rainbow*" (1990:46). I could not agree more; my entire object in the present essay has only been to specify what the relevant "assumptions" and grounds for decision-making are in the case of *Gravity's Rainbow*, and to argue that they derive from modernist codes of reading, which the text then goes on to overturn. McHoul and Wills conclude: "there would be no need for a reader to make such a separation [between the real and the mental] in order to make sense of the novel" (1990: 50). Here, precisely, we part company: for it is my contention that readers *will* need to try (and finally fail) to make such a separation, if "making sense" of *Gravity's Rainbow* is to involve undergoing the experience of learning the inadequacy of modernist codes.

McHoul and Wills would seem to believe that one can simply, as it were, *will oneself* to occupy a position somewhere on the far side of modernist reading, from which perspective *Gravity's Rainbow* would appear not as an unstable world made up of fragments of different onto-logical statuses (some problematically "real," others "mental," still others indeterminable), but only as "text" and "more-text." That this "willing" is not after all so easy is demonstrated by the strenuousness of their own writing, with its many false starts and self-cancellations, switchbacks, improvisations, and neologisms. If their own writing is anything to go by, reading "textually" requires constant vigilance against backsliding into the "normal" reading-habits of one's modernist education. In fact, I might go so far as to argue that reading "textually," as they propose to do, far from being easy, may not (yet) even be possible: for "we are all, still, modernist readers." In any case, we do not reach the position beyond modernist reading by willing ourselves there (like Dorothy tapping her ruby slippers together and reciting "There's no place like home"), but only by passing through some such experience of the failure of modernist codes as the one provided by *Gravity's Rainbow* itself. Part of the meaning of *Gravity's Rainbow* is that it has been designed to *take us to* the place from which McHoul and Wills have proposed to *set out*.

Chapter 4

"You used to know what these words mean": Misreading *Gravity's Rainbow* (1985)

BEING IN UNCERTAINTIES, MYSTERIES, DOUBTS

> You are the second person.
>
> (W.S. Merwin 1970:116)

Thomas Pynchon's *Gravity's Rainbow* holds the mirror up not so much to Nature as to Reading. Wherever we open the novel we find images of our own behavior as readers and critics. Slothrop, descendant of "word-smitten Puritans,"[1] reads raindrops as "giant asterisks [. . .] inviting him to look down at the bottom of the text of the day, where footnotes will explain all" (*GR*:204). Enzian, the Rocket-Kabbalist, thinks of himself and his people as "the scholar-magicians of the Zone, with somewhere in it a Text, to be picked to pieces, annotated, explicated, and masturbated till it's all squeezed limp of its last drop" (*GR*:520). Mr. Pointsman is obsessed with The Book – Pavlov, not Holy Writ (*GR*:47, 87–8). Katje Borgesius correctly interprets Osbie Feel's cryptic movie scenario (*GR*:533–55). Igor Blobadjian of the New Turkic Alphabet G Committee learns how to read molecular structure (*GR*:355). Säure Bummer reads reefers (*GR*:441–2), Miklos Thanatz reads whip-scars (*GR*:484), Pfc. Eddie Pensiero reads shivers (*GR*:641), and Ronald Cherrycoke reads personal effects – cravat, fountain-pen, pince-nez (*GR*:146, 150). All these characters and many others – besides those in Pynchon's other novels (Stencil, Oedipa, Emory Bortz) – perform acts of interpretive criticism. These are didactic, even monitory models: they teach us how hazardous the business of interpretation can be, how prone we are to misread.[2]

Pynchon's critic-heroes engage in two different modes of reading: on the one hand, paranoid reading, "the discovery that everything is connected, everything in the Creation, a secondary illumination – not yet blindingly One, but at least connected" (*GR*:703); on the other hand, antiparanoid reading, "where nothing is connected to anything, a condition not many of us can bear for long" (*GR*:434). Indeed we cannot; so it is hardly surprising that most of the critics *in* Pynchon's fiction (with a few important partial exceptions – Oedipa, Slothrop), as well as most of the critics who have written *about* Pynchon, have tended toward the paranoid pole. One critic (Siegel 1978:15) has gone so far as to suggest that paranoia might be *the* critical mode of modernism; and, indeed, *everything is connected* would make an apposite epigraph for a good many books of literary criticism written since 1925 or so.

The paranoid and antiparanoid modes of reading in fact have a long history, though they have gone under different names in the past. One such set of alternative names was proposed by Keats in the famous letter in which he distinguished between "Negative Capability" – "when a man is capable of being in uncertainties, Mysteries, doubts" – and its opposite, the "irritable reaching after fact & reason" (see Tsur 1975); anti-paranoid and paranoid reading, respectively. We have yet to see much exercise of negative capability in critical interpretations of *Gravity's Rainbow*.[3] Like Coleridge (according to Keats), Pynchon's critics have seemed particularly irritable in their reaching after fact and reason, and particularly incapable of remaining in uncertainties, Mysteries, doubts for very long.

The consequence of the drive for critical certitude, in a text like *Gravity's Rainbow*, is very often simple misreading, not seeing what is before one's eyes because it does not jibe with one's interpretive hypothesis. In the preceding chapter I gave some examples of tendentious critical misreadings, the common denominator being their oversimplification of the complex and problematical ontology of objects and beings in Pynchon's world. In each of these misconstrued passages, an entity or event that we have assumed to be "real" (within the novel's fictional world) is shown not to be "real" after all, but hallucinated, fantasized, or hypothetical: "Of course it happened. Of course it didn't happen" (GR:667). The critics, it seems, resist having to surrender the "reality" of a particularly engaging or stirring or rich passage – a pornographic or slapstick episode, a thematically meaty dialogue. No doubt it would be difficult to live in an ontologically unstable world like that of Pynchon's novel, where things flicker between reality and unreality; but it has proven to be nearly as difficult for the certitude-seeking critic who is forced, like Slothrop, to rely upon "dreams, psychic flashes, omens, cryptographies, drug-epistemologies, all dancing on a ground of terror, contradiction, absurdity" (GR:582). Such a critic, confronted with such material, will almost inevitably misread.

Unless, that is, one chooses an alternative strategy – equally a manifestation of the quest for certitude, and not of negative capability – which involves framing the entire novel as the contents of one or several characters' minds. Prentice, the "fantasist-surrogate" (GR:12), would be a good candidate for this all-encompassing consciousness, as would drug-addled Slothrop, or any of a number of other hallucination-prone characters. This powerful strategy has been used before, notoriously by Bruce Morrissette in his interpretation of Robbe-Grillet's early novels. It eliminates ontological instability by substituting an epistemological and psychological prob-

lem, thus "de-realizing" everything and removing the sting from the question, real or unreal? But the price is exorbitant: the possibility of
entertaining several alternative worlds at once, the need to gauge the
evidential value of any given passage, the whole rich hesitation between
competing hypotheses – all these are lost.

So we see where, in general, the quest for certitude leads us in Pynchon's
fiction: either to misreading, or to premature and deadening naturalization
(see Culler 1975:131–60). But let us look in greater detail at another basic
feature of Pynchon's poetics that seems to provoke certitude-seeking critics' utmost exertions. What are we to make of a passage such as this?

> she looked at him once, of course he still remembers, from down at
> the end of a lunchwagon counter [. . .] both of you, at both ends of
> the counter, could feel it, feel your age delivered into a new kind of time
> that may have allowed you to miss the rest, the graceless expectations of
> old men who watched, in bifocal and mucus indifference, watched you
> lindy-hop into the pit by millions, as many millions as necessary . . . .
> Of course Slothrop lost her, and kept losing her – it was an American
> requirement – out the windows of the Greyhound, passing into beveled
> stonery, green and elm-folded on into a failure of perception, or, in
> a more sinister sense, of will (you used to know what these words
> mean)[. . . .]
>
> (*GR*:472)

Gravity's Rainbow, Edward Mendelson tells us (1978a:8), with passages
like this one in mind, "is in part a second-person novel which periodically
addresses you." Indeed – but who is *you*?

CIRCUITS OF NARRATIVE COMMUNICATION

> A pronoun may seem a small matter, but she matters, he matters, it
> matters, they matter.
>
> (John Berryman 1976:327)

You, in modern English the only pronoun of direct address, always[4]
implies an act of communication. The most reliable sign of narratorial
"voice," it compels the reader, by its very presence in a text, to hypothesize a circuit of communication joining an addressor and an addressee. In
"standard" accounts of textual communication (e.g. Tamir 1976), the
function of *you* is presumed to be symmetrical with that of *I*, each
pronoun necessarily implying the other, and each, on its own or in combination with the other, implying a communicative act. By another influential (and controversial) account, that of Banfield (1982), this relationship
is *asymmetrical*: *I* does not necessarily imply a *you*, and so does not
necessarily imply a communicative circuit; but *you* does necessarily imply
an *I*.[5] By either account, in other words, the presence of *you* always

presupposes two parties to the communicative act, the one to whom *you* is addressed (the referent of *you*), and the one doing the addressing. Wherever *you* occurs in a text, there (if nowhere else) the reader is justified in seeking to identify these two parties, and in reconstructing the communicative circuit that presumably joins them.

In texts of narrative fiction, the second person is potentially ambiguous (indeed multiguous), and this is a potentiality that, as we shall see, the text of *Gravity's Rainbow* systematically exploits, to the reader's discomfiture. The ambiguity arises from the fact that any instance of *you* may function in any of several different communicative circuits, located on different narrative levels or planes of the text. The reader's first challenge is thus to determine, for any instance of *you*, on which plane it functions. To keep our model manageably simple, we can assume that texts (and their readers) operate with a system of three basic narrative planes and several typical circuits of narrative communication.

Author and reader

The first plane does not, strictly speaking, figure in the structure of narrative communication at all, for this is the plane on which (1) *the author addresses the reader*. It is part of the definition of fictionality (and by "narrative communication" I mean *fictional* narrative exclusively) that the empirical author is excluded from the communicative structure: he or she does not command an *I* in the text, and correspondingly, the empirical reader is not available to act as recipient of *you*. This is not to say that empirical authors and readers are irrelevant to a total understanding of texts, for of course they anchor a text in real historical time and space, and hypotheses about the historical cultures that produce and receive texts are crucial to the hermeneutic process. But the empirical author communicates not directly but *indirectly*, using the entire resources of the text, and delegating his or her communicative acts to surrogates: narrators and characters. Some theories of narrative have sought to interpolate an "implied author" in the model of narrative communication, but this is mistaken, for the "implied author" is not a party to an act of communication (see Bal 1981:202–10; Genette 1983:93–107). Rather, the term "implied author" properly serves to designate our hypotheses about the total meaning of the text, in other words, the reader's hypothetical reconstruction of the empirical author's norms and values.[6]

Narrator and narratee

The second plane is the one on which *a narrator addresses a narratee* (see Prince 1973; Piwowarczyk 1976; Rabinowitz 1977). Here we may distinguish two types of communicative circuit, depending upon whether the narrator is located (2a) *outside* the world about which "he" or "she" narrates[7] or (2b) *inside* that narrated world, on the same ontological level as the characters; or, to use Genette's terminology, depending upon whether the narrator is *extra-diegetic* or *diegetic*.

When readers or critics speak casually of the author addressing the reader directly, what they usually have in mind is communicative circuits of the first type, in which (2a) *an extra-diegetic narrator addresses an extra-diegetic narratee*. This casual conflation of roles is justified to the extent that here the empirical author's textual surrogate, the narrator, approximates most closely the functions of the real author, just as the narrator's opposite number, the narratee, approximates most closely the functions of the empirical reader. We are likeliest to infer an act of communication between extra-diegetic narrator and narratee (*you* being identified with the narratee) whenever the act of narration itself or its reception is the topic. Characters are ruled out as plausible recipients of such communications, for they exist *within* the narrated world, and only someone outside of it, capable of reflecting *on* the narrative and its reception, could fill the role of addressee appropriately. The second person functioning as extra-diegetic narratee is typical of eighteenth-century fiction:

> Bestir thyself therefore on this Occasion; for tho' we will always lend thee proper Assistance in difficult Places, as we do not, like some others, expect thee to use the Arts of Divination to discover our Meaning, yet we shall not indulge thy Laziness where nothing but thy own Attention is required, for thou art highly mistaken if thou dost imagine that we intended, when we began this great work, to leave thy Sagacity nothing to do, or that, without sometimes exercising this Talent, thou wilt be able to travel through our pages with any Pleasure or Profit to thyself.
> (Fielding 1974:II, 614)

Such metanarrative acts (or "surjustifications," to use Prince's term (1973:185)), bearing upon the narratee's expectations or supposed extratextual knowledge, are reliable indications that the communicative circuit is extra-diegetic.

In the second type of circuit at this level, (2b) *a diegetic narrator addresses a diegetic narratee*. In this type of circuit, of which Camus's *La Chute* is a paradigmatic example, both the narrator and his or her narratee are characters belonging to the narrated world, though one or both of the parties to the communication may be more or less "effaced" or "invisible." What distinguishes a character-narrator from other characters is simply that he or she narrates about the world they all share. In other words, circuits of this type, joining character-narrators and character-narratees, are distinguishable only by their *narrative function*, not by either their logical or their ontological status, from other communicative circuits joining character-addressors and character-addressees.

Characters

At the third level, that of the narrated world, a communicative circuit operates whenever (3a) *one character addresses another*. The second person in directly reported dialogue between characters is normally unproblematic, and we handle it as we would *you* in real-world conversation. Indirect forms of speech report, and free indirect discourse in particular, are potentially more problematic because they may be formally indistinguishable from sentences attributable to the (diegetic or extra-diegetic) narrator. In such a case, *you* might ambiguously designate either a character-addressee or a diegetic or extra-diegetic narratee. It seems, however, that the second person pronoun itself cannot appear in free indirect discourse (though forms associated with the second person certainly can), so this potential source of ambiguity is presumably ruled out.[8]

A special case of a communicative circuit at the level of the characters is that of (3b) *a character addressing himself or herself*. In this situation, the character has in effect split himself or herself into two, one part acting as the addressor, the other the addressee, of the communication; or, in other words, the communicative circuit has been *internalized*, creating an *interior dialogue*. The second person of a self-addressed discourse is essentially equivalent to the first person of direct interior monologue: "the reader visually records you [but] logically perceives I. The functions of the second person pronoun are dissimulated" (Passias 1976:199). This "dissimulated" second person of interior dialogue, though it has a longer pedigree than one might suppose,[9] is particularly abundant in modernist narrative fiction:

> You told the Clongowes gentry you had an uncle a judge and an uncle a general in the army. Come out of them, Stephen. [. . .] You were awfully holy, weren't you? You prayed to the Blessed Virgin that you might not have a red nose. You prayed to the devil in Serpentine avenue that the fubsy widow in front might lift her clothes still more from the wet street [. . .] You were a student, weren't you? Of what in the other devil's name? [. . .] You seem to have enjoyed yourself [. . .] Whom were you trying to walk like? [. . .] You were going to do wonders, what?
>
> (Joyce 1973:45–7)

Finally, there is one function of English *you* that falls outside any of the communicative circuits we have been describing, and that is its function as (4) *an impersonal pronoun*, roughly equivalent to *one* (or to French *on*, German *man*, etc.): "When he came out of the galley they were further up the river, you could see towns on both sides, the sky was entirely overcast with brown smoke and fog" (Dos Passos n.d.: 32). Here *you* has none of the implications of a communicative act, indeed does not function as a second person pronoun at all; its function, rather, is that of a marker of colloquial style.

Transgressions

It is against this background of "normal" narrative communication that Pynchon's text deploys its second-person pronouns. However, the "normative" model is not the only relevant background for *Gravity's Rainbow*, and before we turn to Pynchon's poetics of the second person we need also to consider some of the characteristic *transgressions* of the normative model that occur in narrative fiction, especially (but by no means exclusively) in the postmodernist period. Exhaustiveness being out of the question here, we will not undertake to calculate all the possible violations (or rather, pretended violations) of narrative level and communicative logic involving the second person,[10] but only to mention those that are most relevant to Pynchon's practice. Of these, one involves a "downward" violation of narrative level, that is, a communicative circuit in which the addressor is located on a level superior to that of the addressee, while the other involves an "upward" violation (addressor inferior, addressee superior).

A "downward" violation of narrative level occurs whenever (5) *an extra-diegetic narrator pretends to address one of "his" or "her" characters.* This is strictly speaking impossible, of course, since characters *do not exist* on the extra-diegetic narrator's level; hence my circumspection in speaking of this as "pretended" address. There are, of course, precedents for this in the classical rhetorical tradition and lyric poetry, where the trope of addressing an absent addressee goes by the name of *apostrophe.* When fictional narrators apostrophize characters, as they have done on occasion throughout the history of narrative fiction, we can be confident that this practice derives from the rhetorical tradition or from lyric poetry, or both:

> And alas (sweet Philoclea) how hath my penne till now forgot thy passions, since to thy memorie principally all this long matter is intended? pardon the slacknes to come to those woes, which, having caused in others, thou didst feele in thy selfe.
>
> (Sidney 1963:I, 168–9)

> Jo, is it thou? Well! Though a rejected witness, who "can't exactly say" what will be done to him in greater hands than men's, thou art not quite in outer darkness.
>
> (Dickens 1971:203)

In both of these examples, the second person is disambiguated by the vocative ("sweet Philoclea," "Jo"). Nevertheless, even in relatively unproblematic cases such as these, we can sense something of apostrophe's transgressive nature, the logical and ontological scandal of its violation of narrative levels (see Culler 1981).

More scandalous still are those cases in which (6) *an extra-diegetic narrator pretends to address the empirical reader directly*. Here the violation is "upward," with an addressor on a lower plane pretending to communicate directly with a superior addressee. The extra-diegetic narrator, we might say, attempts to cast the empirical reader in the role of extra-diegetic narratee. Examples abound in postmodernist fiction:

> You may cut me down in my tracks, you, reader, may close the book or worse, not even buy it, you, editor, may not even publish it, you, agent, may not even try to sell it.
>
> (Sukenick 1969:71)

> The reader! You, dogged, uninsultable, printoriented bastard, it's you I'm addressing.
>
> (Barth 1969:123)

> Now that I've got you alone down here, you bastard, don't you think I'm letting you get away easily, no sir, not you brother.
>
> (Gass 1968:unnumbered p. 21)

The ontological scandal is heightened here by a number of means: first, by the spurious specificity of the address (not just any *you*, but "you, reader," "you, editor," "you, agent," "you . . . printoriented bastard"); secondly, by the emotion which is inappropriately attached to what is, after all, a communication between strangers, whether that emotion is pathos (as in the Sukenick passage) or animus (as in Barth and Gass); and thirdly, by the paradoxical insistence on the textual nature of the addressor ("down here" in the Gass passage is "down here at the bottom of the page, in the footnotes," where this sentence appears).

When one adds these "deviant" communicative circuits to the range of "normal" addressor-addressee circuits predicted by the model of narrative communication, one sees how very wide is the latitude for potential ambiguity in any given instance of the second-person pronoun in narrative fiction. If a text does not choose actively to disambiguate its second-person pronouns – and many postmodernist texts choose not to do so – then the reader is faced with a difficult, perhaps, indeed, intractable, interpretive problem. The latitude for ambiguity in interpreting second-person narrative emerged clearly in the early controversy in French criticism over the interpretation of Butor's *La Modification* (1957), perhaps the paradigmatic second-person novel (for a survey of the controversy, see Morrissette 1985b:126–37). Three different and (at least in part) mutually incompatible naturalizations were proposed for Butor's use of the second person. First, the second person was read as the *protagonist's self-address*, "a variant type of interior monologue" (Morrissette 1985b:135) or, more properly, interior dialogue. Secondly, the second person was read as a case of *an extra-diegetic narrator* (though, in a typical conflation of roles, the critics tended to substitute "author" for "narrator") *addressing the reader*: "It is you yourself, reader, that the novelist seems to implicate politely" (Michel Leiris, quoted in Morrissette 1985b:133).[11] Finally, the second person of *La Modification* was interpreted (by the author himself, among others; see Butor 1964) as a case of the *extra-diegetic narrator addressing* (or apostrophizing) *a character*. This is the naturalization that Morrissette prefers: "The voice that says *vous* is less that of the character than of the author or, better still, that of a persona, invisible but powerfully present, who serves as the center of consciousness in the novel" (1985b:130–1).[12]

The controversy over Butor's *La Modification* is exemplary, for much the same range of intepretive possibilities, and the the same intractable difficulty for the reader in choosing among them, have appeared in other postmodernist texts that are, in whole or in part, second-person narratives. Conspicuous examples include (apart from the texts by Sukenick, Barth and Gass cited above) Carlos Fuentes's "Aura," *La muerte de Artemio Cruz*, *Cambio de piel*, and *Terra nostra*, the opening chapter of John Hawkes's *The Lime Twig*, Giles Gordon's *Girl with Red Hair*, John Ashbery's *Three Poems*, and Calvino's *If on a Winter's Night a Traveler* (see McHale 1987:222–7).[13] Of these, the least tractable of all is perhaps *Gravity's Rainbow*.

THE SECOND PERSON OF *GRAVITY'S RAINBOW*

This poem is concerned with language on a very plain level.
Look at it talking to you. You look out a window
Or pretend to fidget. You have it but you don't have it.
You miss it, it misses you. You miss each other.

(John Ashbery 1981:3)

Flying in the face of everything we know about the obliquity and indeterminacy of narrative communication, Pynchon criticism has for the most part persisted in assuming that the empirical author directly addresses the empirical reader from the pages of *Gravity's Rainbow* (McHoul and Wills 1990:6, 37, 64 and *passim*). Pynchon's critics routinely write as though the addressor in second-person passages of *Gravity's Rainbow* were Thomas Pynchon himself, and the addressee us, his readers. One of them writes, for instance, that "in *Gravity's Rainbow* the words [of direct address] are Pynchon's and they are spoken directly to us" (Schaub 1981:129); another, that "If we refuse to see ourselves in the 'you' Pynchon addresses, we aren't going to get much out of *Gravity's Rainbow*" (Werner 1986:95). One might charitably suppose that in most cases when the critics speak of Pynchon addressing his reader, what they really mean is that "Pynchon" addresses "his reader," that is, that an extra-diegetic narrator, imitating the function of the empirical author, addresses an extra-diegetic narratee; but it is not at all clear that such a charitable construction is merited in every case.

Moreover, second-person passages in *Gravity's Rainbow* are rarely unambiguously reducible to the communicative situation of "extra-diegetic narrator addresses extra-diegetic narratee," or to any other single communicative situation, for that matter. More often, they hover ambiguously among several alternative communicative situations, or switch disconcertingly from one to another. Instead of proceeding reductively ("the words are Pynchon's and they are spoken directly to us"), we need to consider the range of possible interpretations, both "normal" and anomalous, that Pynchon's second-person pronouns seem to invite in one place or another in his (or "his") text.

Interpretations in terms of communication on the first plane, *author addresses reader*, are systematically ruled out (though not all of Pynchon's critics seem to have grasped this). The reasons for this are intrinsic to the logic of fictional communication, as I hope to have made clear in the preceding section. On the second plane of narrative communication, that of narrators and narratees, one of the two options, namely (2b), *diegetic narrator addresses diegetic narratee*, seems to be empirically ruled out, for the narrator of *Gravity's Rainbow*, whatever else "he" might be, does not seem to be a personified character, one who might plausibly share the same narrated world with the novel's other characters.[14] This leaves one other interpretive option at this level, namely (2a) *an extra-diegetic narrator addresses an extra-diegetic narratee*.

Narrator and narratee

As we have just seen, this interpretation is a favorite of Pynchon's critics (though often mistakenly conflated with "author addresses reader"). Unfortunately, the second person of *Gravity's Rainbow* seldom submits unambiguously or unproblematically to this reading. A case in point is the passage (*GR*:695–6) in which some addressee *you*, initially unspecified, is confronted with a roll-call of American placenames: "Dungannon, Virginia, Bristol, Tennessee, Asheville or Franklin, North Carolina, Apalachicola, Florida," and so on. Invited to regard these as "death-towns," "towns of the war dead," the addressee is promptly berated for having done so:

Well, you're *wrong*, champ – these happen to be towns all located on the borders of *Time Zones*, is all. Ha, ha! Caught *you* with your hand in your pants! Go on, show us all what you were doing or leave the area, we don't need your kind around. There's nothing so loathsome as a sentimental surrealist.

It seems safe to assume that this addressee must be the novel's extra-diegetic narratee, who previously has had plenty of occasion to play the "sentimental surrealist" in this abundantly sentimental and surrealist text.[15] However, suddenly a new addressee is proposed, a fictional character: "Which is all our Sentimental Surrealist, leaving the area, gets to hear. Just as well. He is more involved [. . .] with the moment of sun-silence inside the white tile greasy-spoon." Whoever this character is who has experienced the "moment of sun-silence inside the white tile greasy-spoon" (perhaps Slothrop?), he is certainly *not* the narratee.[16] The narratee-oriented *you* of the preceding passage is revealed, retrospectively and disconcertingly, to have been character-oriented after all.

The same pattern of redirected second-person address occurs in the episode entitled "A Moment of Fun with Takeshi and Ichizo, the Komical Kamikazes" (*GR*:690–2). Here some unidentified party (the narratee?) appears to have objected to Kenosho the radarman's haiku. Even though we do not "hear" the objection itself, we infer that there must have been one from the response that it provokes: "– *what*? You didn't like the haiku. It wasn't *ethereal* enough? Not Japanese at all? In fact it sounded like something *right outta Hollywood*?" At this point our hypothesis must be that this is the narrator, responding to a (hypothetical or anticipated) objection on the part of his narratee.[17] The next moment, however, a new addressee is proposed: "Well, Captain – yes you, Marine Captain Esberg from Pasadena – *you*, have just had, the Mystery Insight! (gasps and a burst of premonitory applause) and so *you* are our *Paranoid . . . For the Day*!" As in the "sentimental surrealist" passage, a character-addressee is suddenly introduced, and we are compelled retrospectively to revise our initial hypothesis: *you*, it appears, refers not to the narratee but to "Marine Captain Esberg from Pasadena."

Thus, narratee-oriented address in *Gravity's Rainbow* often switches abruptly to character-oriented address, leaving the reader in the lurch. The opposite pattern is also possible, that is, character-oriented address may be blocked in order to ensure a narratee-oriented interpretation of the second person:

Perhaps you know that dream too. Perhaps It has warned you never to speak Its name. If so, you know about how Slothrop'll be feeling now.
(*GR*:287)

When are you going to see it? Pointsman sees it immediately. But he "sees" it in the way you would walking into your bedroom to be jumped on, out of a bit of penumbra on your ceiling, by a gigantic moray eel, its teeth in full imbecile death-smile, breathing, in its fall onto your open face, a long human sound that you know, horribly, to be a *sexual sigh*.

(*GR*:271–2)

Here contextual features actively preclude the likeliest candidate from serving as character-addressee, leaving only the narratee to do so, by process of elimination. In the first passage, the third-person reference to Slothrop makes it impossible for him to be the referent of the second-person pronoun as well; *you* must therefore designate the narratee. By the same reasoning, in the other passage, *you* in the third sentence must refer to the narratee, although in the first sentence it is ambiguous, and could plausibly refer to Pointsman.

Characters

Pynchon's characters address one another, of course, in direct dialogue exchanges that simulate everyday real-world conversation, *you* behaving here exactly as it does in conversation, that is, "shifting" its referent with each change of speaker (see Jakobson 1971c). This is unproblematical. More problematic types of speech report, such as free indirect discourse, with greater potential for ambiguity, would appear to be ruled out here in any case, on purely formal grounds.[18] But *Gravity's Rainbow* does abound in one problematic type of address between characters, of which the following passage is an example:

> His bare limbs in their metal bondage writhe among the fuel, oxidizer, live-steam lines [. . .] and one of these valves, one test-point, one pressure-switch is the right one, the true clitoris, routed directly into the nervous system of the 00000. She should not be a mystery to you, Gottfried. Find the zone of love, lick and kiss . . . you have time – there are still a few minutes. The liquid oxygen runs freezing so close to your cheek, bones of frost to burn you past feeling. Soon there will be the fires, too. The Oven we fattened you for will glow. Here is the sergeant, bringing the Zündkreuz. The pyrotechnic Cross to light you off. The men are at attention. Get ready, Liebchen.

(*GR*:751)

Whose strange endearments are these?[19] The addressee is specified: Gottfried, Captain Blicero's lover, soon to be his sacrificial victim as the unwilling human payload of a V-2 rocket. The unspecified addressor would appear to be Blicero himself, but if this is directly reported speech, it is anomalous, lacking quotation-marks; and in any case Gottfried would appear to be incommunicado, already sealed in the rocket.[20] A much stronger hypothesis would be that this is Blicero's unuttered, interior discourse, in other words, that he is addressing the absent Gottfried in an interior dialogue, or *apostrophizing* Gottfried.

And, in fact, this possibility for the second person, that of *one character apostrophizing another (absent) character*, recurs throughout *Gravity's Rainbow*, often in contexts much less ambiguous than that of Blicero apostrophizing the seemingly absent Gottfried: "Oh, Wimpe. Old V-Mann, were you right? Is your IG to be the very model of nations?" (*GR*:566); "Well, Bodine, your map is perfect here, except for one trivial detail you sort of, uh, forgot to mention, wonder why that was" (*GR*:380). Tchitcherine mentally addresses Wimpe here years after their alleged intimacy has ended, while Slothrop similarly addresses Bodine in his absence. Clearly, there is little that distinguishes such unuttered apostrophes from the special case of interior dialogue or self-address.

But, if another character can serve as one's imagined addressee in an interior dialogue, so too can one's *self*, and the result might be described as *self-apostrophe*:[21]

> "Lemme at least tell you my story," blithering fast as he can [. . .] wondering meantime, in parallel sort of, if that Oberst Enzian wasn't right about going native in the Zone – beginning to get ideas, fixed and slightly, ah, erotic notions about Destiny are you Slothrop? eh?
>
> (*GR*:576)

The context makes it plain that this must be interior discourse ("wondering [. . .] in parallel sort of"), Slothrop taunting himself mentally. Taken out of context, however, the vocative passage here at the end ("beginning to get [. . .] erotic notions about Destiny are you Slothrop?") would be indistinguishable from cases of (5) *the extra-diegetic narrator apostrophizing one of "his" characters* (see below). Once again we are faced with potential for confusion.

In *Gravity's Rainbow* there are few second-person passages that can unequivocally be identified as "interior dialogue"; persuasive competing hypotheses can almost always be proposed. Perhaps the only completely unequivocal examples are those that are explicitly introduced *as* interior discourse:

> Slothrop's dumb idling heart sez: The Schwarzgerät is no Grail, Ace, that's not what the G in Imipolex G stands for. And you are no knightly hero. The best you can compare with is Tannhäuser, the Singing Nincompoop – you've been under one mountain at Nordhausen, been known to sing a song or two with uke accompaniment, and don'tcha feel you're in a sucking marshland of sin out here, Slothrop?
>
> (*GR*:364)

Here the hypothesis of "interior dialogue" is reinforced by dialectal features appropriate to Slothrop ("Ace," "Nincompoop," "uke," "don'tcha"; but also, problematically, "sez," *outside* the presumed interior-discourse passage) and by the vocative of self-address.

Impersonal "you"

As any reader can attest, *Gravity's Rainbow* is a text of multiple styles, and one of its many styles (one is tempted to call it the dominant style, but that would be an unjustified assumption) is that of colloquial spoken American English. Accordingly, the text abounds in instances of *you* in its colloquial use as an impersonal pronoun (as Smetak, for one, has noticed (1987:103 n. 13)): "Reception tonight is perfect, the green return 'fine-grained as a baby's skin,' confirms Spyros ('Spider') Telangiecstasis, Radarman 2nd Class. You can see clear out to the Azores" (*GR*:389). Substituting *one* for *you* in "You can see clear out to the Azores" confirms that this is impersonal *you*. In French, the equivalent construction would have *on*, or perhaps the reflexive of the verb, and another way of corroborating our hypothesis about this instance of *you* would be to consult Michel Doury's French translation of *Gravity's Rainbow*: "Ce soir, la propagation est parfaite, l'onde verte de retour est «comme une peau de bébé», si l'on en croit Spyros (Spider) Telangiecstasis, Radarman 2nd Class. On voit jusqu'aux Açores" (Doury 1975:341).[22]

But even this apparently unproblematic, noncommunicative use of the second-person pronoun is usually susceptible of more than one reading; often, indeed, alternative hypotheses crowd upon the reader thick and fast. Consider the following passage describing the approach to "The White Visitation," in which *you* seems, at first glance, to have its impersonal function:

> from a distance no two observers, no matter how close they stand, see quite the same building in that orgy of self-expression, added to by each succeeding owner, until the present War's requisitioning. Topiary trees line the drive for a distance before giving way to larch and elm: ducks, bottles, snails, angels, and steeplechase riders they dwindle down the metaled road into their fallow silence, into the shadows under the tunnel of sighing trees. The sentry, a dark figure in white webbing, stands port-arms in your masked headlamps, and you must halt for him. The dogs, engineered and lethal, are watching you from the woods. Presently, as evening comes on, a few bitter flakes of snow begin to fall.

> (*GR*:83)

The hypothesis of impersonal *you* seems to be confirmed by the scrupulous impersonality of the perspective in this passage: no particular observers are evoked, but merely any two anonymous, typical observers, any two observers at all. Try substituting *one* for *you*; the reading this yields is not in the least implausible: "The sentry [. . .] stands port-arms in one's masked headlamps, and one must halt for him." This, in effect, is Doury's solution as translator, although here he has the advantage of being able to use the reflexive: "La sentinelle, silhouette sombre en treillis, se dresse dans la lumière masquée des phares. Il faut s'arrêter" (Doury 1975:86).

But Doury's solution is a limiting one, for it proves impossible to maintain this impersonal reading to the exclusion of all other hypotheses. The menace at the end of this passage is too pointed, too directed, for the second person here not to take on some sense of address; but who is the addressee? We may be tempted to construe this (though on meager enough grounds) as one of those cases in which *the extra-diegetic narrator pretends to address the empirical reader* (see below). Or perhaps we begin casting around for some likely character to play the role of addressee in this threatening communication. Mr. Pointsman? But we have just left him at a meeting *inside* "The White Visitation"; surely he cannot be approaching from outside the grounds at the same time. Roger Mexico? It seems likely that he would be attending the same meeting (although he has not in fact been mentioned by name). Katje? She will be brought to "The White Visitation" eventually, but presumably not until somewhat later than this. Slothrop? Jessica? No, neither of them ever enters "The White Visitation" at all, so far as we can know.[3] And so on; hypotheses multiply, to no definite conclusion.

Transgressions

The transgressive use of the second person pronoun in which (5) *the extra-diegetic narrator apostrophizes a character* is actually routine in *Gravity's Rainbow* – or, if not exactly routine (since it never entirely loses its aura of ontological scandal), then at least recurrent. Narratorial apostrophe is rarely unambiguous, however. Its least equivocal instances are those in which the character-addressee of the narratorial apostrophe is explicitly named:

> You can't swim upstream, not under the present dispensation anyhow, all you can do is attach the number to it and suffer, Horst, fella.
>
> (*GR*:452)

> No, Klaus, don't drift away, please, not onto dreams of kindly Soviet interrogation that will end in some ermine bed, some vodka-perfumed stupor, you know that's foolish.
>
> (*GR*:518)

Strikingly, in both of these instances the character-addressees (Horst

Achtfaden, Klaus Närrisch) are about to undergo interrogation (Achtfaden by the Schwarzkommando, Närrisch by the Russian Tchitcherine). It is almost as if the narrator were, in some sense, anticipating the coming interrogations by first interrogating his characters himself (see note 12 above).

Relatively unequivocal though they may be, in both these examples the evidence of the vocative is to some degree counterbalanced by other evidence in the general context suggesting that this may not be narratorial apostrophe at all, but self-addressed interior dialogue (on the Närrisch passage, see Purdy 1988:14). Thus we are left with (at least) two competing hypotheses, apparently equally strong: narratorial apostrophe or character self-address. It would appear, then, that even the least ambiguous instances of the narrator apostrophizing a character in *Gravity's Rainbow* prove to be thoroughly ambiguous after all.

While it is true that Pynchon's critics have tended to be naively willing to see in Pynchon's highly ambiguous second-person mode evidence of a communicative circuit joining author and reader, it is also true that the *Gravity's Rainbow* narrator (*not* Thomas Pynchon, the empirical author) sometimes seems to invite or provoke us to identify with "his" narratee. By this act of narrative seduction (and like all seductions, this one is *transgressive* (see Chambers 1984)), we are made the recipients of an illegitimate address; we become *you*. Pynchon criticism has generalized this transgressive function of *you* far too widely, to the point of making every narratorial address an instance of (pseudo-)direct communication with the reader. In fact, cases of what might plausibly be construed as reader-oriented *you* occur only rarely, mainly in those metanarrative comments ("surjustifications") in which the tone of address is, for one reason or another, particularly arresting (engaging or off-putting): "You will want cause and effect. All right" (*GR*:663); "Well, and keep in mind where those Mysteries came from in the first place. (Check out Ishmael Reed. He knows more about it than you'll ever find here.)" (*GR*:588).Whenever Pynchon critics discuss address to the reader, these two passages (and a few others) are sure to be cited.[24] The reasons for this are clear enough: not only do these comments bear on issues of expectations and extratextual knowledge that belong to the reader's province, but their indecorous tone (overt hostility in the first, smugness and exclusivity in the second; see Leverenz (1976:243, 247)) seems designed to provoke a response.

Nevertheless, McHoul is right to object, apropos of the first of these examples, that, far from being addressed by Pynchon (or his surrogate) to the reader, it is "not clearly addressed by anyone to anyone at all" (1987:31). Indeed, it might be argued that it is precisely the indeterminacy, the *vacuousness*, of this address that seduces us into identifying (however briefly) with the narratee. Interpretation abhors a vacuum; where *Gravity's Rainbow* leaves an unspecified, free-floating *you*, we rush in.[25]

MISREADING *GRAVITY'S RAINBOW*

> But why am I always baiting my readers? That's a nasty habit. This
> is not *Notes from Underground* after all. Why am I so hostile and
> defensive?
>
> (Ronald Sukenick 1969:71)

So ubiquitous are Pynchon's second-person pronouns that it seems
unlikely that any critic, whatever interpretation he or she might be pursuing, and however indifferent he or she might be to linguistic detail, would
be able to avoid having to propose, if only incidentally, a reading for
some second-person passage or other. Inevitably, the critics misread. Or
perhaps it would be fairer to say that they *under*-read; that is, they fail
to entertain the entire range of possible interpretations for any given
instance of *you*, but instead opt for one of them – the one, obviously,
that is most compatible with whatever general interpretive hypothesis they
happen to be pursuing – suppressing the other, perhaps equally plausible
alternatives. In their reaching (irritable or otherwise) after fact and reason,
the critics do not so much misconstrue the text as construe it *prematurely*.
What is significant and revealing about these critical under-readings is
which alternatives are suppressed, why they are suppressed, and in the
interests of what general hypotheses about the text.

"Which do you want it to be!"

It is important, at this point, that we look in some detail at a few of the
second-person passages which seem to attract critical misreadings or under-
readings. One of them occurs in the first part of the novel (*GR*:127–36)
when the young lovers Roger Mexico and Jessica Swanlake stop off at a
church somewhere in Kent to hear a choir sing a vespers service during
Advent. There is a long digression from the vespers scene to a general
panorama of wartime life, with several local shifts into the second person:
"Is the baby smiling, or is it just gas? Which do you want it to be?"
(*GR*:131); "Leave your war awhile, paper or iron war, petrol or flesh,
come in with your love, your fear of losing, your exhaustion with it"
(*GR*:134). Eventually the passage circles back to the scene in the church,
heightened now by the use of the second person:

> no counterfeit baby, no announcement of the Kingdom, not even a try
> at warming or lighting this terrible night, only, damn us, our scruffy
> obligatory little cry, our maximum reach outward – *praise be to God!*
> – for you to take back to your war-address, your war-identity, across
> the snow's footprints and tire tracks finally to the path you must create
> by yourself, alone in the dark. Whether you want it or not, whatever
> seas you have crossed, the way home. . . .
>
> (*GR*:136)

Who is *you* in this passage?

The interpretive options here would appear to be the same as the ones that emerged from the controversy over Butor's second-person novel *La Modification* (see "Circuits of narrative communication", above); namely, either an extra-diegetic narrator addresses an extra-diegetic narratee; or the narrator apostrophizes a character; or a character addresses himself or herself in interior dialogue. Interestingly, the critics seem not to have entertained the possibility of narratorial apostrophe, opting instead for one or the other of the two remaining hypotheses. Thus, one group of critics (including Siegel 1978:21, 52; Quilligan 1979:178; Fowler 1980:24–8; Schaub 1981:62, 66–7, 127–8; Tanner 1982:88; Tölölyan 1983:65) favors the hypothesis that the referent of *you* here is the narratee (most of them say "the reader") and that the Advent vespers passage is communicated by the narrator (many of them say "Pynchon") directly to this narratee without being routed through the consciousness of any character whatsoever. "Pynchon," writes one of these critics, in an uncharacteristically explicit formulation of this hypothesis,

> develops the whole experience of the Advent service at this little Kent church far beyond his young lovers' perception of it – he shares its meaning only with us, just as a poet does, and his characters have no contact with the images and experience he creates.
>
> (Fowler 1980:24)

A second group (including Sanders 1976:154; Plater 1978:185–6; Newman 1986:112; Smetak 1987:96–7) favors the alternative hypothesis, namely that here, as one of them phrases it, "A character meditates" (McConnell 1977:178).

But if so, *which* character? For, as it turns out, there are really *two* cruxes here. The first crux, as we have just seen, has to do with determining which communicative circuit is involved, the one joining narrator and narratee, or the internalized circuit of a character's self-address. The other crux emerges in the case of the self-address hypothesis: *which* character's self-address? (Incidentally, the same crux would also arise in the case of narratorial apostrophe: *which* character is being apostrophized? who is the referent of *you*?)

The likeliest candidate, and the critics' almost universal favorite, would appear to be Roger Mexico (see, e.g., Plater, Newman, Smetak). According to this reading, it is Mexico who experiences the vision of used toothpaste tubes recycled into war materiel (*GR*:130), Mexico who mimics the style of the "manly, haggard" chaplains at the front ("what kind of a world is it [. . .] for a baby to come in tippin' those Toledos at 7 pounds 8 ounces thinkin' he's gonna redeem it, why, he oughta have his head examined" (*GR*:135)), and finally, Mexico who is the addressee of these self-addressed second-person pronouns. Certainly, there is nothing inherently implausible in this attribution. Pynchon's characters are capable on occasion of visions of connectedness even vaster than the one attributed to Mexico here (cf. Enzian's vision, (*GR*:520–1), or Tchitcherine's (*GR*:566)), and readily accommodate themselves to styles at least as distant from their own as this "manly" chaplain's from Mexico's.

What might lead us to speak of misreading, or under-reading, here is not any inherent implausibility in this hypothesis, but rather the way it in effect interdicts other, equally plausible hypotheses. Several critics, for instance, have seen in this passage a *merger* of voices, ascribing it to Roger and Jessica jointly (Sanders 1976:154) or even to Roger, Jessica *and* the narrator (or "Pynchon") jointly or in alternation (Slade 1983:185, 186; Werner 1986:96). There is much to be said in particular for the reading that makes Roger and Jessica joint referents of *you*.[26] After all, they do have moments of "eerie confusion" when, we are told, they are "merged into a joint creature unaware of itself" (*GR*:38). But why leap to the exotic alternative of a merged addressee without first considering the option of Jessica as addressee in her own right, independent of Roger? Although no critic (to my knowledge) has actually argued this hypothesis, a good case could be made for it as well. Certainly there is at least one passage early in the episode that openly adopts Jessica's perspective:

> No, Jessica's never seen his face exactly like this, in the light of a few hanging oil lamps [. . .] Roger's skin more child-pink, his eyes more glowing than the lamplight alone can account for – isn't it? or is that how she wants it to be?
>
> (*GR*:129)

and another one, more anonymous, which is at least strongly suggestive of her perspective, and contains an instance of the second-person pronoun:

> Another year of wedding dresses abandoned in the heart of winter, never called for, hanging in quiet satin ranks now, their white-crumpled veils begun to yellow, rippling slightly only at your passing, spectator . . . visitor to the city at all the dead ends . . . Glimpsing in the gowns your own reflection once or twice, halfway from shadow, only blurred flesh-colors across the peau de soie, urging you in to where you can smell the mildew's first horrible touch, which was really the idea – covering all trace of her own smell, middleclass bride-to-be perspiring, genteel soap and powder.
>
> (*GR*:131)

Thus, in the case of the Advent vespers episode we are left with a range of interpretive hypotheses for the episode's second person pronouns – narrator addressing narratee or narrator apostrophizing character or character self-address; Roger or Jessica as addressee, or Roger *and* Jessica as joint addressee – but no obvious grounds for deciding conclusively among them, perhaps no grounds at all, obvious or otherwise. Nevertheless, the critics have usually been willing to impose a conclusion in the general interests of certitude. They have not, however, done so in the *particular* interests of one or another interpretive hypothesis about *Gravity's Rainbow* at large, or at least not so far as I can see.[27] We will need to look elsewhere for examples of how critical misreadings of Pynchon's equivocal second-person passages can subserve broader, *global* interpretations of the text, and how these global readings end by locking the novel in a stranglehold of imposed certitude.

"You used to know what these words mean"

We could begin with the example of Slothrop's leavetaking from Bianca (*GR*:471–2), part of which was quoted at the very end of the first section above. The passage opens in the third person, with the third-person pronouns at first clearly referring to Slothrop and Bianca ("Her look now [. . .] has already broken Slothrop's seeing heart") but gradually becoming more equivocal and anonymous; Bianca, born and bred in Europe, could not actually have been the girl whom Slothrop saw and lost at an American lunchwagon counter. Next the passage modulates into the second-person mode ("both of you, at both ends of the counter, could feel it"), then back again to the third person ("Of course Slothrop lost her, and kept losing her"), except for the parenthetical "you used to know what these words mean." Finally, after two intervening paragraphs the second-person mode is resumed:

> Of all her putative fathers – Max Schlepzig and masked extras on one side of the moving film, Franz Pökler and certainly other pairs of hands busy through trouser cloth, that *Alpdrücken* Night, on the other – Bianca is closest, this last possible moment below decks here behind the ravening jackal, closest to you who came in blinding color, slouched alone in your seat, never threatened along any rookwise row or diagonal all night, you whose interdiction from her mother's water-white love is absolute, you alone, saying *sure I know them*, omitted, chuckling *count me in*, unable, thinking *probably some hooker* . . . She favors you, most of all. You'll never get to see her. So somebody has to tell you.
> (*GR*:472)

Scattered thoughout *Gravity's Rainbow* are several comparable elegaic passages about lost girls, cast in the second-person mode: two further elegies for the lost Bianca (*GR*:577, 672) and one for Katje (*GR*:303). They form among themselves an isolable textual strand or constellation, a kind of dispersed micro-text in the *Gravity's Rainbow* macro-text. In none of them is it unambiguously clear who *you* is; there are always several plausible candidates. What about the passage before us? Who is *you* here?

The strongest candidate would appear to be Slothrop himself, either as the addressee of a narratorial apostrophe or as his own interior addressee. Evidence for this attribution of *you* is to be found in the deictic elements of the passage, which seem to locate the addressee in precisely the temporal and spatial position occupied by Slothrop. Relative to the chronology of the narrated world, the leavetaking passage constitutes a temporal *pause*, occupying the brief interval between the moment when Slothrop, ascending the ladder to the deck above, loses sight of Bianca ("The last instant their eyes were in touch is already behind him" (*GR*:471)) and the moment when, "Halfway up the ladder" (*GR*:473), he encounters Ensign Morituri. This is the interval that the phrase "this last possible moment" in our passage must refer to. It would appear, then, that this passage represents a flashback, unfolding in Slothrop's memory in no more "real time" than it takes him to climb a few steps of the ladder. Similarly, the spatial deixis in "below decks here behind the ravening jackal" places the addressee on board the yacht *Anubis* (whose figurehead is "a gilded winged jackal" (*GR*:459)) in exactly the position occupied by Slothrop during "this last possible moment."[28]

Given the way the addressee's position is made to coincide with Slothrop's, it is surprising that the critics (e.g. Plater 1978.18; Clerc 1983h:150; Rosenheim 1985:48–9) have preferred to identify this addressee not with Slothrop, but with the extra-diegetic narratee ("the reader").[29] Or, if not with the narratee exclusively, then with the narratee *as well as* Slothrop. Thus, for example, Kaufman (1976:215) seems to acknowledge the strength of Slothrop's claim to being addressee of these second-person pronouns, but then goes on to discern a further addressee behind or beyond him: "with the reiterations of the pronoun [you], Pynchon expands its referent outward; not only to Slothrop, but to the reader, also." Why should the Slothrop option be ignored or qualified in this way, in defiance of all the countervailing evidence?

Kaufman provides the clue. This point about the expansion of reference "outward . . . to the reader" is of some importance to her larger argument, for she is intent on demonstrating the reader's complicity in the novel's victimizer-victim relationships: "So, not just Slothrop, then [. . .] but all of us have joined in the corporate act of the murder of exploitable innocence" (1976:215). In other words, her solution of this particular, local ambiguity dovetails into a larger, *global* interpretation involving relationships of victimization everywhere in the novel. It is the global hypothesis that has dictated which of the alternative solutions to the local crux will be preferred, and which ignored or suppressed.

Nor is this particular global hypothesis about Pynchon's second-person mode exclusive to Kaufman (though she may have been the first to articulate it). Other critics, too, have noticed how the second-person pronouns of *Gravity's Rainbow* implicate the reader in a pattern of victimization spanning the whole novel. Fine; but *on which side* of the victimizer-victim relationship do they implicate us? For there are two options here. Hite (1983a:146–7) follows Kaufman in treating the text's second-person pronouns as a means for securing "the reader's" complicity with the victimizers (e.g. Mr. Pointsman): "The narrator tends to modulate into direct address whenever a character says or does something that might alienate the reader and provoke an unsympathetically pejorative judgement." Seed (1988:179), on the other hand, regards Pynchon's *you* "as an inclusive device to unite reader with character, particularly with character as victim" (e.g. Pökler). It is not a question here of choosing the "right" interpretation, for they are, of course, both "right"; that is, the second-person pronoun sometimes seems to be associated with the victimizers (e.g. in the leavetaking passage, where Slothrop can be construed as Bianca's victimizer), sometimes with the victims.[30] In either case, it is the global interpretive hypothesis – complicity with victimizers or identification with victims – that determines which second-person passages will be selected for interpretation, and which interpretive hypotheses about those passages will be entertained. Local reading subserves global reading.

Moreover, there is another, and even more powerful, global interpretive hypothesis that the passage in which Slothrop takes his leave of Bianca can be made to subserve.[31] In order to see what this might be, we need first to establish that Slothrop's leavetaking from Bianca belongs to more than one textual strand; that is, in addition to the micro-textual pattern of recurrent elegies for lost girls, it also forms a constellation with a different set of second-person passages dispersed throughout the text, including, for instance, this one:

> once again the floor is a giant lift propelling you with no warning toward your ceiling – replaying now as the walls are blown outward, bricks and mortar showering down, your sudden paralysis as death comes to wrap and stun *I don't know guv I must've blacked out when I come to she was gone it was burning all around me head was full of smoke* . . . and the sight of your blood spurting from the flaccid stub of artery, the snowy roofslates fallen across half your bed, the cinema kiss never completed, you were pinned and stared at a crumpled cigarette pack for two hours in pain, you could hear them crying from the rows either side but couldn't move.
>
> (*GR*:49)

What are the common denominators of these two passages, aside from the second-person mode itself? The new passage seems to represent the "spoken dreams," the "pain-voices of the rocketbombed" lying in a ward of St. Veronica's Hospital (unless these voices are actually only imaginative projections of Mr. Pointsman's, a possibility the context allows). Apparently, the rocket-bomb victims conflate memories of the original bomb-blast with anticipations of a second bombing yet to come ("once again," "replaying now") – and, in fact, their anticipations prove prophetic, for St. Veronica's will be struck by a V-2 (*GR*:138). Thus, the setting is simultaneously a hospital ward ("the snowy roofslates fallen across half your bed") and the site of the original bombing: a movie theater ("the cinema kiss never completed," "the rows [of seats] either side").[32] Here, then, is the connection with the "*Alpdrücken* Night" (i.e. the night on which "you [. . .] slouched alone in your seat" watching the German Expressionist film *Alpdrücken*) in the leavetaking passage. Both passages contain instances of what we might call the "cinema-seat second person" (see Clerc 1983b:150).

"Old fans who've always been at the movies (haven't we?)"

"The image of someone, alone in a theater," one critic writes, "helplessly watching their film-illusion of reality is a crucial motif all through *Gravity's Rainbow*" (Fowler 1980:201). The motif recurs sometimes as an actual episode (e.g. *GR*:114, 252, 384–5, 542–3), sometimes as a conceit (*GR*:150, 663; see Clerc 1983b:136–40): "none of it was real before this moment: only elaborate theatre to fool you. But now the screen has gone dark, and there is absolutely no more time left. The agents are here for you at last" (*GR*:267). A number of these passages, both literal and figurative, are cast in the second person, the addressee being the moviegoer. This motif culminates, of course, on the novel's final page, where an audience waits impatiently for the movie to resume while the rocket that will destoy them "reaches its last unmeasurable gap above the roof of this old theater" (*GR*:760). The fact that this scene, too, is cast in the second person ("There is time, if you need the comfort, to touch the person next to you, or to reach between your own cold legs"), as well as the first-person plural, has escaped no one, and the critics have almost universally drawn the same conclusion from it (see, e.g., Siegel 1978:27; Quilligan 1979:289–90; Cowart 1980:57–9; Simmon 1981:126; Smith 1982:32; Tate 1983:5–6; Kharpertian 1990:137):

> Suddenly, Pynchon draws us directly into the novel, and we find ourselves sitting in a movie theatre (the theatre of war, one wonders?) watching a film.
>
> (Schwarzbach 1978:66)

the death-sequence Pynchon presents in the last pages of his novel includes but exceeds the suicide of one young German soldier, for the experience is enlarged to include us, "old fans who've always been at the movies (haven't we?)."

(Fowler 1980:80)

"Includes but exceeds," "the experience is enlarged to include us" – we have seen this sort of formulation before, in Kaufman's reading of Slothrop's leavetaking from Bianca. The inference seems irresistible: if *you* (and *we*) in the novel's climactic movie theater scene is identifiable with the narratee, the reader-surrogate, then why not extend this identification to every *you* in *all* the movie theater scenes throughout *Gravity's Rainbow*? Indeed, why stop there – why not extend the identification to every *you* in the novel?

From this inference it is but a short step to a global interpretive hypothesis powerful enough to naturalize and thoroughly domesticate this maddeningly equivocal text, reducing it to univocal order. "It's all theatre", we are told at the novel's outset (*GR* 3), and many critics have been more than willing to take the text at its word. *Gravity's Rainbow* "functions as a movie"; it is "the imitation of a movie" (Plater 1978:124, 97). "Pynchon presents evidence that the novel presents a view, not of reality, but of film reality – that the novel is indeed a film" (Smith 1982:28). "Pynchon identifies the reader not as a reader but as a viewer; not of a book, but of a film" (Marriott 1985:47). "At novel's end we take the events to have occurred on screen – we have been witness to a movie about World War II and its aftermath" (Clerc 1983c:10–11). And so on; *Gravity's Rainbow*, it would appear, is not the direct representation of a world, but a mediated, *second-order* representation, the representation *of a representation* of the world: specifically, the representation of a movie.[33]

Like the interpretive strategy, mentioned in the first section above, of framing the novel as the contents of its characters' minds, this strategy of framing it as the contents of a movie is both powerfully integrative and economical.[34] Novel-as-hallucination or novel-as-movie, either reading effectively "solves" *Gravity's Rainbow*. On the positive side, the novel-as-movie naturalization serves to motivate and integrate some of the most provocative and otherwise unintelligible features of Pynchon's text. It allows us to read its stream of allusions to real films, characters, actors, and directors, as well as the fictional film careers of various characters (von Göll, Greta Erdmann), as signs of the novel's cinematic nature. More importantly, it motivates the imitation of motion-picture generic conventions – slapstick routines, musical-comedy numbers, chase scenes (*GR*:637), and so forth – and the use of cinematic devices in making transitions and juxtapositions: movie music in general (*GR*:196 and *passim*; see Tate 1983), "bridge music" (*GR*:222–3), travelogue voiceover (*GR*:527–8), and so forth. Finally, it gives us the key to certain motifs that have clearly been inspired by the film medium. I am thinking especially of the reversal of processes – of Slothrop's family history (*GR*:203–4), or of rocket-production ("faired skin back to sheet steel back to pigs to white incandescence to ore, to Earth," *GR*:139) – which seems to presuppose the extension to reality itself of film's capacity to be run backwards.[35]

Negatively, however, this "solution" seems to me seriously to falsify our experience of the text. If *Gravity's Rainbow* is "the imitation of a movie," then its *entire world*, from the first page to the last, must be understood as having undergone a global ontological "demotion," "lowering" it one level to the status of a secondary, nested representation. I wonder whether it is possible for anyone to read *Gravity's Rainbow* consistently in this way, at two removes, as it were. Even for readers apprised of this possibility, most episodes, surely, will continue to be apprehended directly, without any sense of a further level of mediation, the outer frame of the novel and the inner frame of the movie merging, the movie frame fading from the reader's awareness. It is only when some incongruously cinematic feature intrudes – a musical-comedy number, a passage of soundtrack – that we are jarred into recollecting the movie-frame hypothesis.

But, more importantly, reading *Gravity's Rainbow* as a movie, while it undoubtedly increases the intelligibility of the text, also reduces its *strangeness*; and it is its strangeness, after all, that we especially prize. If, for instance, we "solve" the problem of musical-comedy and slapstick routines by declaring the context to be that of a 1940s movie – the appropriate, predictable, "natural" context of such routines – then we have preempted all the other hypotheses that might be entertained, including, say, the hypothesis that Pynchon is asking us to imagine a "real" world (a world in this respect rather like Sidney's Arcadia or Alice's Wonderland or looking-glass world) in which people break spontaneously into song, anywhere, any time.

Or, to return to our problem with the second person: if we hold consistently to the movie-frame hypothesis, then we have a readymade formula for determining who *you* is in every instance. *You* will always be read as addressed to a narratee imagined to be sitting in a movie theater – in short, a character-narratee, located within the world of the fiction. If, however, resisting the temptation to prejudge the case, we undertake, as I have undertaken here, to calculate the range of possibilities for the second-person pronoun in this text; if we apply the moviegoer hypothesis sparingly and tentatively, experimenting with alternative hypotheses – that *you* is the sign of the narrator's apostrophe of "his" character, or of an imagined address of one character to another, or of a character's interior dialogue, or even of a transgressive address to the reader that seeks to implicate him or her in the role of victimizer or victim; if we do these things, then we may not satisfy our drive for certitude, but we will have exercised our negative capability, and will have preserved the text's strangeness in the process.

METAREADING

> Reader, take care, I have unadvisedly led thee to the Top of as high a Hill as Mr. *Allworthy's*, and how to get thee down without breaking thy Neck, I do not well know.
>
> (Henry Fielding 1974:I, 43–4)

It has not been my intention to correct Pynchon's critics, or to expose their misreadings. From a certain perspective, there is nothing either to correct or expose. If they have misread, they have done so in the name of the best interpretive practices. They have tried to construct interpretive hypotheses of the greatest possible explanatory power and broadest possible scope, capable of accommodating the largest number of facts without self-contradiction. Confronted with a range of possible readings, they have chosen the one most in accord with their hypothesis. They have sought to maximize integration and intelligibility. In short they have behaved like good paranoid readers, as we all do when we undertake to interpret according to the (modernist) norms of literary criticism. If, in the process, they (as we) have ascribed a greater degree of ontological stability to the fictional world than the text actually warrants, or have interdicted certain readings of the second-person pronoun, then the fault is less theirs than criticism's. More than merely justifiable, the critics' misreadings are in fact both intelligible and inevitable, even necessary. Intelligible, because they are the consequence of habits of reading of which we can give an account; indeed, it is these very misreadings that help us to formulate that account. Inevitable, because these habits of reading have developed in response to texts radically unlike *Gravity's Rainbow*, while the habits that would enable us to read texts like *Gravity's Rainbow* adequately are still scarcely conceivable. And necessary, because it may well be part of Pynchon's purpose to provoke just such misreadings. I have no argument with Pynchon's critics; but Pynchon has an argument with criticism.

Certainly there is a large measure of truth in the naturalizing critics' contention that Pynchon "draws us directly into the novel," "includes" or "implicates" us, through his reiterated use of the second-person pronoun. *You* is a sign of dialogue, conveying some vocative appeal, some sense of address, even in its most "innocent," impersonal instances, and we cannot help but respond dialogically to it in some measure. Thus, through our surrogate in the text, the narratee, a role we both identify with and distance ourselves from, we the readers are constantly being solicited to participate in the text structure and the text's world.

"To play the critic's game with Pynchon," Levine writes,

is not only to read but to participate in his scenario. That is, we become either the manipulated We to his uncannily ingenious They (which, I think, is part of his fun as it might be part of ours), or, more solemnly, play They to the We of multifarious and discontinuous experience. Obviously, there's no way to escape participation in the game. We should play it carefully.

(Levine 1978:182)

Pynchon, in other words, engages our paranoid tendencies as readers in at least two ways: by stimulating our drive for certitude, inviting us to demonstrate how "everything is connected"; and by making us the target of his direct, menacing appeal. We see ourselves mirrored in Pynchon's characters, at whom menacing fingers are repeatedly pointed, towards whom ominous faces turn to gaze. When a finger points threateningly at one of them (like Oedipa's vision of Uncle Sam telling her, "I want you" (Pynchon 1967:7)), we feel the text pointing past her at us; when a face turns towards one of them (like the nightmare dog turning to face Mr. Pointsman (*GR*:142–3)), we feel the text turning disconcertingly to gaze at us.[36] We are the second person.

But Pynchon also solicits our participation at a higher, reflexive level of reading: "the text constantly invites and then exposes the reader's imposition of meaning" (Quilligan 1979:277). By confronting us with irreducibly ambiguous, or, better, multiguous features such as the second-person pronoun, Pynchon compels us to reflect upon our own critical practices, inviting us to become metareaders, readers of our own (and others') readings – and, more to the point, of our own inevitable *mis*readings.

Metareaders, we now no longer seek solutions to the cruxes of Pynchon's fiction, but rather *meta*solutions, accounts of the range of possible solutions and of what is at stake when any one particular solution is preferred over the others. Pondering a problem in Pynchon interpretation analogous to the one I have been discussing here, one critic writes, "A metasolution is possible, but it requires ignoring the evidence of the novels" (Plater 1978:188). What I am suggesting is that, with problems like that of Pynchon's ubiquitous second-person pronouns, not only is a metasolution possible, it is the only possible solution; and, far from requiring us to ignore the evidence, it is the only means we have even of determining what might *count as* evidence, and what it might count as evidence of.

Finding ourselves, like Pynchon's own Captain Blicero, locked inside the limits of a game whose possibilities we begin to feel we have exhausted – in Blicero's case, the game of sexual domination; in ours, the game of literary interpretation – perhaps, like him, we begin to dream of a superior kind of game-player. Blicero dreams of a sexual partner who would be the diametric opposite of his lover Katje, black and African where Katje is blonde and northern, mistress of the game where Katje appears to be its victim, free where Katje is trapped. "Perhaps," he muses, "the black girl is a genius of meta-solutions – knocking over the chessboard, shooting the referee" (*GR*:102). Metareaders of *Gravity's Rainbow*, we are solicited at every turn ("*what*? You didn't like the haiku," "Perhaps you know that dream too," "You will want cause and effect. All right," "Which do you want it to be?," "you used to know what these words mean") to transform ourselves into just such overturners of chessboards and shooters of referees, just such geniuses of metasolutions.

Chapter 5

Zapping, the art of switching channels: on *Vineland*[1]

MEDIATED LIVES

> Now you can say that I've grown bitter
> But of this you may be sure
> The rich have got their channels in the bedrooms of the poor
> And there's a mighty judgment coming
> But I may be wrong . . .
>
> (Leonard Cohen, "Tower of Song")

Pynchon's *Gravity's Rainbow* begins, notoriously, with the sound of screaming in the sky; but this is revealed to have been *mediated* sound, heard not in the "real" world but in a dream; perhaps doubly mediated, since the dreamer is Pirate Prentice, a *medium* able somehow to tap into other people's fantasies, and this dream may well have originated with someone else and merely been channeled through Prentice. Seventeen years later, Pynchon's next novel, *Vineland*, also builds up throughout its opening episode to a climactic mediated sound: the sound of breaking glass, as Zoyd Wheeler leaps through the plate-glass front window of the Cucumber Lounge, just off Highway 101 in Vineland County, California. Climactic, or anti-climactic? for there is something distinctly wrong about this sound: "He knew the instant he hit that something was funny. There was hardly any impact, and it all felt and sounded different, no spring or resonance, no volume, only a sort of fine, dulled splintering."[2] The sound is wrong because the window is not, as Zoyd supposes, of plate-glass but clear sheet candy; it is, in other words, the kind of window used by television stunt-men to *simulate* bursting through a plate-glass window. Of course, Zoyd knows perfectly well that his leap is in a sense a television stunt, that it is being videotaped for later broadcast on the television evening news. Indeed, it is a condition of his continuing to receive mental-disability benefits that he should annually make a televized spectacle of himself in this way,[3] and he has conscientiously prepared his performance with the television medium in mind, for instance dressing in colors ("Day-Glo orange, near-ultraviolet purple, some acid green, and a little magenta"

(*V*:15)) he expects "would look good on television" (*V*:4). But even Zoyd is unaware, until a bystander proves it to him by eating a shard of the shattered window, of how completely the medium has evacuated his performance of its reality, of how thoroughly his leap has been transformed into what Daniel Boorstin would call a "pseudo-event," and Jean Baudrillard a "simulacrum."

Thus, just as the opening episode of *Gravity's Rainbow* establishes the pattern of the reader's experience throughout that novel, so, seventeen years later, does the opening episode of *Vineland* establish the pattern of *its* reader's experience; and that experience, in both cases, is one of an ambiguously *mediated* representation of a world. Among the media of *Gravity's Rainbow* are dreams, hallucinations and movies; in *Vineland*, the medium of choice is television.

Television world

Vineland, as every reader will attest, is TV-saturated. It is peppered with allusions to TV programs, and not to sophisticated or serious TV, either. Apart from a handful of references to news or public-affairs broadcasts (*The MacNeil–Lehrer News Hour* (*V*:88); *60 Minutes* (*V*:373); the Watergate hearings (*V*:72)), the allusions are all to American commercial entertainment programs of the most unserious and ephemeral kinds, many of them reruns of series long since canceled: celebrity talk-shows, game-shows, situation comedies, cop-shows and other "action" programs, Saturday-morning cartoon shows and, ubiquitously, *Star Trek*.[4] In addition to the many authentic TV references, there are also a few invented ones, including references to an apocryphal Japanese sitcom called *Babies of Wackiness* (*V*:159–61) and others to a number of apocryphal made-for-TV "docudramas." These constitute a kind of running gag involving incongruous mismatches between stars and roles – the joke being, of course, that these are just the sort of weirdly appropriate casting mismatches we have learned to expect from commercial TV. Hence, Pia Zadora in *The Clara Bow Story* (*V*:14), Pat Sajak in *The Frank Gorshin Story* (*V*:48), Sean Connery in *The G. Gordon Liddy Story* (*V*:339), John Ritter in *The Bryant Gumbel Story* (*V*:355), Pee-Wee Herman in *The Robert Musil Story* (*V*:370–1), and *The Magnificent Disaster*, a basketball docudrama with a cast including Paul McCartney as Kevin McHale of the Boston Celtics, Sean Penn as his teammate Larry Bird, Lou Gossett, Jr. as Kareem Abdul-Jabbar of the L.A. Lakers, and "Jack Nicholson as himself" (*V*:371, 377–8).

Many, though by no means all, of these allusions occur in the context of characters actually watching TV. In this respect, if in no other, Pynchon is a verisimilar realist, for he faithfully represents Americans doing what Americans do more often, perhaps, than they do anything else, namely watching TV. More interestingly, from a sociological perspective, he also represents them doing some of the other things they do *while* ostensibly watching TV, that is, he represents some of the "illicit" or "unauthorized" uses we routinely make of TV ("illicit" and "unauthorized" only from the point of view of TV advertisers, who presumably would prefer to have our undivided attention). Pynchon's characters fall asleep in front of the TV (*V*:234), smoke dope in front of the TV (*V*:21, 59), watch TV with the audio turned off (*V*:21, 141), masturbate while watching TV (*V*:59, 83, 278), have sex with the TV on (*V*:212), watch TV while listening to the radio (*V*:197, 270) or even while driving a car (*V*:335).

Vineland, in other words, reflects the routine interpenetration of TV and "real life," the intimate interaction between what has been called "TV flow" (the succession of program segments, commercials, etc.) and "household flow" (the succession of domestic tasks and activities; see Altman (1986)). This is, no doubt, a relatively shallow interpenetration; but it is by means of its routine ubiquity in our everyday domestic life that TV has come to pervade our lives in more profound ways, shaping and constraining our desires, our behavior, and our expectations about others. *Vineland* mirrors this "modeling" function that TV has come to serve in our culture. Many of its characters are preoccupied with conforming their lives to TV models. Some, the more self-conscious among them, reflect on the adequacy or inadequacy of TV models to reality, but even the self-conscious ones seem unable to free themselves from TV's grip on their lives. Zoyd Wheeler's adolescent daughter Prairie, for instance, is on the one hand self-conscious enough to be troubled by the images of ideal adolescent girls proffered by TV (*V*:327), but on the other hand unselfconsciously models her relationship with her best friend Ché on the "star-and-sidekick" pattern of TV action programs (*V*:327). Similarly, the narcotics agent Hector Zuñiga seeks to disabuse Zoyd of any illusions he may have about the adequacy of TV models to real undercover police-work (*V*:31), but still cannot avoid shaping his own behavior to conform to these same cop-show models (*V*:51, 345).

Reality is experienced by no-one in the world of *Vineland* in a "raw," unmediated state; it always reaches one already shaped by TV models, "framed" by the Tube. Certain characters achieve such a level of TV saturation that their lives become wholly "mediated," their "authentic" selves preempted by TV models. Hector Zuñiga is an extreme case: so pathologically addicted is he to TV that he must undergo forcible TV detoxification, parodically modeled on therapies for alcohol and drug dependency (*V*:33, 43, 335–7). In fact, the therapy fails, and Hector is soon back on the street again, as much a TV addict as ever. But Zoyd Wheeler himself is only slightly less TV-saturated than Hector, and the children raised in this TV-saturated culture – Prairie, Justin – behave routinely in TV-modeled ways that, in the adult Hector, appear pathological. *Vineland* grotesquely mirrors this TV-based culture and TV-shaped selfhood in its fantastic community of Thanatoids, people caught in a limbo between life and death, their deaths "mediated" in the same way that normal American lives are "mediated." Thanatoids do little apart from watch TV (*V*:170–1). Ironically, these quasi-dead compulsive TV-viewers prove to be indistinguishable from "normal" TV-addicted Americans: certain "normal" citizens, stumbling upon the Thanatoid community by accident, opt to stay, having "discover[ed] that they were already Thanatoids without knowing it" (*V*:384).

One consequence of the intimacy of our everyday interaction with TV is that we are apt to think of the boundary between our domestic space and the space *inside* the TV screen, between the world "out here" and the world "in there," as a relatively porous one; thus TV-viewers may address the figures on the TV screen, or otherwise behave towards TV figures as though their space were continuous with ours (see Morse 1986). Pynchon's characters are shown interacting with the TV in this way (*V*:41, 61, 348, 371); they even fantasize climbing through the screen into the TV world (*V*:368), or the other way around, TV figures passing through the screen and entering "reality" (*V*:227). Thus Frenesi experiences a "primal Tubefreek miracle" when police officers from a TV cop-show (objects of her masturbatory fantasies) seem to materialize outside her front door (*V*:84), and Hector Zuñiga, watching what appears to have been the accidental broadcast of a rehearsal for a declaration of martial law, imagines the TV addressing him directly and threateningly: "As if the Tube were suddenly to stop showing pictures and instead announce, 'From now on, I'm watching you' " (*V*:340).[5] Such transgressive paradoxes are, of course, a staple of postmodernist fiction (see McHale 1987:115–24); in the world of *Vineland*, however, they occur only in characters' fantasies.

Television discourse

TV pervades not only the represented world of *Vineland*, but also the linguistic level of the text; it "mediates" the lives of the characters not only in the sense that they compulsively consume TV, fantasize about it, model their behavior and expectations on it, and so on, but also in the sense that the reader's access to these characters' lives is by way of a verbal medium itself saturated by TV. Least problematic are the idioms actually spoken by characters which are based on or derived from TV viewing. Many of these appear to be original with Pynchon, though he passes them off as familiar idiomatic expressions. Such idioms serve to reflect and confirm the deep penetration of TV into the characters' everyday behavior and sense of themselves and others. For example:

Only a couple more commercials, just hold on.

(*V*:105)

Maybe you should start to think – about beaming out of this.

(*V*:176; see also *V*:345)

please, save that for Saturday morning with the Smurfs and the Care Bears and them, OK?

(*V*:341)

[the] easiest thing might just be to go find the son of a bitch and cancel his series for him, ever think about that?

(*V*:374)

More problematic are the figurative expressions, some of them elaborate conceits in the style of *Gravity's Rainbow* and *The Crying of Lot 49*, occurring outside the characters' direct speech. Presumably these TV-based figures reflect the presence of TV models in the characters' consciousness, and we ought to attribute them to the characters themselves, even though they are transmitted obliquely through some form or other of "combined" (free indirect) discourse in which the characters' voices and the narrator's mingle:

It was like being on "Wheel of Fortune," only here there were no genial vibes from any Pat Sajak to find comfort in, no tanned and beautiful Vanna White at the corner of his vision to cheer on the Wheel, to wish him well, to flip over one by one letters of a message he knew he didn't want to read anyway.

(*V*:12–13)

This look from brand-new Prairie [. . .] would be there for Zoyd more than once in years to come, to help him through those times when the Klingons are closing, and the helm won't answer, and the warp engine's out of control.

(*V*:285)

Our "natural" inclination would probably be to attribute such metaphors to the characters *just because* they draw on TV materials, as though it were impermissible to think of the novel's narrator as a TV-viewer in whose own "voice" TV conceits might occur. By this interpretation, the narrator necessarily maintains an ironic distance from his TV-obsessed characters and their TV-saturated language. Such an interpretation rests on a subtle form of high-culture snobbism, and in any case is undermined by the precedent of the *Gravity's Rainbow* narrator, whose own discourse is promiscuously open to all the discourses of the text's world, high and low, technical and colloquial, poetic and obscene, hackneyed and exotic. So we may well be forced to concede, against our inclinations to read ironically, that the *Vineland* narrator's "natural" idiom is as TV-saturated as that of his characters.

Finally, TV's ubiquity in *Vineland* gives rise to a number of neologistic coinages, mainly based on the colloquial expression for television, "the Tube." These neologisms (not all of them strictly original with Pynchon) include the adjective "Tubal" (*V*:15), and its negative, "non-Tubal" (*V*:46); "Tubefreeks" (*V*:33) and "Tubeheads" (*V*:42), for obsessive TV consumers; "Tubeflicker" (*V*:278) and "Tubelight" (*V*:286), for the characteristic illumination cast by the TV screen; "Tubed out" (*V*:345) for an overdose of TV consumption, and "Tubaldetox" (*V*:335) for its cure; and so on. There are also a number of TV-oriented neologisms not based on the expression "the Tube," e.g., the verb "to pixeldance" (*V*:226).

Here it is no longer possible to exculpate the narrator, for these coinages belong for the most part unambiguously to him, not to the characters' discourse. Such neologisms are clear evidence of how deeply TV has penetrated the discursive medium of this text. TV in *Vineland* in effect constitutes a kind of secondary language, a code supplementary to the linguistic codes of American English, functioning analogously, perhaps, to the way classical mythological allusion functioned in Renaissance and Neoclassical literary discourse. Or, closer to home, TV functions in *Vineland* analogously to the way movies function in *Gravity's Rainbow*.

Big screen, little screen

The cinema-oriented reading of *Gravity's Rainbow* has become something of a topos of Pynchon criticism, and by now that novel's plethora of allusions to specific movies, film genres, directors, stars, techniques, and so on, its cinematic models of behavior and movie-based metaphors and idioms, its transgressions of the boundary between cinema and real life, have all been very fully documented.[6] To say that TV functions in *Vineland* as the movies do in *Gravity's Rainbow* is not, however, to say that TV has entirely displaced the movies in the new novel. There are some movie allusions, though relatively few compared to TV allusions, and often to the types of films likely to be seen on late-night TV (e.g. *Gidget* (*V*:17); *Godzilla* (*V*:65)). Movies do in one or two instances function in the present time of *Vineland* (viz. 1984) in the same way TV does, to intervene in and even preempt "reality"; e.g. the *Return of the Jedi* film crew, filming in Vineland County, has provoked a "change of consciousness" there (*V*:7), and Hector Zuñiga lends his identity and life-story to a film project, becoming literally absorbed in it (*V*:51, 337ff.). More typically, however, film functions in this way in the novel's past, or plural pasts: the 1960s, the 1940s. The sole instance of a representation of movie-viewing (by contrast with the many instances of TV-viewing) occurs when Prairie in 1984 watches footage filmed in the 1960s by her mother's revolutionary film collective.

Film, thus, is associated here with the revolutionary aspirations and betrayals of the 1960s, and with the generation of Prairie's parents, and even further back, with Prairie's grandparents and the Left-wing Holly-wood of the 1940s and early 1950s, and *that* generation's revolutionary aspirations and disillusionment.[7] Significantly, the renegade cop Brock Vond, in 1984, vindictively burns the remaining film archives of the long-defunct collective, thus symbolically destroying the last revolutionary legacy of the '60s, which had been preserved on film (*V*:33–4). So, although certain key events in *Vineland* are mediated not by TV but by film (notably the murder of Weed Atman, in fact preserved only on the film soundtrack, the camera having missed the actual shooting), the general tendency here is to associate film with an irrecoverable past, and TV with the present, in effect demonstrating or enacting the displacement of cinema (the privileged medium of *Gravity's Rainbow*), and everything associated with it, by the ubiquitous Tube.

The displacement of film by TV ephemera must be a cause for alarm among those committed to canonizing Pynchon as a serious literary author. Some misgivings had already been expressed (see, e.g., Clerc 1983b:149) about Pynchon's use of film in *Gravity's Rainbow* as a kind of "shorthand" (or what I have called a secondary or supplemental code). The anxiety is that Pynchon's writing will not endure as literature if it relies too heavily on ephemeral or merely topical popular-culture materials. Film, at least, has proven to be relatively durable (culturally speaking), and many of the films and genres on which Pynchon relies most heavily (German Expressionism, *film noir*) have themselves already attained a secure canonical status in their own right, so perhaps the threat of *Gravity's Rainbow* lapsing eventually into mere topicality is less than it might be.[8] The risks, however, would be heightened if in future writers were to come to rely on TV ephemera as Pynchon in *Gravity's Rainbow* relies on film. This, of course, is exactly what Pynchon himself has done now in *Vineland*. Presumably, then, *Vineland* is doomed to subside into mere topicality as the cultural memory of these ephemeral TV programs fades. Evidently Pynchon has fatally compromised his candidacy for canonical status by writing such a TV-saturated novel.

Redeeming TV

Unless, of course, there is some way of "redeeming" *Vineland* from its debilitating association with TV ephemera. One way of "redeeming" the TV presence in *Vineland* – one which we can confidently expect to see critics employing before long (if they have not already begun to do so) – would be to argue that Pynchon does not simply "use" TV here, still less endorse it, but rather mounts a critique of it and its role in our culture. There is certainly evidence to support such a reading. For one thing, as we have just seen, film is associated in *Vineland* with the revolutionary aspirations of the 1960s, a positive value for Pynchon, and its displacement by TV functions as a kind of synecdoche, simultaneously symbol and example, of the betrayal and collapse of the revolutionary ethos. Nor need we rely solely on our inferential skills as readers to arrive at this political analysis, for it is one that the characters themselves explicitly develop. Mucho Maas explains to Zoyd Wheeler how the State will counteract the subversive insights afforded by acid trips: "Easy," he tells Zoyd:

> They just let us forget. Give us too much to process, fill up every minute, keep us distracted, it's what the Tube is for, and though it kills me to say it, it's what rock and roll is becoming – just another way to claim our attention, so that beautiful certainty we had starts to fade.
>
> (V:314)

A member of the younger generation, a certain Isaiah Two-Four (named for the Biblical verse about beating swords into plowshares), corroborates Mucho's analysis:

> "Whole problem 'th you folks's generation," Isaiah opined, "nothing personal, is you believed in your Revolution, put your lives right out there for it – but you sure didn't understand much about the Tube. Minute the Tube got hold of you folks that was it, that whole alternative America, el deado meato, just like the Indians, sold it all to your real enemies, and even in 1970 dollars – it was way too cheap."
>
> (V:373)

Throughout the novel, the 1960s are characterized as a period before TV began to preempt reality, "the Mellow Sixties, a slower-moving time, predigital, not yet so cut into pieces, not even by television" (V:38). Conversely, the repressive regime that, according to Pynchon, America in 1984 was fast becoming, the disciplined, well-policed, homogeneous America projected by conservative ideologues, is often expressed here in terms of domination by TV and TV models. The Reaganite vision, Pynchon tells us, is of

> a timeless, defectively imagined future of zero-tolerance drug-free Americans all pulling their weight and all locked in to the official economy, inoffensive music, endless family specials on the Tube, church all week long, and, on special days, for extra-good behavior, maybe a cookie.
>
> (V:221–2)

"The perennial question" for radicals in 1984 is

> whether the United States still lingered in a prefascist twilight, or whether that darkness had fallen long stupefied years ago, and the light they thought they saw was coming only from millions of Tubes all showing the same bright-colored shadows.
>
> (V:371)

Moreover, the characters most addicted to TV viewing are represented as damaged personalities: the Thanatoids, in every respect ambiguous characters, suspended in a limbo symbolized by their compulsive TV-viewing; Hector Zuñiga, whose TV addiction is clearly comic, but also disturbing and pathological (his wife names the Tube as corespondent when she files for divorce and he, in turn, tries to have her charged with homicide for destroying the TV set in question, "since she'd already admitted it was human" (*V*:348)). The parallelism between TV addiction and alcoholism or drug addiction may be comic hyperbole, but it also has a dimension of Swiftian satirical denunciation.

TV, finally, as we already know from Mucho Maas's analysis, is designed to distract attention, and "attention" appears throughout *Vineland* as a positive value term. In this context, anything that promotes inattention can only be negative.[9] And what exactly does television distract our attention from? From our subversive, acid-borne insights and our revolutionary aspirations; but also, perhaps even more sinisterly, from the natural world, here, as everywhere in Pynchon, an unequivocally positive value, so that whatever intrudes upon nature or obscures our vision of it must presumably be negatively valued.[10] And this, precisely, is what TV does:

> Up and down that street . . . televison screens had flickered silent blue in the darkness. Strange loud birds, not of the neighborhood, were attracted, some content to perch in the palm trees, keeping silence and an eye out for the rats who lived in the fronds, others flying by close to windows, seeking an angle to sit and view the picture from. When the commercials came on, the birds, with voices otherworldly pure, would sing back at them, sometimes even when none were on.
>
> (*V*:82; cf. *V*:194)

American jeremiads

Thus, it is possible to "redeem" Pynchon's preoccupation with TV so long as we interpet it as a jeremiad against TV's corrosively negative influence on American public life. This reading has the advantage of allowing us to see *Vineland* in the perspective of a familiar rhetorical tradition, that of the "American jeremiad" (Bercovitch 1978). Deeply rooted in American Puritan culture, subsequently secularized as a vehicle of national self-criticism and self-reassurance, the jeremiad genre continues to flourish in American public discourse. It is regularly revived whenever rituals of self-examination seem called for, for instance in the recent debates over American education, and of course in the ongoing ritual denunciations of TV (see, e.g., Boorstin 1985 (1961); Postman 1985;

Kroker and Cook 1986).[11] If *Vineland* is a jeremiad against TV, it is in distinguished company.

There are also, however, reasons for not wanting to embrace too hastily this jeremiad reading of *Vineland*. For one thing, as Bercovitch has taught us to see, the American jeremiad is an ideologically loaded and suspect genre: in the process of denouncing the shortcomings of American culture, it has historically served to enforce consensus and to deflect or preempt genuinely radical critique. This is clearly the case with jeremiads against TV. Postman, for instance, demonizes TV in order to mystify the print culture which it displaces and renders obsolete, in particular American print-oriented culture of the eighteenth and nineteenth centuries. This culture engaged in rational public discourse of a kind no longer available to us, or so Postman claims, conveniently forgetting that this allegedly rational discourse-culture ultimately broke down into civil war. Demonizing TV relieves Postman of the obligation to examine the "rationality" of print culture too closely or critically.

But there is an even more persuasive reason for not wanting to assimilate Pynchon's attitude too quickly or completely to that of the anti-TV jeremiad, and this is the fact that Pynchon's denunciation of TV is far from unequivocal.[12] At some level, no doubt, *Vineland* is a jeremiad against TV and its politically-motivated distractions, and that jeremiad is explicitly voiced by spokesmen strategically planted in the text itself. Nevertheless, at the same time it seems hard to avoid the conclusion that *Vineland* is fascinated with TV, and that Pynchon is, at the very least, equivocal about its value. TV in this text is clearly a "mindless pleasure" of the same kind as those which throughout *Gravity's Rainbow* (originally to have been titled *Mindless Pleasures*) are associated with the evasion of Puritanism, bureaucratic rationalization, and technologization. Zoyd Wheeler, the schlemiel figure of *Vineland* (kin to Slothrop in *Gravity's Rainbow* or Benny Profane in *V.*), and clearly a sympathetic character, is not only a TV addict but, as we have seen, himself a TV "entertainer." The Thanatoids, too, are TV addicts, and they too are basically schlemiels and basically sympathetic. More tellingly still, the children of *Vineland* – Frenesi's daughter Prairie and son Justin – speak a TV-inflected idiom and are saturated with TV-modeled desires and expectations, and children for Pynchon, as we know not only from *Gravity's Rainbow* but also from such early texts as "The Secret Integration," are almost inevitably bearers of positive value (see Fowler 1980:16–19 and *passim*). Finally, let us return to the passage of lyrical nature description quoted above ("Up and down that street . . . television screens had flickered," etc.) in which, it was alleged, TV is represented as intruding upon the natural world. What if we suppressed our automatic inclination to read denunciation into such a passage, and instead tried to read it "neutrally" or "innocently"? What would prevent our seeing in this passage, and others like it, not the intrusion of TV upon nature but its *integration* in the natural scene? not a jeremiad against TV but TV's reclamation by nature, its provisional redemption?

In the end, though, the most intractable evidence of all is simply the density of *Vineland*'s saturation with TV allusions and representations, and what can only be called the loving attention lavished on TV throughout. But, if Pynchon is not after all conducting a jeremiad against TV, is he then merely passively registering the ubiquity of TV in our culture, or worse, making himself the accomplice, witting or unwitting, of TV's cultural domination? Perhaps there is some other way to understand the ubiquity of TV in *Vineland*. Before we can see what that might be, we will need to digress to a consideration of the uses of TV in postmodernist fiction in general.

REPRESENTING TV

TV, as we have seen, tends to displace cinema in *Vineland* as a privileged or paradigmatic object of representation. In this respect, *Vineland* faithfully reflects the general tendency in postmodern culture to displace cinema by TV as "cultural dominant." Where the movies had arguably functioned in the modernist period as cultural dominant, modernism's preferred model or metaphor for itself, TV has come to function as postmodern culture's privileged model or metaphor (see Jameson 1991b:69). TV, it might be argued, is the medium in which postmodern culture prefers to represent itself *to* itself. This does not mean that representations of movies disappear from postmodernist novels; the example of *Gravity's Rainbow* shows how fallacious that assumption would be. In fact, film has continued to play a conspicuous role in postmodernist fiction.[13] Nevertheless, there is a sense in which representations of TV are somehow more "typical" of postmodernist fiction, while postmodernist representations of movies either seem faintly "retrograde," or seem to have been modeled on representations of TV.

Typical or retrograde, representations of TV and of movies often function equivalently in postmodernist texts. Common to both is their function of introducing a second ontological plane or level within the plane of the fictional world. In other words, representations of film and TV figure among the range of postmodernist motifs and strategies that might collectively be called "ontological pluralizers." This term covers a variety of formal or stylistic devices and narrative motifs all designed to introduce secondary worlds within the world of the fiction, or to split and multiply the primary ontological plane (see McHale 1987).

Among the formal and stylistic strategies of pluralization are (1) self-contradiction and self-erasure, which split the plane of the text into a "garden of forking paths" of parallel, branching, alternative states of affairs (e.g. Barth's "Lost in the Funhouse," Coover's "Magic Poker," Brooke-Rose's *Thru*); (2) ambiguously metaphorical expressions which seem to "hover" between the figurative and literal planes (e.g. García Márquez, Brautigan); and (3) the aberrant use of the second-person pronoun, which creates plural, fluctuating ontological planes, some interior to the fictional world, others apparently straddling the boundary between it and the readers' empirical world (see above, " 'You used to know what these words mean' "). Among the narrative motifs of pluralization are (1) visitors from other worlds (angels, ghosts, extraterrestrials), whose irruption into our world shatters its ontological homogeneity (e.g. Disch's *The Business-man*, Rushdie's *The Satanic Verses*), or "mediums" who give access to other worlds (e.g. *Gravity's Rainbow*); (2) doors, mirrors, and other points of intersection or ingress between our world and some adjacent one (e.g. Borges, Cortázar, Angela Carter); (3) dreams, visions, hallucinations, etc. (see above, "Modernist reading, postmodernist text"); and (4) inset or "nested" texts or representations, including novels-within-the-novel, ekphrastic descriptions of paintings, photographs, comics, etc., and of course representations of movies or TV programs.

Towards an ontology of television

However, if representations of TV in fiction are in some respects functionally equivalent to representations of movies, there are also differences. These differences between the functions of film and TV in fiction can be traced to the differing ontological structures of film and TV themselves. One could summarize the relevant dimensions of TV's ontological difference from cinema (from the point of view of their respective functions in prose fiction) under three headings: (1) the "flow" of worlds (see Williams 1974); (2) the intimate interaction between TV "programming flow" and real-world "household flow" (see Altman 1986:40, 43–4); and (3) the "precession of simulacra" (see Baudrillard 1983b, 1988).

   (1) By contrast with the monolithic ontological character (one film/one world) of most commercial film genres, in particular "classical" Holly-wood realist film (see Kaplan 1987:148), TV is characterized by an ongoing "flow" of segments (commericals, programs of different genres, etc.) projecting worlds of radically different kinds, from verisimilar realism to many varieties of non-realism (stylized realism, "magic realism," surrealism, etc.), making different kinds of truth-claims (fact, fiction, "docudrama," etc.), inhabited by beings of differing ontological status, governed by different sociological and psychological norms and even, in some cases, by different physical laws (think of the physics of cartoons). This "flow" characterizes both the interior structure of individual programs (think of news or sports programs with their studio anchors, prerecorded footage,

"live" action, commercial spots, etc.) and the overall structure of a day's programming schedule.

(2) The boundary between the fictional worlds of cinema (or of live theater, for that matter) and the empirical "real world" of the viewer is very heavily signposted. In approaching that ontological divide one undergoes a whole series of elaborate rituals: traveling to the theater, buying the ticket, negotiating the lobby, locating the seat, viewing certain "threshold" representations (previews of coming attractions, maybe a cartoon, in some countries advertisements), etc. (see Berger and Luckmann 1966:24–5). Not so in the case of TV: the "televisual apparatus" is right there in one's own home, its worlds instantly accessible without any preliminary ritual. The worlds of TV unceremoniously mingle with the ongoing empirical-world activities of the household (or bar, student center, etc.). Far from interrupting the flow of activity in such viewing sites by demanding undivided attention, TV encourages "selective inattention"; its tendency is to mesh with rather than override ongoing activities in the empirical world. Because of the casualness with which TV interacts with empirical-world viewing sites, TV viewers are apt to regard the TV screen not as some absolute ontological boundary (like theater footlights), but rather as a kind of semipermeable membrane, and even to engage in pseudo-dialogue exchanges with TV announcers, as though these latter shared the same world-space with the viewers (Morse 1986:69).

(3) TV intervenes in empirical reality not only in the context of domestic TV consumption, however; it also, and more profoundly, does so at the source, so to speak. Already some decades ago, relatively early in what Baudrillard calls the "era of communication," Boorstin (1985 (1961)) presciently observed how certain categories of people ("celebrities") and events ("pseudo-events," he called them) exist only as a function of the communications media that supposedly "report" but actually generate them. Such media phenomena of course predate commercial TV – Hollywood "movie stars" are a textbook example – but it is only with the advent of TV and its apparently irresistible rise to cultural dominance that we begin to experience the wholesale evacuation of reality by its mass-media simulations.

Boorstin cited, as prime examples of mass-media pseudo-events, press-conferences, presidential debates, opinion polls, and the like; interestingly, however, he exempted sport and crime, suggesting that our fascination with such "spontaneous events" is to be explained by our recognition that in them lingers a residue of spontaneity and first-hand reality, by contrast with the glut of second-hand, media-generated events. Perhaps Boorstin was unwilling to follow the logic of his own analysis to its limit, or perhaps mass-media simulation had not yet come to pervade sport and crime as thoroughly as it has done since then; but one need only reflect on the packaging of the Olympic Games, or the reciprocal adaptation of

American football to the televisual apparatus and the televisual apparatus to football, or the marketing of sports "celebrities," to realize how completely sport has become "simulacral." And, as for crime, the mass-media have called into being an entire category of crime that would not even exist but for the media presence, namely (post)modern terrorism. Indeed, Baudrillard argues that all major crime is simulacral now:

> all hold ups, hijacks and the like are now as it were simulation hold ups, in the sense that they are inscribed in advance in the decoding and orchestration rituals of the media, anticipated in their mode of presentation and possible consequences. In brief . . . they function as a set of signs dedicated exclusively to their recurrence as signs, and no longer to their "real" goal at all . . . hyperreal events, no longer having any particular contents or aims, but indefinitely refracted by each other.
>
> (Baudrillard 1988:179)

More outrageously still, Baudrillard goes on to argue that even war (he has in mind the war in Vietnam) is subject to the law of the precession of simulacra whereby the simulacrum precedes, indeed preempts, the reality it is supposed to simulate. Not that wars do not cause real deaths, dismemberment, devastation; but these horrors have come increasingly to be reduced to the status of gruesome side-effects, strictly ancillary to the real business of TV representation, or rather simulation. Perhaps, indeed, this is no longer as outrageous a proposition as it once seemed; for not only do we now have the evidence of witnesses to the Vietnam War (such as Herr 1978; on Herr, see Jameson 1991a:44–5) as to the "mediated" character of that conflict, but we have seen, in the 1991 Persian Gulf campaign, how the true arena of conflict, the "theater of war," has shifted from the battlefield to the competition between the broadcast networks and cable news.[14]

TV as ontological pluralizer

These three ontological dimensions of TV are variously foregrounded and exploited in postmodernist fiction. The "flow" of TV worlds, for instance, is foregrounded in texts such as Robert Coover's "The Babysitter" (from *Pricksongs and Descants*, 1969), in which an entire evenings's TV programming (7:40, variety-show dance number; 8:00, Western; 8:30, spy thriller; 9:00, various options on different channels, including a ballgame, a melodrama, and a murder mystery; 10:00 news, followed by an aspirin commercial and the late movie) unfolds in the background, and sometimes the foreground, of a multi-branched "forking paths" narrative, adding substantially to the complexity of the whole.

Other texts, e.g., Pynchon's *The Crying of Lot 49* (1966), Clarence Major's *Reflex and Bone Structure* (1975), Ascher/Straus's *The Menaced*

Assassin (1982), and Don DeLillo's *White Noise* (1985), emphasize TV's ubiquity and the interaction between TV programming flow and the flow of reality itself, demonstrating how TV worlds insinuate themselves into the real world to pluralize the latter. For example, the characters in Major's *Reflex and Bone Structure* watch TV continuously – in bed, in bars, etc. – and the constant presence of various TV "sub-worlds" further complicates the heterogeneous ontological texture of a world already riddled with segments of diverse and often indeterminate ontological status (fantasies, speculation, dreams, alternative scenarios, etc.): "Rita Haywood is screaming in the room. Canada looks around. Oh. The television" (Major 1975:46). Similar interventions of TV sub-worlds recur throughout DeLillo's *White Noise*: "Upstairs a British voice said: 'There are forms of vertigo that do not include spinning'" (DeLillo 1985:56); "The voice at the end of the bed said 'Meanwhile here is a quick and attractive lemon garnish suitable for any sea food'" (DeLillo 1985:178).[15]

Already as early as 1971, Jerzy Kosinski had undertaken a fictional analysis of the precession of simulacra in the political sphere. In *Being There*, his novel of that year, a mentally-handicapped gardener learns so perfectly to imitate TV representations of responsible, authoritative public men that he succeeds in displacing "real" politicians; Chauncey Gardner is in effect nothing but a simulacrum – but then, so are the politicians he imitates. A finer-grained analysis is to be found in Walter Abish's "Ardor/Awe/Atrocity" (1977). Here the simulated reality of a TV private-eye show, "Mannix," preempts and displaces the reality of the empirical world:

> People watch Mannix carefully, in order better to emulate the wealthy people he frequently visits in the graceful-looking haciendas of San Diego. Without Mannix, Southern California would have no entrée to the wealth and power in L.A. and San Diego. Without Mannix Southern California would be bereft of the distinction between ardor, awe, and atrocity.
>
> (Abish 1977:45)

Southern Californians, Abish tells us, convert the world around them into its simulation, into images on a screen:[16]

> At what stage does the Southern Californian convert the world around him into the flatness that resembles a movie [*sic*] screen. Everything the mind focuses on may be something it might have, on a prior occasion, spotted on a screen. In time, the Southern Californian will no longer ask, can I also do it? Instead he or she will want to know where, at what movie house, can it be seen?
>
> (Abish 1977:50)

"Mannix," we are assured, provides a "pleasure map" of Southern

Californian reality (Abish 1977:45). This metaphor of mapping recurs throughout Abish's text:

> The immediate future, the immediate immaculate future, lies *mapped out* in the brain cells as the suntanned people on the Coast carefully observe Mannix's arrival at an airport. It resembles their own arrival.
>
> (Abish 1977:47; my emphasis)

> Mr. and Mrs. Down pore over the *map* of L.A. It is a *landscape* filled with the recollection of Mannix.
>
> (51–2; my emphases)

Surely we are meant to remember Korzybski's admonition, "The map is not the territory." The irony of this story is that, in fact, the map *is* the territory here, as it turns out: the "Mannix" world of sex, drugs, crime, and violent death is the world Abish's character Jane enters when she moves to L.A., and in which she ultimately perishes. Clearly, Abish's attitude toward TV, like that of Kosinski and other postmodernists who have explored the precession of simulacra, tends to be that of the anti-TV jeremiahs (Boorstin, Postman, Kroker and Cook, *et al.*). This is one possible postmodernist attitude, though not the only or inevitable one.[17]

TV-en-abyme

The ontological plurality of texts such as Coover's "Babysitter," Major's *Reflex and Bone Structure* or Abish's "Ardor/Awe/Atrocity" is aggravated and complicated by the presence, among their other manifold sub-worlds (dreamed, hallucinated, speculative, alternative "forkings," etc.), of the plural and heterogeneous worlds of TV. The worlds of these texts, in other words, have something like the ontologically plural, centrifugal structure of TV itself. So when TV appears *in* the worlds of these texts, it not only contributes to and further aggravates the plurality of their worlds, but also reflects in miniature the ontological structure of the texts themselves. TV, in other words, functions not only as ontological pluralizer in these texts but also as *mise-en-abyme*, or reduced scale-model, of ontological plurality itself.[18]

No doubt it is for this reason that TV as such – the TV "set," the object itself – so often appears in these texts as something uncanny, almost other-worldly, associated (if only figuratively) with angelic visitors from some other order of being. For instance, angels and TV are juxtaposed, and in some sense equated, in Rushdie's *Satanic Verses*. Prompted by an interviewer to reflect on how, in the contemporary world, "TV is a medium as much as an angel is," Rushdie remarks, "[T]he television in the corner is a kind of miraculous being, bringing a kind of revelation . . . television is what we now have for archangels" (Rushdie 1989:17–18).

Elsewhere TV is associated with what in our real-world experience has always been the most salient example of "another order of being," namely death. TV is systematically associated with death throughout Thomas Disch's *The Businessman* (1984), as it is also in DeLillo's *White Noise* and Pynchon's *The Crying of Lot 49*. Thus, for instance, in *The Businessman*, Disch's postmodernist fantastic novel, the newly dead watch the earthly doings of their surviving loved ones on an other-worldly version of Home Box Office. In *White Noise*, a text that is as death-obsessed as it is TV-obsessed, the two are routinely equated; thus, for instance, seeing one's wife on TV gives a kind of foretaste of her death, while new medical imaging techniques are described as death "rendered graphically," "televised so to speak" (DeLillo 1985:104–5, 141–2).[19] Similarly, in *The Crying of Lot 49*, Mr. Thoth, who complains of TV contaminating his dreams, awaits the Angel of Death (*Lot*:136); Oedipa and the lawyer Metzger watch Metzger himself, as a child actor, simulate dying in an old movie on TV (*Lot*:27); while the late Pierce Inverarity's manifold commercial interests are ubiquitously advertised on TV, as though in a kind of televisual haunting. Moreover, on the very first page of *The Crying of Lot 49* TV is associated, albeit obliquely and figuratively, with both death (the death of Pierce Inverarity) and the divine: having just learned of Pierce's death, and that she has been appointed executor of his will, "Oedipa stood in the living room, stared at by the greenish dead eye of the TV tube, [and] spoke the name of God" (*Lot*:1; see Schaub 1981:33).[20]

Such images, uncannily assimilating TV to the numinous, to angelic visitations, or even to death itself, graphically demonstrate that TV functions in postmodernism not just as one pluralizer among others, but as the figure of ontological plurality itself. TV in these texts thus functions simultaneously at two different levels, at one level serving to *represent figuratively* that very ontological plurality to which, at another level, TV itself contributes. Here TV is a *figure of itself*, a kind of strange loop.

There is a sense in which all forms of self-reflexivity in TV, all the strategies whereby the televisual apparatus "lays bare its own devices" (as the Russian Formalists would have said), can be seen as cases of TV figuring itself, troping on itself. I have in mind here not only TV's self-parodies – e.g. *Monty Python's Flying Circus*, *The Muppet Show*, *Sesame Street* and so on – but also certain tendencies in TV commercials and in the regular fare on MTV, as well as, at the opposite institutional extreme from commercial music videos, video art.[21] Video art, as Jameson (1991b:71) has observed, serves to expose the inherent characteristics of TV, commercial TV included, and this means, among other things (though Jameson himself does not say so) its distinctive ontological characteristics.

Zapping

There is, moreover, yet another means of troping on TV, one that produces what might be called a "homemade" or "guerilla" equivalent of video art, and which postmodernist fiction in its turn exploits in a characteristic way. This familiar "abuse" of the televisual apparatus ("abusive," presumably, only in terms of the interests of those who buy and sell TV commercial time) is a recurrent object of representation in postmodernist fiction. One finds a conspicuous instance of it in DeLillo's *Players*:

> Lyle passed time watching television. Sitting in near darkness about eighteen inches from the screen, he turned the channel selector every half minute or so, sometimes much more frequently. He wasn't looking for something that might hold his interest. Hardly that. He simply enjoyed jerking the dial into fresh image-burns. He explored content to a point. The tactile-visual delight of switching channels took precedence, however, transforming even random moments of content into pleasing territorial abstractions. Watching television was for Lyle a discipline like mathematics or Zen.
>
> (DeLillo 1984:16; cf. also 40, 123)

This, of course, is a description of so-called "channel-hopping," or "zapping."

Zapping also occurs conspicuously in Rushdie's *The Satanic Verses*, where Saladin Chamcha, we are told,

> watched a good deal of television with half an eye, channel-hopping compulsively, for he was a member of the remote-control culture of the present . . . . he, too, could comprehend, or at least enter the illusion of comprehending, the composite video monster his button-pushing brought into being . . . what a leveller this remote-control gizmo was, a Procrustean bed for the twentieth century; it chopped down the heavyweight and stretched out the slight until all the set's emissions, commercials, murders, game-shows, the thousand and one varying joys and terrors of the real and the imagined, acquired an equal weight.
>
> (Rushdie 1988: 405)

In an interview, Rushdie has undertaken to explain the relevance of TV channel-hopping in *The Satanic Verses*:

> Take the image of channel hopping, sitting there with a remote control and pushing the buttons and getting fractions of fifty worlds which blur into each other as you sit there. Well, the novel [*The Satanic Verses*] in a way does some channel hopping; it takes a large number of different kinds of narrative and puts them up against each other and darts between them. . . . What one can learn from [this] is that people are willing now to take literature in a kind of mosaic form, that you

can take a number of stories and juxtapose them . . . the fact that people are used to performing the other act [i.e. channel-hopping] helps, it actually clarifies and simplifies the act of reading such a book, which a hundred years ago might have been harder to do. So you can use the techniques of other forms and find out what they mean for your own.

(Rushdie 1989:19–20)

Or, in other words, zapping in *The Satanic Verses* is a reduced scale-model, or *mise-en-abyme*, of the textual poetics of *The Satanic Verses* as a whole, in particular its juxtaposition and orchestration of disparate worlds, its ontological plurality. This, it seems to me, is an insight that can readily be generalized to many of the other texts featuring the channel-hopping motif, including Coover's "The Babysitter," Ted Mooney's *Easy Travel to Other Planets* (1981), Bruce Sterling's cyberpunk SF novel *Islands in the Net* (where the TV scans automatically through the channels while a couple make love in front of it), as well as Pynchon's *Vineland*, as we shall see. If the normal flow of TV worlds is a good scale-model or *mise-en-abyme* of postmodernist ontological plurality, then the heightened, intensified flow produced by zapping is that much better, a model with even higher visibility and sharper "resolution."

Moreover, zapping, this "illicit" or "guerilla" practice of homemade video art, not only serves better as a scale-model (*en abyme*) of postmodernist verbal art, it also performs better the larger cultural modeling functions of TV. More than a technology or even an institution, TV is a privileged model or metaphor for the whole of the society that produces and consumes it; at least, that would seem to be the consensus among the contemporary jeremiahs of TV culture (see, e.g., Baudrillard 1983a:127, 128; Postman 1985:10, 92–3, 111; Kroker and Cook 1986:274–5). If Jameson and the anti-TV jeremiahs are right, and TV really can be seen as a privileged model of postmodern culture, postmodernism's principal means of representing itself *to* itself, then zapping, as a heightening and intensification of TV's specific ontological structure, functions in a heightened way to model the "difficult whole" of postmodern culture at large.

With this in mind, we can now finally return to the specific postmodernist representation of TV from which we began, namely, Pynchon's *Vineland*; but not before we have made one last brief detour through *Gravity's Rainbow*.

MEDIATED DEATHS

TV makes only two appearances in *Gravity's Rainbow*, both of them highly instructive. In one (*GR*:691–2), what had seemed to be a "real" episode of daily life among Japanese kamikaze pilots on a remote Pacific atoll abruptly "loses" its reality, undergoing a sudden demotion of ontological status to that of a "World War II situation comedy," presumably the "Takeshi and Ichizo Show." Indeed it is doubly demoted, for the situation comedy seems itself to have been "quoted" in the course of a TV quiz-show, "Paranoid for a Day." TV will make another appearance later on when somebody identified as Slothrop's "chronicler" – presumably a fictional surrogate of the author himself – abandons his Tarot fortune-telling cards and, disheartened by what he has read there, settles down in front of the Tube "to watch a seventh rerun of the Takeshi and Ichizo Show, light a cigarette and try to forget the whole thing" (GR: 738).

These are instructive episodes because in both TV is associated with other characteristic ontological pluralizers: in the first, with "nested" representations and the transgressive use of the second-person pronoun ("– what? You didn't like the haiku");[22] in the second, with the metafictional interpolation of the author (or rather his surrogate) into the fictional world. Moreover, both episodes feature appearances by "Takeshi and Ichizo, the Komical Kamikazes" (GR:690), who thus acquire, by their association with these moments of ontological disruption, the function of metonymic figures of ontological plurality itself.

It is a function which they retain in Vineland – or at least one of them does. Takeshi, one of the Komical Kamikazes of Gravity's Rainbow, returns in Vineland as Takeshi Fumimota, insurance investigator turned "karmic adjuster."[23] He is, evidently, the "same" Takeshi: "I keep forgetting," his new partner remarks maliciously, "suicide used to be your old lifestyle."

> She was referring to what he had a way of calling his "interesting work with airplanes" during World War II. "Though to be frank," she continued, "I can't imagine you in anybody's air force, let alone the kamikaze, who, I understand from the history books, were fairly picky about who flew for 'em."
>
> (V:175)

Merely by the fact of his appearance here, Takeshi exemplifies one of postmodernism's devices of ontological pluralization, namely retour des personnages.[24] Moreover, here as in Gravity's Rainbow Takeshi continues to be associated metonymically with TV. It is he alone, of all the many TV-fixated characters in Vineland, who is shown practicing the paradigmatic postmodernist art of zapping: "He . . . checked into one of the airport motels, put on the air-conditioner and the Tube, hit the Search button on the remote, and lay watching the channels crank by, two seconds apiece" (V:160). Takeshi, himself a metonymic figure of ontological plurality, reliably orients us toward what is in some sense Vineland's center of gravity, not only its primary device of ontological pluralization but the very model of its plurality: the Tube.

Genre-worlds

TV's ubiquity in *Vineland* has already been established; it remains to clarify its function. In nearly every instance, at every level of the text, TV's primary function in *Vineland* (though not its only one) is to complicate, diversify, and destabilize the ontological structure of the fictional world. We have seen, for instance, how TV models saturate the characters' consciousness and language, constituting a kind of alternative "ghost" reality shadowing all their real-life interactions. Behind and alongside everything they say or do in "real life" loom ideal models of behavior based on TV representations (the TV cop, the TV adolescent, the TV parent, etc.) which their real behavior can only approximate more or less imperfectly. But it is not just the characters whose behavior conforms (or fails to conform) to TV models, and not just the characters' consciousnesses that are shaped by TV. Rather, the very world of *Vineland*, the outside "real world" existing independently of any particular character's consciousness of it, is itself modeled on TV.

Different "regions" of this world seem to be modeled on the norms of different TV genres. These regions, while independent of the characters' consciousnesses, nevertheless are typically "keyed on" specific characters. Thus, the region of the fictional world around Zoyd Wheeler seems to conform to the genre norms of TV sitcoms, the region around Brock Vond to the norms of TV cop-shows, the region around Frenesi and her husband Flash to those of soap-operas, and so on.[25] Each genre-world posits different character-types and psychologies, and obeys different reality-norms, even to some extent different physical laws: pratfalls, for instance, do not hurt in sitcoms as they would if they occurred in soaps. Thus, mingling TV genres in the same fictional world yields effects analogous to the casual juxtapositions of genre-worlds produced by the TV flow itself – or, better, to the heightened incongruities produced by zapping.

The disparities among genre-worlds are somewhat camouflaged by the fact that cop-show, soap-opera, and even sitcom norms are all more or less assimilable to realist verisimilitude. But there is no hiding such disparities in the case of regions modeled on animated cartoons, which do not conform to realist norms. The cartoon world is "home" to no single character of *Vineland*, but several of them pass at one point or another through a cartoon region: Zoyd seems in one episode to have stumbled into the infinitely malleable world of a Warner Brothers Bugs Bunny or Daffy Duck cartoon (*V*:62–7); Prairie meets a cute talking refrigerator reminiscent of Disney (*V*:193); Mucho Maas encounters a VW busload of freaks straight out of an R. Crumb "underground" comic (complete with "speech balloon emerging from their tailpipe as they rolled away," *V*:311); and so on.[26] When a character from a different world-region enters such cartoon worlds, or when cartoon-modeled episodes are juxtaposed with verisimilar episodes, the effect is one of extreme ontological incongruity and disjuncture. An example of juxtaposing naturalistic and cartoon episodes is Frenesi's vision or fantasy, in bed with Weed Atman, of worms playing pinochle on his snout (V:238). Weed, a tragic figure of failed revolution, has just been betrayed by Frenesi, and will shortly be shot dead as a consequence of her betayal. Spliced into the sequence between these desperately serious episodes, the worms allude to a traditional piece of juvenile gallows humor ("The worms crawl in/The worms crawl out/ The worms play pinochle on your snout"), and, except for their dimension of black comedy, could almost belong to the anthropomorphic world of a Disney cartoon.[27]

TV also contributes to the ontological plurality of Vineland by supplying the vehicles for many of the text's elaborate conceits (see "Mediated lives", above), some of them amounting in effect to semi-autonomous metaphorical micro-worlds.[28] Ontological pluralization perhaps also underlies and helps to explain Pynchon's apparently trivial running gag about apocryphal Movies of the Week. Pynchon's jokey casting for these made-for-TV movies serves to foreground the weirdness (see Polan 1986:181–2, 1988:53–4) of this genre, a weirdness which passes almost unremarked by the TV-viewing public, so acclimatized have we become to it, and which ultimately derives from the genre's ontologically hybrid nature. Films of the Movie-of-the-Week genre are typically "docudramas," i.e. fictionalizations (or "dramatizations") of real-life situations or the biographies of real persons. Constrained at least as much by the norms of TV fictional genres as by the "facts" of the lives they fictionalize, they are factual-fictional hybrids. Moreover, they typically cast high-profile stars in the roles of the biographical protagonists, so that there is a further ontological tension in the competition of two "real-life" figures (the protagonist of the biography on the one hand, the star on the other) for the same quasi-fictional character. These are the sorts of ontological tensions that Pynchon's parodic mismatching of casts and roles serves to foreground and heighten.

Moreover, TV in Vineland is not just a pluralizing device in its own right; as in other postmodernist texts described above in "Representing TV" ("The Babysitter," Reflex and Bone Structure, White Noise, etc.), here too it also functions as the model for the text's other pluralizing devices, for its ontological plurality in general. TV's ontological plurality, its "flow" of worlds, mirrors that of Vineland as a (difficult) whole, so that TV functions here at two levels, at one and the same time contributing to ontological plurality and modelling that plurality en abyme. This mise-en-abyme function is made explicit in a key scene in which Darryl Louise (DL), killing time while waiting for her chance to assassinate Brock Vond, falls into an ontological meditation whose "objective correlative" is the TV:

> Sometimes, waiting in her room, she'd wonder if this was all supposed to be some penance [. . .] Was it a koan she was meant to consider in depth, or was she finally lost in a great edge-to-edge delusion, having only read about Frenesi Gates once in some dentist's waiting room or standing in line at the checkout, whereupon something had just snapped and she'd gone on to make up the whole thing? And was now not in any Japanese whorehouse waiting to kill Brock Vond at all, but safely within a mental institution Stateside, humored, kindly allowed to dress up as the figure of her unhappy fantasies? For company while she waited she left the Tube on with the sound off. Images went rolling in and out of the frame as she sat, quiescent, sometimes teasing herself with these what-is-reality exercises.
>
> (*V*:141)

"What-is-reality exercises" constitute, indeed, the very fabric of *Vineland*. Some of these exercises involve television directly, others do not, but either way they all find their ultimate reflection, as DL's does here, in the "images . . . rolling in and out of the frame" of the TV screen, postmodernism's preferred model of its own plurality.[29]

In the zone

For the space of *Vineland* is a multiple-world space, a heterotopia or "zone" (see McHale 1987:43–58), and its ontological plane is split along several different axes. Like *Gravity's Rainbow*, *Vineland* is pervaded by the alternative realities not only of the mass media (movies in *Gravity's Rainbow*, TV here), but also of dreams and hallucinatory visions.[30] These increase in frequency in the novel's final chapter, as all the major characters converge on Vineland County, and indeed the pervasiveness of dreams and hallucinations in this part of the novel attests to the special ontological plurality which this text attributes to Northern California in general, and fictional Vineland County in particular. "Crossing the Golden Gate Bridge represents a transition, in the the metaphysics of the region," we are told, "there to be felt even by travelers unwary as Zoyd" (*V*:314). The infant Prairie responds to the forested landscape she and her father pass through on the far (northern) end of the bridge "as if this were a return for her to a world behind the world she had known all along" (*V*:315; cf. *Lot*:136–7; *GR*:202). Evening shadows in the backwoods of Vineland County provoke "easy suspicion of another order of things"; at this hour the two adjacent worlds "draw . . . closer, nearly together, out of register only by the thinnest of shadows" (*V*:220). The light in Vineland seems to issue a "call to attend to territories of the spirit" (*V*:317), a call to which the aboriginal inhabitants, the Yurok and Tolowa peoples, had responded by locating the entrance to their underworld of Tsorrek, "the world of the dead," in the backwoods of what would later come to be known as Vineland (V:186–7). It is to this underworld, still evidently accessible despite the disappearance of those who once believed in it, that the renegade cop Brock Vond is delivered in the novel's closing pages (V:378–80).[31]

Parallel or alternative worlds, though likeliest to be encountered in Vineland County, are not exclusively restricted to this region. Prairie, for instance, evidently encounters one in a walk-in freezer at the hilltop retreat of the Kunoichi Attentives (V:189–90), while back in the sixties in Los Angeles, Weed Atman had experienced the waiting-room of the sinister dentist Dr. Elasmo as a kind of limbo, separate from the real world:

> Weed at the close of the workday would go back down the chipped and crumbling steps, back across a borderline, invisible but felt at its crossing, between worlds. It was the only way to say it. Inside [. . .] was an entirely different order of things.
>
> (V:228)

In addition to such parallel worlds, there are also worlds of unrealized possibilities, the branchings not taken in history's garden of forking paths. The most elaborately developed of these is the scene in which Weed Atman and Rex Snuvvle, reunited in a pastoral landscape years after the traumatic events at the College of the Surf, reminisce about their campus-revolutionary days (V:232–3). In fact, this scene, with all its circumstantial detail of setting and conversation, would never occur in "reality," having been preempted by the real events of the College of the Surf, where Rex Snuvvle shoots his friend Weed Atman dead, mistakenly believing him to have betrayed the revolution to Brock Vond's police (V:246). This episode, in other words, has been edited out of the actual sequence of events, placed *sous rature*, under erasure: it occurs, in a sense, but only as unactualized potential, literally a might have-been.[32]

Finally, in a more diffuse way, the presence of other worlds, of "another order of things," is indicated by the pervasiveness in *Vineland* of certain recurrent figures of speech. Symbols of some higher order's intrusion upon our mundane existence, these figures include metaphors of angels, of UFOs, or of "another planet" (even, in one case, "another dimension" (V:283)):[33]

> She waited . . . standing at the window and trembling, moonlight from a high angle pouring over her naked back, casting on it shadows of her shoulder blades, like healed stumps of wings ritually amputated once long ago, for some transgression of the Angels' Code.
>
> (V:261)

DL's [puberty and adolescence] were . . . turning out to be like vacationing on another planet and losing her traveler's checks.

(V:123)

A special case of ontological plurality in *Vineland* is the juxtaposition of the ontological states of life and death, being and not-being. Elsewhere (McHale 1987:227–32) I have contended that all foregrounding of ontological difference in postmodernist fiction is in effect a displaced modeling of the ultimate ontological disjunction between life and death. Insofar as this is so, then it follows that the multiplication of ontological planes and regions throughout *Vineland* must necessarily function, in however displaced a way, and apart from any other functions it may also serve, to model death. But this function of modeling death is not merely inferential in the case of *Vineland*, as it sometimes is in other cases, for here the text underscores its death-modeling function by explicitly thematizing death, and by staging encounters between states of life and death, for instance in the episode of Brock Vond's descent to the aboriginal land of the dead. Indeed, most of the central motifs of the novel prove on inspection to be means, however displaced, of modeling death.[34]

Death and television

And this includes the TV motif. If TV in *Vineland* functions as a model *en abyme* of the text's plurality in general, then it follows that among the other ontological differences that it models, TV here also models death. Striking intimations of TV's death-modeling function occur in the novel's middle chapters, in episodes which, paradoxically enough, involve neither TV as such nor death as such. These are the episodes of Prairie's quest to recapture the mother she never knew and the lost world of the Sixties that was her mother's milieu. To do so, she must rely on various media, first that of a computer monitor, on which she reviews her mother's file (including photographs (V:113–15)); then that of film, though, belonging as she does to a TV-oriented generation, Prairie would have preferred videotape. In any case, she brings her video instincts to bear even when she watches movies:

"Can you put it on pause, freeze it?"
"Sorry. We did transfer it all to videotape, and there are duplicates around, but the idea was to disperse the archives so they'd be safer, and I got stuck with all the film."

(V:199)

The experience is, in more than one sense, a mediumistic one, as though Frenesi were already dead and Prairie were attempting to contact her through the apparatus of computer screen and film projector. It is, the text tells us, "as if Frenesi [Prairie's mother] were dead but in a special way, a minimum-security arrangement, where limited visits, mediated by projector and screen, were possible" (V:199).

Dead but in a special way: mediated death. "If mediated lives," the text asks rhetorically, "why not mediated deaths?" (V:218). The "mediated" lives of so many of the characters in *Vineland* – lives in which TV simulations have effectively preempted direct experience – is explicitly connected with the "mediated deaths" of the strange beings called Thanatoids. The Thanatoids of *Vineland* occupy the excluded middle ground between the one and the zero of life and death.[35] Neither fully alive nor fully dead, they inhabit a kind of posthumous limbo, "like death only different" (V:170), awaiting rectification of the imbalances in cosmic justice and injustice that prevent them "from advancing further into death" (V:171); by a system of adjustments and deferments of karmic rewards and punishments, "Death . . . got removed from the process" (V:175), leaving the Thanatoids stranded. To conclude, as DL somewhat hastily does, that they must be ghosts (V:173) is hardly to do justice to the equivocal, amphibious state in which they persist.

In fact, the Thanatoids are nothing more nor less than Pynchon's tool – his *medium* – for exploring the paradoxical ontology of death. By positing these liminal beings, and locating them, not incidentally, in the frontier region between worlds in the backwoods of Vineland, Pynchon is attempting to imagine death by imagining instead a displaced state *just this side* of it.[36] And if the Thanatoid state is an attempt to model death, then TV – "mediated life" – is in turn an attempt to model the Thanatoid state. Thanatoids, it will be recalled, "watch a lot of Tube":

> While waiting for the data necessary to pursue their needs and aims among the still-living, Thanatoids spent at least part of every waking hour with an eye on the Tube. "There'll never be a Thanatoid sitcom," Ortho Bob confidently predicted, "'cause all they could show'd be scenes of Thanatoids watchin' the Tube!"
>
> (V:170–1)

If death is finally beyond the grasp of our imaginations, then perhaps the only way we can even approach the thought of it, sample or "taste" the thought of it, is by displacement, through the experience of *other* forms of ontological difference; and in our culture, the most readily accessible experience of ontological difference, and at the same time the most comprehensive model of *all other* forms of ontological difference, is provided by the TV.

This, then, I want to propose, is how Pynchon undertakes to use TV. Instead of engaging in yet another jeremiad against it (a gesture, as we have seen, fatally compromised from the start anyway) or, alternatively, merely passively acquiescing in its seductions and distractions, Pynchon sets out to make TV into a tool in a perhaps quixotic cognitive enterprise. By representing the ontological plurality *of* TV, and its pluralizing effect on the world of which it forms a part, Pynchon seeks to model the ontological plurality of postmodern culture itself, including the final, intractable ontological difference, the ultimate limit to all modeling and all representation, death. Much in the same way, perhaps, that Jameson has sought to convert the spaces of postmodernist architecture into a tool for thinking about ("cognitively mapping") the otherwise elusively unrepresentable world system, Pynchon may be seeking to convert TV into a tool for cognitively mapping the place of death in a postmodern culture. And much as Jameson has strangely, and controversially, redeemed even so unlikely a building as John Portman's egregious Bonaventure Hotel by appropriating it in this way to his (and our) cognitive use, so Pynchon has, perhaps more strangely still, "redeemed" TV.

Part III

Reading postmodernists

Chapter 6

The (post)modernism of *The Name of the Rose*

Proverbs for Paranoids, 3: If they can get you asking the wrong questions, they don't have to worry about answers.

(Thomas Pynchon 1973:251)

Umberto Eco is properly skeptical about the term "postmodernism": "I have the impression," he writes in his *Postscript to The Name of the Rose*, "that it is applied today to anything the user of the term happens to like" (Eco 1984:65). This does not prevent him from offering his own definition of it, a characteristically witty and perspicacious one. "I think of the postmodern attitude," he writes,

> as that of a man who loves a very cultivated woman and knows he cannot say to her, "I love you madly," because he knows that she knows (and that she knows that he knows) that these words have already been written by Barbara Cartland. Still, there is a solution. He can say, "As Barbara Cartland would put it, I love you madly." At this point, having avoided false innocence, having said clearly that it is no longer possible to speak innocently, he will nevertheless have said what he wanted to say to the woman: that he loves her, but he loves her in an age of lost innocence. If the woman goes along with this, she will have received a declaration of love all the same. Neither of the two speakers will feel innocent, both will have accepted the challenge of the past, of the already said, which cannot be eliminated, both will consciously and with pleasure play the game of irony . . . But both will have succeeded, once again, in speaking of love.
>
> (Eco 1984:67–8)

This definition bears a good deal of resemblance to the one proposed by John Barth in his much-cited essays on the "Literature of Exhaustion" (1967) and the "Literature of Replenishment" (1979).[1] Eco acknowledges Barth, but expresses some misgivings about Barth's willingness to "grade" writers according to their degree of postmodernism (Eco 1984:71). No doubt he would be even less satisfied with Charles Jencks, the architecture critic who, in a little book called *What Is Postmodernism?*, cites both Barth and Eco as corroborating his own definition of postmodernism. Jencks defines postmodernism as *double coding*: the postmodernist building or art-work simultaneously addresses an elite minority audience through high-art codes, and a mass public through popular codes (Jencks 1986:14–15 and *passim*).[2] Not satisfied with merely defining, Jencks devotes most of his book to policing the boundaries of postmodernism and denouncing other critics for failing to distinguish sufficiently sharply between modernism (or late-modernism) and postmodernism; that is, between these other things and *his* postmodernism, of course.

Despite the formidable authority of Barth, Eco, and Jencks, this definition of postmodernism is not the one I prefer to use. I find corroboration for my preferred definition in the avant-garde poet, composer, performance artist, and sometime publisher Dick Higgins, who actually avoids the terms "modernism" and "postmodernism" altogether. Nevertheless, his categories of "cognitive art" and "postcognitive art" evidently correspond rather closely to the more familiar categories. Higgins' definition runs like this:

> *The Cognitive Questions*
> (asked by most artists of the 20th century, Platonic or Aristotelian, till around 1958):
> "How can I interpret this world of which I am part? And what am I in it?"
>
> *The Postcognitive Questions*
> (asked by most artists since then):
> "Which world is this? What is to be done in it? Which of my selves is to do it?"
>
> (Higgins 1978:101)

By contrast with Jencks's dogmatic definition, Higgins's is appropriately playful and fictional. To fix on precisely the year 1958 as the watershed, instead of more obviously symbolic years such as 1945 or 1960, is to signal that this little story of Higgins's is just that, a story – not a map whose boundaries need policing.[3]

This is not to say that Higgins's distinction, however playful, is not a useful tool for doing literary history. I have used it myself elsewhere (McHale 1987:xii, 3–25 and *passim*), though I have substituted my own terminology for Higgins's "cognitive art" and "postcognitive art." In my version of Higgins's opposition, modernist fiction is fiction organized in terms of an epistemological dominant, fiction whose formal strategies implicitly raise issues of the accessibility, reliability or unreliability, transmission, circulation, etc., of knowledge about the world (compare Higgins's "cognitive" question, "How can I interpret this world of which I am a part?"). Postmodernist fiction, on the other hand, is fiction organized in terms of an ontological dominant, fiction whose formal strategies implicitly raise issues of the mode of being of fictional worlds and their inhabitants, and/or reflect on the plurality and diversity of worlds, whether "real," possible, fictional, or what-have-you (compare the "postcognitive" question, "Which world is this?"). Thus, for Higgins's "cognitive art" read "epistemological poetics"; for his "postcognitive art," "ontological poetics."

If these are our working definitions, then what, in the first place, does a modernist novel look like in the light of them?

EPISTEMOLOGY ("HOW CAN I INTERPRET THIS WORLD . . .?")

The short answer is, a modernist novel looks like a detective story.[4] Classic detective fiction is the epistemological genre *par excellence*. Its plot is organized as a quest for a missing or hidden item of knowledge: classically, "whodunit," or, in its more sophisticated forms, "*why* was it done?" and even "what kind of person would do such a thing?" The detective-story protagonist is a "cognitive hero" (Krysinski 1981:168; cf. Fokkema and Ibsch 1987:1–47), the hero as cognizer of the world and agent of *recognitions* (Aristotelian *anagnorisis*); he or she is reduced synecdochically to the organ of visual perception, the (private) eye. This detective-story structure underlies modernism's epistemological quests from the earliest modernist phase through the phase of "high modernism" to its latest phases – from, say, *The Sacred Fount* and *Lord Jim* through *Absalom, Absalom!* and *The Great Gatsby* to *The Real Life of Sebastian Knight*, *La Jalousie*, *The Crying of Lot 49*, Pinget's *L'Inquisitoire*, and the late-modernist epistemological quests of Joseph McElroy.[5] All these fictions, and many others which we have learned to call modernist, revolve around problems of the accessibility and circulation of knowledge, the individual mind's grappling with an elusive or occluded reality.

Among many other things, Umberto Eco's *The Name of the Rose* is, of course, a detective story. Its principal intertextual model, as the name of its hero, William of Baskerville, proclaims, is Conan Doyle's *The Hound of the Baskervilles*, though other paradigmatic detective stories also contribute to its plot (notably Dorothy Sayers's *Gaudy Night* and Poe's "The Purloined Letter" (see De Lauretis 1985)). Eco himself, in his *Postscript*, has described *The Name of the Rose* as a "story of investigation and of conjecture" – or, indeed, of conjectures in the plural, for the "basic story (whodunit?) ramifies into . . . many other stories, all stories of other conjectures" (Eco 1984:54, 57). The main epistemological quest in *The Name of the Rose* is, of course, William's quest for "whodunit" at the mountain-top monastery – and not only who, but how and especially why as well. This quest gives rise, in turn, to a second one focused on the identity of the book for which the murders have been committed, then for the book itself (which twice in the course of the action is hidden, purloined-letter style, in plain sight). The murders also generate a third quest – or a third and a fourth, William's less coercive inquisition paralleling the misguided "official" one conducted by Bernard Gui – into the recent history of the Franciscans and their relations with millenarian and heretical movements. Thus a "local" mystery story deepens and ramifies into a form of historical research and reconstruction – another kind of epistemological quest – in the manner of Faulkner's *Absalom, Absalom!*, Pynchon's *The Crying of Lot 49*, or John Banville's *The Newton Letter*.

There is yet another epistemological quest here, one less indebted to the detective genre per se and more directly modeled on high-modernist fiction, namely, Adso's epistemological quest as a retrospective narrator seeking to recover the experiences of himself as a young man (see Coletti 1988:39–72). Eco, in his *Postscript*, has identified the model for this narrative structure as Thomas Mann's *Doktor Faustus*, but in the same passage he also alludes to Proust's *Recherche* (Eco 1984:33), and in fact it is in Proust that we recognize the most striking analogue with Adso's quest to recover his "lost time." Adso's epistemological quest perhaps emerges most saliently in the episode of the maiden "beautiful and terrible as an army arrayed for battle." As Adso the narrator prepares to recount this experience of Adso the young protagonist, he claims that reconstructing the past is unproblematic, merely a matter of copying out the contents of memory:

> I can do so [i.e., tell what he saw and felt then] with the fidelity of a chronicler, for if I close my eyes I can repeat not only everything I did but also what I thought in those moments, as if I were copying a parchment written at the time.[6]

The past is fully known, fully accessible; it is just a matter of telling (or indeed *re*telling) it. But, as he proceeds with his reconstruction of his one and only sexual experience, Adso finds himself "gripped by the vortex of memories" (*NR*:248), and he ends up not merely telling what he already knew but discovering aspects of his past experience that he did not know, or did not know that he knew. In short, his experience of narrating the past is very much that of Proust's Marcel in the *Recherche*.[7]

Nevertheless, if Adso is modeled on high-modernist narrators – Mann's Serenus Zeitblom or Proust's Marcel – it is clearly William who is the most fully "modernist" figure in *The Name of the Rose*. He is so not only in my sense – the cognitive hero of an epistemological quest – but also in the medieval sense. In his confrontations with Abbot Abo, the librarian Jorge, and the inquisitor Bernard Gui, William speaks as one of the *moderni* in the ideological quarrel between the *via moderna* and the *via antiqua*. A follower of Roger Bacon and friend of William of Occam, he represents nominalism and a proto-empiricism in opposition to an ideology founded on *auctoritas* (see Coletti 1988:155–9). It is a question whether William's "modernity" in this medieval sense has anything to do with the "modernity" of twentieth-century modernism, whether the "modern" which functions in opposition to "antiquity" coincides with the "modernism" we distinguish from "postmodernism."[8] Eco himself suggests that categories such as "postmodernism" and "the avant-garde" (which he identifies with modernism) are in fact transhistorical, not period styles but perpetually available possibilities (Eco 1984:66; cf. Lyotard 1984a); and I think a case could be made (though this is not the place to make it) for seeing William's medieval "modernity" as substantially continuous with the "modernity" of modernist epistemological poetics (Higgins's "cognitive art").[9] From this perspective, postmodernist onto-logical poetics can be seen as recovering certain elements of the "antiquity" that William's medieval "modernity" stood in opposition to.

Can we safely conclude, then, that *The Name of the Rose* is a typically modernist novel? No; for this would be to overlook certain "defects" (deliberately contrived) in its detective-story structure. "The ingenuous reader," writes Eco, "may not even realize that this is a mystery in which very little is discovered and the detective is defeated" (1984:54). This "ingenuous reader" is reflected in Annaud's film version of *The Name of the Rose*; the film, in effect, both *is* the ingenuous reader and caters for him/her in the shape of the mass-distribution movie audience. For the William of Baskerville whom we encounter in the film is a *successful* detective. He suffers a defeat, of course, in the burning of the library and particularly of the lost volume of Aristotle; but he has not been defeated *as a detective*, but rather (like Sherlock Holmes himself in story after story) vindicated in the end. By contrast, Eco's original William of Baskerville conspicuously *fails* as a detective. He discovers the truth, yes, but by stumbling upon it, not by a successful chain of deductions:

"There was no plot," William said, "and I discovered it by mistake. . . . I arrived at Jorge through an apocalyptic pattern that seemed to underlie all the crimes, and yet it was accidental. I arrived at Jorge seeking one criminal for all the crimes and we discovered that each crime was committed by a different person, or by no one. I arrived at Jorge pursuing the plan of a perverse and rational mind, and there was no plan, or, rather, Jorge himself was overcome by his own initial design and there began a sequence of causes, and concauses, and of causes contradicting one another, which proceeded on their own, creating relations that did not stem from any plan. Where is all my wisdom, then?"

(*NR*:492)

Jorge, no friend of rationality, gets the point: "You are proud to show me how, following the dictates of your reason, you arrived at me, and yet you have shown me you arrived here by following a false reasoning. What do you mean to say to me?" (*NR*:471).

What, indeed? Of course, as William's faithful Dr. Watson, Adso, hastens to point out, William has successfully solved, through pure ratiocination, a number of subsidiary mysteries: he has cracked Venantius' code, deduced the structure of the labyrinth, established the identity of the fatal book, and so on. Nevertheless, the trail that leads to Jorge and the solution of the main mystery is a false trail, and only by chance arrives at the right place. There is no pattern of murders based on the scenario of the *Apocalypse*. Though four of the six deaths are directly or indirectly Jorge's doing, only in the case of Malachi's poisoning has any deliberate effort been made to echo the apocalyptic pattern, and in this case only in order to plant a red herring to mislead William. As for the other two deaths, one (the first, Adelmo's) is suicide, the other (Severinus's) has been caused by Malachi the librarian. Furthermore, even if William's hypothesis were sound, which it is not, there are some downright irrational leaps in his chain of reasoning. In order to identify the mysterious book, William needs to have his memory jogged by Adso's recounting of a dream based on the *Coena Cypriani*. Similarly, in order to interpret correctly Venantius's instructions for gaining access to the sealed room (*finis Africae*), William needs to be reminded, through a Latin error committed by the vagabond Salvatore – again reported by Adso – of the possibility of a *de dicto* reading of the cryptic text instead of the *de re* reading he has been taking for granted.

Thus the champion of reason in this text, its Sherlock Holmes figure, can only solve the mystery through consistent misinterpretation of the evidence, and even then only thanks to irrational associational leaps prompted by a dream and a grammatical error, both recounted by an adolescent novice! This is the most painful irony of Eco's novel, more painful even than the irony of the library's inadvertent destruction by the one most committed to its values.

This element of irrationality in William's detective work is not to be dismissed as merely a question of red herrings, for it actually undermines the basic assumption of the detective story from Poe's Dupin through Sherlock Holmes to Hercule Poirot and Miss Marple and beyond, namely, the assumption of the adequacy of reason itself, of ratiocination. So profoundly has the rationality of detection been compromised here that *The Name of the Rose* qualifies as an "anti-detective story," one which "evoke[s] the impulse to 'detect' . . . in order to violently frustrate it by refusing to solve the crime" (Spanos 1972:154) – or, I would add, by inverting, suppressing, or occluding other essential features of the detective-story model (crime, victim, detective), ultimately by undermining its very rationality.[10] The anti-detective story has proliferated in postmodernist writing, from Gertrude Stein's *Blood on the Dining Room Floor* through Borges and Robbe-Grillet to Puig (*The Buenos Aires Affair*), Fuentes (*La Cabeza de la hidra*), Clarence Major (*Reflex and Bone Structure*), Richard Brautigan (*Willard and His Bowling Trophies, Dreaming of Babylon*), Walter Abish ("Ardor/Awe/Atrocity," *How German Is It*), and many others.[11]

By deliberately crippling the detective story's epistemological structure, these texts in effect evacuate the detective story of its epistemological thematics. But, like nature, literary history abhors a vacuum; if epistemology has been evacuated from these anti-detective stories, what rushes in to take its place? *The Name of the Rose* shows us the answer. The final irony of the breakdown of reason in *Name of the Rose* is that the events which William mistakenly construes as an apocalyptic pattern do finally really conform to an apocalyptic pattern, climaxing in the destruction of the library and the monastery. Who is the author of this pattern? Jorge convinces himself that it is a divine plan after all, that God is its author, and in a certain sense he is right; but which god? "Writing a novel," Eco tells us, "is a cosmological matter, like the story told by Genesis (we all have to choose our role-models, as Woody Allen puts it)" (Eco 1984:20). The final irony of *The Name of the Rose* is Romantic irony (see Gorak 1987), and it reveals to us, behind the layers of patterns of events and misconstructions of patterns and retrospective reconstructions, the presence of the real author himself: smiling, bearded Umberto Eco, cosmologist and labyrinth-builder.

ONTOLOGY ("WHICH WORLD IS THIS?")

Thus *The Name of the Rose* is, at least in this respect, a metafictional text, laying bare its status *as* text and *as* fiction. In other words, to revert to the language of my definition of postmodernism, *The Name of the Rose* foregrounds its own ontological status, its mode of being, in this case its relative ontological "weakness" *vis-à-vis* its own author, whose presence it reveals "behind" it. What rushes in, then, when the anti-detective story empties the detective model of its epistemological structure and thematics? What else but ontological structure and thematics: postmodernist poetics.

The Name of the Rose draws on several strategies from the postmodernist repertoire, apart from its deconstruction of the detective-story pattern. These strategies fall into two groups: first, strategies for staging confrontations among two or more worlds, thus laying bare the plurality of worlds (see Calinescu 1983) and focusing attention on the boundary or interface between worlds; and, secondly, strategies for destabilizing the projected world of the novel itself, thus foregrounding the very process of world-construction, what Nelson Goodman (1978) calls the "ways of worldmaking."

Confrontations among worlds

(1) The most conspicuous ontological confrontation in *The Name of the Rose* is the one between the novel's fictional world and real-world historical "fact." In a certain sense, *Name of the Rose* has been designed precisely for the purpose of staging a tense, prolonged face-off between fact and fiction. Another way of saying this, of course, is simply to call it a historical novel; not, however, a historical novel of the classic type made canonical in the nineteenth century by Scott, Tolstoy and others, and now largely practiced as a best-selling entertainment genre, but a historical novel of the postmodernist type, the type that Hutcheon (1988) has called "historiographic metafiction" (see Eco 1984:74–5). Where the classic historical novel sought to ease the ontological tension between historical fact and fictional invention, and to camouflage if possible the seam along which fact and fiction meet, postmodernist historical fictions such as those written by Pynchon, Barth, Fowles, Coover, Grass, Fuentes, Ishmael Reed, Salman Rushdie, Russell Hoban, John Banville, Guy Davenport, T.C. Boyle and others, aim to exacerbate this tension and expose the seam. They do this, for instance, by contradicting familiar historical fact, by mingling the realistic and fantastic modes, and by flaunting anachronism.

It is in particular this last strategy, deliberate anachronism, that Eco exploits in *Name of the Rose*. Eco has defended his anachronism, arguing that when one of his characters generates what appear to be "modern" ideas from medieval ones, he is only doing what his culture in fact did, as history confirms: the Middle Ages generated modernity. This may be so, but it fails to account for the disorienting effect Eco's anachronism has on the reader. Eco boasts that when readers charge him with anachronism it is invariably on the grounds of some passage actually quoted from a fourteenth-century text, while when they praise him for his historical authenticity they cite what he himself regards as modern interpolations (Eco 1984:76–7). We can be certain of deliberate anachronism when Eco has William quote Wittgenstein, but we may feel a good deal queasier when he has him anticipate Freud's interpretation of dreams or propose a "strange concept of temporal government" (*NR*:492, 438, 352ff.). Do these passages authentically represent advanced late-medieval thought, or have they been projected back into the Middle Ages from the modern world? This queasiness of ours is precisely an ontological queasiness, a symptom of our uncertainty about the exact boundaries between historical fact and fiction in this text.

(2) The presence of real-world historical personages in a fictional text – such as Michael of Cesena or Bernard Gui in this one – is a case of

what Eco himself has called "transworld identity" (Eco 1979:229 and *passim*). Transworld identity is always a sign of the penetration of one world by another, the violation, in some sense, of an ontological boundary. Apart from the incorporation of historical personages, other kinds of transworld identity are possible, for instance the "borrowing" of fictional characters from other fictional worlds. Thus, for example, Gilbert Sorrentino in *Imaginative Qualities of Actual Things* borrows Lolita from Nabokov's novel, Alejo Carpentier in *El recurso del metodo* lifts several characters from Proust, Fuentes in *Terra Nostra* borrows from a number of fellow Latin-American novelists, and Kathy Acker pirates characters (Pip, Hester Prynne, Don Quixote, Temple Drake) and even authors (Genet, Rimbaud) from world literature to populate her fictional worlds. There is also the possibility of *roman-à-clef*, in which fictional characters are understood to be thinly-disguised surrogates for real-world personages. The sense of scandal which typically accompanies the *roman-à-clef* is precisely an ontological scandal, arising from an "illegitimate" mingling of worlds. Both of these forms of transworld identity are discernible in *The Name of the Rose*, the first (the borrowing of characters from other fictional worlds) in William of Baskerville and his faithful sidekick Adso/Watson, the second (*roman-à-clef*) in Jorge of Burgos and in sly allusions to "the great Lyotard" and the scholars of Paris who are experts on difference and "are very sure of their errors" (*NR*:434, 196–7, 306).[12]

(3) If such transworld identities are rather marginal to *The Name of the Rose*, there is another strategy of ontological confrontation which has greater centrality, involving as it does the very linguistic texture of the text. That texture is *polyglot*: even in translation, *The Name of the Rose* is a multilingual text, "contaminated" throughout with the Latin of the medieval cultural context, which has been integrated to varying degrees with the main language of the text (sometimes set off typographically, sometimes not; sometimes translated, sometimes left untranslated, etc. (see Kurzon 1989)). Moreover, the world projected in *The Name of the Rose* is even more polyglot than the text itself. Adso does not report the speech of the peasant girl because he cannot understand her dialect (*NR*:244, 330), and for the same reason does not transcribe Greek or Arabic passages from the books he and William examine (*NR*:362, 366); nevertheless, the spaces which these "absent" languages occupy in the world of the novel are mapped out.

Different languages, different registers of the same language, different discourses each construct the world differently; in effect, they each construct *different worlds*. This is a hypothesis of twentieth-century reflections on language which may be traced, with varying emphases and intonations, through Baxtin and Wittgenstein and Benjamin Lee Whorf to Berger and Luckmann and Michel Foucault and beyond (see McHale 1987:162–75). If we accept this hypothesis, it follows that to juxtapose or superimpose different languages, registers, or discourses is to place different, perhaps incommensurable worlds in tense confrontation. "Polyphonic" texts which stage such confrontations are especially likely to arise in cultures or periods in which a plurality of languages and discourses, and their associated world-views, jostle and mingle. Such a period is our own; think of *Finnegans Wake* or *The Cantos*, or the polyglot, poly-discursive postmodernist texts of Burroughs, Butor, Roche, Barthelme, Acker, Brook-Rose, Ashbery, the L=A=N=G=U=A=G=E poets and many others. The late Middle Ages in which *The Name of the Rose* is set was another such period (see Vance 1986:152–83), so here Eco's postmodernism and his historical authenticity converge. Eco's text reflects the linguistic struggles of the period – in particular between Latin and the vernacular languages, but also between Latin and the other learned languages (Greek and Arabic) and among the various vernaculars – and uses them as a vehicle for staging confrontations among the corresponding world-views.

The plurilingualism of the world of *The Name of the Rose*, simultaneoulsy postmodern and late-medieval, is reflected in the vagabond Salvatore. Ultimately modeled, perhaps, on Pantagruel's polyglot sidekick Panurge, and speaking "all languages, and no language" (*NR*:46), Salvatore is in effect a synecdoche for the tense interaction among languages and world-views in late-medieval Europe. He is a walking site of his culture's heteroglossia, a one-man polyphony,[13] and from his narrative of picaresque adventure Adso reconstructs an image of the vagabond populations of Europe, captured in one of Eco's most astonishing catalogues ("false monks, charlatans, swindlers, cheats, tramps and tatterdemalions, lepers and cripples, jugglers, invalid mercenaries, wandering Jews . . . lunatics, fugitives under banishment, malefactors with an ear cut off, sodomites," and so on for a further twenty-odd lines (*NR*:189–90)).[14] Salvatore "*is* the face of Europe," writes Coletti (1988:133).

He is also a one-man carnival, reflecting, and in turn reflected by, all the other images of the carnivalesque throughout Eco's text: the "upside-down world" of the marginalia in the illuminated manuscripts, Adso's dream or vision of the *Coena Cypriani*, the monastery kitchen, the "magnificent carnival" of the days of the Dolcinian uprising, and so on.[15] An authentically late-medieval *topos* (or indeed bundle of *topoi*) of ontological plurality and confrontation – polyphony made literal – carnival is also a postmodernist *topos*. Examples abound: *Gravity's Rainbow*, *Terra Nostra*, *Midnight's Children* and *Satanic Verses*, García Márquez's "Los funerales de la Mama Grande," Juan Goytisolo's *Conde Julian* and *Makbara*, texts by Burroughs, Acker, Ishmael Reed, Angela Carter, and the cyberpunk science-fiction writer William Gibson, and postmodernist films such as Scott's *Blade Runner*, Tsukerman's *Liquid Sky*, Kureishi and Frears's *Sammy and Rosie Get Laid*, and Greenaway's *The Cook, the Thief, His Wife and Her Lover*.

Destabilization of the projected world

Just as staging confrontations among worlds serves to raise and explore ontological issues, so too does robbing the fictional world of its stability *as* a world. In *The Name of the Rose*, this destabilization of the fictional world is accomplished mainly through two strategies, one considerably more efficacious than the other.

(1) The first strategy, the less powerful of the two, involves "weakening" the fictional world by placing it at several narrative removes (see Füredy 1989). The world of *The Name of the Rose* is not directly projected for us by an authorial voice, or even indirectly through the mediation of a fictional narrator (Adso). Rather, according to the frame-tale that prefaces the narrative proper, this world has been mediated by no fewer than *four* intermediaries: first Adso, whose text has then been edited by Mabillon, whose text in turn has been translated by Vallet, whose text has in its turn been "transcribed" by "Eco."[16]

Obviously, this narrative distancing has a certain effect of robbing the fictional world of its solidity, dissolving it into mere intertextuality, hearsay, dubious scholarship. Just as obviously, however, that effect is relatively short-lived, attenuating as we proceed deeper into Adso's densely-specified late-medieval world. In any case, such multiple narrative embedding is not necessarily a tool of ontological foregrounding, though it does serve that function in postmodernist "Chinese-box" texts such as Barth's *Giles Goat-Boy*, "Menelaiad," and "Life-Story," Flann O'Brien's *At Swim-Two-Birds*, Gilbert Sorrentino's *Mulligan Stew*, Calvino's *If on a Winter's Night a Traveller*, and the texts of Raymond Federman. However, it is just as likely to serve to foreground epistemological issues of narrative mediation, transmission, and reliability, as it does in epistemologically-oriented texts from *Wuthering Heights* to Conrad's *Chance* and Faulkner's *Absalom, Absalom!* and beyond.

(2) More threatening to the solidity of the fictional world is the strategy which we have learned to call by its French name, for lack of a good equivalent in any other language, *mise-en-abyme*. *Mise-en-abyme* involves the paradoxical reproduction ("mirroring" is the metaphor favored by critics) *within* the fictional world *of* the fictional world itself.[17] Familiar examples include the play-within-the-play in *Hamlet*, the tale-within-the-tale in "The Fall of the House of Usher," or the various paintings and sculptures which partially reproduce the narrative worlds throughout the fiction of Hawthorne, Melville, and James.

The Name of the Rose is riddled with instances of *mise-en-abyme*, and their cumulative effect is to infiltrate paradox, corroding the fictional world's solidity and stability. The most conspicuous instances are the two tympanums, that of the abbey church and the one in the chapter-house.

The first, in particular, is understood by Adso to reproduce the apocalyptic pattern of events in the monastery. It provokes in him a vision:

> I realized the vision was speaking precisely of what was happening in the abbey, of what we had learned from the abbot's reticent lips – and how many times in the following days did I return to contemplate the doorway, convinced I was experiencing the very events that it narrated. And I knew we had made our way up there in order to witness a great and celestial massacre.
>
> (NR:45)

Indeed, the very architecture of the church portal warns us that this tympanum is, literally as well as figuratively, a *mise-en-abyme*:

> Two straight and unadorned columns stood on either side of the entrance, which opened, at first sight, like a single great arch; but from the columns began two embrasures that, surmounted by other, multiple arches, led the gaze, as if into the heart of an abyss, toward the doorway itself, crowned by a great tympanum.
>
> (NR:40)

Similarly, Adso interprets the labyrinthine marginal decorations in an illuminated manuscript in the library as a *mise-en-abyme*, mirroring the labyrinthine structure of the library as well as that of the baffling tangle of events in which he has been caught up:

> My eye became lost, on the page, along gleaming paths, as my feet were becoming lost in the troublous succession of the rooms of the library, and seeing my own wandering depicted on those parchments filled me with uneasiness and convinced me that each of those books was telling, through mysterious cachinnations, my present story. "De te fabula narratur," I said to myself, and I wondered if those pages did not already contain the story of future events in store for me.
>
> (NR:241)

And there are further elements of this world which seem to invite interpretation as structures *en abyme*: the damaged and gory armillary sphere, the murder-weapon in Severinus's death, which seems to mirror the violence soon to be inflicted on the monastery-microcosm (NR:359); and Adso's vision during the singing of the *Dies irae* on the sixth day, in particular his vision of the fragmented "macrobody" in the crypt, which seems to echo the imminent dissolution of the abbey, its library, and its world, and to foretell the moment, narrated in Adso's epilogue, when he collects the fragments (significantly called "relics") of the burned library (NR:432–4; cf. NR:500).

But of course the most important instance of *mise-en-abyme* in *The Name of the Rose* is the library itself. The Aedificium which houses the library inspires Adso to meditate on architecture, the art "that most boldly tries to reproduce in its rhythm the order of the universe, which the ancients called 'kosmos' " (*NR*:26). Indeed, the library does reproduce the cosmos; its structure is a scale-model of the known world, its floor-plan reproducing the map of the world (*NR*:314); it is "a great labyrinth, sign of the labyrinth of the world" (*NR*:158). This doubling of the world of *Name of the Rose* by the world-within-the world which is the library opens up an abyss of potentially infinite regress, thereby radically destabilizing the world of the novel, and in the process laying bare its ontological structure. The threat of infinite regress arises when we consider that the library, scale-model of the world, contains a book whose decorations constitute a scale-model *en abyme* of the library: world-within-world-within-world . . .[18]

TOPOLOGY AND ESCHATOLOGY

But the structure *en abyme* of the library has other functions as well, and a consideration of them will lead us on to certain specific themes which are characteristic of postmodernist writing, in particular the thematics of postmodernist space and the theme of apocalypse.

Postmodernist space

The film version of *The Name of the Rose* is "false" to Eco's novel in many ways, of course, but one way in which it is strikingly faithful to the spirit of Eco's original, if not exactly to its letter, is in the representation of the interior space of the library. Eco's library labyrinth occupies a single floor, while Annaud's film shows us a deep but densely crowded space on several levels, connected by ramps and stairs. Yet the film does capture in its own medium the experience of complexity, disorientation, and combined claustrophobia and agoraphobia which Eco projects in his verbal medium, and it does so partly by directly drawing on some of the same visual sources discernible, if only remotely, behind Eco's representation: Piranesi's *Carceri*, Escher's topological paradoxes. These two visual sources are models or (in the case of Escher) analogues for what are in turn the main literary models of Eco's labyrinth, namely Borges's "Library of Babel" and the interior spaces of the law-courts in Kafka's *The Trial*. These texts of Borges and Kafka are, it might be said, founding-texts not only of Eco's representation of a disorienting, paradox-ridden interior space, but of an entire postmodernist topology. For postmodernist fiction is full of paradoxical and labyrinthine spaces, both interior spaces (as in Robbe-Grillet's *Maison de rendez-vous* and *Topologie d'un cité fantôme*, Calvino's "The Count of Monte Cristo," Flann O'Brien's *The Third Policeman*, Don DeLillo's *Ratner's Star*, and others) and urban spaces or cityscapes (as in Robbe-Grillet's *Dans le labyrinthe* and *Projet pour une révolution à New York*, Calvino's *Invisible Cities*, and Burroughs's Interzone, Minraud, and *Cities of the Red Night*).[19]

Moreover, this disorienting postmodernist space appears not only in verbal, fictional representations, but also in actual built structures. Charles Jencks, architecture critic and apologist for postmodernist architecture, contrasts the space of modernist architecture with this characteristically postmodernist space. Where modernist space – the space of Le Corbusier, the Bauhaus, Mies van der Rohe – is homogeneous, isotropic, oriented within right-angled grids, and sharply bounded, postmodernist space – the space of Peter Eisenman, Charles Moore, or Frank Gehry – is apt to be skewed or distorted, subject to abrupt shifts and transformations, and ambiguous as to its boundaries (Jencks 1984:118–26). Jencks compares it to the space of a Chinese garden:

> Post-Modern, like Chinese garden space, suspends the clear, final ordering of events for a labyrinthine, rambling "way" that never reaches an absolute goal. The Chinese garden crystallises a "liminal" or in-between space that mediates between pairs of antinomies, the Land of the Immortals and the world of society being the most obvious mediation. It suspends normal categories of time and space, social and rational categories which are built up in everyday architecture and behaviour, to become "irrational" or quite literally impossible to figure out. In the same manner Post-Modernists complicate and fragment their planes with screens, non-recurrent motifs, ambiguities and jokes to suspend our normal sense of duration and extent.
>
> (Jencks 1984:124)

The liminal, in-between space of the Chinese garden and of postmodernism is also the space of Eco's library-labyrinth: "For these men devoted to writing, the library was at once the celestial Jerusalem and an underground world on the border between terra incognita and Hades" (*NR*:184).

The difference between the Chinese garden and postmodernist space, as Jencks is quick to point out, is of course that Chinese garden space is sustained by a particular metaphysics, of which it is in effect the sign, while it is not at all clear what, if anything, postmodernist space might be a sign of. Or at any rate Jencks himself is not disposed to pursue this issue.

But it seems an issue well worth pursuing. What might postmodernist space, whether built space or that of literary labyrinths, reflect or represent? How might it be "read"? Fredric Jameson has recently proposed that we undertake to read the complex, disorienting spaces of postmodernist buildings – John Portman's Bonaventure Hotel in Los Angeles, Frank Gehry's house in Santa Monica – as allegories or "cognitive mappings" (Jameson 1988) of the almost unthinkably complex world system within which we live under the regime of multinational capitalism. In the case of the Portman hotel, this space is (no doubt inadvertently) overwhelming, numbing, ungraspable – an appropriate built representation of our inability to master the immensely complicated, interdependent world in which we find ourselves (Jameson 1983, 1991a(1984)). On the other hand, the Gehry house offers a different kind of experience: disorienting, yes, but stimulating rather than anaesthetizing. It seems to hold out the possibility of our getting a critical grip on the conditions under which we live, instead of being submerged in them (Jameson 1991c).

Eco quotes an "ingenuous reader" of *The Name of the Rose* who, failing to following the theological controversies developed in the book, nevertheless understood them – properly, in Eco's view – as extensions of the labyrinthine space of the library (Eco 1984:58). In this respect, the library can be seen as a synecdoche for the labyrinthine world of late-medieval Europe in which *The Name of the Rose*, as a historical novel, is set. At the same time in can also be read as a different figure, a metaphor or *mise-en-abyme*, in the postmodernist context. In this context the library functions, like other postmodernist labyrinthine spaces, whether verbal representations or actual constructions, as an attempt to draw a "cognitive map" of the world of late-capitalism which Umberto Eco shares with us, his contemporaries.[20]

If Eco's library-labyrinth can be read as a cognitive map *en abyme* of the postmodernist world, then what aspects of that world, specifically, does it map? Among other things, its imminent end.

Displaced apocalypse

The final image of Thomas Pynchon's postmodernist masterpiece *Gravity's Rainbow* is that of a nuclear warhead uncannily poised the last incalculable sliver of time and space above the roof of the theater in which we, the readers of the book, presumably sit. Metaphor for the imminence of nuclear holocaust, this immeasurably narrow gap is the space in which we have lived since 1945. But Pynchon has not only given us a definitive emblem of life under the nuclear threat; he has also done so in a way which recapitulates (or anticipates) many of the strategies by which postmodernist writing has endeavored to represent the unrepresentable scene of nuclear apocalypse. In its suspension of time and motion, this last episode of *Gravity's Rainbow* is another fantastic moment in a novel which promiscuously mingles the realistic and the fantastic. It is also a metafictional moment, involving a transgression of narrative levels: the text seems to address us ("There is time, if you need the comfort") and to include us ("It was difficult even for us, old fans who've always been at the movies"), as though striving to draw us into its world (Pynchon 1973:760).[21] Finally, the missile poised above the theater is not one missile but, uncannily, three missiles, three repetitions of the same event collapsed into one: the V-2 launched by the mad German rocket commander Blicero in the last days of the Second World War, carrying his beloved Gottfried to his extinction; the re-enactment of that sacrifice by Enzian and his *Schwarzkommando* some months after the war's end; and the final rocket, the one yet to come – the ICBM of nuclear holocaust.

At the risk of sounding frivolous or grotesque, one might say that implicit in the closing pages of *Gravity's Rainbow* is the problem of how to represent apocalypse, and several proposals for its solution – an entire postmodernist poetics of nuclear war. But why frivolous or grotesque? For any writer aspiring to address the prospect of nuclear war, out of whatever motives – warning, exorcism, or simply the desire to come to grips with this enormous fact of our existence – apocalypse, whatever else it may be, is also a representational problem: how do we go about representing what seems to lie beyond the scope of our forms of representation? How do we express the inexpressible?[22]

Precedents show that realistic representations of nuclear apocalypse, however thoughtful and earnest (e.g. Lynne Littman's film *Testament*), let alone the more sensational exploitations of the theme (e.g. Nicholas Meyer's made-for-TV movie *The Day After*), can only be inadequate. Consequently, postmodernist fiction has developed a range of strategies for *displacing* nuclear apocalypse in ways which, potentially at least, might make this theme available to the imagination while preventing it from lapsing into the merely familiar, the automatic, the cliché.[23] One such strategy, for instance, involves the displacement of nuclear holocaust onto some other apocalypse scenario, some other form of large-scale or global disaster, natural or man-made;[24] another involves its displacement to distant places or times – the distant past or future, some other planet.[25] In one powerful version of this latter form of displacement, the future apocalypse proves to be an uncanny *repetition* of apocalypse – as though the world could end more than once. Apart from *Gravity's Rainbow*, this is also the strategy of Walter M. Miller's *A Canticle for Leibowitz* and Russell Hoban's *Riddley Walker*, in both of which the apocalypse is restaged (in Hoban's case, in a displaced form, namely, through the rediscovery of gunpowder) by descendants of the survivors of a twentieth-century nuclear war. In both these texts the repetition is exceptionally complex, for the future in which the apocalypse is restaged is itself a repetition of earlier phases of human history: in *A Canticle*, the Middle Ages and Renaissance; in *Riddley Walker*, prehistoric hunting-and-gathering society.[26]

Nuclear apocalypse may also be displaced into the fantastic mode, notably in the case of James Merrill's verse trilogy, *The Changing Light at Sandover*, with its campy (though ultimately serious) Ouija-board communications from the Other World warning of nuclear war. Or it may be displaced into the metafictional mode, as in the closing pages of *Gravity's Rainbow* or in Maggie Gee's novels *Dying, in Other Words* and *The Burning Book*, where the metafictional gesture of breaking the fictional frame and exposing the text's fictionality functions as a metaphor for nuclear apocalypse. A minimalist example of this latter strategy is the story "Apocalypse" by Peter Sagamore, the fictional author in John Barth's postmodernist extravaganza, *The Tidewater Tales*. This text is brief enough to be quoted in full:

> Apocalypse
> One drizzly Baltimore November forenoon, as from an upstairs work-room window of our little house I mused over the neighbors' lawns – some raked clean, some still leaf-littered – and considered whether
>
> (Barth 1987:142)

End of story; end of world.[27]

Finally, and most radically of all, there is the displacement of nuclear apocalypse into the very language of the text. Here language itself is pulverized, fused, ruined, reconfigured, both as a realistic consequence of the nuclear destruction visited on the culture of which this language is a vehicle, and as a kind of text-length metaphor of apocalypse. This is the strategy of William Burroughs's apocalyptic text *Nova Express*, in which language has been deliberately "cut up" and "folded in" on itself, and of Hoban's *Riddley Walker* and Denis Johnson's *Fiskadoro*, both of which (Johnson's text somewhat less radically) project future forms of scrambled, mutated English.[28]

Apocalypse, of course, is a conspicuous theological theme of *The Name of the Rose*, and a major intertextual motif, and as such contributes to the authenticity of Eco's novel as a historical fiction. But the novel's climax, the burning of the library, needs to be read not only in terms of medieval apocalypticism but also in the context of the postmodernist poetics of nuclear war.[29] Like those of his postmodernist contemporaries, Eco's too is a displaced apocalypse. It involves, in the first place, a *figurative* displacement, a troping on apocalypse. The library is a scale-model of the world, in both its horizontal and vertical dimensions: horizontally, of course, it reproduces the map of the medieval world; but vertically it reflects the hierarchy of medieval culture, with the official culture of order and *auctoritas* (the library itself) at the top, the kitchen, site of corporeality (food, sex) and the lower orders, at the bottom, and in between the mediating space of the scriptorium (see Coletti 1988:128–9).[30] When the library burns, the world is figuratively destroyed in its geographical extension as well as in its hierarchical strata (the library collapses into the kitchen).

Furthermore, nuclear apocalypse in *The Name of the Rose* also undergoes a temporal displacement to the late Middle Ages, with a corresponding scaling-down of its scope (from nuclear war to "ecpyrosis," from a world destroyed to a monastery) which serves to bring the unrepresentable within the range of representation. This strategy of temporal displacement involves a form of repetition, as in Miller's *A Canticle for Leibowitz*, a text which *The Name of the Rose* parallels in striking ways. Like Eco's, Miller's novel restages apocalypse in the context of monastic life, and the texture of Miller's text, also like Eco's, is polyglot, incorporating swatches of untranslated Latin. The difference, of course, is that Miller's apocalypse lies in the future and *repeats* a twentieth-century nuclear war, while Eco's late-medieval apocalypse *anticipates* nuclear war while it recapitulates a *different* end of the world. For the burning of the abbey library literally destroys the ancient world all over again by destroying that world's written remains, its archive. The library's fiery end uncannily repeats the disastrous episodes which brought the classical Mediterranean cultures to an end: the fall of Rome, the burning of the library at Alexandria. Thus the destruction of the library is in this sense doubly apocalyptic, involving the (metonymic) destruction of the ancient world at the same time as the (metaphorical) destruction of our world, the postmodern world.

Finally, the burning of the library in *The Name of the Rose* also involves a metafictional displacement of apocalypse. To destroy a text – figuratively, by exposing its fictionality, or literally, by burning it – is in effect to destroy a world. Multiply the destruction of a book many-fold and one has the destruction of a library of books; multiply *that* destruction in turn and one arrives at the ultimate destruction, the ruination of what Derrida (1984:26–8) has called the "juridico-literary archive," the storehouse of our culture from which, if it were to survive intact, our world could be reconstructed. Thus Maggie Gee, in *The Burning Book*, establishes a parallelism between the metafictional destruction of a fictional world and the physical destruction of a book; while as early as 1935 Elias Canetti, in *Auto da Fé* (*Die Blendung*), had allegorized the destruction of the cultural archive in the burning of a library.

Eco follows Canetti and anticipates Derrida in making a burnt-out library the symbol of the loss of a world. The final, memorable image of *The Name of the Rose*, an emblem of displaced apocalypse as definitive as Pynchon's arrested rocket, is that of Adso collecting the debris of the burned library:

> Poking about in the rubble, I found at times scraps of parchment that had drifted down from the scriptorium and the library and had survived like treasure buried in the earth; I began to collect them, as if I were going to piece together the torn pages of a book.... Along one stretch of wall I found a bookcase, still miraculously erect, having come through the fire I cannot say how; it was rotted by water and consumed by termites. In it there were still a few pages. Other remnants I found by rummaging in the ruins below. Mine was a poor harvest, but I spent

a whole day reaping it, as if from those disiecta membra of the library a message might reach me.

(*NR*:500)[31]

Adso is at the end of the fictional world that has given him a kind of existence, and simultaneously at the end, in a different sense, of his medieval world, the world consumed with the library. But in another, equally metafictional sense he is at the beginning of a world, for he is about to commence the project of world-making. From this debris Adso will compose, as he says, a *cento*, a book of remnants, "a kind of lesser library . . . made up of fragments, quotations, unfinished sentences, amputated stumps of books" (*NR*:500) – none other than the book we have in front of us, *The Name of the Rose*.

POSTSCRIPT TO *THE NAME OF THE ROSE*

Finally, then, is Eco's *The Name of the Rose* better thought of as a modernist (perhaps late-modernist) text or as a postmodernist one? On the one hand its central spine, the narrative armature on which it is constructed, is the epistemological quest typical of modernist fiction, and both its hero William of Baskerville and its narrator Adso of Melk, as well as its nastiest villain, Bernard Gui, are "cognitive heroes" of the type found in modernism. On the other hand, this epistemological structure has been deliberately sabotaged, crippled in a way typical of many postmodernist anti-detective stories, and the text has been opened to a range of characteristically postmodernist strategies – of transworld identity, Chinese-box nesting, *mise-en-abyme*, and so on – and has been made the vehicle of certain characteristically postmodernist themes of space and displaced apocalypse. Which is it, then, modernist or postmodernist? Or could it be both?

This is the wrong question, of course. The case of *The Name of the Rose* is not interesting because it requires us to choose between identifying the text as modernist and identifying it as postmodernist, but rather because it calls into question the entire opposition of modernist vs postmodernist. *The Name of the Rose* demands to be seen not as a puzzle to be solved unequivocally one way or the other, but as a challenge to the entire enterprise of distinguishing period styles (if that's what modernism and postmodernism are) or, more generally, to the entire enterprise of literary history. The real question is, if a text can be as "amphibious" as this one, simultaneously and in about equal measure modernist and postmodernist, then what consequences does this fact have for our literary-historical categories of "modernism" and "postmodernism"?

A deconstructive move might be to assert the amphibiousness – irreducible doubleness, indeterminacy – of *all* texts, thus dissolving all such literary-historical distinctions as "modernism vs postmodernism" into a general textuality. But this move is *too* powerful, I think; unhelpfully so. For it seems clear that some texts, at least, including many of the ones mentioned in this chapter, *are* satisfactorily accounted for as predominantly either modernist or postmodernist in their strategies and orientation. Of the texts that do not yield readily to such a description, some may be made literary-historically intelligible by embedding them in some higher-order narrative, for instance by placing them in the context of the story of a writer's career. This is the kind of story that Eco himself tells about Joyce, in the *Postscript*: *A Portrait of the Artist* is pre-modernist, *Dubliners* is fully modernist, *Finnegans Wake* is already postmodernist; *Ulysses*, however, is "on the borderline" (Eco 1984:68).[32]

But of course there are texts for which this contextualizing move will not work. A conspicuous example is Faulkner's *Absalom, Absalom!*, an ambiguously modernist-postmodernist text from which, however, Faulkner does not subsequently "advance" into postmodernism, as the literary-historical narrative would seem to require. Another example, of course, is *The Name of the Rose*. Ambiguously modernist-postmodernist, it is nevertheless a first novel, and thus hardly a candidate for insertion into the before-and-after scenario; unless, that is, we choose to regard Eco's earlier critical and semiotic work as typically modernist – but then the narrative coherence of the story would depend on what he would do next. (What he in fact did next was, of course, *Foucault's Pendulum*; see below.)

What Eco's text, so finely poised between modernist and postmodernist poetics, serves above all to remind us is that period terms such as these (or, e.g., "the Renaissance," "Romanticism," etc.) are after all *only* constructs, convenient literary-historical counters, figments generated by the discourses of critics, literary historians, reviewers, publishers, professors, and (sometimes) writers themselves. If we reify such categories, turning them into pseudo-objects with sharp outlines and unambiguous identities, we will inevitably get "amphibious" texts such as *The Name of the Rose* wrong; but worse than that, we will delude ourselves about the epistemological and ontological status of all our literary-historical discursive constructs, and in that sense will get *all* our "modernist" and "postmodernist" texts wrong. Thus, apart from anything else, an investigation of *The Name of the Rose* from the point of view of its literary-historical affiliations should have a sobering influence on our claims and ambitions as literary historians and critics. It should teach us to adopt Dick Higgins's playful attitude toward our own literary-historical constructs, rather than Charles Jencks's proprietary and dogmatic attitude. The literary historian as performance-artist, rather than as policeman: this is the role to which *The Name of the Rose* teaches us to aspire.

Chapter 7

Ways of world-making: on *Foucault's Pendulum*

In 1983 Umberto Eco published a postscript to *The Name of the Rose* (*Postille a Il nome della rosa*), a commentary on his own text, which I have had occasion to cite more than once in the preceding chapter. Five years later he published a postscript of a different kind, namely his second novel *Il pendolo di Foucault* (1988; *Foucault's Pendulum*, 1989). *Foucault's Pendulum* is a postscript to *The Name of the Rose* in the sense that it continues, supplements, completes, and pursues to their logical conclusion certain aspects of the earlier novel. In doing so, it confirms the affiliations I have described above between Eco's fiction and the postmodernist repertoire of motifs and strategies, even as it develops new affiliations with other elements of that repertoire. The purpose of the present chapter is to document some of the relationships between Eco's first novel and his second, and to explore some of the affinities between *Foucault's Pendulum* and the poetics of postmodernism.

In particular, there are two salient aspects of *The Name of the Rose* that have been continued and developed in *Foucault's Pendulum*, namely (1) reflection on the practice of paranoid reading, and (2) foregrounding of the ontological dimension of conspiracy.

PARANOID READING

The Name of the Rose, as we have seen, is an anti-detective story. In this respect, as in a number of others, it would appear to have been partially modeled on the stories of Jorge Luis Borges, in particular Borges's "Death and the Compass" ("La muerte y la brújula," 1942).[1] In this story, let me remind you, the detective Lönnrot thinks he has solved a series of three murders, and prevented a fourth, by discovering their underlying pattern, namely, that the victims' initials spell out three of the four letters of the Tetragrammaton (yod-heh-vav-heh), that lines drawn between the murder sites form an equilateral triangle, and that the murders occur on the fourth day of three consecutive months. Lönnrot conjectures where the next murder will occur (the point at which lines drawn from two of the other murder-sites would converge to complete a rhombus) and when (the fourth day of the fourth month). His conjectures prove to be correct, but only because he has fallen into a trap set for him by the gangster Scharlach: although the first murder was unpremeditated, the second and third had been planned by Scharlach to establish a pattern which he knew Lönnrot would discover. The fourth victim, of course, is Lönnrot himself.

The similarities between this ironic scenario and that of *The Name of the Rose* are sufficiently obvious that I need not specify them in detail here: there is the same series of conjectures which, though leading to a "solution," are nevertheless misguided, the same motif of entrapment by a sinister mastermind (Scharlach in one case, Jorge of Burgos in the other), the same fatal confrontation (though in one case it is fatal to the detective, in the other to the criminal). There is also, however, at least one crucial difference between the Borges model and Eco's transformation of it. Scharlach, like many sinister masterminds before and since, boasts to Lönnrot of his ingenuity in contriving the pattern, apart from that first fortuitous murder. Jorge of Burgos, by contrast, disclaims all responsibility for the pattern of six deaths (in four of which he has been instrumental); rather, he tells the detective William of Baskerville, as further murders occurred, "I became convinced that a divine plan was directing these deaths" (Eco 1983: 470). William replies, "You are trying to convince yourself that this whole story proceeded according to a divine plan, in order to conceal from yourself the fact that you are a murderer" (Eco 1983: 471). But William is wrong: Jorge, no hypocrite, really does believe that the pattern, based on the *Apocalypse*, has been arranged by God; indeed, he believes *all* patterns in this world are ultimately of God's making, whoever or whatever might have been their instruments. For Jorge, in effect, pattern always attests to the activity of the divine (super-human) pattern-maker. Human intermediaries, conspirators such as himself, are more or less irrelevant, mere tools in the divine conspiracy.

Modeled on the mad masterminds of popular fiction, Jorge is represented as melodramatically insane; a "paranoid," we might casually call him, using the term in its colloquial, not its clinical sense. But who is more paranoid really, William or Jorge? After all, it is William who persuades himself of the existence of a conspiracy motivating all the murders, which does not in fact exist. Jorge does not need "conspiracy theories" to motivate events, because for him all events are ultimately willed by God. In one of the epigraphs in *Foucault's Pendulum*, Eco quotes Karl Popper: "The conspiracy theory of society . . . comes from abandoning God and then asking: 'Who is in his place?' "[2] Jorge has not abandoned God, and so does not need to construct conspiracy theories. And of course there is a sense in which Jorge is strictly, literally right: in the world in which he exists, every pattern, including the apocalyptic pattern of the murders, has indeed been willed by an all-powerful pattern-maker. That pattern-maker, of course, is none other than the author of *The Name of the Rose*.[3]

This conclusion – that it is not the "madman" Jorge who is paranoid, but the "sane" William – has disturbing implications. For in *The Name of the Rose*, as in other epistemological fictions, the detective is our surrogate in the world of the text, and his "cognitive quest" of crime-detection parallels and mirrors our own cognitive quests as readers. His methods of conjecture, so self-consciously expounded to his side-kick Adso, in effect double as reading-instructions to us, guidelines for the proper construal of this text. But, if our reading of the text of *The Name of the Rose* mirrors William's reading of the world of *The Name of the Rose* – the world *as* text – and if William's reading of his world is "paranoid," then are we implicated in William's paranoia? Does this text expose us as paranoid readers?

Diabolical reading

Here is the point where *Foucault's Pendulum* takes up the theme. Consider its situation: three intellectuals – Casaubon (the narrator), Belbo, and Diotallevi – associated with the Milanese publishing house of Garamond become aware of the existence of an entire subliterature of occultism and secret societies, produced and consumed by a heterogeneous subculture on the margins of mainstream cultural institutions. This subculture, whose members they nickname "the Diabolicals," constitutes what Stanley Fish might call an "interpretive community": possessing its own canon of (esoteric, hermetic) texts, this community has developed its own methods for reading and interpreting these texts, and its own practices of writing. It is, in effect, a community of paranoid readers. Casaubon, Belbo and Diotallevi become obsessed with this Diabolical subliterature, teaching themselves how to read according to Diabolical norms, i.e. paranoiacally, and eventually even beginning to produce their own pastiche of Diabolical writing based on those norms ("parodying the logic of our Diabolicals," Casaubon calls this (*FP*:467)).

How, exactly, does one go about reading Diabolically or paranoiacally? The fundamental rule, it would appear, parodies E.M. Forster's slogan in *Howard's End*: "Only connect." The corollary is "Only suspect," i.e., read suspiciously, in the expectation of overlooked or occult connections. Belbo explains to Casaubon:

> Any fact becomes important when it's connected to another. The connection changes the perspective; it leads you to think that every detail of the world, every voice, every word written or spoken has more than its literal meaning, that it tells us of a Secret. The rule is simple: Suspect, only suspect. You can read subtexts even in a traffic sign.
>
> (*FP*:377–8)

Casaubon puts these reading-instructions into practice when he undertakes to interpret Diabolically texts belonging to the Diabolicals' own canon, namely the seventeenth-century Rosicrucian manifestoes of Johann Valentin Andreae:

> I read, not to believe what the manifestoes said, but to look beyond them, as if the words meant something else. To help them mean something else, I knew I should skip some passages and attach more importance to some statements than to others . . . . this was exactly what the Diabolicals and their masters were teaching us . . . .
>
> Taken literally, these two texts were a pile of absurdities, riddles, contradictions. Therefore they could not be saying what they seemed to be saying . . . . They were a coded message to be read by superimposing them on [sic] a grid, a grid that left certain spaces free while covering others . . . . Having no grid, I had to assume the existence of one. I had to read with mistrust.
>
> (FP:394)

Further corollary rules for paranoid reading emerge as Casaubon and his colleagues become increasingly intimate (fatally so, in the end) with Diabolical habits of thought. Casaubon summarizes them:

> Rule One: Concepts are connected by analogy. There is no way to decide at once whether an analogy is good or bad, because to some degree everything is connected to everything else . . .
>
> Rule Two says that if tout se tient [everything hangs together] in the end, the connecting works . . .
>
> Rule Three: The connections must not be original. They must have been made before, and the more often the better, by others. Only then do the crossings seem true, because they are obvious.
>
> (FP:618)[4]

Foucault's Pendulum is a compendium of Diabolical or paranoid readings. Notable examples, apart from Casaubon's reading of the Rosicrucian manifestoes, include Colonel Ardenti's interpretation of a cryptic fourteenth-century French text, supposedly documentary evidence of a Templar conspiracy (FP:135–40), and Belbo's parodic close reading of an automobile owner's manual according to paranoid rules (FP:377–80). Belbo goes so far as to program his personal computer (nicknamed "Abulafia") to generate random collocations of "facts" for use in practical exercises in paranoid interpretation; for, in accordance with the principles that "everything is connected to everything else" and "any fact becomes important when it's connected to another," even random collocations can be made to yield Diabolical sense (FP:376.)

Interpretive communities

But how "crazy" is paranoid reading, really? The example of William of Baskerville's interpretive practices in *The Name of the Rose* should already have disabused us of the idea that paranoid reading is the exclusive preserve of "crackpots." On the contrary, far from being restricted to "lunatic fringe" groups like the so-called Diabolicals, Diabolical-style reading is routinely practiced by other, thoroughly "respectable" and mainstream interpretive communities as well. There is, for instance, what might be called the subculture of data-collection and data-collation. This is the subculture to which Casaubon, a professional researcher, belongs, and even before his exposure to the Diabolicals his own research practices already exhibit a characteristically Diabolical logic:

> I was accumulating experience and information, and I never threw anything away. I kept files on everything. I didn't think to use a computer (they were coming on the market just then [. . .]). Instead, I had cross-referenced index cards. . . . Even the sloppiest manuscript would bring twenty new cards for my hoard. I had a strict rule, which I think secret services follow, too: No piece of information is superior to any other. Power lies in having them all on file and then finding the connections. There are always connections; you have only to want to find them.
>
> (*FP*:225)

Casaubon's casual reference here to secret services identifies for us the main constituent groups of this subculture, namely intelligence organizations and police departments (and of course private detectives like William of Baskerville). Police detective DeAngelis confirms this identification when he tells Casaubon, "If you look at the world in a certain way, everything is connected to everything else" (*FP*:315) – a classic formulation of the paranoid world-view. Thus, apart from the Diabolical fringe of society, paranoid reading is also practiced professionally and institutionally by groups of readers very near the centers of power, namely the professional conspirators and conspiracy theorists of the so-called "intelligence community." This is institutionalized paranoia of a kind that, as we shall see, preoccupies postmodernist writers both in itself and as a metaphor for the global conspiratorial order in which we live.

The other contemporary subculture which conspicuously practices paranoid reading is one whose assumptions you, gentle reader, presumably share with the author of this essay; for I doubt that anyone would have gotten this far in the present chapter (let alone in this book) who did not belong to one or other of the interpretive communities that together make up what might be called the literary-critical and literary-pedagogical subculture. Professional readers (reviewers, critics, scholars, instructors) and apprentice professionals (students) practice paranoid reading very much in accordance with the rules as formulated by Eco (who is himself, of course, in another capacity a member of this same subculture). To be more exact, they (we) have acquired paranoid reading skills in response to the challenge of modernist verbal art, through the process of learning how to read modernist texts properly and, by extension, how to read pre-modernist text modernistically. For before modernism (or, as we shall see, before the *institutionalization* of modernism) such skills were called for only in the interpretation of sacred scripture; not until modernism did it seem necessary to transfer them wholesale from scriptural interpretation to the practice of reading secular literature.

Consider, for example, the case of Joyce's *Ulysses* (a text about which, not at all incidentally, Eco himself has written). "The ideal-reader response to *Ulysses*," says Leo Bersani, is "one of extreme – or extremely nervous, perhaps even somewhat paranoid – vigilance" (1990:156). No doubt those who taught us how to read Joyce were not so indiscreet as explicitly to recommend paranoid vigilance; but they did teach us, more or less implicitly (or we taught ourselves by studying the text and its critics) to assume that everything connects (*tout se tient*); to assume that every detail, however trivial, probably has more than its literal meaning; to seek analogies among apparently unrelated details; to isolate patterns by imposing a grid that blocks out some elements, emphasizes others; above all, to read suspiciously.

Take the Joycean crux of the Man in the Macintosh. At Paddy Dignam's funeral ("Hades"), Leopold Bloom is asked by a newspaper reporter to identify an unknown fellow-mourner; failing to recognize him, Bloom casually refers to him as the man in the macintosh (raincoat), and the newspaperman mistakenly writes down "M'Intosh," a proper name. It is as M'Intosh that the unknown is identified later that day in the published list of mourners. Later still, in the phantasmagorical "Circe" episode, M'Intosh, who strictly speaking does not exist except as something between a slip of the tongue and a typographical error, returns as a character.

This has become a classic crux of Joyce criticism and scholarship: who is this M'Intosh/the Man in the Macintosh? who is he "really"? A variety of "solutions" has been proposed – symbolic-allegorical, referential, inter-textual (e.g. he is Mr. James Duffy of "A Painful Case," from *Dubliners*, visiting the grave of Mrs. Sinico), and so on. Note, first of all, that all the proposals for "solving" the M'Intosh "mystery" (the detective-fiction metaphor is irresistible here) faithfully apply the rules of paranoid reading: everything connects, read suspiciously, and, in the case of the intertextual solution in particular, assume that Joyce's texts (as Signor Garamond says of the Diabolical canon) "confirm one another; therefore they're true." Secondly, note that "Joyce" himself (not the biographical James Joyce, but the implicit authority "underwriting" the text, so to speak) expects us, perhaps in a sense even requires us, to regard M'Intosh as a "mystery" and to undertake (however futilely) to "solve" it. He does so by "thematizing" the M'Intosh mystery in the text itself, and by foregrounding it through the uncanny "materialization" of M'Intosh in the "Circe" episode. Thus, in proposing solutions to the M'Intosh mystery, we are following Joyce's program for us; we have, in effect, been "programmed" by the text – an appropriately paranoid insight into a paranoid process.

Meta-paranoia

Thus high-modernist texts such as *Ulysses* amount to instruction manuals for reading "modernistically" (that is, paranoiacally); in effect, high-modernist texts create (or even "program") modernist readers. In a later phase, criticism and pedagogy, especially the so-called New Criticism in Britain and the United States, legitimate and institutionalize modernist (paranoid) reading practices (see Newman 1984; van Delden 1990). After modernism – or, better, after the New-Critical institutionalization of modernism – paranoid reading comes to be taken for granted, assumed to be *the* appropriate norm of reading, whether of modernist texts or premodernist texts (see above, "Modernist reading, postmodernist text"). Consequently, in the next phase of this development, *post*modernist texts appear which assume and anticipate paranoid reading-habits on the part of their readers. Such texts incorporate representations of (fictional) paranoid interpretations (conspiracy theories) or paranoid reading practices, or they thematize paranoia itself, thereby reflecting on and anticipating, and perhaps preempting, actual readers' paranoid readings. Think, for example, of Robbe-Grillet's *La Jalousie*, Nabokov's *Pale Fire*, Pynchon's *The Crying of Lot 49* and *Gravity's Rainbow*, DeLillo's *Running Dog*, *The Names*, and *Libra*, and, of course, Eco's *The Name of the Rose* and *Foucault's Pendulum*.

Consider the complexity of the postmodernist reader's situation. If paranoid reading is the institutionalized norm, the practice of reading in which one has been trained, then how is one to read paranoid postmodernist texts that, having themselves internalized the same norm, anticipate and preempt paranoid reading itself? Perhaps the challenge is to imagine a way to read paranoid texts paranoiacally, to read, so to speak, *meta*-paranoiacally. Perhaps such a meta-paranoid practice of reading, paranoia raised to the second power, is the only viable response to a text like *Gravity's Rainbow*, in which the paranoid world-view, overflowing the limits of the fictional world, spills into the real world, fictitious conspiracies mingle indistinguishably with real-world conspiracies (or at least conspiracy theories), and the elusive author himself seems part of a conspiracy every bit as paranoid (and as paranoia-inducing) as any in his text.[5] The naive response to such a totalizing paranoid world-view, which seems to efface the boundary between the textual and the extra-textual, is to buy into it, to surrender to it and allow oneself to be swept along by it; thus, the pages of journals such as *Pynchon Notes* are full of the kinds of paranoid readings that seek to substantiate Pynchon's conspiracy theories, or that exploit rumors or speculations about Pynchon himself.[6] What is needed is not further faithful reproductions of the paranoid structures of *Gravity's Rainbow*, but some form of paranoiacally skeptical reading *of* those paranoid structures – a reading practice which, to date, barely exists.[7]

The same is true, to a lesser degree, of *Foucault's Pendulum*, a text which similarly mingles real and fictitious conspiracies, or conspiracy-theories, and which similarly risks (or invites) the effacement of the boundary between the textual and the extra-textual, the apparently true but actually apocryphal and the apparently apocryphal but actually true. The crucial difference here is that, unlike *Gravity's Rainbow*, Eco's text does not solicit our participation in its own paranoia. *Foucault's Pendulum*, indeed, is *about* the risks of effacing boundaries and participating in paranoia, and in that sense might almost be said to anticipate, not just paranoid reading, but even the meta-paranoid reading I have been advocating.

But I have gotten ahead of myself; for we cannot begin to speak about the effacement of textual boundaries and the merger of real and fictitious conspiracies until we have first investigated the ontological dimension of conspiracy itself.

"THE PLAN" AND WAYS OF WORLD-MAKING

Foucault's Pendulum begins, like *The Name of the Rose* before it, as an epistemological quest. Like *The Name of the Rose*, too (see the preceding chapter), it has not one but several "cognitive heroes." The narrator, Casaubon, is one of them. He appears at the outset in the role of a scholar (a type of cognitive hero), researching the mysteries of the Knights Templars' fall; later he goes into business for himself as an independent researcher, "a kind of private eye of learning" (*FP*:224), modeling himself on Chandler's Philip Marlowe (*FP*:225), in other words merging another cognitive-hero role, that of the detective, with his original role of scholar. Another cognitive hero is Col. Ardenti, one of the Diabolicals, who claims to have uncovered the Templars' master-plan for world domination; a third is police detective DeAngelis, who is trying to solve the case of Ardenti's mysterious disappearance. But if, as we saw in the preceding chapter, the epistemological quest ultimately collapses in *The Name of the Rose*, it collapses (or rather they collapse, for there is more than one) much earlier in *Foucault's Pendulum*, indeed almost immediately. Ardenti disappears; DeAngelis remains a marginal figure; and Casaubon joins his colleagues Belbo and Diotallevi in a different sort of project, not an epistemological quest for the truth about the Templars, but the fabrication of "The Plan."

Not content to remain passive observers of the Diabolical subculture and students of its interpretive habits, Belbo, Casaubon, and Diotallevi carry their obsession further, into actual practice, collaborating on a parody of the Diabolicals' manifold conspiracy-theories in proper Diabolical style. How does one go about parodying the Diabolicals, who seem already parodies of themselves? one might well wonder. Only by pushing Diabolical practice to the limit; in other words, not by parodying one or other of the Diabolicals' conspiracy-theories (how would one distinguish between the parody and the original?), but by undertaking to integrate the full repertoire of Diabolical secret societies, occult knowledge and conspiracy-theories – *all* of them, many of them mutually contradictory – into a single monster conspiracy, embracing the Knights Templars, the Freemasons, the Rosicrucians, the Bavarian Illuminati, the Jesuits, the International Jewish Conspiracy, the Nazis, even the King of the World who is reputed to dwell in the subterranean kingdom of Agarttha, and so on. "The idea," explains Casaubon, "is not to discover the Templars' secret, but to construct it" (*FP*:383); no longer, in other words, an epistemological quest, but an enterprise unconstrained by criteria of truth and evidence. The enterprise is that of "reconstructing the history of the world" (*FP*:405), or, better, of *creating* the world. Says Belbo, "It took seven days to make the world. And now *we'll* give it a try" (*FP*:450). Thus, unlike in *The Name of the Rose*, where the epistemological quest only conclusively fails late in the text, and the epistemological focus of attention competes throughout on fairly equal terms with the ontological focus, here the epistemological quest is aborted very early in favor of a project which is from the outset explicitly ontological: an experiment in self-conscious world-making, "a cosmological matter," as Eco (1984:20) says of the novel-writing enterprise, "like the story told by Genesis."

Ontological side-effects

This world-making project begins, as we have just seen, as derisive parody, but it develops unintended ontological side-effects. There are historical precedents for this, which the text itself recounts. Col. Ardenti, who wants to publish his "findings" about the Templars in order to provoke some response from them, to bring them out into the open, was evidently anticipated in this strategy by Johann Valentin Andreae, who in the seventeenth century published his Rosicrucian "manifestoes," inviting the real Rosicrucians (whoever they might have been) to contact him. The ontological side-effects of this invitation to communicate were startling: whether or not any such body as the Rosicrucians pre-dated Andreae's manifestoes, a Rosicrucian Brotherhood was certainly *called into being* in response to them. The manifestoes, in effect, "projected" the Rosicrucians. Later, it appears, the English Templars similarly "projected" Masonism (Chapter 76), just as the Jesuits, later still, "projected" neo-Templarism (Chapters 89, 90), and Rachkovsky of the Tsarist secret police (the Okhrana) "projected" the Franco-Russian Anti-Semitic League: "To ensure its success [Rachkovsky] uses a technique similar to that of the Rosicrucians: he declares that the league exists, so that people will then create it" (*FP*:492). Casaubon explains to detective DeAngelis, "There exists a secret society with branches throughout the world, and its plot is to spread the rumor that a universal plot exists" (*FP*:317). DeAngelis thinks he's joking, but by this point Casaubon is beginning not to be amused; he will be even less amused before the novel is finally over.

All these historical precedents amount, in effect, to degraded versions of St. Anselm's "ontological proof" of God's existence, discussed by Belbo and Casaubon at the very beginning of their acquaintance. Anselm defined God as that than which no greater can be thought. If that than which no greater can be thought existed only in the mind, then a greater could still be thought after all, namely a being who existed in extra-mental reality. Therefore God must exist not only mentally but also in reality: the necessity of the concept of God is proof of the existence of God. Belbo objects: "St. Anselm's ontological argument is moronic. . . . The saint confuses existence in thought with existence in reality."[8] Throughout history, it appears, the Diabolicals, too, have confused existence in thought with existence in reality, but they have also gone on to project *into reality* those non-existent entities (such as the Rosicrucian Brotherhood, the Masons, the Franco-Russian Anti-Semitic League, and the rest) which they had first conceived in thought.

Belbo and Diotallevi themselves produce a degraded version of the ontological proof when, in the innocent days before the emergence of The Plan, they play their private game of inventing nonexistent and nonsensical or internally contradictory scholarly disciplines and university departments (e.g. the history of Easter Island painting, contemporary Sumerian literature, crowd psychology in the Sahara, Urban Planning for Gypsies). Casaubon suggests that the public will want to pursue these disciplines if they hear of them, and Diotallevi agrees: "Unwittingly, we've drawn up a real prospectus for scholarship. We've shown the necessity of the impossible" (*FP*:75).[9]

This innocent game anticipates the greater and, as it turns out, much less innocent game of The Plan, and the side-effects which Casaubon jokingly imagines, and for which there is historical precedent in the cases of the Rosicrucians, the Masons, neo-Templarism, the Franco-Russian Anti-Semitic League, and so on, actually occur. When the Diabolicals learn of The Plan, far from recognizing it as parody and merely resenting it, they eagerly *conform themselves to it*, "realizing" in the empirical world the fictitious master-conspiracy that Casaubon and his colleagues (with the assistance of the computer Abulafia) have fabricated:

> We invented a nonexistent Plan, and They not only believed it was real but convinced themselves that They had been part of it for ages, or, rather, They identified the fragments of their muddled mythology as moments of our Plan, moments joined in a logical, irrefutable web of analogy, semblance, suspicion.
>
> But if you invent a plan and others carry it out, it's as if the Plan exists. At that point it does exist.
>
> (*FP*:619)

Projecting worlds

Here, too, as in *The Name of the Rose*, there is a relevant Borges intertext to be noted, not, this time, "Death and the Compass," but the equally well-known story "Tlön, Uqbar, Orbis Tertius."[10] Indeed, "Tlön" actually mentions Johann Valentin Andreae, the author of the Rosicrucian manifestoes (and consequently the "author" of the Rosicrucian Brotherhood itself?), who figures in the historical background of *Foucault's Pendulum*. Andreae, according to Borges's account, belonged to a secret society calling itself Orbis Tertius, dedicated to the invention, down to its smallest details, of a wholly imaginary country, Uqbar. Later the scope of the project would broaden to that of inventing an entire imaginary world, Tlön. This world-making project, an international conspiracy spanning centuries, would finally take the form of an encyclopedia, *A First Encyclopedia of Tlön*, on which some three hundred contributors would secretly collaborate. At the end of his text, Borges's narrator reveals that the Tlön project has had ontological side-effects of a kind with which we are already familiar. The projected world of Tlön has begun to contaminate the real world: "Contact with Tlön and the ways of Tlön have disintegrated this world" (Borges 1962c:34). The narrator predicts a time when Tlön will have supplanted the real world: "The world will be Tlön" (1962c:35). The parallels with *Foucault's Pendulum* are obvious: "if you invent a plan and others carry it out, it's as if the Plan exists. At that point it does exist."

"Tlön" is a paradigmatic "ontological fiction," a fiction about, a demonstration of, ontological projection, or what Nelson Goodman has called the "ways of world-making." All fictional texts (but not *only* fictional texts) project worlds, of course; this is one of the necessary conditions (though not a sufficient condition) for our identifying them *as* fiction. But not every fictional text is *about* world-projection; not every fictional text reflects on its ways of world-making. "Tlön," however, does: at one level, it represents world-making, namely the making of the fictional world of Tlön by the Orbis Tertius conspirators; while at another level it itself undertakes to make a fictional world, the world *in which* the Orbis Tertius conspirators fabricate Tlön. In exactly the same way, *Foucault's Pendulum*, too, is an ontological fiction. Like Borges's "Tlön," it projects a world in which a circle of conspirators (Casaubon and his colleagues) in turn project a world, namely The Plan; and, also as in "Tlön," that projected world ends up by becoming, in some sense, real.

There is another, even more disturbing ontological dimension, or at any rate ontological *potential*, to conspiracy in *Foucault's Pendulum*. Unlike the Orbis Tertius conspirators of Borges's story, who do finally produce their forty-volume encyclopedia, Casaubon and his fellow-conspirators never actually complete the writing of their Plan. That is left to Eco, who has in effect written the book of The Plan which his characters, interrupted by the murderously impatient Diabolicals, fail to finish; that book, of course, is *Foucault's Pendulum* itself. The Plan, as we have seen, calls into being a "real" conspiracy corresponding to the one it fabricates; will *Foucault's Pendulum*, in its turn, one wonders queasily, reach out into the real world and call into being the conspiracy that *it* fabricates? It would be interesting to know how the actual Diabolical subculture (for there is one) has received *Foucault's Pendulum*; whether, for instance, Eco has been receiving letters from crackpot readers who have taken his fiction seriously; in short, whether anyone has undertaken to realize Eco's Plan as the Diabolicals in the novel realize the Plan concocted by Belbo, Casaubon, and Diotallevi.[11]

If so, Eco may be in danger. In *Foucault's Pendulum*, Belbo is horribly murdered by Diabolicals seeking to extract from him secrets which he does not, of course, really possess, because they do not really exist; Casaubon, we assume, will also be murdered by them (sometime after the point at which his narrative ends). Of the three, only Diotallevi apparently dies of natural causes. Could we imagine real Diabolicals pursuing Eco for secret knowledge which, like Belbo's, he does not possess because it does not exist? "If you invent a plan and others carry it out, it's as if the Plan exists. At that point it does exist." Beware of ontological side-effects, Professor Eco!

THE POSTMODERNISM OF *FOUCAULT'S PENDULUM*

The Name of the Rose, as I tried to show in the preceding chapter, is poised on a cusp between modernist and postmodernist poetics: on the one hand structured around a typically modernist epistemological quest, on the other it sabotages that quest, and its affinities are as much with the characteristic strategies and motifs of postmodernism (destabilized world and *mise-en-abyme*, the representation of postmodernist space, the thematics of apocalypse) as with those of modernism. Eco's first novel, in other words, *can be* constructed as a postmodernist text – and not only according to my model of postmodernism, but also, e.g., according to Jencks's criterion of "double coding" [12] – but *need not* be so constructed. In the case of *Foucault's Pendulum*, the option of constructing the text *otherwise than as* postmodernist seems to me weaker, less persuasive. Here the epistemological quest is almost immediately transposed into an ontological key: not "mystery," but "conspiracy," and in particular the "world-making" dimension of conspiracy. Moreover, the affinities between *Foucault's Pendulum* and the postmodernist motif repertoire are, if anything, stronger than in the case of *The Name of the Rose*. Interestingly, however, Eco's second novel intersects with different areas of the postmodernist repertoire than his first; and it is this different sub-repertoire that we must now try to specify.

The sub-repertoire in question is the one brought to our attention, and decisively placed on the postmodernist critical agenda, by Fredric Jameson's ground breaking essay, "Postmodernism, or the Cultural Logic of Late Capitalism" (1984; now reprinted, Jameson 1991a). Postmodernist artworks and art-forms, in Jameson's view, are for the most part merely *symptomatic*, reflections or expressions, in the cultural realm, of late-capitalist social and economic relations: postmodernism *is*, as his title has it, the cultural logic of late capitalism. But there are certain postmodernist works and tendencies which undertake to *reflect on*, and not merely passively reflect, late capitalism, seeking to transcend the merely symptomatic and become *diagnostic*. Such works aspire to produce, for the uses of our imaginations, some image or figure or representation of the unrepresentably complex multinational world-system in which we live. Extrapolating from a concept developed in a different context by the urbanist Kevin Lynch, Jameson calls this "cognitive mapping." No fully satisfactory cognitive mapping of the late-capitalist world-system, it would appear, has yet been achieved, and Jameson does not venture to predict what one would look like. To date, the most nearly successful attempts have been in architecture, that is, at the level of architectural *form* (e.g. the Frank Gehry house in Santa Monica (see Jameson 1991c)), and Jameson is willing to say only that he expects that "achieved cognitive mapping will be a matter of form" (1988:356).

Meanwhile, less than fully successful attempts at cognitive mapping have been made at the level of *content*, involving elements of the represented world or explicit themes. Among these more or less inadequate, more or less "degraded" (but nevertheless characteristic and revealing) cognitive mappings of the late-capitalist world-system, Jameson (1991a:36–8) mentions what he calls the fiction of "high-tech paranoia," and what, paraphrasing him, we might call the "thematics of mechanical reproduction." Mechanical reproduction is not, however, only a privileged theme of postmodernist fiction, it is also a postmodernist textual procedure, so when we have finished investigating the thematic repertoire of *Foucault's*

Pendulum we will need briefly to consider this text's relation to postmodernist practices of "procedural" writing.

High-tech paranoia

"Conspiracy," says Jameson, "is the poor person's cognitive mapping in the postmodern age" (1988:356). What he has in mind is the contemporary entertainment literature of conspiracy, whose practitioners include, among others, Robert Ludlum and Tom Clancy, and in the preceding generation Ian Fleming and Len Deighton, in other words, the high-tech thriller genre; and now also, more recently, cyberpunk science fiction (William Gibson, Bruce Sterling, Pat Cadigan, Rudy Rucker, Lewis Shiner, Walter Jon Williams, Richard Kadrey, *et al.*).[13] Such narratives, typically involving secret criminal or terrorist organizations (the Mafia, the Yakuza, neo-Nazis, the PLO, Ian Fleming's SPECTRE), foreign secret services, renegade government intelligence agencies, unscrupulous and all-powerful multinational corporations, and, inevitably, computers, communications networks and high-tech weapons, attempt, according to Jameson, by means of "figuration," i.e., at the level of the represented world, to "think the impossible totality of the contemporary world system" (1991a:38).

Jameson's analysis is corroborated by postmodernist reworkings of high-tech thriller motifs in conspiracy fictions such as those of Don DeLillo (*Players*, 1977; *Running Dog*, 1978; *The Names*, 1982; *White Noise*, 1985; *Libra*, 1988). In *Players*, for instance, a terrorist cell targets the New York Stock Exchange because, one of their number explains, they had

> wanted to disrupt their system, the idea of worldwide money. It's this *system* that we believe is their secret power. It all goes floating across the floor [of the Stock Exchange]. Currents of invisible life. This is the center of their existence. The electronic system. The waves and charges. . . . It was this secret of theirs that we wanted to destroy, this invisible power. It's all in that system, bip-bip-bip-bip, the flow of electric current that unites moneys, plural, from all over the world.
>
> (DeLillo 1984:107)

Here, as in other postmodernist paranoid fictions – e.g. the novels of Burroughs and Pynchon, Robbe-Grillet's mock-thrillers of the seventies, John Barth's conspiracy-obsessed novels of the seventies and eighties, Joseph McElroy's *Lookout Cartridge* and *Women and Men* – conspiracy and counter-conspiracy, terrorist network and government intelligence agency, are clearly conceived of as displaced representations, at the content level, of the global capitalist network itself. All these texts illustrate in various ways the "cross-over" of thriller motifs from entertainment literature to "advanced" postmodernist fiction, and the more or less self-conscious use of such motifs as tools of cognitive mapping.[14]

Conspiracy paranoia, it might plausibly be argued, is a recurrent cultural phenomenon, especially in American political life, with its successive waves of anti-Illuminism, anti-Masonism, anti-Catholicism, anti-Communism and so on (the classic account is Hofstadter 1967); it is hardly an accident that nearly all the postmodernist conspiracy fictions I have mentioned so far are by Americans. One hypothesis might be that whenever the complexity of the social-economic system outstrips our capacity to represent it to ourselves, conspiracy theory arises to fill the gap as the "poor person's cognitive mapping." The recurrence, at intervals since at least the early-modern period, of crises of cognitive mapping (cf. Harvey 1989:260–1 and *passim*) helps to explain the phenomenon of "waves" of paranoid conspiracy fiction. Earlier waves (Rosicrucianism, anti-Masonism, anti-Jesuitism, anti-Semitism, etc.), evidence of which is mostly to be found in uncanonical writing or subliterature, in fact make up the archive of Diabolical texts which the researches of Casaubon and his colleagues bring to light in the course of *Foucault's Pendulum*. Occasionally, however, traces of this type of response to crises in cognitive mapping have appeared in canonized literature as well. One example is the British "Rosicrucian novel" of the late-eighteenth through early-nineteenth centuries (e.g. William Godwin's *St. Leon*, Percy Shelley's *St. Irvyne*, Mary Shelley's *Frankenstein*, Charles Maturin's *Melmoth the Wanderer*, and Bulwer-Lytton's Rosicrucian novels (Roberts 1990)); another is American sensationalistic fiction of the 1840s and 1850s, especially that of George Lippard, which left its traces in the canonical literature of the mid-century "American Renaissance" (Poe, Hawthorne, Melville, even Whitman (see Ziff 1981:87–107; Reynolds 1988)).

So these earlier waves, responses to successive crises in society's self-imagining, have left deposits behind them in the form of a "tradition" of earlier conspiracy theories, outdated and now "fossilized" attempts at the cognitive mapping of contemporary social-economic relations. *Foucault's Pendulum* (to continue the metaphor) might be said to sink a shaft through the sedimentary layers of historical conspiracy theories, extracting a core sample. In fact, this historical archive of conspiracy theories has served as a resource for a number of postmodernist cognitive mappings, apart from Eco's. Thus, in addition to late-capitalist "high-tech" versions of conspiracy, we need to take into account here the postmodernist resurgence of "traditional" conspiracy theories (Templar, Masonic, Illuminatist, Rosicrucian, Jesuit, Jewish, etc.) in, e.g., Ishamel Reed's *Mumbo Jumbo*, Lawrence Durrell's *Avignon Quintet*, and Milorad Pavić's *Dictionary of the Khazars*. Borges's well-documented fascination with heresies and secret societies (as in "Tlön, Uqbar, Orbis Tertius") is another variant of the same phenomenon. All these conspiracy narratives would appear to endorse Reed's slogan: "beneath or behind all political and cultural warfare lies a struggle between secret societies" (1973: 19–20). The suspicious reader, however (and suspicion is, of course, the appropriate paranoid attitude) might choose to invert the slogan: beneath or behind all representations, at the content level, of struggles between secret societies lies the reality of political and cultural warfare. In other words, though they lack the high-tech component that Jameson specifies for this form of cognitive mapping, these "traditional" conspiracy theories seem to function in the postmodernist context much as the high-tech variants do, as more or less distantly displaced "figurations" of the contemporary world-system.

"Shall I project a world?"

Conspiracy, as we have seen in the case of *Foucault's Pendulum*, can have an ontological dimension or ontological side-effects: conspirators, or conspiracy theorists like Casaubon and his colleagues, can in effect "project a world." Itself a form of ontological plurality (at least potentially), conspiracy thus appropriately co-occurs with other motifs and strategies of ontological plurality: alternate, parallel, or "other" worlds (e.g. Borges's "Tlön," Pavić's *Dictionary of the Khazars, Gravity's Rainbow*);[15] metafiction, *mise-en-abyme*, and the transgression of narrative levels (e.g. Robbe-Grillet's conspiracy fictions, Durrell's *Avignon Quintet*); etc. In other words, conspiracy belongs to the umbrella category of "ontological pluralizers" (see above, "Zapping, the art of switching channels").

Evidence of conspiracy's ontological side-effects is to be found throughout the postmodernist literature of conspiracy. *"Shall I project a world?"* is, of course, Oedipa Maas's anguished question in Pynchon's *The Crying of Lot 49*, where to the end (and beyond) it remains unclear who is doing the projecting, the conspiracy theorist herself (Oedipa) or the conspirators (and if the conspirators, *which* ones? For there are at least two sets of candidates). More than once in *Gravity's Rainbow*, conspiracy theories or hoaxes appear to have generated solid realities, bits of world. The most notable example is the Allied psychological warfare unit that, hoping to undermine Nazi morale, fabricates evidence of the presence in Nazi Germany of black African rocket-troops, the *Schwarzkommando* (Pynchon 1973:74–5, 112–13), only subsequently to discover that such troops really do exist (Pynchon 1973:275–6; see above, "Modernist reading, postmodernist text"). Similarly, in DeLillo's *Libra*, a CIA conspiracy intended to simulate a "fake" assassination attempt on President Kennedy (in order to provoke him to retaliate against Cuba) generates a real assassination conspiracy and, of course, a successful assassination.

Finally, there are a number of instances of ontological side-effects that are uncannily akin to those in *Foucault's Pendulum*, indicating not the direct influence of one text on another (which can be ruled out in most of these cases) but rather an internal logic that, inhering in the postmodernist repertoire itself, manifests itself differently in different texts. In McElroy's *Lookout Cartridge*, for instance, Cartwright pretends to know more than he really does about a terrorist conspiracy in order to induce others (who believe, wrongly, that he already knows it all) to tell him what *they* know. Consequently, the real conspirators begin to regard him as a fellow conspirator himself – but on whose side? Cartwright's pretence of knowledge may not exactly create the conspiracy, but it certainly catalyzes it. In Durrell's *Avignon Quintet*, on the other hand, the clerk Quatrefages really does generate a conspiracy *ex nihilos* when, playing a confidence trick on his employer, Lord Galen, he pretends to be on the verge of discovering the whereabouts of a (non-existent) Templar treasure, and is taken seriously by Nazi agents. Torturing him in order to force him to reveal knowledge he does not really possess, the Nazis ultimately drive Quatrefages mad, so that he comes to believe in the spurious treasure himself. Cartwright's and especially Quartrefages's situation is of course Belbo's as well at the end of *Foucault's Pendulum*: the pretence of knowledge about a conspiracy has called that conspiracy into existence, with dangerous or fatal consequences. And perhaps not just the conspiracy, but its object as well: for the *Avignon Quintet*, at least, ends inconclusively, when the entire cast of characters descends into what is supposedly the Templar treasure-cave to find . . . something, or nothing? Has Quatrefages also brought the treasure itself into being through his hoax? We shall never know.

Thematics of mechanical reproduction

It will be recalled that Jameson identifies two related (but for our purposes distinguishable) cognitive mappings at the level of narrative content. One is high-tech paranoia, the subject of the preceding section; the other is what we might call the thematics of mechanical reproduction, that is, "narratives which are *about* the processes of reproduction and include movie cameras, video, tape recorders [and computer monitors and simulations, one might add], the whole technology of the production and reproduction of the simulacrum" (Jameson 1991a:37). Like modernist machine aesthetics, the postmodernist thematics of mechanical reproduction affords us a glimpse of what Jameson calls the "technological sublime," but one clearly different from the modernist technological sublime of speed and power.[16]

The technology of mechanical reproduction is also the technology of surveillance, deception, and "data control" – staple ingredients of the high-tech thriller. It follows that the postmodernist conspiracy fictions discussed in the preceding section ought also to involve the thematics of mechanical reproduction, and indeed many of them do. A number of them are to some greater or lesser extent "about" film and film-making (*Gravity's*

Rainbow, McElroy's *Lookout Cartridge*, Barth's *LETTERS*, DeLillo's *Running Dog* and *The Names*).[17] Only a few are "about" television (Pynchon's *The Crying of Lot 49* and *Vineland*, DeLillo's *Players* and *White Noise*), unless we also take into account the postmodernist "wave" of science fiction, so-called cyberpunk SF (Sterling's *The Artificial Kid*, Gibson's cyberspace trilogy, Cadigan's *Synners*). Still fewer of the postmodernist conspiracy fictions represent technologies of audio-taping, though there are important examples in the novels of William Burroughs ("This Horrible Case" from *Nova Express*, *Cities of the Red Night*). Finally, representations of the newest, computer-based technologies of mechanical reproduction, rare as yet in the postmodernist literature of conspiracy (but see William T. Vollmann's *You Bright and Risen Angels*), are of course absolutely central to cyberpunk (e.g., Gibson, Cadigan, Sterling's *Islands in the Net*, Rucker's *Software* and *Wetware*, etc.).[18]

In many of these examples, technologies of mechanical reproduction are not just objects of representation but also function as what, in an earlier chapter, I have called "ontological pluralizers." That is, they introduce a second ontological plane, a world one level "down" from the primary narrative world, or they otherwise fissure the plane of the fictional world. This pluralizing function is performed in a particularly radical way in *Gravity's Rainbow*, in which (at least according to one reading) the entire verbal text, from the first page to the last, represents the contents of a movie, so that the whole narrative world has in effect been "demoted" one level. In other, less radical cases, certain narratological functions that would normally be carried out directly by the verbal text have been entrusted to some secondary medium (movie, television, computer) represented *in* the verbal text. Thus, for example, in Pynchon's *Vineland* certain major flashbacks are literally "mediated," transmitted to the reader indirectly as verbal representations, in one case of computer files, in another of film footage; while in Vollmann's *You Bright and Risen Angels*, the very function of narration itself is "mediated," for here the entire verbal text of the novel supposedly represents an electronic computer-file.[19] Finally, there are a number of examples (e.g. *Gravity's Rainbow*, Burroughs's *The Wild Boys* and *Exterminator!*, Robbe-Grillet's *Projet pour une révolution à New York*, Reed's *Mumbo Jumbo*) in which the discourse of film-making or of shooting scripts or scenarios (e.g. "cut," "retake," "voice-over," "freeze frame," "fadeout," "music under") substitutes for more typically novelistic verbal devices of segmentation and transition.

Foucault's Pendulum shares with these other texts the postmodernist thematics of mechanical reproduction, and it does so primarily through the motif of "Abulafia," Belbo's personal computer. Large blocs of verbal material, supposedly composed by Belbo and entered into his machine's memory, are "mediated" by Abulafia, to whose files Casaubon gains access after Belbo's disappearance. Here, in other words, several traditional narratological functions have been entrusted to a secondary medium, namely the representation of computer-files (first flashed on a monitor screen, then printed out as "hard copy"). The first of these functions is shift of point of view. Since Casaubon is the first-person narrator of *Foucault's Pendulum*, we would have access only to his point of view were it not for the files stored in Abulafia's memory, which give him (and us) access also to Belbo's alternative perspective on the same events. This alternative perspective often differs from Casaubon's, yielding the sort of perspectival effects that are characteristic of modernist poetics, but here "mediatized" or "technologized" in a characteristically postmodernist way.[20]

Not only does characterological perspective shift when Casaubon accesses Abulafia's memory, but also temporal perspective, for Belbo's computer files constitute his diary or journal, and each file reflects a specific past moment, which is interpolated in the present time of the narrative when the file is recovered. In other words, the Abulafia motif subsumes and updates the flashback function of more traditional narrative structures. Finally, of course, the Abulafia motif also subsumes the traditional function of the inset tale: the found manuscript of traditional narratives (including *The Name of the Rose*) here becomes the accessed computer-file of the literature of mechanical reproduction.

Apart from its narratological functions, the computer Abulafia also participates in the conspiratorial plot of *Foucault's Pendulum*; "he" is, in more than one sense, an accessory to The Plan. As we saw above, Belbo uses Abulafia to generate raw material for practice exercises in paranoid interpretation, programming the computer to juxtapose "facts" at random so that he and his colleagues Casaubon and Diotallevi can practice making connections where none exist, an essential paranoid reading-skill. Eco's model here would appear to have been the language-machine of Laputa from the third voyage of *Gulliver's Travels*, which in fact is cited as an epigraph to Chapter 65 of *Foucault's Pendulum* (*FP*:373). Equally apposite, however, would be William Burroughs's writing-machine, described in *The Ticket That Exploded*, which cuts up texts at random and splices them together to form new texts, or indeed the audio-tape splicing techniques described and evidently practiced in *Nova Express*, *Cities of the Red Night*, and elsewhere in Burroughs. If Burroughs is not exactly a model for Eco here, he is certainly an analogue.

Procedural writing

Indeed, this function of Abulafia as a language-machine or writing-machine suggests an oblique affiliation between *Foucault's Pendulum* and a different wing of postmodernist poetics altogether, not the conspiracy fiction wing but what might be called the poetics of "procedural" writing. Procedural writing, as practiced by many poets (John Cage, Jackson MacLow, the L=A=N=G=U=A=G=E poets) and a few prose writers (especially the OuLiPo group, including Queneau, Calvino, Georges Perec, Harry Mathews and others) involves partial (rarely total) surrender of authorial control over the production of the text, as a means of evading or overriding the constraints of literary and cultural norms and personal psychology. This is *not*, at least not in postmodernist practice, a form of surrealist "automatic writing," but in fact its opposite, *mechanical* writing: it taps, not the unconscious, but the potential of the literary or linguistic system, or the latent possibilities of a corpus of verbal "raw material."

In procedural writing, as the name implies, textual production is entrusted to a fixed procedure – an acrostic is a simple example, a highly constraining verse-form such as a sestina is another – which generates, automatically as it were, strings of language, which in turn become the raw materials for building narrative worlds. The procedure involved can be rigorously mechanical, as in the case of the "algorithms" and *combinatoires* of the OuLiPo group, or, alternatively, based on chance or found objects, as in the case of Burroughs's cut-ups, fold-ins, and splices. Either way the effect, from the writer's point of view, is much the same: unanticipated combinations, surprise, the evasion of the internal "censor." The effect for the reader partly depends on the recoverability or otherwise of the procedure used to generate the text. MacLow's acrostics and Cage's mesostichs, for instance, can literally be "read off" their texts; but, though we know in general how Raymond Roussel generated his texts (thanks in part to his own revelations in his posthumous *ars poetica*, *Comment j'ai écrit certains de mes livres*), most of the specific procedures involved are, and must remain, finally irrecoverable.

In this context, Eco's Abulafia appears as a kind of literalization of the mechanical procedures of procedural writing, a *literal* writing-machine, and perhaps even as a kind of witty homage to OuLiPo and Oulipian poetics. Moreover, there is also a striking correlation between procedural writing and postmodernist conspiracy fiction generally. In certain cases, the conspiracies themselves, the objects of representation of conspiracy fiction, prove to have been determined or guided by arbitrary linguistic patterns akin to the generative procedures of procedural writing. For instance, in DeLillo's *The Names*, the conspiracy involves a cult of murderers who, obsessed with languages and alphabets, build up a linguistic pattern by ritually murdering their victims at sites bearing the same initials as the victims' names (e.g. *M*ichalis *K*alliambetsos at *M*ikro *K*amini). In effect, the cultists use murder as a kind of writing implement to inscribe letters on the landscape and, not incidentally, to "write" the conspiracy whose discovery and interpretation is narrated in *The Names*.

In other texts, arbitrary linguistic procedures are used in a more radical way to shape the very narrative world of the conspiracy fiction itself. In this case, of which Barth's *LETTERS* and Harry Mathews's *The Sinking of the Odradek Stadium* are examples, the generative procedures involved operate on a level "above" that of the narrative world itself; imposed from "outside," they are (unlike the "readable" conspiracy of *The Names*) invisible to any of the inhabitants of that world. What distinguishes *The Sinking of the Odradek Stadium* from *LETTERS* is the recoverability or irrecoverability of the specific procedures involved in generating the text. While Barth's procedure (superimposing the letters of the word "LETTERS" on a calendar in order to determine who, in this epistolary novel, writes to whom and when) is reproduced and explicated in the text of *LETTERS* itself, Mathews's procedure is irrecoverable (or at any rate its specific details are (see Mathews in Motte 1986:126–39)).

What could possibly explain this (on the face of it) unlikely correlation between procedural writing and conspiracy fiction, to which Eco's motif of Abulafia seems obliquely to allude? Procedural writing, one might venture to hypothesize, actually complements conspiracy fiction because it constitutes a kind of *metaconspiracy*: a conspiracy between the author and the reader, in cases where the procedural constraints are "invisible" to the characters but visible to the reader; but in cases where the generative procedure is irrecoverable (as in Roussel or Mathews), a conspiracy in some sense *by* the author *against* the reader. "Beyond the words being read," writes Mathews (1986:126), "others lie in wait to subvert and perhaps surpass them. Nothing any longer can be taken for granted; every word has become a banana peel." Indeed, what could be more conducive to paranoia than the suspicion that the text before one amounts to a kind of "inside joke" which one will never finally fathom? And what could be more appropriate to the conspiratorial content of conspiracy fiction than a form based on compositional principles of secrecy, deceit, and the deliberate withholding of information?

ANTI-PARANOIA

Conspiracy, mechanical reproduction, procedural writing: these, then, are some of the areas of the postmodernist repertoire of motifs and strategies with which *Foucault's Pendulum* intersects, just as its predecessor, *The Name of the Rose*, had intersected with such areas as the representation of postmodernist space, the thematics of apocalypse, and the genre of historiographic metafiction. Moreover, both of Eco's novels, as I have tried to demonstrate, belong to postmodernist poetics in the sense that they share with other postmodernist texts (somewhat equivocally in the case of *The Name of the Rose*) postmodernism's ontological dominant.

But there may be a different, and paradoxical, sense in which *Foucault's Pendulum* can be thought of as postmodernist, a sense in which a certain kind of postmodernity may be achieved precisely by *resisting* postmodernism itself, or at any rate the version of postmodernism I have sought to construct here.

Foucault's Pendulum, as I have tried to show, demonstrates the practice and consequences (ontological side-effects) of paranoid reading, but this does not necessarily mean that it *endorses* paranoid reading. Quite the opposite, Eco's novel produces a counter-reading-strategy more persuasive than paranoid reading, and one which the "author" (again, not the professor of semiotics at Bologna but the "authority" implicit in this text) evidently prefers.

When Casaubon presents his girlfriend Lia (Chapter 63) with the myriad analogies he has collected linking ritual and occult practices around the world, supposedly evidence of a worldwide tradition of secret knowledge of great antiquity, Lia offers an alternative interpretation whereby the analogies derive not from some occult tradition but from the bedrock facts of bodily experience shared by all human beings everywhere: one penis, one vagina, two eyes, two ears, two breasts, four limbs, five fingers, eight orifices, etc., yielding all the "magic" numbers, and all the other "mystic" orientations and resemblances as well. Lia is pregnant, and it is her heightened awareness of her body in pregnancy, Eco implies, that enables her to achieve this skeptical insight. Later on (Chapter 106), it will also be Lia who successfully reinterprets the cryptic document, discovered by Colonel Ardenti and supposedly revealing the Templar plan for world domination, upon which the fabrications of Casaubon and his colleagues ultimately rest. Using, this time, not any special maternal insight, but only sound philology, responsible historical research, and common sense, she demonstrates that the "Templar" document is not a coded blueprint for world mastery, but . . . a merchant's laundry list! What Lia proposes (and through her Eco) is, in effect, an alternative to paranoid reading, a counter-occult, resolutely quotidian and this-worldly reading strategy.

Recall that paranoid reading is, in the first instance, a *modernist* reading practice, one which has been institutionalized, becoming first normative and then self-reflexive, in the postmodernist period. Consequently, there is a sense in which *resisting* paranoid reading, indeed reading "against the grain" of paranoid reading, is more genuinely "postmodernist" than reading paranoiacally. Moreover, this "postmodernist" gesture of reading counter to paranoid reading practice has, like paranoid reading itself, ontological consequences: it "dissolves" the world projected (constructed) by paranoid reading, the world where everything connects, where *tout se tient*. Reading counter-paranoiacally, against the grain of paranoid reading, places conspiracy (including The Plan fabricated by Casaubon and his co-conspirators) *sous rature*, under erasure. That is, the conspiracy really does exist – it can be "read" under the marks of erasure – because The Plan has brought it into being: "If you invent a plan and others carry it out, it's as if the Plan exists. At that point it does exist." Yet at the same time it does *not* really exist – it has been erased – because it depends for its existence on discredited reading practices: it rests on nothing.

"Contact with Tlön and the ways of Tlön," Borges tells us at the end of the story that is one of the intertextual models for *Foucault's Pendulum*, "have disintegrated this world." Conspiracy theories yield only "thin" descriptions of experience – schematic, diagrammatic, plot-oriented (in both senses of the word); while "thick" description of lived experience – body-oriented, here-and-now, this-worldly – entails something like an anti-paranoid world-view. The ontological experiments in world-making narrated by Borges in "Tlön, Uqbar" and by Eco in *Foucault's Pendulum* both end up by eroding the "thick" reality of this world, thinning it out. Eco's Belbo and Casaubon, like Pynchon's Slothrop before them, resist the erosion of this world in their anti-paranoid moments. Might not their this-worldly (anti-paranoid) resistance to world-making (conspiracy theory, The Plan) constitute a form of postmodernism after all?

I would seem, at this point, to have exchanged my story of postmodernism for another one, or at any rate to have coupled a different story onto mine, by way of epilogue. The ontological dominant which has been the keystone of my narrative of postmodernism seems to have metamorphosed into an ontological dominant in a different sense, something closer to Alan Wilde's sense of ontological dominant when, for instance, he writes of Barthelme that the latter's "concerns are . . . ontological in their acceptance of a world that is, willy-nilly, a given of experience" (1981: 173). Here at the end, my story about Eco's career seems to have strayed out of the orbit of my own master-narrative of postmodernism, according to which postmodernist poetics foregrounds world-making and unmaking, and to have entered the gravitational field of a different master-narrative, something like Wilde's, for whom the ontological preoccupations of postmodernism issue in an endorsement of *this* world.

Chapter 8

Women and men and angels: on Joseph McElroy's fiction

Joseph McElroy's *Women and Men* (1987) is the most typical novel of contemporary literature. When Viktor Shklovsky made a similar claim about *Tristram Shandy*, in his 1929 *Theory of Prose*, he meant to draw attention to the way Sterne's novel "laid bare" the devices of prose fiction, as all literary fiction does to some greater or lesser degree.[1] When I make this claim about *Women and Men*, I mean to suggest that McElroy's novel lays bare the history of the modern novel. *Women and Men* is a kind of *summa* of modern fiction, a text of recapitulation: it recapitulates the successive phases in the development of the poetics of the novel – realist, modernist, (perhaps) postmodernist. McElroy's five earlier novels, too, were summative, in their more limited ways, so that, in recapitulating the history of the novel, *Women and Men* also recapitulates McElroy's own career.[2] This is not a "horizontal" recapitulation – realist chapters followed by modernist chapters followed by postmodernist chapters, joined end-to-end – as, for instance, *Ulysses* is, according to some accounts;[3] rather, recapitulation in *Women and Men* is "vertical" – postmodernist layer on top of modernist layer on top of realist layer. To undertake a reading of *Women and Men* as *summa* is thus to read geologically (archeologically?) by prising apart the text and scrutinizing in turn each of its sedimentary strata.

METONYMY; OR, REALISM

"We have friends in common," says the ubiquitous Spence, introducing himself to McElroy's female protagonist, Grace Kimball.[4] This is an understatement: in the world of *Women and Men*, neither of these characters has *any* friend who is not also a friend of the other, or at least "a friend of a friend." This last phrase echoes throughout the text (see *WM*:158, 462, 920), along with other cognate phrases: "they had acquaintances in common" (*WM*:883), "We share a messenger" (*WM*:1153), and so on. In one richly comic scene (*WM*:33–40, 182–3), various diners in a Mexican restaurant study one another with interest without any of them being

aware that they are all connected through one or two intermediary "friends
in common." As in a Dickens novel (think how appropriate the title *Our
Mutual Friend* is), the world of *Women and Men* is constituted by a web
or network of people related, connected, contiguous with one another
(see Mathews 1990:221 and *passim*) – a world, in short, constituted by
metonymy.

Metonymy, of course, is the trope of contiguity, involving substitution
of, for instance, the maker for the thing made ("She was reading Virgil"),
the instrument for its user ("A hired gun"), the place for those in the
place ("Wall Street panicked"), and so on (Bredin 1984). Roman Jakobson
(1971d), in a classic paper on aphasia, identified metonymic relations (contiguity in general) as the constitutive principle of realist prose,[5] and this
insight has subsequently been elaborated by David Lodge (1977) into an
entire history of modern prose fiction.[6] Whatever reservations we may
have about Lodge's historical account, Jakobson's hypothesis does seem
to capture some of our soundest intuitions about "classic" nineteenth-
century realist poetics. Selection in realist fiction proceeds by synecdoche
(a trope closely related to metonymy, if not a sub-type of it), combination
by metonymy; that is, details stand for absent continua or complexes (cf.
"slice of life"), while the ordering of these details in the text reflects (or
gives the illusion of reflecting) local spatiotemporal relations in some
model of the world. Ordering according to the principle of similarity, i.e.,
metaphor, is not ruled out in realist texts, but it does seem to go against
the grain of realism – which, of course, is why metaphorical organization
proved to be such a powerful tool in the modernist "revolution" against
realist poetics.

Before *Women and Men*, McElroy had already explored the metonymic
organizing principle of realist prose in his earlier novels. His first, *A
Smuggler's Bible* (1966), has often been regarded as a text dominated by
metaphor; smuggling itself, the text's master-trope, is, as Richard Howard
(1986:n.p.) has cannily observed, "a metaphor for metaphor." Nevertheless, it is striking that David Brooke, the novel's narrator, reacts strongly
against his mother's insistent metaphorizing of the Manhattan skyline:
"That skyline is just a skyline. Don't talk to me about organ pipes. You
might just as well call that skyline a graph, and you could make it show
anything you wanted."[7] David, in editing his eight narratives of different
episodes from his past, aims to "work out the connections" (*SB*:136)
among them, to develop, in other words, a network of metonymic relations
that will integrate all eight. According to one character, this is just what
David has done in his private life: "(partly through your efforts to bind
people to you) you had created a cat's cradle of relations among them quite
independent of you yourself" (*SB*:370). This "cat's cradle of relations" is
actualized in the chain letter which circulates among David's friends in
part VII – a "realized metaphor" *of* metonymy.[8]

Although David's drive to make connections among the people and episodes of his life has its sinister side, *A Smuggler's Bible* is largely free of any oppressive sense of connectedness as conspiracy – surprisingly so, since conspiracy is such a characteristic topos of contemporary writing.[9] But if paranoia is conspicuously absent from *A Smuggler's Bible*, it begins to make its presence felt peripherally in McElroy's next novel, *Hind's Kidnap* (1969), with its mysterious Center for Total Research and other labyrinthine institutions. Paranoia reaches its peak in McElroy's *Lookout Cartridge* (1974), surely one of the paranoid classics of our time, surpassed only by Pynchon for its vision of the conspiratorial connectedness of everything.

Connecting

Women and Men recapitulates both the metonymic poetics of realism and McElroy's own earlier recapitulations (see Walsh 1988:265). It is *about* connectedness, like *A Smuggler's Bible*, only more so; like *Lookout Cartridge*, it is informed by a paranoid vision. *Women and Men* has a double center, two protagonists, Jim Mayn and Grace Kimball, both of them "connectors" by profession as well as inclination. Mayn is a science journalist, a mediator of information between knowledge specialists and the general public. Grace leads feminist consciousness-raising workshops where people are put "in touch" with themselves, their bodies, and each other. Between these two professional connectors stretches a tangled network of personal connections, mutual friends and friends of friends and friends of friends of friends; Grace calls it her "periodic cluster" (*WM*:117).

This network is arranged in concentric circles of proximity around the double center of Mayn and Grace. Nearest is the New York apartment house, an "articulate structure that can accommodate a multiplicity of small-scale units" (*WM*:40 and *passim*), in which Grace, Mayn, and a number of their mutual friends and acquaintances live. This circle is in turn surrounded by what is for McElroy perhaps the most important circle of contiguity relations, the city: New York, specifically Manhattan. McElroy has a highly-developed sense of the city as metonymic site, a zone of spatial contiguity, interdependence, and circulation. It is especially through his poetics of urbanism that McElroy recapitulates classic realism (see Tanner 1987:220–1), for there has long been an intimate relation between novelistic realism and urbanism: think of Balzac's Paris, Dickens's London, Dreiser's Chicago and New York.

McElroy constructs the city as metonymic site through the device of the urban pedestrian (cf. Baudelaire's *flâneur*): he walks one of his characters through the city, and uses this character's consciousness to register the contiguous fabric of city space. Both *Hind's Kidnap* and *Lookout*

Cartridge open with set-piece walking-tours of districts of New York, and McElroy devotes many pages throughout his fiction to similar urban itineraries in London (in *Lookout Cartridge*), Manhattan, and, obsessively, Brooklyn Heights. In *Women and Men*, the urban itinerary is several times covered not on foot but by bicycle – by Grace (*WM*:126–9), Larry (who calls this itinerary his "Manhattan Project," *WM*:412), and Jimmy Banks the messenger. But there are also properly pedestrian itineraries: Mayn on Second Avenue (*WM*:995–1000), Norma on Park Avenue (where a rolling orange briefly connects her with other pedestrians in an actualized metonymic chain, *WM*:479–80), and Mckenna, in a variation of the pedestrian device, standing still on Times Square while the urban crowd (including a number of characters to whom he is variously "connected") flows by him (*WM*:444–63).

Finally, outside the circle of the city lies the widest circle of all, the "world," the global network of which the city is itself a metonymy: "This global network looked so compact, but put yourself in it and your neighborhood is endless" (*WM*:1013). The web of densely interconnected lives ranged around the double center of Grace and Mayn, extending in space as far as Pinochet's Chile (Chilean refugees and government agents play a large role) and in time at least as far back as the Mexican War, and as far ahead (the novel's present is 1976–7) as a distant sci-fi future that Mayn has either imagined or somehow, inexplicably, experienced, intersects or interlocks with other, more impersonal metonymic continua: "Earth and its chains (food chain, profit-tradeoffs chain, crisis-intuiting chain, et al)" (*WM*:1104).

But this world-spanning network proves to be incomplete: there is a missing link, a missed connection. Despite all the friends they have in common, despite all the opportunities that shared spaces and intersecting itineraries place in their way, despite their (and our) suspicions that they might in some sense be "made for each other," Grace and Mayn never actually meet. The doorman mentions Mayn to Grace, but she "didn't have a picture" of him (*WM*:144). Norma describes Grace to Mayn, urging him to look her up (*WM*:661, 902); "have to get around to meeting this woman," says Mayn (*WM*:874). A spiritualist medium predicts that Grace will meet a man who fits Mayn's description (*WM*:472, 938). Grace even catches sight of Mayn (without knowing it is him) during her bicycle itinerary (*WM*:126; cf. 545), and, on the last pages of this very long novel, Mayn actually rings Grace's doorbell, but then changes his mind and walks away before she answers (*WM*:1185; see also 32, 380). The irony here is insistent, even somewhat heavy-handed, and seems to echo Grace's women's-separatist program (which in turn echoes the novel's title): "Get it together: keep generally women and men apart" (*WM*:108). The ironic near-misses of *Women and Men* also echo the near-misses of *Ulysses* (Bloom dodging Boylan throughout the day, Bloom's and Stephen's paths

intersecting several times before the decisive meeting at the lying-in hospital) and the climactic mis-recognitions of Pynchon's *V.* and Gaddis's *The
Recognitions*.

To what purpose? The conspicuous failure of Grace and Mayn to
"connect" serves to foreground the contiguity principle itself, and the very
metonymic network which, through this one failure of connection, falls
short of completeness. This is not McElroy's only foregrounding strategy
in *Women and Men*. For instance, there is also an entire cast of subsidiary
characters who in a sense personify metonymy: go-betweens, networkers,
mediums, forgers (in both senses) of connections. Mayn, himself a professional connector, has a sinister double (who may even be his brother),
a certain disreputable photojournalist named Spence. Spence makes his
living by "putting one source in connection with another source in the
covert interest of gaining information that was to be sure news for coverage
but for money-like leverage, too" (*WM*:671). He even manages to implicate Mayn and his daughter Flick in an anti-Pinochet conspiracy which
may not actually exist outside the minds of Spence and DeTalco the
Chilean agent.[10] Other personified metonymies include DeTalco himself,
whose job is to make and break conspiracies; Pearl Myles, Mayn's high-
school journalism teacher and self-appointed investigator into Mayn family
secrets; Jimmy Banks, the bicycle messenger "shared" by a number of
characters in the novel; and Senora Wing and her twin sister, literally
"mediums." There is even a woman journalist named Linc (short for
Lincoln) who, yes, links Jim Mayn and Grace Kimball; a friend of Mayn's
daughter, she attends one of Grace's workshops.

Circulating

Another device for calling attention to the metonymic network itself
involves objects which circulate through the network, passing from hand
to hand. There are a number of these, including a white Cadillac sold by
Grace's friend Cliff to Mayn, who gives it to his daughter; a bicycle sold
by Larry to Grace, who gives it to Jimmy Banks to enable him to go into
business as a messenger; the fragmentary score of an opera version of
Hamlet, which traces a possibly apocryphal itinerary through the Western
United States and South America, to end up being performed in New
York before an audience composed of most of the major characters in this
novel; and a Colt pistol (if it isn't actually two pistols) which passes from
hand to hand and place to place from the days of the Mexican War to
the year 1894, when it is evidently fired once with fatal effect, subsequently
becoming a Mayn family heirloom and ultimately a kind of lost Grail. Of
all the itineraries traced by such circulating objects through the networks
of *Women and Men*, none is more conspicuous than the "tapeworm track"
(*WM*:606). A tapeworm is, of course, like the chain letter of *A Smuggler's*

Bible, a realized metaphor *of* metonymy. This particular tapeworm, retrieved by a Native American fisherman from a Great Lakes pike, has been shipped to a fashionable East Coast physician, who in turn has administered it to an opera diva as a desperate weight-loss strategy; "after it got flushed away down the diva's silver toilet, its track clung like experience to the insides of the slowly self-understanding society we're in" (*WM*:321).

Finally, the structure and operation of the network of contiguities in *Women and Men* are made particularly conspicuous by the circulation of knowledge. Not only objects, but information, especially information organized as narrative, travels along the metonymic chains which constitute the densely interconnected world of *Women and Men*. Mayn and the other journalists in the novel (Spence, Linc, Mayn's girlfriend Jean, among others) are circulators of information by profession, but Grace, too, is a "central agency of information-sharing power" (*WM*:674), and so, in lesser ways, are many other characters:

> a newspapermen I had known some years before who had moved back into the building was reported to have told a fellow tenant who announced classical music on a small but surviving radio station who had told it to his wife's lawyer also living in the building who had told it to *his* wife, who told it to me in the incredible basement laundry . . . and back to its *original* source (who told *my* source that it was better than what he had originally said)

and so on (*WM*:921). This particular circuit is peripheral to the main events of the novel, but it is duplicated on a larger scale, and with profounder consequences, by the circuit along which the stories told by Mayn's grandmother Margaret are transmitted. As a young unmarried woman in the 1890s, Margaret returns from a daring, not to say scandalous, trip to the Southwest with strange tales of her adventures among the Navajo. These she tells half a century later to her grandson Jim as bedtime stories. He takes possession of them, changing them to suit his own imaginative reconstruction of events, and tells them in turn to his daughter Flick, who transmits them to her friend the journalist Linc, who repeats some of them at Grace Kimball's workshop. Margaret's stories finally turn up as episodes in Grace Kimball's dreams, assimilated to her own unconscious – ironically, since Mayn himself, collaborator on these stories at their inception, apparently never dreams. These same stories pass along a different chain by way of the egregious Spence, ultimately reaching the ears of the Chilean agent DeTalco, who interprets them as coded subversive messages.

But at the point at which what circulates is not Cadillacs, bicycles, or tapeworms but knowledge, we pass from a realist poetics of metonymy to a modernist poetics of epistemology.

EPISTEMOLOGY; OR, MODERNISM

Lodge (1977), following Jakobson, has attempted to construct a history of modern writing based on the pendulum-like alternation between metonymic and metaphoric "poles": after a metonymically-oriented realism comes a metaphorically-oriented modernism, followed by a metonymically-oriented antimodernism, and so on. In fact, Lodge's story breaks down almost immediately, for, while some modernist prose is indisputably metaphorical in orientation, other modernist texts (as Lodge himself admits) "radicalize" metonymy; examples include the metonymic interior monologues of Bloom and Molly, or Stein's *The Making of Americans* (Lodge 1977:144).[11] A better hypothesis, then, might be this: modernist poetics "reinterprets" the contiguity principle of realist fiction, subordinating it to a new organizing principle, a new "dominant."[12] Think of the web of interconnected lives in Proust's *Recherche*, Joyce's sense of the city as metonymic site in *Ulysses*, Musil's deterministic vision of a modern world constituted by systems: here the metonymic organizing principle of classic realist prose persists, but it has undergone a radical transformation. Now it becomes a vehicle for characteristic modernist preoccupations, which are predominantly cognitive or epistemological.[13]

McElroy's *Women and Men* recapitulates modernist poetics as well as classic realist poetics. *Women and Men* is not just about contiguity; it is also about epistemology. Consider the titles a number of its chapters bear: "division of labor unknown," "the unknown sound," "dividing the unknown between us," "sisters sharing information," "known bits," "the unknown saved," "the message for what it was worth," "news." Such titles direct our attention to the fact that the circulation of information through the metonymic network of *Women and Men* is not free and unimpeded: there are blockages, gaps; certain "bits" are known to some characters, unknown to others; some "bits" will never be fully known. For those characters who are driven to know, this tantalizingly uneven distribution of knowledge transforms the static network of contiguities into pathways along which they may pursue their epistemological quests. In short, it turns *Women and Men* into a detective story.[14]

Investigating

The detective-story model of epistemological quest underlies much classic modernist fiction, from the earliest modernism of James (*The Sacred Fount*, *The Ambassadors*) and Conrad, through the high modernism of Faulkner,[15] to the "late modernist" texts of Robbe-Grillet (*Les Gommes*, *La Jalousie*), Pynchon (*V.*, *The Crying of Lot 49*), Manuel Puig (*The Buenos Aires Affair*), John Hawkes, Don DeLillo, and many others. McElroy had already recapitulated this classic modernist model in his earlier novels.

David Brooke of *A Smuggler's Bible* is a "snooper," an obsessed amateur detective (see Tanner 1987:212–13); so, too, is the nameless narrator of *Ancient History* (1971). *Hind's Kidnap* is an epistemological quest closely modeled on the Oedipus detective-story. Here Jack Hind, another amateur detective, resumes after seven years his freelance investigation of an unsolved child kidnapping, following a trail of obviously planted clues that leads him from friend to friend as in a treasure-hunt. His investigation proves inconclusive, but in the process Hind uncovers the truth of his own parentage. Similarly, in *Lookout Cartridge*, the narrator-protagonist Cartwright goes in search of the persons and motives behind the destruction of a film on which he has collaborated, in the process bringing to light an international conspiracy of American draft-resisters and expatriates.

Detectives both amateur and professional abound in *Women and Men*. These include, among others, Spence, DeTalco, Pearl Myles, and especially Mayn himself, another of McElroy's obsessed amateur detectives, but also a reluctant one (he is "locked into some obsessional reluctance" towards the mysteries around him, says his girlfriend Jean (*WM*:264)). There are two major interlocking mysteries. The first is a private one, the Mayn family mystery – did Mayn's mother commit suicide, and if so, why? Or did she survive, and if so, where? And who is really buried in her grave-plot? The second mystery is public and political, and involves an alleged conspiracy to free an anti-Castro Cuban (or is he really pro-Castro?) from prison so that he may infiltrate the Chilean secret service; there are a number of subsidiary disappearances and murder-mysteries, and also, as in *Hind's Kidnap*, a child kidnapping. As in *A Smuggler's Bible* and *Ancient History*, detection here is often indistinguishable from simple snooping, especially when it takes the form of that cliché of melodrama, eavesdropping. DeTalco eavesdrops on the diva's telephone conversations; Spence is a chronic eavesdropper who seems always to be standing at the bar when Mayn is exchanging confidences with friends (e.g. *WM*:410, 429); Mayn as a child eavesdrops on his grandfather (*WM*:1027), and on one occasion even turns the tables and eavesdrops on Spence (*WM*:1023–5).

Representing consciousness

But the modernist detective-story structure is itself only a dramatization of the more general and more basic modernist epistemological preoccupation with the mind in its cognitive engagement with reality: the fine-grained interaction between consciousness and the world outside consciousness. Modernist fiction is at least as interested in our everyday epistemological quests – "an ordinary mind on an ordinary day," as Virginia Woolf put it – as it is in the adventures of detectives, amateur or professional. In other words, the detective-story emplots what appears elsewhere in modernist poetics as the project of seizing and representing the activity of consciousness itself.

McElroy shares this modernist preoccupation with the interaction between world and consciousness, and the modernist project of representing consciousness in action.[16] Already in *A Smuggler's Bible* he has given us a narrator who, hoping to escape the epistemological cul-de-sac of solipsism (see *SB*:36, 470), undertakes what amounts to a series of epistemological experiments, "projecting" himself (see *SB*:98, 392) into the minds and experiences of eight friends and relatives. These eight acts of projection involve eight different formal means for representing consciousness.[17] Experimental representation of consciousness is pursued more subtly in the first-person narrative of *Lookout Cartridge*, where the entire substance of the fictional world has been passed through the filter of Cartwright's probing consciousness.[18] The most radical of all McElroy's experiments, however, occurs in *Plus* (1977). Centered in a disembodied human brain which has been launched into earth orbit as the onboard "wet computer" of a satellite, this text is entirely organized around epistemological themes and motifs: solipsism and the problematic interface with the world outside consciousness; the recovery and revision of memory (already a major motif in *A Smuggler's Bible* and *Lookout Cartridge*); the acquisition and loss of self.

The epistemological experimentation continues in *Women and Men*, where McElroy undertakes to represent consciousness in action through a range of formal means, some of them classically modernist, others extensions of modernist strategies, or new hybrids. For instance, he presents the interior monologue of a mentally retarded bicycle messenger, Jimmy Banks (*WM*:464–77, 948–55, 1059–64). A "revised" version of Faulkner's Benjy, Jimmy is canny and street-smart, active in his engagement with his urban environment where Benjy is passive and locked in the grip of his past. Formally, Jimmy's monologue is composed of sentences from which the grammatical traces of the monologuing subject have been almost entirely effaced.[19] Also innovative is the first-person narrative of the convict Foley (*WM*:690–782), a variant on the epistolary form, but evidently transmitted to its addressee, Mayn, by telepathy (see *WM*:693, 707, 741, 779), unless it represents the contents of a series of letters from Foley after they have been "boiled down" in Mayn's own consciousness (see *WM*:719).[20] But McElroy also uses classically modernist strategies for representing consciousness, such as the "free indirect" meditation by Grace Kimball during which she reviews her memories, waiting for their hidden coherence to reveal itself (*WM*:100–47; see Mathews 1990:218). A sort of *A la recherche du temps perdu* in miniature, this chapter also recapitulates the "loops" and "inserts" of *Lookout Cartridge*, remembered scenes which Cartwright reviews for overlooked bits of evidence.

Not satisfied merely to explore the operations of a single consciousness, modernists such as Joyce, Faulkner, Woolf, Gide, Huxley and Dos Passos developed strategies for juxtaposing different consciousnesses, and McElroy also recapitulates these strategies of perspectivism or parallax. The simplest examples are binary ones, in which the same objective situation is represented as experienced by first one character, then another: thus, we are given Grace's experience of the first encounter between herself and Clara Mckenna (WM:100–47), then Clara's version as reported to her husband (WM:148–58), or an "interior" view of Jimmy Banks (WM:464–77), followed by a rather shocking "exterior" view from Norma's perspective: "A messenger, a retarded man she'd seen up and down Madison Avenue with wall eyes and a jaw like a shovel, limped by, carrying a manila envelope" (WM:482). More complex examples of perspectivism involve multiple, often oblique perspectives on a single event, for instance the recovery of a young woman's body (Amy's?) from the East River, an event withheld from us except insofar as it has been refracted through a number of characters' awareness of it (e.g. WM:501–2). The parallax structure is comically "laid bare" in an episode in which two women, near-strangers, discuss their relationships with men, specifically one woman's present boyfriend, the other's ex-, only to find that they have been discussing the same man (WM:216–32)! A third perspective is provided by a male eavesdropper, who understands quicker than the women do that the two versions refer to one and the same objective "Dave."[21]

Modernist reading

The presence of the eavesdropper in this scene directs our attention to a further dimension of the epistemological structure of *Women and Men*, for we readers in effect occupy the position of this eavesdropper: he is our surrogate within the fictional world. In other words, the various epistemological quests of the characters are ultimately transferred to us, the readers. As in the texts of Faulkner and other modernists,[22] the "mysteries" of this fictional world are organized in such a way that we investigate them in tandem with the characters themselves, and solve them (or fail to solve) them along with the characters.

This particular epistemological structure also characterizes McElroy's earlier fiction. In *Ancient History*, for instance, it takes the classically modernist form (exploited to the full in late-modernist texts such as Nabokov's *Pale Fire*) of the need to determine the first-person narrator's reliability or unreliability: as he pursues his epistemological quest within the fictional world, so we pursue the parallel quest of evaluating the epistemological worth of his statements. Much more radical is the reader's epistemological quest in *Plus*. Here we begin in a state of mystification, baffled by the experiences evidently being undergone by Imp Plus;

gradually, as Imp Plus acquires (or rather remembers) the language for describing these experiences, we come to understand his situation better, until finally, in the closing chapter, we are able to "eavesdrop" on the telepathic exchange between him and the project scientist he thinks of as "the Acrid Voice," when all (or as much as can be) is revealed.

A similar transfer of epistemological responsiblity to the reader occurs throughout *Women and Men*. On a small scale, it occurs in chapters such as the one (described above) in which Grace Kimball passes her memories in review: we review these loops of memory along with her, waiting along with her for the retrospective pattern to emerge, as indeed it finally does, though not until the chapter's last sentence. On a larger scale, the same transfer is accomplished through the systematic withholding or displace-ment of key evidence required to solve this novel's various "mysteries." In the case of the "private" mystery involving the secret history of the Mayn family, the key events of the year 1894 are delayed, in a strategy reminiscent of Faulkner's *Absalom, Absalom!*, until the novel's penultimate page (page 1191!), when it finally becomes clear (or does it?) that it must be the body of the Navajo prince, shot dead by Jim Mayn's grandfather Alexander, that occupies Mayn's mother's grave-plot. As for the political mystery involving the anti-Pinochet conspiracy (if there is one), this would appear to have been resolved by the chaotic events at the dress-rehearsal of the *Hamlet* opera. Unfortunately, these events reach us only obliquely and retrospectively, refracted through an imperfect post-factum reconstruc-tion of events by Mckenna and Clara (*WM*: 1170–77), so that we will never learn whether DeTalco was murdered, whether the kidnapped child was recovered, or in general what transpired in the aftermath of the disrupted rehearsal. In this case the strategy is less that of *Absalom, Absalom!* than of *The Crying of Lot 49*: we are left with a permanently suspended resolution, and an insoluble epistemological crux.

ANGELOLOGY; OR, POSTMODERNISM?

The difficulties we experience in reading those chapters of *Women and Men* in which McElroy represents his characters' consciousness in action are difficulties of a familiar kind; they are modernist difficulties. Here form is (as the Russian Formalists used to say) deliberately "impeded" – gaps are opened, information withheld or obliquely presented – for the purpose of drawing us into the text's epistemological quests. But between these chapters of represented consciousness lie other chapters in which the difficulties are of a different order altogether. The analogues of these "interchapters" are less the modernist strategies of *Absalom, Absalom!* or *Ulysses* than the strange, shifty, sliding, punning discourses of, say, *Tender Buttons*, *Finnegans Wake*, *Texts for Nothing*, or the texts of Raymond Federman, Ron Sukenick, or Christine Brooke-Rose:[23]

And this tapeworm in its steady state takes in along a multiplicity of small-scale units that are its nervous system's segments a homogenized menu of the godly diet – read *sacred* – *divine* – read *diva* suddenly which is opera for goddess. But wait: what diet is this? We have to know. Oh it is food digested by her the tapeworm's host then processed by the worm her guest plus helpings of a new para-placenta that lines the linings of this diva's – read *songbird's* – read *opera singer's* – gut: so as the worm makes its way, and its way makes the worm, the diva gets hers, her way, which eats up her surplus and empowers her to shed really a lot of weight, sundry reported amounts upwards of a hundred foolish pounds.

(WM:12)

Such a passage would not seem out of place in a text like *Between* (1968), Brooke-Rose's novel about a professional translator suspended between languages, cultures, and selves, written entirely without any form of the copula *to be* (since here everything is *in between* states, in a process of *becoming*).[24] McElroy's interchapters, too, lie "between" – "BETWEEN US," "BETWEEN HISTORIES," as their titles announce, or, in other words, between the chapters proper; but above all between Grace Kimball and Jim Mayn, whose lives these interchapters simultaneously connect and separate (see Mathews 1990:215–16):

Now, they two aren't to be thought of in the same breath here. Yet if the chance remains that they should never meet to our satisfaction, still we ourselves are their relation, think of them as being like married folk who have so much between them they need friends to be between them too.

"So much between them"? So once more we caught ourselves saying two things at once. . . .

(WM:32)

McElroy has long been fascinated with in-betweenness in general (see Tanner 1987:233–4), and with the space between chapters in particular. He had already experimented with interchapters as early as *A Smuggler's Bible*, and had returned to these experiments again in the "inserts" of *Lookout Cartridge*. But in *Women and Men* the experiment seems to have gotten out of hand, like Frankenstein's monster. Here the interchapters have ballooned to gigantic proportions, to the point that the space "between" threatens to swamp the chapters proper (if it is even possible to speak of "chapters proper" any longer). Called "breathers," ironically implying a respite or moment of relaxation, these interchapters actually dominate the text: "But breathers aren't what they – *or* we --used to be: once marginal, the breather came to take up major space like a friend in need whom you have to listen to for weeks of personal crisis" (*WM*:663).

Among its many other curious features, the discourse of the *Women and Men* interchapters regularly uses the first-person plural – "We already remember what's been going on" (*WM*:8), "We have to know" (*WM*:12), "So once more we caught ourselves saying two things at once" (*WM*:32) – prompting us to ask, along with the text itself, "Who is this 'We'?" (*WM*:16).[25] The jacket blurb answers, somewhat preemptively, that this "we" is "a kind of collective voice, the novel's chorus." The answer which the text itself supplies is stranger, and harder to take seriously: this voice which utters the discourse of the "breathers," which uses the first-person plural pronoun, belongs to – angels:

> Are these merely our angels? They angle into and out of our speech like some advanced listening advice we recognize because we remember from somewhere. And what *is* this community – this large We we ourselves voice? It will be a community for one thing and capable of accommodating even angels real enough to grow by human means.
>
> (*WM*:11; cf. also 9, 10, 25–6, 27, 30 and *passim*)

Postmodern angelology

Angels? Not long ago, Alexander Theroux made the protagonist of his Menippean satire, *Darconville's Cat* (1981), an angelologist – rather an unlikely specialization for a late-twentieth-century academic, one might think, but no doubt intended (along with so much else in this novel) to signal Darconville's distance from the values of his, and our, time (see Moore 1986).[26] But this will hardly help to explain why Donald Barthelme, too, of all people, practices angelology in his text, "On Angels" (from *City Life*, 1970), or why J.H. Prynne does in his important poem "Of Sanguine Fire" (from *Brass*, 1971), or Milan Kundera in *The Book of Laughter and Forgetting* (1978), or Harold Brodkey in "The Angel" (1985), or Salman Rushdie in *The Satanic Verses* (1988), or Don DeLillo at the end of *White Noise* (1985), or why Wyndham Lewis did, and on such a massive scale, in his late masterpiece, the *Human Age* trilogy (*Childermass*, 1928; *Monstre Gai*, 1955; *Malign Fiesta*, 1957), or why so many other postmodernist writers have similarly found uses for angels.[27]

For the fact of the matter is that angels have been making a strange kind of come-back in postmodernist writing. Inevitably, many of these postmodernist angels are parody angels, "hollow" angels emptied of their otherworldliness and brought ingloriously down to earth (figuratively or literally). Such is the case with Barthelme's angels, for instance, who have been left "in a strange position" by news of the death of God; or García Márquez's angel, who is no more than "a very old man with enormous wings" in the story by that name (from *The Incredible and Sad Tale of Innocent Eréndira and Her Heartless Grandmother*); or the angel of death and other celestial flunkies in Stanley Elkin's travesty of the world to come, *The Living End* (1980); or the winged dogs (a Golden Retriever, a Rotweiler, and a St. Bernard) who guard the pearly gates in Steve Katz's "Mongolian Whiskey" (from *Stolen Stories*, 1984). Hollow, too, in various ways, are such quasi-angelic figures as the winged insurance agent who tries to take flight from the roof of No Mercy Hospital in the opening pages of Toni Morrison's *Song of Solomon* (1977); or the winged aerialiste, a low-life cockney adventuress, in Angela Carter's *Nights at the Circus* (1984); or, most tellingly of all, the angel found with its throat slit on the first page of Patchen's *The Journal of Albion Moonlight*. God having been killed off, how can angels hope to survive?

Strikingly, though, they do. Even those texts which parody or travesty angelic figures turn out to attest, in their backhanded way, to the continued viability of angels; for who would ever have imagined, without the appearance of such parodies, that angels were still worth parodying, so late in the twentieth century? The presence in fiction even of degenerate and parodic angels means that angels are still with us after all, despite (or because of?) the death of their Creator. Furthermore, not all these parody angels are unequivocally parodic. In some cases, having been "hollowed out" at the beginning of the text, the angelic figures are found to be "full" again by the end: Toni Morrison's protagonist recovers stories of an ancestor who, unlike the winged but flightless insurance agent, really did (it is said) fly away home to Africa; and Angela Carter's Fevvers survives abuse and degradation to prove that her wings are genuine, and her powers of flight real.

There are, moreover, postmodernist texts in which angels appear to function from the outset in their full traditional roles, relatively free of parodic taint. Such (so to speak) "full-fledged" angelic texts include two which many would rank among the most important of their generation, namely, Thomas Pynchon's *Gravity's Rainbow* (1973) and James Merrill's verse trilogy, *The Changing Light at Sandover* (1976, 1978, 1980, 1982). Both these texts project angelic hierarchies, "bureaucracies of the other side," as Pynchon puts it (1973:411). In *The Changing Light*, the poet and his partner David Jackson receive instruction from successive mentors each located higher in the otherworldly hierarchy than his (or its) predecessor. Evidently less orderly, and certainly less accessible, the angelic hierarchy of *Gravity's Rainbow* is implied rather than fully realized. Angels tend to be disruptive, threatening forces in Pynchon's world, bursting in upon it like the Angel of Lübeck, or looming over it like the "watchmen of world's edge" who monitor Slothrop's progress (Pynchon 1973:150–2, 214–15, 217).[28]

In the course of their long migration from ancient scripture (often apocryphal) to postmodernism,[29] the angels have undergone radical transformations. "Like earlier artists," writes William S. Wilson, "postmodernists use religious images – crosses, nuns, angels – but the implications are different because the context is different. . . . Today, a religious image . . . seems more provisional than providential, changing with the circumstances which change it" (Wilson 1989:18). Nevertheless, throughout these transformations angels have also retained a certain persistent core of meaning. Indeed, it might be more helpful to speak not of "angels" as such but of an enduring angel-function which is fulfilled in similar ways by different beings at different times. For instance, the message-bearing function of angels in Christianized epic was anticipated by the function of messenger-gods (Hermes, Mercury) in classical epic; in effect, the angels systematically took over the functions of their pagan precursors (see Greene 1963). In our own time, it might be argued, the angel-function has been largely "science-fictionized," ceded to aliens from outer space.[30] But, if there has been a certain stability to the angel-function over time, there has also been constant change. From epoch to epoch, the angels have always served immediate ideological needs dictated by the times in which they find themselves. Appropriated and reappropriated by different and often incompatible systems of thought, they have functioned as a kind of secondary language in which angelologists could conduct coded discussions of a range of this-worldly issues (see Jameson 1979:152–4).[31] As Barthelme says, "It is a curiosity of writing about angels that, very often, one turns out to be writing about men" (Barthelme 1982c:136).

Toward an ontology of angels

In postmodernist poetics, angels evidently serve, among other things, as realized metaphors of the violation of ontological boundaries.[32] Ambassadors from what Pynchon calls "the Other Order of Being" (Pynchon 1973:222 and *passim*), angels call attention to the plurality of worlds and world-versions in postmodernist texts, and to the ontological "seams" or "rifts" between adjacent or rival worlds which often fissure these texts.[33] This is particularly conspicuous in those texts in which the presence of angels correlates with metafictional boundary-violations or frame-breaking, for instance in William T. Vollmann's *You Bright and Risen Angels* (1987), where the metafictional "author" refers to his characters, puppets under his god-like control, as his "angels"; or in Sam Shepherd's play *Angel City* (1976) where, apart from the joking allusion to Los Angeles, the presence of "angel" in the title correlates with the blurring of levels between "real life" and "the movies" in the world of the play.

A boundary may be crossed in either direction, of course, so if the presence of angels signals the breaching of some ontological boundary, then this motif yields two possible basic scenarios: either an angel has penetrated our "lower" world, or a human being has penetrated (or aspires to penetrate) the "higher" angelic world. Both of these scenarios have been elaborated in postmodernist fictions. On the one hand, there is a class of texts, for which Rilke's *Duino Elegies* is perhaps the most influential model, in which angels symbolize the human aspiration to achieve a state beyond the human. This is their function in *The Changing Light at Sandover* and (somewhat less certainly, because of the ironies involved) *Gravity's Rainbow*, as well as in many of the "science-fictionized" versions (Tsukerman's *Liquid Sky*, Clarke and Kubrick's *2001*).[34] On the other hand, there is another class of texts in which the direction of the boundary-violation is reversed, and angels consort with humans or, indeed, aspire *to be* human. This is the case, for instance, in Wyndham Lewis's *Human Age* trilogy, Wenders and Handke's *Wings of Desire*, Lem and Tarkovsky's *Solaris*, and, most scandalously of all, in Juan Goytisolo's *Makbara* (1980), where an androgynous angel, fleeing the boredom of an oppressively bureaucratic paradise, descends to earth to become a transvestite prostitute and conceives a grotesque passion for a Moroccan "guest-worker."

Clearly, then, McElroy's angels are not without precedent, from the point of view of postmodernist angelology in general. They do, however, seem to be without precedent in McElroy's own writing – or nearly so. The only possible exception might be *Plus*, where the satellite brain Imp Plus seems to bear a resemblance to some of the science-fiction adaptations of the angel-function.[35] If this is so, then Imp Plus belongs to the Rilkean angelic paradigm: under bombardment from space, he undergoes a transformation into a trans-human – angelic? – state, developing into a "lattice" capable of generating energy and communicating telepathically with earth-bound humans. Ultimately Imp Plus merges with "thought" itself. Strikingly, it is in this text, with its quasi-angelic protagonist and center of consciousness, that we find language closest to the shifting, polysemous discourse characteristic of the "angelic" interchapters of *Women and Men*.

Angelic consciousness

The angels of *Women and Men* are elusive beings, and we must pursue hints and fragmentary evidence dispersed throughout this immensely long text in order to get at their nature. Evidently they belong to the opposite paradigm from the Rilkean scenario of *Plus*: where Imp Plus transcends the human, these angels, like those of *The Human Age* or *Makbara*, aspire to become human. This is an insight that comes to both Grace Kimball and the convict Foley: "*angels get to be humans*," thinks Grace (*WM*:110), and Foley reflects that "all they want is to be like us and live only inside our limits, change their lives" (*WM*:690). "Change their lives": this phrase recurs in various versions throughout the text (e.g. *WM*:159, 374), and seems to echo and deliberately to invert Rilke, who counsels *us* to desire to be changed to some other (higher) order of being.[36]

"I sometimes hear angels talking talking talking nearby," says Foley

(*WM*:690), and Jim Mayn corroborates, quoting a stranger he once encountered at a Tigers-Yankees game:

> A plural voice. Not at all *"voices,"* though a man . . . told him "voices" of that schizophrenic species while they drove him nuts (which he already was) gave him this friendly sense of his mind being endlessly settled by colonists who changed their career goals and departed, then moved back vociferously.
>
> (*WM*:859)

These angels who aspire to be human manifest themselves as voices – or, better, they *are* voices: "the voices . . . boiled down from a cloud of near-angel voices (awfully like ours on a good day) to now and then one voice" (*WM*:27); "some reasonable invading voices, mysterious We, angels perhaps if there were angels anyplace but inside us, saying the words she hears" (*WM*:364). Confirmation comes towards the end of the text, from the angelic "we" itself: "We had learned we were a language" (*WM*:1113).

Angels are discourse, then; but how is it that they "change their lives"? in what sense do they become human? "Angels exist in thought," we are told, ambiguously enough, near the beginning of *Women and Men* (*WM*:11). Once again, it is Grace Kimball who gropes toward the elusive truth: "she feels others, like angels trying to get in on her act, trying to catch up, speaking like her language, speaking *her*" (*WM*:102); she feels herself "invaded by these – hmmm, well, *angels* she had to reckon with . . . she thought that's what these humdingers might be, for they felt like more than one" (*WM*:137).³⁷ The clincher comes immediately after Grace has her insight that "angels get to be humans": "She knew where she was coming from and it was all the breathing spaces, each breath-pulse point: she was coming from what found her! Someone had said, doubtfully, *Consciousness*. Who was it?" (*WM*:110). "Consciousness": Graces comes from and finds herself in consciousness, the consciousness that saturates the "breathers" ("the breathing spaces") between the chapters of *Women and Men*. This consciousness "invades" her and "speaks" her – it constitutes her – and then moves on, leaving Grace in order to constitute other characters, dipping ("swerving" or "curving" is the text's own preferred metaphor) into them and back out again: "We can't answer – for we changing from angel into Jim sometimes find or hear only the moment and the words of its impulse" (*WM*: 635); "this diva with all her paraphernalia has gotten she *feels* quite real – we hadn't been looking for it, she was our transit, and now it has just happened . . . " (*WM*:327).³⁸

In other words, the angels of *Women and Men* are personifications, realized metaphors, for consciousness in this novel: the consciousness of the characters, but also the medium of consciousness in which the characters' individual consciousnesses are suspended, and which washes around them and spreads between them, penetrating everywhere. The imagery here has been supplied by Foley, who develops an entire theory of the "Colloidal Unconscious," the collective mind in which individual minds are suspended like particles dispersed in a colloid (*WM*:82, 698, 1129). Foley's is a crackpot theory, but, in point of fact, true in a strictly literal sense – not necessarily of the real world, but certainly of *this text* (and textuality in general), where characters' minds literally are dispersed and suspended in a discursive medium – the language of *Women and Men*, its "angelic" discourse (see Mathews 1990:202).[39] "Do you ever feel," Mayn's girlfriend asks him, "that we fit into a large life that doesn't much know us but – holds us? And that this is better than its being more aware of us?" (*WM*:266). Of course they literally do "fit into a large life," and that larger life is the discourse *of* this novel, which is also its (angelic) consciousness.

Who, then, is this "We" who speaks the characters and the "in-between" spaces of *Women and Men*? Ultimately, of course, it is *us* – the readers, we who allow this discourse to occupy and preoccupy *our* minds, who invest this novel with *our* consciousness, constituting by our acts of reading both the characters' various consciousnesses and the discursive connective tissue in which they are suspended.[40] The reader's consciousness is the literal *locus* of the world of this text: *we* are the colloid in which these characters are suspended, the weather which blankets this world and bathes it on all sides. The angelic discourse is our vehicle for penetrating the world and the minds of this text; it is, in effect, our surrogate in the text, holding open for us the space which we will come to occupy when we read. Producing this text through our acts of reading, we provisionally adopt the angelic position and the first-person plural pronoun associated with it, the "We" of the angelic discourse, as our own. We give *Women and Men* life, *our* lives – no mere figure of speech when one calculates how many hours must have gone into reading (let alone rereading!) a difficult text over 1200 pages long. We are, literally, the angels of *Women and Men*.[41]

WOMEN AND MEN; OR, LATE-MODERNISM

Finally, is McElroy's *Women and Men* a postmodernist text? A vacuous question, deserving an equally vacuous answer: It all depends. For the question implies that there is something "out there" in the world which is "postmodernism," and that in order to determine whether *Women and Men* is "postmodernist" all one would need to do is compare it with that object "out there." But of course there is no such "thing" as postmodernism: postmodernism is a discursive construct produced in and by the discourses of (among others) critics, philosophers, art historians, journalists, public-relations people, even (sometimes) writers and artists. Or rather it is not one construct but many, not all of them compatible with each other, not all of them equally coherent or valuable or useful.

So determining whether *Women and Men* is a postmodernist text does in fact "all depend" on which construct of postmodernism one is operating with. There is at least one such construct according to which it would certainly qualify, namely the version of postmodernism so strenuously promoted by the architectural critic Charles Jencks (1986), and more circumspectly by John Barth (1984c) and Umberto Eco (1984).[42] According to this version, postmodernism is characterized by "double coding": the postmodernist text (or artwork, or building) simultaneously addresses a popular audience through the codes of familiar, popular art, and an elite audience through "high-art" codes; it is simultaneously "readerly" and "writerly." This, as I hope to have shown, is the case with *Women and Men*: at one level it deploys the historical code of classic nineteenth-century realism, still the basis of popular fiction, while at other levels it appeals to much more restricted audiences schooled in the codes of high-modernist epistemological fiction and contemporary ontological fiction.

But Jencks's is not the only version of postmodernism, nor is it the one I endorse. I prefer to construct a postmodernism with an ontological orientation, that is, a poetics subordinated to an ontological dominant. It is within such a poetics that angels function as I have described above, as devices for foregrounding the plurality of worlds and the boundaries between them. McElroy's angels do not function this way: they are not strategies for foregrounding ontological preoccupations, but rather strategies for exploring consciousness in fiction – consciousness in and of fictional characters, consciousness in and of the text itself, the consciousness of the reader. By my reading, in other words, *Women and Men* is not after all a postmodernist text but one devoted to radical explorations of modernist issues of consciousness; call it "late-modernist," if you will, or "aggravated modernism."

Thus *Women and Men* does not move "forward" into postmodernism (if I may be permitted a misleadingly progressivist metaphor), but "laterally" into still-unexplored spaces of modernist poetics. Others have ventured into these late-modernist territories – Nathalie Sarraute, Manuel Puig, Peter Handke, Thomas Bernhard, John Hawkes, William Gaddis, Don DeLillo – but none more adventurously than Joseph McElroy.[43]

Chapter 9

"I draw the line as a rule between one solar system and another": the postmodernism(s) of Christine Brooke-Rose

TELLING POSTMODERNIST STORIES OTHERWISE

In the world of Tlön, Borges tells us, "A book which does not include its opposite, or 'counter-book,' is considered incomplete" (Borges 1962c:29). Tlön, Borges predicted, would contaminate and in the end supplant our world, and of course he was right: nowadays Tlön is the world we live in, a world where simulacra preempt reality and nothing is more fictitious than "real life"; the postmodern world, as we have learned to call it. This essay is about two books which, from a Tlönian point of view, must be considered incomplete; books which do not contain their counter-books but only the traces of them, from which the contours of the missing counter-books must be inferred. Interestingly, the missing counter-book of each of these defective books actually exists; more interestingly still, it is the *same* book.

One of these defective books is my own *Postmodernist Fiction* (McHale 1987). In it I told a misleadingly progressivist story about how, once upon a time, a modernist poetics of fiction gave way to a postmodernist poetics. I illustrated that story with cases of writers (Joyce, Beckett, Robbe-Grillet, Fuentes, Coover, Nabokov, Pynchon) whose careers seemed to follow the same trajectory from modernism through a transitional phase to postmodernism. What is missing from *Postmodernist Fiction* (though its traces may be detected there) is the counter-story according to which modernism and postmodernism are not successive stages in some inevitable evolution from less advanced to more advanced aesthetic forms, but rather alternative contemporary practices, equally "advanced" or "progressive," equally available, between which writers are free to choose. This alternative story, had it been told, could have been illustrated with writers (e.g. Hawkes, Barth, perhaps also Abish, García Màrquez, Fuentes in his later career) who have seemed to "zig-zag" between modernism and postmodernism instead of following a smooth evolutionary trajectory from one to the other.[1]

The other incomplete book is Christine Brooke-Rose's *A Rhetoric of the Unreal* (1981). This book tells the story of the historical continuity among the varieties of modern "unrealism," from the "classic" fantastic of Poe's "The Black Cat" and James's *The Turn of the Screw* to such contemporary forms as the "new" science fiction (Vonnegut, McElroy) and the *nouveau* and *nouveau nouveau roman*.[2] What is missing from *A Rhetoric of the Unreal* is the extension of this story to include (American) postmodernist fiction, for, just at the point where the story arrives at postmodernism, Brooke-Rose abruptly abandons her narrative paradigm of continuity and takes up instead a different paradigm, one based on the parasitism of postmodernism on historically prior modes (see McHale 1982 and above, "Telling postmodernist stories"). She seems unable to imagine how the principle of hesitation, upon which all the previous varieties of unrealist poetics had been based, might be extended to postmodernist fiction, and it is this failure of imagination that explains the abrupt change of paradigms at the end of *A Rhetoric of the Unreal*.

Ironically, what Brooke-Rose lacks in her theory of unrealist fiction she might readily have found in her own *practice* of unrealist fiction. That is, she might have found in her own fiction of the late sixties and seventies a poetics based on the principle of hesitation, but not, as in the "classic" fantastic described by Todorov, hesitation between alternative explanatory hypotheses (natural or supernatural); rather, hesitation between alternative *worlds* (levels of reality, orders of being). More accurately, she would have found this poetics of *ontological* hesitation in *some* of her texts of that period: in *Such* (1966) and *Thru* (1975). In the others – *Out* (1964), *Between* (1968) – she would no doubt have recognized the same forms of *epistemological* hesitation that have, by her own account, characterized earlier modes of unrealism (the "classic" fantastic, the *nouveau roman*, etc.). In other words, Brooke-Rose's fiction of the late sixties and seventies zigzags between epistemological hesitation and ontological hesitation; between, to revert to my own categories in *Postmodernist Fiction*, modernist poetics and postmodernist poetics.[3]

It is in this sense that the missing counter-book to both my own *Postmodernist Fiction* and Brooke-Rose's *A Rhetoric of the Unreal* is the same book, conveniently assembled between two covers by Carcanet Press, namely *The Christine Brooke-Rose Omnibus* (1986), comprising the four novels from *Out* to *Thru*. It is the counter-book of my book because it reflects a different, nonlinear, non-progressivist story about the relation between modernist and postmodernist poetics; it is the counter-book of *A Rhetoric of the Unreal* because it completes, by enacting it, Brooke-Rose's unfinished story about the historical varieties of hesitation and the continuity from the classic fantastic to postmodernism.

A brief survey of what lies between the covers of *The Christine Brooke-Rose Omnibus* should serve to establish its claim to being doubly a counter-book, the book that, if our world were Tlön (which of course it is), ought to have been contained in both *Postmodernist Fiction* and *A Rhetoric of the Unreal*.

FROM *OUT* TO *THRU*: POSTmodernISM[4]

Apart from her academic career as critic and narratologist, Christine Brooke-Rose has had, in a sense, two (and now three) careers as a novelist. Her first career spans the four early novels of the fifties and early sixties, which she seems now almost to have repudiated, namely *The Language of Love* (1957), *The Sycamore Tree* (1958), *The Dear Deceit* (1960), and *The Middlemen* (1961; see Martin 1989:112–14). Her second career, from *Out* (1964) to *Thru* (1975), is the one that concerns me here. It traces a zigzag itinerary from novel to novel: first modernist (*Out*), then postmodernist (*Such*), then modernist again (*Between*), then postmodernist again (*Thru*).[5]

Out: "Knowledge certain or indubitable is unobtainable"

Out (1964) is, as Brooke-Rose herself acknowledges (Brooke-Rose 1989:102; Friedman and Fuchs 1989:82), heavily indebted to the phenomenological fiction of the early Robbe-Grillet, in particular *La Jalousie* (1957) and *Dans le labyrinthe* (1959). As in *La Jalousie*, its subject or center of consciousness is ubiquitous but effaced, deprived of a proper name or pronoun through which its (his) presence could even be indicated. Nevertheless, we "share the mental content" of this effaced subject, as Brooke-Rose (1981:309) says of Robbe-Grillet's *Dans le labyrinthe*; the entire substance of the text is attributable to his obsessive, damaged consciousness. Since we are always "inside" his consciousness, events and conversations which he has only imagined or anticipated, or which he has really experienced but misperceived or misunderstood, are indistinguishable from "objective" events and conversations. Sometimes the text explicitly signals the "unreality" of a segment: "This dialogue does not necessarily occur"; "This fantasy is . . . ruled out of order by the Silent Speaker."[6] At other times, conversely, it signals the objective status of a segment that otherwise might be treated as subjective delusion or speculation: "The sequence has occurred" (O:48); "The conversation is real, repeat real" (O:101); "Somewhere in the archive there will be evidence that this occurred, if it is kept, and for those who wish to look it up" (O:79). Elsewhere, however, the status of a segment is left indeterminate, or worse, the text itself confuses the issue by multiplying alternatives:

> Either the conversation has partially occurred, the beginning, for instance, the remainder being suppressed, selected, manipulated, transformed, schematised, because inunderstood. Or the conversation has

wholly occurred, and been wholly manipulated, transformed, schematised, because inunderstood . . . . A corollary to that is that the conversation has wholly occurred and that Mr. Swaminathan is mad . . . . A second corollary is that the conversation has wholly occurred and is wholly sane but beyond the grasp of sick white reasoning.

(O:108–09)

Thus the phenomenological organization of this novel undermines the reliability of every narrative proposition in it. The result is epistemological hesitation, on the reader's part as on the protagonist's, and indeed problems of epistemology are an explicit theme throughout: "Knowledge certain or indubitable," the protagonist thinks at one point, "is unobtainable" (O:60).

As if this were not disorienting enough, a further complication arises from the fact that the events of *Out* are set in a future, dystopian world, in the aftermath, evidently, of a (nuclear?) disaster that has decimated Europe and North America. In a novel set in a version of the familiar present-day world we could rely on familiar standards of verisimilitude to decide which segments could "really" have occurred and which could not, and indeed the text seems to urge us to do just that: "It is sometimes sufficient to imagine but only within nature's possibilities" (O:22). But when the background reality is an unfamiliar future world, and when the text makes no effort to "familiarize" that future for us (which is the case here), then we are unable to rely on criteria of verisimilitude to resolve ambiguities; in effect, we do not know what "nature's possibilities" might be in this world. Thus, when the protagonist is sent for "psychoscope" treatment, evidently a form of electronic mind-reading, we cannot know whether this is subjective delusion or whether, on the contrary, psychoscopy is an extrapolated technology belonging to the background reality of this world. In other words, the science fiction premise of *Out* introduces an element of hesitation in a different dimension: ontological hesitation, hesitation over the make-up of this fictional world and the norms of verisimilitude appropriate to it.[7] Here, in this science fiction dimension of *Out*, we may discern a postmodernist cross-current or undertow in what is, nevertheless, predominantly a modernist, epistemologically-oriented novel.

Such: ". . . between one solar system and another"

What was only undertow in *Out* becomes the main current of Brooke-Rose's next novel, *Such* (1966), her first fully postmodernist fiction. Literally a text of ontological hesitation, *Such* projects a two-tier ontology, juxtaposing two incommensurable worlds – this world and the world to come – and foregrounding the boundary between them ("I draw the line as a rule between one solar system and another," (*S*:203)). Its protagonist, Larry (or Lazarus) literally "hesitates" between the two worlds: dying in our world, he experiences a bizarre, dream-like wonderland in the world to come, only to return to life after three days, strangely altered. Thereafter he "relapses" into the death-world in intervals of dream or hallucination, evidently dying a second time (but the text is ambiguous on this score) in the last sentence.

The world-to-come of *Such*, which identifies this novel as an exemplar of a characteristic postmodernist topos,[8] has a haunting familiarity, for all its strangeness – a *déjà vu* (or, better, *déjà lu*) quality, arising from its intertextual allusiveness. The presence of Lewis Carroll's *Alice* books, in particular, is strong; but more interesting for our purposes is the apparent presence of another intertext, namely that of the "Circe" chapter of Joyce's *Ulysses*. Echoes of "Circe" seem to be everywhere, in the general phantas magoric texture of Brooke-Rose's world-to-come but also in a number of specific details. For instance, Larry's first ordeal in the other world is that of having a heavy woman squat on his chest, "her huge buttocks in my face" (*S*:203), just as, in Nighttown, Bella (metamorphosed into Bello) Cohen squats on Bloom's upturned face. Similarly, Larry gives birth to, or at any rate assists at the delivery of, five children (who are also planets) with the names of classic blues songs – Dippermouth Blues, Gut Bucket Blues, Potato Head Blues, Tin Roof Blues, Really the Blues – much as Bloom fantasizes giving birth to eight miraculous children, Nasodoro, Goldfinger, Chrysostomos, Maindorée, Silversmile, Silberselber, Vifargent, and Panagyros.

There are several ways we might understand the presence (or apparent presence) of the "Circe" intertext in *Such*. One would be to argue that *Such* deliberately parodies "Circe," and that in this respect it is typically or characteristically postmodernist, exemplifying in its specific parody of Joyce the general parodic relation obtaining between postmodernist poetics and modernism (see Hutcheon 1988:124–40). This approach appears less than compelling, however, first of all on biographical grounds: Brooke-Rose, a late-comer to Joyce, denies having read *Ulysses* until *after* the publication of *Such*.[9] More to the point, perhaps, is the peculiar character of the "Circe" chapter itself, which makes it all but immune to postmodernist parody. For "Circe" is itself already a parody of modernism; it already stands in a parodic relation to the modernist poetics of the earlier chapters of *Ulysses*. "Circe," that is, is one of those chapters of Joyce's text (together with "Cyclops," "Oxen of the Sun," "Eumaeus," and "Ithaca," perhaps also "Sirens") in which Joyce seems already to have outstripped modernist poetics (including the normative modernism of other chapters of *Ulysses* itself) and to anticipate postmodernism. Thus, in appearing to allude to "Circe" (even without the author's having intended to do so!), *Such* does not so much parody "Circe" as it implies a continuity with the postmodernist strain which we are able (retrospectively) to identify in Joyce's strangely hybrid, modernist-postmodernist text.[10]

But the postmodernism of *Such* manifests itself not only at the other-world level of this novel's two-tier ontology, or in the tension between the worlds, but also at the this-worldly level. The language of the "real" world is often as bizarre as that of the phantasmagoric world-to-come; here, for instance, is how an evening of conversation among friends is rendered from the protagonist Larry's point of view:

> – Yes, look at him, says [Brenda] less remotely, and the words rebound from inside the map-like contours emanating from her, filling the room, the street no doubt, the entire sky. Their internal combustion has pushed her out of their banal untender story that throttles her . . . .
> – I meant to say something a little different, the professor says gently, or pretends to say inside the latitudes and longitudes he shows to men . . . . Despite his small eyes, one of them almost blind, the other watery, he has an undoubted presence on the screen of social intercourse that flickers its arpeggios like harp-strings up and down our subliminities. . . .
> Remote [Brenda] looks out with her naked eye, suddenly in an anguish only I can see. And Professor Head perhaps, who closes his blind eye and cocks his giant telescope to catch the radiation of the bursting galaxies. But [Stanley's] wife sips her drink and looks with glazed not naked eyes. She cannot hope for an eternal quadrangle, though she bombards the square room with the particles of a vague discontent . . . . [H]is wife's anger . . . disturbs the flickering harp-strings on the screen of social intercourse.
>
> (*S*:280–83)

How are we to understand this strange discourse which seems to dissolve "social intercourse" into interacting wave-forms or lines of force ("map-like contours," "latitudes and longitudes," "arpeggios like harp-strings," etc.)?

One approach, obviously, is to treat this language as figurative, a series of metaphors for Larry's estranged, de-familiarized experience of his fellow human beings since his "resurrection." Such metaphors might be understood to capture social intercourse "above or below the verbal level as well as within it" (*S*:213), or what people know "full well below their thoughts" (*S*:257); they capture, in other words, the level that Nathalie Sarraute calls "subconversation." Brooke-Rose herself has described Sarraute's poetics of subconversation in language that seems to echo the language of *Such*:

> These half-conscious movements and murderous impulses are viewed like organisms caught and enlarged in an electron microscope. But

the metaphoric title [*Le Planétarium*] swoops the perspective from submicroscopic to giant-telescopic, our psychic energies being implicitly seen also in terms of planets revolving around stars, galaxies receding from one another or colliding through the forces of gravitation, electromagnetism and nuclear reactions.

(Brooke-Rose 1981:324)[11]

But understanding it metaphorically is not our only option for interpreting this language. Another option is suggested, presumably by Brooke-Rose herself, in the jacket-blurb from the original edition (1966) of *Such*: Larry, runs the blurb, as a consequence of his near-death experience, "has acquired a peculiar perceptive faculty, he sees . . . people as a radio-telescope 'sees' the stars, in terms of radiation, planetary systems, the colours of the spectrum, atoms and waves of particles." In other words, however much it may formally resemble Sarraute's metaphors of subconversation, this discourse is not figurative at all, but a literal account of how Larry physically perceives others. By this reading, the discourse of *Such* converges with that of certain science fiction representations of characters who "see" the world much as Larry is said to "see" it, according to the jacket blurb. Here, for instance, is Olivia Presteign, the albino heiress of Alfred Bester's classic SF novel *Tiger! Tiger!* (1955):

> She was beautiful and blind in a wonderful way, for she could see in the infra red only, from 7,500 Angstroms to one millimeter wavelengths. She saw heat waves, magnetic fields, radio valves [*sic*], radar, sonar and electro-magnetic fields. . . . She looked like an exquisite statue of marble and coral, her blind eyes flashing as she saw and yet did not see.
> She saw the drawing-room as a pulsating flow of heat emanations ranging from hot highlights to cool shadows. She saw the dazzling magnetic patterns of clocks, phones, lights and locks. She saw and recognized people by the characteristic heat patterns radiated by their faces and bodies. She saw, around each head, an aura of the faint electro-magnetic brain pattern, and sparkling through the heat radiation of each body, the ever-changing tone of muscle and nerve.
>
> (Bester 1979:42–3)

In *Such*, says Brooke-Rose in an interview, metaphors from scientific discourse (such as, presumably, "the map-like contours emanating from her," "the radiation of the bursting galaxies," "she bombards the square room with the particles of a vague discontent," etc.) are "treated as ontological in the world of the fiction, like a sunset or a tree" (Friedman and Fuchs 1989:83.) That is, they are actualized or realized, made literal like Bester's infra-red-sighted girl, rather than left figurative like Sarraute's subconversations.

Nevertheless, we need not regard this literal reading as authoritative (despite its having been proposed by the author herself!). The alternative figurative reading continues to seem at least as plausible. In effect, we remain with two hypotheses, and no way to decide conclusively between them: real in this world, that is (as Brooke-Rose says), ontological? or figurative, a flower of rhetoric, not a flower (or tree) of reality? This is a difference of ontological status, of course, and our inability to decide between these alternatives is, as much as Larry's "hesitation" between worlds, a form of ontological hesitation.

Between: "one alleinstehende Frau"

Between (1968), as its title suggests, is another novel of hesitation, but not hesitation between worlds, or at least not between worlds in the literal sense of the term: between "worlds," one might say, but not between worlds. Its heroine, like Larry in *Such*, vacillates, not between this world and the one to come, but between the "worlds" of different cultures (that of her French mother, her German father's family, her English husband) and the disparate world-views encoded in the various languages and professional and technical discourses to which, as a simultaneous translator, she is continually exposed. In its construction of the world as plural, *Between* itself stands, we might say, somewhere between two other British novels with similar premises: on the one hand Brigid Brophy's *In Transit* (1969), which tends to actualize this plurality in an ontological direction, dissolving the unitary real into a number of competing alternative realities governed by different physical laws, observing different norms of verisimilitude, populated by beings of different orders, and so on; and on the other hand, David Lodge's *Small World* (1985), which tends on the contrary to recuperate plurality in terms of differing cultures and discourses, differing epistemologies. *Between* stands closer to the epistemological pole than the ontological one: closer, that is, to modernism than to postmodernism.

Certainly the central self around which the novel is organized, this woman poised uneasily between (or among) worlds, seems characteristically modernist: fragmented, self-divided, threatened with dispersal, perhaps on the verge of a nervous breakdown. In the course of the novel, "layers" of her past experience (the metaphor is that of a friend of hers (*B*:515)) are brought successively to light, apparently through the operation of some version of Proustian involuntary memory. An elaborate analogy is drawn with the archeological layers excavated at the site of Troy (*B*:469–70), but even more apt, and more indicative of the modernist orientation of this novel, are the intertextual allusions (e.g. *B*:548) to another "archeological" text in which successive layers of cultural memory are brought to light and fragments are shored against the ruins of the self, namely, of course, Eliot's *Waste Land*.

As in the earlier novel *Out*, the subject of consciousness has been effaced here, deprived of proper noun or pronoun; nevertheless, again as in *Out*, the entire substance of the text is attributable to her. The discourse of the text, though it seems to float free of any producer, must, we suppose, be her interior discourse. This hypothesis seems to be confirmed when, late in the novel, as the heroine approaches what apparently will be her ultimate breakdown, she begins to speak aloud in a style with which by now we are very familiar but which up until now has never appeared in directly quoted dialogue:

– Have you taken a pep pill or something?
– The stones contain the temple, cavern, sepulchre which contains one alleinstehende Frau sitting cross-legged on a prayer-rug, a miniature temple you know, prêt-à-porter, with her fingers forming a squat diamond space through which the pattern on the prayer-rug, say, blue, red, green, has no significance beyond itself. The stones contain the space and the space contains the presence of no more than centuries of mankind's need to love even eine Abwesenheit die nur eine Abwesenheit bedeutet.
– Yes, well . . . Do you feel all right? You look absolutely washed out.

(*B*:564–5)

Here for the first time the characteristic discourse of this text is explicitly connected with a personified speaker, and that speaker is its heroine. From this I think we are justified in concluding that she must have been the source of this discourse all along.

As in *Out* too, however, there is also a postmodernist undertow tugging at the predominantly modernist poetics of this novel. The entire discourse of *Between* has been shaped by a blanket constraint on the appearance of any form of the copula *to be*. Arbitrary, blanket stylistic constraints such as this one have the effect, as Brooke-Rose herself explains, of making the "physical signifier . . . more physical, the signified less important" (Friedman and Fuchs 1989:84). Or, in other words, they serve to foreground the disparity and asymmetry between the textual stratum of language and the stratum of the world projected by the text, i.e., such a constraint foregrounds the ontological structure of the text itself. Ontologically speaking, the make-up of the fictional world is always subordinate to the shape of the language that projects it, but in cases like that of the arbitrary exclusion of all *to be* forms (or of the letter *e* in Georges Perec's *La disparition*, 1969), this subordination is made conspicuous. Here language visibly has the upper hand, occupying a position of clear ontological "strength" or superiority relative to the fictional world (cf. McHale 1987:148). This is a strategy which Brooke-Rose shares not only with Perec but with others of his OuLiPo circle (Queneau, Calvino, Mathews *et al.*; see Motte 1986) and other postmodernists as well; it is, in short, a characteristic postmodernist strategy.

Nevertheless, as Brooke-Rose herself acknowledges, this global constraint on the language of *Between* has by and large escaped the notice of its readers (Brooke Rose 1989:103).[12] It is, one might say, a subliminal constraint, or perhaps a constitutive constraint, that is, one valuable for the writer in the process of composition but on the whole invisible or irrelevant to the reader. In effect, the dominant modernist poetics of *Between* overrides and eclipses its constitutive postmodernist strategy for everyone except the author (and the occasional prying narratologist).

Thru: "Danger. You are now entering the Metalinguistic Zone"

The case for reading *Between* as a modernist novel is strengthened if one turns to Brooke-Rose's next novel, *Thru* (1975). For *Thru* is in a sense what *Between* would look like if it were fully "postmodernized." Two examples will have to suffice to illustrate this relation. First, intertextual allusions: in *Between* these occur either in the direct speech of the protagonist or her interlocutors (e.g. the allusion to *The Waste Land* mentioned above) or, more ambiguously, in the protagonist's thoughts. That is, such allusions have an entirely *discursive* status – they belong to the level of language, whether interior or exterior – and their immediate source (not, of course, their ultimate intertextual source) is located *within* the fictional world of *Between*, in the mouths or minds of the novel's characters. Not so in *Thru*, where intertextual allusions (e.g. to Diderot's *Jacques le fataliste* and Coleridge's "Kubla Khan") are frequent, and their status and level paradoxical or indeterminate. Jacques and his Master, for instance, appear first (*T*:591) in a "free-floating" quotation from Diderot – "free-floating" in the sense that one cannot attribute it to the spoken or interior discourse of any particular character or narrator – only to return a few pages later (*T*:595) as characters not of *Jacques le fataliste* but of *Thru*. They belong, that is, to the *world*, and not just the *discourse*, of *Thru*; or rather, they belong to *one* of its worlds, for evidently they do not share the same world with the other characters of *Thru*, with whom they never interact. In other words, intertextual figures such as Jacques and his Master, or the "man from Porlock" (a quasi-fictional "character" from the notorious prefatory note to Coleridge's "Kubla Khan"), are not entirely discursive in *Thru* as they were in *Between*, but manage to obtain an ontological foothold here.

This is more radical than it sounds, for when one plagiarizes (or, more politely, "appropriates") a character from another text, that character comes trailing fragments of its own world, the world of its "home" text. To introduce realized intertextual characters in this way is to violate the norm of textual-ontological unity (one text/one world), in effect producing an ontologically composite or heterogeneous text, one that mingles or straddles worlds. It produces, in short, a characteristically postmodernist text in which multiple worlds coexist in uneasy tension.[13]

A second example is the relative status of metalanguage in *Between* on the one hand and *Thru* on the other. In *Between*, metalanguage, language about language, is firmly lodged within the fictional world: it appears, for instance, in the professional discourse of the linguists and semioticians whose conference lectures it is the protagonist's job to translate (*B*:426 and *passim*). Metalanguage plays a similar role in *Thru*, where it occurs as the professional discourse attributed, realistically enough, to characters who happen to be university lecturers in narratology and poetics. Here, however, unlike in *Between*, such metalinguistic discourse refuses to "stay put": it keeps jumping levels, shifting or slipping from the characters' pedagogical discourse about other texts (*Tristram Shandy*, *La Princesse de Clèves* or what-have-you) to metafictional discourse about *this* text, about *Thru* itself. Relative to this higher-level metalanguage, the characters themselves, what they do and say, and the world in which they do and say it have all been reduced to the status of discursive artifacts, ontologically "weaker" than the higher-level discourse of which they are themselves no longer the sources but merely the objects. It is this disorienting freedom of metalanguage in *Thru* to jump out of the fictional world to an ontologically superior level that gives point to the joke someone proposes during a classroom discussion: "There should be placards saying: Danger. You are now entering the Metalinguistic Zone" (*T*:629).

There are no such placards in *Thru*, whether to warn us of the presence of metalanguage or to signal the other forms of ontological instability that make reading this text so disorienting an experience. For throughout this text a similar instability of status and reversibility of level infects nearly every narratological category we normally rely on for novelistic coherence and legibility: character, narration, space, time, event, etc. *Thru* displays the full postmodernist repertoire of destabilizing strategies, including self-contradiction; the placing of episodes or descriptions "under erasure"; so-called "strange loops"; *trompe-l'oeil* effects, such as "demoting" an event, character or object to a lower narrative level or, conversely, "promoting" one to a higher level; *mise-en-abyme*; irresolution or hesitation between mutually-exclusive alternative scenarios; and so on (see Rimmon-Kenan 1982:21–32; McHale 1987:99–130). *Thru*, in other words, is a text of radical ontological hesitation: a paradigmatic postmodernist novel.

FROM *AMALGAMEMNON* TO *VERBIVORE*: AS IF SF

It would have been convenient, as far as the present narrative of the zigs and zags of Brooke-Rose's career is concerned, if she had ceased writing fiction after *Thru*. Inconveniently enough, after a nine-year hiatus she resumed, publishing three more novels and promising a fourth to round out a projected "computer quartet." Brooke-Rose's "third career" appears to be both continuous and discontinuous with her second, as her second was with her first. How, if at all, are we to accommodate this third career of hers to the story thus far?

Amalgamemnon: "as if"

The first obstacle to be surmounted is *Amalgamemnon* (1984), the inaugural novel of this new phase, and the least tractable of the three that have appeared to date. It is perhaps the only one of Brooke-Rose's novels that properly deserves to be called "experimental" – not "experimental" as book-reviewers typically use that term (namely, as a dismissive label for any innovative or unconventional writing whatsoever (see Johnson 1973:19–20; Sukenick 1985a:47–8)), but experimental in a stricter sense, for in this novel in particular Brooke-Rose seems to be reconnoitering for new possibilities, new materials, new discourses, a new way forward. Yet, at the same time that it is experimental in this sense, *Amalgamemnon* also recapitulates the four preceding novels, from *Out* to *Thru*, echoing certain elements of their plots and fictional situations. For instance, the basic situation of *Amalgamemnon* is that of a humanist scholar, a university lecturer in classics, made redundant by the shift of university priorities to the training of scientists and technologists. Her situation recalls those of *Such*, *Between*, and even (in a few episodes) *Thru*, in all of which a person trained in the humanities is forced to come to terms with, and to "eavesdrop" on, scientists and their discourses. There is also the recurrent erotic situation of the heroine's being courted by an inappropriate, importunate suitor; in *Amalgamemnon*, as in *Between*, the suitor is older than the heroine, while in *Thru* the ages are reversed and the suitor is younger (but just as inappropriate).

More significantly, *Amalgamemnon* exploits in a conspicuous way the discourses of science and technology, as did all four of the "second career" novels.[14] In *Out*, it is the discourse of chemistry that is exploited in this way; in *Such*, that of astrophysics; in *Between* a whole range of technical discourse and jargons, including genetics, linguistics, and structural anthropology; in *Thru* it is the quasi-scientific discourse of narratology; and in *Amalgamemnon*, the discourse of computer science (see below).

Finally, like *Between*, *Amalgamemnon* has been composed subject to a blanket stylistic constraint, not, as in *Between*, a ban on the copula *to be*, but rather a blanket obligation for all verbs (including those uttered by characters in direct discourse) to appear in some "nonrealizing" form (tense or mood): future, conditional, hypothetical, etc.[15] Similar hypothetical or speculative passages appear in *Out* and *Between*, but in both these texts they are readily recuperated as projections or fantasies of the respective protagonists, and hence not incorporated into the reader's reconstruction of the text's "real world": they are, in effect, edited out of the reality-picture. Such a recuperation is not available in the case of *Amalgamemnon*, for here everything, including the narrator-protagonist herself, is framed by this hypothetical-speculative mode, so there are no grounds either for editing any particular sequence or detail out of the reality-picture or, for that matter, for including it. Thus, this blanket constraint has radical ontological consequences: in effect, the entire world of *Amalgamemnon* – its narrator, characters, events, time and space, etc. – dangles in ontological limbo, subject to an implicit (and sometimes explicit) "as if."[16] It is, in short, like *Thru*, a paradigmatic postmodernist novel of ontological hesitation.

Is *Amalgamemon*, then, merely recapitulative, a recycling of materials and strategies from the *Omnibus*, a mere appendix or coda to Brooke-Rose's second career? This is indeed the way it is likely to appear if one reads through Brooke-Rose's *oeuvre* in chronological order, starting with the novels collected in the *Omnibus* and moving on from them to *Amalgamemnon*; but the picture changes significantly if one reads in reverse, so to speak, looking back at *Amalgamemnon* from the perspective of Brooke-Rose's latest novel, *Verbivore* (1990).

For *Verbivore* is a sequel to *Amalgamemnon*, and exploits the ontological effects that are possible when characters from an earlier text by the same author return in a sequel. These effects, familiar from realist (e.g., Balzac) and modernist (e.g. Faulkner) as well as postmodernist poetics (e.g. Barth, Pynchon), arise because characters who exist "between" texts, intertextually, seem to approach the ontological status of beings who exist "outside" texts, in the real world. In the case of the intertextual relations between *Verbivore* and *Amalgamemon*, this effect is intensified, because the characters who return in *Verbivore* (Mira Enketei, Perry Hupsos, Nelson Nwankwo) never fully "existed" in their "home" text in the first place: that is, their status there was relativized and in a sense weakened by the blanket "as if" mode that governs the whole of *Amalgamemnon*. Thus, by bringing these characters back sequel-fashion, *Verbivore* has the effect of *actualizing* them retroactively. It is as if these characters, ontologically so enfeebled by their "native" context, somehow acquired a degree of ontological robustness "between" texts, in the passage from their home text to its sequel.

Xorandor: SF

But *Verbivore* is not a sequel to *Amalgamemnon* alone; it also functions as a sequel to the intervening text, *Xorandor* (1986), a novel generically quite distinct from the two that flank it. For *Xorandor* is Brooke-Rose's science-fiction novel.[17] Not only does *Xorandor* exploit SF motifs, it does

so in full awareness of their ontological consequences. SF is a self-consciously ontological or "world-building" genre, juxtaposing (sometimes
explicitly, sometimes only implicitly) the world of contemporary reality
with an alternative world that differs from it in certain specified ways.
What differentiates the *Xorandor* world from contemporary reality is, of
course, the presence of silicon-based intelligences, computer-rocks, and
Brooke-Rose uses the computer-rock motif not only to build up a new
(fictional) reality but, even more conspicuously, to "solve" certain formal
problems. There is, for instance, the problem of how to maintain the
limited point of view of the two child-narrators while at the same time
supplying information not directly accessible to them but essential if the
reader is to understand the scope of the crisis precipitated by the computer-rocks. The computer-rock motif itself yields a solution: the smaller
computer-rocks are present, as exhibits, at the conferences where high-
level scientific and governmental policies not otherwise accessible to the
narrators are being debated; "eavesdropping" on these conferences, the
rocks transmit what they "overhear" to their parent-rock, Xorandor itself,
who in turn communicates them to the child-narrators, who transcribe
them in the text we are reading. In a similar way, as Martin (1989:120–1)
has observed, the narrators' use of computer memory and tapes solves the
"age-old problem of the perfect recall of the narrator who is limited by
age or education." In both these case, in other words, SF novelties – an
absolute novelty in the case of the computer-rocks, a relative one in the
case of the narrators' use of tapes and computers – serve to motivate
formal solutions to problems of access to and circulation of information:
ontological propositions affecting the make-up of the extrapolated world
"solve" epistemological problems.[18]

Verbivore "revives" characters and situations from *Xorandor* as well as
from *Amalgamemnon*, integrating them all in the same fictional world. As
the joint sequel to both *Amalgamemnon* and *Xorandor*, *Verbivore* in effect
folds together in the same text the postmodernist poetics of the one
and the SF poetics of the other, the postmodernist "as if" ontology of
Amalgamemnon and the extrapolated SF near-future world of *Xorandor*.
Now, this mingling of the *Amalgamemnon* and *Xorandor* worlds in the
world of its joint sequel recoils upon *Amalgamemnon* itself. Reading in
reverse, looking back at *Amalgamemnon* from the perspective of *Verbivore*, we are compelled to see the postmodernist poetics of *Amalgamemnon* as converging with the SF poetics of *Xorandor*; we are compelled to
see *Amalgamemnon*, retrospectively, as somehow potentially compatible
with SF, "as if SF."

At the interface

In what ways, then, does *Amalgamemnon* converge with SF poetics? First of all, and most superficially, in certain elements of content. A major *topos* of modern SF is of course apocalypse, man-made or natural, and its aftermath; indeed, it may well be SF's larger function in our culture to equip us with tools (imagery, typologies, scenarios) for rehearsing in imagination the otherwise unimaginable prospect of our collective end.[19] *Xorandor* is in part a thriller about a nuclear disaster narrowly averted, and thus belongs to this SF topos; while *Out*, it will be recalled, is based on the premise of a post-apocalypse world of survivors. *Amalgamemnon*, too, has an apocalyptic element, but here the perspective is pre- rather than post-apocalypse. The narrator anxiously anticipates nuclear or environmental disaster, and her anxieties are continually fed and confirmed by alarming radio news broadcasts: "in a little while the voice will announce the end of the World News" (Brooke-Rose 1984:11).

Anticipation has often been claimed as the special province of SF, so there is a sense in which the grammar of anticipation in *Amalgamemnon* – its future tenses and hypothetical and conditional moods – relates it to SF poetics. Actually, of course, as Brooke-Rose herself several times remarks, SF does not normally resort to future-tense narration, almost always opting for the "epic preterite," the "postdated" narrative tense of conventional novel-writing.[20] In this respect, then, *Amalgamemnon* literalizes, in the futurity and conditionality of its grammatical forms, what is in effect only figuratively future and conditional or hypothetical in "normal" SF, *Xorandor* included.

Above all, however, it is the presence of computer-science discourse in *Amalgamemnon* that enables one to see it as converging with SF. In the context of *Amalgamemnon* itself, this discourse is only one, albeit a conspicuous one, in the "amalgam" that also includes, for instance, discourses of myth and history persisting from the classical world (Herodotus), discourses of broadcast news and entertainment, and so on. Here cybernetics serves mainly as a rich source of metaphors and puns; in the transition from *Amalgamemnon* to *Xorandor* it is promoted to the dominant discourse in the text. Substantial passages of *Xorandor* are cast in an invented programming language, Poccom, while the language of the novel's joint narrators is saturated with computer-oriented slang and figures of speech.[21] If *Amalgamemnon* is properly regarded as an "experimental" novel it is in this respect, namely, in its function as a necessary first stage in the development of the new cybernetic style that would only emerge fully in *Xorandor*.

From this perspective, reading in reverse chronological order, *Amalgamemnon* thus appears as a member of a class of postmodernist texts that have developed on a track parallel to recent developments in SF proper.

So ubiquitous is SF in contemporary culture that it would be hard to say that this type of postmodernism is entirely free from direct SF influence; nevertheless, I want to insist on the notion of parallel and independent development because for the most part these texts set out from a different starting-point, operate with a different poetics, yet converge with contemporary SF preoccupations and motifs. We might call this type of postmodernism "interface fiction," for it arises from the confrontation between the discourses and world-view of those trained in the humanities (including most writers of fiction) and the new computer technologies and their discourses.[22] Examples include Russell Hoban's *The Medusa Frequency* (1987), James McConkey's *Kayo* (1987), William Vollmann's *You Bright and Risen Angels* (1987), even Umberto Eco's *Pendolo di Foucault* (1988) – and of course, as we are now in a position to see, Christine Brooke-Rose's *Amalgamemnon*, *Xorandor* and *Verbivore*.[23]

Thus Brooke-Rose's computer trilogy (and, I think we can assume, the full "quartet" once it is completed) intricately mingles the poetics of demanding, "advanced," "elite" postmodernist fiction and the poetics of popular "genre" writing, namely SF. A parallel development has emerged in SF proper during the 1980s, in the form of a new "wave" of SF writing, so-called "cyberpunk" SF, which intricately mingles "advanced" postmodernist poetics and familiar SF motifs and topoi, but on the "popular" side of the elite-art/popular-art divide.

In this respect, the novels of Brooke-Rose's "third career," from *Amalgamemnon* to *Verbivore*, constitute another, different counter-book to the two incomplete books which served as my starting-point. In *A Rhetoric of the Unreal*, Brooke-Rose, apart from telling the unfinished story of the persistence of the hesitation principle from the classic fantastic to postmodernism, also began a story about the convergence of "popular" SF and "elite" avant-garde fiction; but this narrative, too, was left unfinished.[24] The trajectory of convergence which she sketched there is the very trajectory traced, and completed, by her own novels from *Amalgamemon* to *Verbivore*. Similarly, in *Postmodernist Fiction* I suggested a relation of complementarity and mutual influence between "elite" postmodernism and "popular" SF, but my narrative of the dynamics of change from modernism to postmodernism, fixated on high-art forms, left no room for the dynamics of *interchange* between elite and popular art-forms. The case of Brooke-Rose's computer trilogy compels me to revise my story to make room for the traffic, already heavy and sure to be heavier in the future, across this elite/popular divide.

Part IV

At the interface

Chapter 10

POSTcyberMODERNpunkISM[1]

A reader in search of a reliable and authoritative account of contemporary fiction in the United States, turning to the relevant chapter in the *Columbian Literary History of the United States* (1988), would find there an essay in which no fewer than seven out of twenty-two tightly-budgeted paragraphs were devoted to science fiction (SF), including, conspicuously, the fiction of the so-called "cyberpunk" SF novelist William Gibson. According to the *Columbia Literary History*, science fiction is "arguably the most significant body of work in contemporary fiction," and its "emergence . . . as a major literary genre" is among the "most significant new directions in recent American fiction" (McCaffery 1988b:1167, 1162.) The *Columbia Literary History* represents, if not a breakthrough, then at least a striking advance in the process of science fiction's legitimation. What explains this new "official" acceptability of SF? The present essay proposes a partial answer to this question. It aims to describe, not all of the conditions for the current legitimation of SF, many of which are institutional, but only one of the *necessary* conditions, namely what might be called the condition of *aesthetic contemporaneity*.

CROSS THE BORDER? CLOSE THAT GAP?

Larry McCaffery, author of the chapter on "The Fictions of the Present" in the *Columbia Literary History*, explains SF's new legitimacy in terms of the alleged collapse of hierarchical distinctions between high and low art, between "official" high culture and popular or mass culture, in the postmodern period. This is one of the most potent myths of postmodernist culture and cultural critique (see Jameson 1983, 1991a:2–3; Huyssen 1986), and one that postmodernist writers themselves (including SF writers) seem to find irresistibly attractive. For instance, the cyberpunk novelist William Gibson unreservedly endorses this myth in an interview with McCaffery: "This process of cultural mongrelization," he tells McCaffery, "seems to be what postmodernism is all about . . . . I know I don't have a sense of writing being divided up into different *compartments*" (McCaffery 1990b:132–3).

Nevertheless, it would be easy to demonstrate that not only Gibson's own writing but cyberpunk SF in general relies on the continuing viability of cultural compartmentalization. Without such "compartments" there is no possibility of incongruity, and cyberpunk in general, and Gibson's fiction in particular, functions at every level, down to the "micro" structures of phrases and neologisms, on the principle of incongruous juxtaposition – of American culture with Japanese culture, high tech with low tech, the dominant "official" culture with youth and criminal subcultures, and so on. Indeed, the very term "cyberpunk" itself (evidently coined by the SF critic Gardner Dozois) exemplifies this incongruity principle.

In fact, of course, the myth of the collapse of hierarchical distinctions in postmodern culture is just that, a myth, and the institutions for the production, distribution, and consumption of high culture continue to be distinct from those for popular culture, regardless of whatever promiscuous minglings of cultural strata may occur *inside* certain texts (see Kaplan 1988b:4). Moreover, the thesis of postmodernism's effacement of the "great divide" between high and low culture depends for much of its potency and persuasiveness on a particularly tendentious construction of modernism, one designed to throw into high relief the novelty and difference of postmodernism. Historical "high modernism," by this account, sought to seal high culture off from "contamination" by mass culture (see Huyssen 1986). A little reflection will show, however, the degree to which even the most self-assertively "artistic" modernist writers exploited popular-art models and genres, and not just by ironically quoting or parodying them. In Anglo-American modernism, think of Henry James's reliance on melodrama and romance, or Conrad's on adventure-story models; Faulkner's exploitation of historical "costume" romance, detective fiction, horror stories, pornography, and just about every other currently available popular-art genre; and the almost universal impact of cinematic models and strategies, especially in the United States (Hemingway, Faulkner, Dos Passos, Fitzgerald, Nathanael West; in Britain, Graham Greene, etc.).

This is not to say that there is no significant difference between modernism and postmodernism on this issue, for of course there is, but it is mainly a difference of their respective self-descriptions: where the modernists repudiated and sought to camouflage their reliance on popular-art models, the postmodernists have tended openly to advertise theirs. But we must try not to confuse cultural polemics with actual practice.

Moreover, the constant traffic between low and high – the high-art appropriation of popular-art models, and the reciprocal assimilation by popular-art genres of "cast-off" high-art models – far from being a distinctive feature of the postmodern period is one of the universal engines driving the history of literary (and, more generally, cultural) forms. What is distinctive of postmodernism is not the fact of "contamination" of high culture by mass culture but rather the technologically-enhanced speed of the traffic in models between the high and low strata of culture. Popular-art models are assimilated by high art (and vice-versa) more quickly now than ever before; and this has the further consequence of producing an ever more intimate interaction, an ever-tighter feedback loop, between high and low. Such speed and intimacy of interaction is not, however, to be confused with the collapse or effacement of hierarchical distinctions. For the engine to continue to turn over the high culture/low culture distinction must persist, in however problematic or attenuated a form.[2]

FEEDBACK IN THE LITERARY SYSTEM

Science fiction is a case in point. It has been over a decade now since critics first began to note the "convergence" or "cross-fertilization" between recent science fiction and "serious" or "mainstream" postmodern-ist fiction (e.g. Ebert 1980; Mathieson 1985; McHale 1987:59–72).[3] How-ever, so steadily has the tempo of this interaction accelerated from decade to decade that at the same time critics were beginning to notice this phenomenon the youngest generation of SF writers, the so-called cyber-punks, were both corroborating and preempting the critics. In any case, the trajectory of convergence can now be extended through the 1980s.

In order to describe the systemic relations relevant to SF's situation through the 1980s we need, minimally and in a preliminary way, to draw two categorial distinctions: first, between SF, as one of the species of so-called "genre" fiction (other species include, e.g., detective fiction, horror fiction, women's romance fiction, and so on), and what SF writers and critics themselves call "mainstream" fiction, i.e. canonical literary fiction;[4] and, secondly, within the "mainstream" category, between its conservative (norm-observing) wing and its "advanced" or "innovative" or "state-of-the-art" (norm-violating) wing. These are certainly not the only distinc-tions that would have to be made in a fully-developed account of the literary system (see Even-Zohar 1990a), but they are adequate to the more limited purposes of the present essay.[5]

In the earliest phases of modern SF history, from its re-emergence in the 1920s through the 1940s, SF and mainstream fiction existed in mutual isolation from one another. Modern SF crystallized and developed as a sub- or paraliterary "ghetto" enclave, largely out of touch with contempor-ary mainstream fiction, just as the latter was in turn largely unaware of and unresponsive to SF. The first important inter-species contacts occurred in the 1950s, with the "leveling-up" of SF's stylistic norms to something approaching those of conservative mainstream fiction. Heinlein, Asimov, Clarke, Sturgeon, Bester and others of their generation modeled their prose style, narrative strategies, etc., on the poetics of bestseller fiction (itself a "trickle-down" version of the poetics of mainstream "art" fiction), while, reciprocally, a few mainstream bestseller writers (e.g. Nevil Shute) began occasionally to adopt typical SF motifs, themes and materials. It is partly due to the success of the SF novelists of this generation that the poetics of the leveling-up phase has come to be perceived (not entirely accurately) as the SF genre norm (see Brooke-Rose 1981:72–102).

Interaction between SF and advanced or state-of-the-art mainstream fiction does not, however, begin until the next phase, in the 1960s and early 1970s, with so-called "New Wave" SF and the first wave of postmodernist mainstream fiction. While SF of the "New Wave" of the 1960s and early 1970s does begin to absorb models from state-of-the-art mainstream fiction, it seeks its models not in contemporary state-of-the-art fiction (e.g. Heller, Hawkes, Pynchon, the *nouveau roman*) but in that of an earlier generation of advanced mainstream writing. That is, SF of the "New Wave" generation finds its mainstream models in high-modernist fiction: J.G. Ballard in Conrad, Philip J. Farmer in Joyce, John Brunner in Dos Passos, Thomas Disch in Mann, and so on. Similarly, advanced mainstream fiction in the 1960s and early 1970s (e.g. Burroughs, Vonnegut, Pynchon, Calvino), while it does begin to draw on SF for materials, themes, imagery, etc., draws not on SF in its contemporary phase but in an earlier phase of its development: the dated SF of pulp-magazine "space opera," superhero comics, SF disaster and monster movies, and so on. Thus, there is a peculiar relation of *nonsynchronization* between SF and advanced mainstream fiction in this period, with each reflecting an *outdated* phase of the other.[6]

Only in the course of the 1970s do SF and postmodernist mainstream fiction really become one another's contemporaries, aesthetically as well as chronologically, with each finally beginning to draw on the current phase of the other, rather than on some earlier and now dated phase. It is during this period, beginning in the late 1960s (e.g., Aldiss's *Report on Probability A*, 1968; Dick's *Ubik*, 1969; Ballard's *The Atrocity Exhibition*, 1969) and continuing through the 1970's and into the early 1980s (e.g. Samuel Delany's "big" novels of the period, *Dhalgren*, 1974; *Triton*, 1976; and *Stars in My Pocket Like Grains of Sand*, 1984) that we start to encounter SF incorporating elements of postmodernist poetics. Reciprocally, it is during this phase that postmodernist texts can first be seen to incorporate contemporary SF motifs and materials, beginning with, say, Angela Carter's *Heroes and Villains* (1969) and Nabokov's *Ada* (1970) and continuing down to Alasdair Gray's *Lanark* (1981), Raymond Federman's *The Twofold Vibration* (1982), John Fowles's *A Maggot* (1985), Christine Brooke-Rose's *Xorandor* (1986) and beyond.[7]

As this phase of the interaction prolongs itself into the 1980s, a feedback loop begins to operate between SF and postmodernist fiction. That is, we find postmodernist texts absorbing materials from SF texts that have already been"postmodernized" to some degree through contact with mainstream postmodernist poetics. Reciprocally, we find SF texts that incorporate models drawn from postmodernist fiction that has already been "science-fictionized" to some degreee through its contact with SF poetics. Thus certain elements can be identified as having cycled from SF to mainstream postmodernism and back to SF again, or in the opposite direction, from mainstream fiction to SF and back to the mainstream again. It is this latest phase of the interaction between SF and postmodernist fiction that, on the SF end of the feedback loop, has acquired the label of "cyberpunk" SF.

Cyberpunk SF can thus be seen, in this systemic perspective, as *SF which derives certain of its elements from postmodernist mainstream fiction which itself has, in its turn, already been "science-fictionized" to some greater or lesser degree.*

IN THE LOOP (1): POSTMODERNISM RECYCLED AS CYBERPUNK

The cycling of materials between cyberpunk SF and postmodernist mainstream fiction can be observed at either end of the feedback loop; but let's begin at the cyberpunk end.

The fiction of the cyberpunk school (if that's what it is; see below, "Towards a poetics of cyberpunk") draws heavily, as the cyberpunk novelists themselves freely admit, on the motifs, models, and styles of certain postmodernist mainstream writers who have themselves already exploited the models, motifs and imagery of earlier SF writing. The two examples that no-one ever fails to mention in this context are William Burroughs and Thomas Pynchon, their traces are everywhere in cyberpunk writing.

Burroughs

Indicative of Burroughs's place in the feedback loop is the itinerary that one of his titles traces from SF to postmodernism and back again. A 1979 Burroughs text in the form of a film script bears the title *Blade Runner (a Movie)*. On his copyright page, Burroughs acknowledges his title's ultimate source in a science fiction novel by Alan E. Nourse, *The Blade Runner*. Ridley Scott, of course, subsequently appropriated the title for what is undoubtedly the most influential example of cyberpunk poetics in any medium, his film version, not of Burroughs's text, but of Philip K. Dick's SF novel *Do Androids Dream of Electric Sheep?* Burroughs is duly acknowledged in the film's credits, but *not* Nourse. Thus, beginning its career in the SF genre, the title *Blade Runner* cycles through postmodernism and back to SF again (though its earlier identity as an SF title seems to have fallen victim to Hollywood's notorious lack of historical memory).

Meanwhile, the title *Blade Runner* having been appropriated for other uses, the narrative motif to which it had originally been attached has pursued its own independent itinerary through the feedback loop. Nourse's *The Blade Runner* concerns the smuggling of contraband medical supplies in a dystopian future world in which access to medical care is restricted. It is this motif that Burroughs takes over in his text (along with Nourse's title), subjecting it to his characteristically postmodernist manipulations, e.g. fragmenting the story-line and intercutting it with unrelated segments, introducing secondary "nested" representations, changing narrative levels, etc. The plot motif that began as Nourse's and then became Burroughs's, that of medical smuggling and outlaw doctors in a plague-stricken city of the future, eventually reappears in a recycled form in Richard Kadrey's cyberpunk SF novel *Metrophage* (1988). It would be hard to prove that Kadrey had been specifically aware of the rather obscure Burroughs text from which his motif seems to have derived, but this in any case is not the interesting point. For, whether or not he was familiar with *Blade Runner (a Movie)* in particular, Kadrey is demonstrably aware of Burroughs' texts and motifs in general, and could readily have "reconstructed" what we might call the "blade runner" motif from other elements of Burroughs's repertoire.[8]

Another Burroughs motif, or motif complex, that pursues a similar itinerary through the feedback loop is that of the "lost civilization." Appearing early in Burroughs's fiction (see, e.g. "The Mayan Caper" in *The Soft Machine*, 1961) and persisting in various forms throughout his career, the "lost civilization" motif, too, like the "blade runner" motif, originates in SF – or, rather, it is the common property of pulp-magazine SF and some of the other "pulp" genres adjacent to it ("weird" tales, jungle-adventure thrillers, etc.). Its elements, in Burroughs's version of it, include an ancient civilization "lost" somewhere in the jungles of Central or South America; a tyrannical priestly caste that dominates the populace through thought-control; drug use; exotic religious and sexual practices; etc. Burroughs assembles his version of the motif from materials he could have found in such places as H. Rider Haggard's jungle romances or the Tarzan series of the *other* novelist Burroughs, Edgar Rice, then literally manipulates these materials, cutting them up and folding them in to produce a "postmodernized" version of pulp SF. When the "lost civilization" motif resurfaces in the 1980s in cyberpunk SF (e.g. Bruce Sterling's "Spook," 1983; Lucius Shepard's *Life During Wartime*, 1987; Lewis Shiner's *Deserted Cities of the Heart*, 1988), the version we find there is not the original pulp-SF version but the "postmodernized" one – Burroughs's version, in short. These cyberpunk treatments of the motif have Burroughs's fingerprints all over them; his characteristic obsessions and emphases – thought-control, drugs, weird sex, etc. – are there to be traced in the cyberpunk texts. Here, then, we have a clear case of the circulation of motifs from SF sources back to SF again by way of a postmodernist intermediary.[9]

Pynchon

Thomas Pynchon's position in the feedback loop between SF and post-modernist fiction is, if anything, even more crucial than Burroughs's. The presence of Pynchon's texts, *Gravity's Rainbow* (1973) in particular, is pervasive in cyberpunk fiction at all levels, from the minutest verbal details right up to the paranoid world-view and conspiracy theory of history characteristic of most cyberpunk fictional worlds. So ubiquitous is the Pynchon presence in cyberpunk that only a fraction of the evidence for it can be mentioned here.

Of all the traces of Pynchon's presence, the least equivocal are verbal echoes of names and coinages from Pynchon's texts, which may even function in their new context as direct allusions to their source in Pynchon. Thus, for instance, Pynchon is the source for the name of the fictional plastic, "Imipolex G," in Rucker's *Software* (1982) and *Wetware* (1988), as well as the names of two of the industrial cartels, "Yoyodyne" and "Pointsman Pharmaceuticals A.G.," in Williams's *Hardwired* (1986). In the same Williams text, the neologistic phrase "riding the eye-face," i.e. operating a machine (automobile, aircraft) through the interface (I-face) between one's own nervous system and the machine's electronics, proves also to have been a Pynchon coinage (see Pynchon 1973:731).

More equivocal are various motifs which, though not necessarily derived from Pynchon directly, nevertheless have strong Pynchon associations because of the frequency and salience of their occurrence in his texts. One example is the motif of the slowly turning face, a recurrent gesture of nightmarish menace and dread throughout *Gravity's Rainbow* (e.g. Pynchon 1973:22, 142–3, 196, 222, 635, 714; see above, " 'You used to know what these words mean' "). The nightmarish turning face reappears, for instance, in Cadigan's *Synners* (1991:89, 335) and, with associated details even more strongly reminiscent of Pynchon, in Shepard's *Life During Wartime* (1987). Here the averted face belongs to a helicopter pilot who can never remove his flight helmet because he is literally wired into it:

> As the pilot completed the bank, a ray of sun slanted into the cockpit, illuminating the copilot's visor, and for a split second Mingolla could make out the vague shadow of the face beneath. It seemed lumpy and malformed. His imagination added details. Bizarre growths, cracked cheeks, an eye webbed shut. Like a face out of a movie about nuclear mutants.
>
> (Shepard 1987:89–90; and cf. 5–7)

Now compare Pynchon:

The pilot is turning to Rószavölgyi, who is still strapped in safety harness behind him. The face is covered with helmet, goggles that reflect too much light, oxygen mask – a face of metal, leather, isinglass. But now the pilot is raising the goggles, slowly, and whose eyes are these, so familiar, smiling hello, I know you, don't you know me? Don't you *really* know me?

(Pynchon 1973:635)

Pynchon would also seem to have supplied the models for a number of specific episodes in various cyberpunk texts. Examples include Bobby Newmark's queasy epiphany in an empty nightclub in Gibson's *Count Zero* (1987b:163), which seems to have been modeled on a similar epiphany that comes to Slothrop in an empty gambling casino (Pynchon 1973:202–3), and the disgusting dinner-table conversation, intended to discourage enemies seated at the same table, in Swanwick's *Vacuum Flowers* (1987:153), which recalls a similar tactic in *Gravity's Rainbow* (1973:715–17). Other cyberpunk texts seem to echo *The Crying of Lot 49*: the episode of sex with the television on in Sterling's *Islands in the Net* (1988:324) recalls similar scenes in *Lot 49* (1967:25–7, 79), just as the episode of the "smart bomb" caroming around a room in Rucker's *Wetware* (1988:128–9) echoes Pynchon's runaway can of hairspray (1967:22–3).

Finally, at the most general level of textual organization, it is tempting to speculate on the degree to which Pynchon's plots might have served as models for the main story-lines of various cyberpunk texts. For instance, Slothrop's inconclusive quest for the truth of his own origins might be suspected of having served as a model for Shepard's *Life During Wartime* and Williams's *Voice of the Whirlwind* (1987), while it is rather Oedipa's quest in *The Crying of Lot 49* that seems to underlie Sterling's *Islands in the Net*.

The ubiquity, but also elusiveness, of Pynchon's intertextual presence in cyberpunk might aptly be symbolized by a single one of its instances, involving a verbal echo that is at one and the same time almost subliminal and, once one's attention has been drawn to it, seemingly incontrovertible. That echo occurs in a sentence which has already in a few short years acquired an intertextual history of citation and imitation of its own, so that it has come to be identified as a kind of stylistic touchstone of cyberpunk. I am thinking of the opening sentence of Gibson's path-breaking cyberpunk novel *Neuromancer*: "The sky above the port was the color of television, tuned to a dead channel" (Gibson 1984:3).[10] On one level, this sentence signals Gibson's affiliation with postmodernism in general, for the figurative association of television with death ("a dead channel") has become something of a topos of postmodernist fiction (see above, "Zapping, the art of switching channels"). More specifically, however, one seems to hear somewhere behind this sentence the distant echo of another sentence from the first page of a different book. Here, too, death and television are juxtaposed, for the sentence I have in mind is the one in which, having just learned of the death of a former lover and her own appointment as executrix of his will: "Oedipa stood in the living room, stared at by the dead eye of the TV tube, [and] spoke the name of God" (Pynchon 1967:1).

The putative relationship between these two sentences captures the paradox of Pynchon's relation to cyberpunk in general. On the one hand, echoes of Pynchon's texts can seemingly be detected everywhere in cyberpunk; but on the other hand, apart from a few incontrovertible verbal allusions (Imipolex G, Yoyodyne, riding the eye-face, etc.), these alleged "echoes" might just as plausibly derive from the general postmodernist intertextual network, in which both Pynchon and the cyberpunks participate, as from Pynchon's texts in particular. If Pynchon is at one and the same time everywhere and nowhere in cyberpunk, this is because he is everywhere and nowhere in the general postmodernist intertext. In this perspective, identifying Pynchon's presence (or Burroughs's, for that matter) in cyberpunk texts is less a question of "source-hunting" (a dubious and ultimately uninteresting exercise anyway) than of tracking the circulation of motifs, models and materials through an intertextual network that includes both Pynchon and the cyberpunks, and in which Pynchon's texts are not so much "sources" as reservoirs or catchment basins.

IN THE LOOP (2): CYBERPUNK RECYCLED AS POSTMODERNISM

Just as on one end of the feedback loop between postmodernist mainstream fiction and SF we find a mode of SF which exploits the already "science-fictionized" postmodernism of Burroughs, Pynchon, and other state-of-the-art mainstream writers, so on the other end of the loop we begin to find postmodernist mainstream writers who exploit the already "postmodernized" SF of the cyberpunks. An example is Kathy Acker, in particular her postmodernist text *Empire of the Senseless* (1988), which appropriates and rewrites material from William Gibson's cyberpunk SF novel, *Neuromancer* (1984).

Already in *Don Quixote* (1986), Acker had introduced SF materials into her postmodernist mix of pastiches and appropriations. Here the source was Japanese SF monster movies (*Megalon, Godzilla*; Acker 1986:69–77.)[11] In other words, *Don Quixote* belongs to that earlier phase of interaction, typical of the 1960s and early 1970s, in which advanced mainstream fiction drew upon already long outdated SF models. By the time of *Empire of the Senseless* (1988), however, Acker seems to have become aware of cyberpunk, and of Gibson's *Neuromancer* in particular. She appropriates and extensively reworks two episodes from Gibson's novel, and a close comparison of Gibson's originals with Acker's reworking of them reveals much about the latter's postmodernist methods and priorities, as well as about the circulation of materials between cyberpunk and postmodernist fiction.

The first of these episodes is the one in which Gibson's protagonists, the computer hacker (or "cowboy") Case and his partner, the female ninja Molly, break into a closely-guarded corporate headquarters in order to steal an electronic storage unit housing the taped memory and personality-construct of a long-dead fellow computer cowboy (Gibson 1984:55–69). It is in fact Molly who does the actual breaking in, Case supporting her at his computer console and, most interestingly, able through an electronic broadcast link ("simstim") to experience vicariously not only what she is seeing and hearing (as he would if she were outfitted with present-day video broadcast technology) but also what she smells, tastes, and feels. "Simstim," in other words, is a technological realization of the formal literary device of change of point of view.[12]

It is, we might speculate, this feature of the episode, namely Case's access to the sensory experience of his female partner (who happens also to be his lover), with its potential for gender disorientation, that might have attracted Acker to this episode in the first place. Whether or not this is so, Acker does not actually preserve the simstim motif in her rewriting of the episode (Acker 1988:31–42; see Appendix 10.1). Instead, she copies several key sentences more or less verbatim from Gibson's text, relocating them in quite different contexts in her own text and thus radically altering their meaning. For instance, she transfers the description of Molly recovering from her wounds ("A transparent cast ran from her knee," etc.) to a point in her narrative *before* the break-in, thus robbing it of its narrative motivation. Acker also somewhat gratuitously alters details of this description, slightly diluting the SF effect of the original by deleting the neologism "micropore" and the brand-name "Akai," converting Molly's bruises into something that, enigmatically, "looked like bruises but weren't," and displacing the colors of these bruises to "spots" on the fingernails and toenails.

This does not seem to be a parody of Gibson's text, exactly, for it lacks the *pointedness* of parody. What interpretation or evaluation of Gibson's text could possibly be implied by, say, converting bruises into something that only *looked* like bruises (but without specifying what that something else might be)? What *point* is being made about Gibson's original? None whatsoever, so far as I can see. In other words, Acker's strangely untendentious rewriting of this passage from *Neuromancer* is an example of what Jameson (1991a:17) has called "blank parody." Literally "pointless," Acker's rewrite has no discernible purpose apart from that of producing the "sampling" effect itself.

The second episode is an inset story, told in Gibson's original by the Finn, the character most often entrusted with such story-telling duties throughout Gibson's cyberpunk trilogy. This story (Gibson 1984:73–6) involves a fence who runs afoul of a sinister and shadowy organization, in Gibson the powerful Tessier-Ashpool family, in Acker American Intelligence, or AI (which is of course the acronym, in Gibson, for Artificial Intelligence, not American Intelligence). This time Acker's strategy of appropriation is different (Acker 1988:39–41; see Appendix 10.2), for here she preserves intact Gibson's situation and original context, but rewrites his craftsmanlike prose, transposing it into her own characteristic anti-craftsmanlike register of deliberately "bad" writing or "back-broke" sentences.[13] Even in this case the verbal details are closely modelled on those of the original. For instance, where *Neuromancer* has "Smith sat very still, staring into the calm brown eyes of death across a polished table of Vietnamese rosewood" (Gibson 1984:75), Acker writes: "I knew he was a real man because I knew I was staring into the eyes of death" (Acker 1988:40).

Apart from these two specific episodes, many other details have been lifted from Gibson's text and subjected to various displacements and substitutions. Thus, for Sense/Net, the communications corporation whose headquarters Molly and Case raid, Acker substitutes American Intelligence, conflating its acronym, AI, with that of Artifical Intelligence (see above); for the Panther Moderns, the name of a gang of urban terrorists in *Neuromancer*, Acker substitutes simply the Moderns; for Wintermute, the codename of an artificial intelligence in *Neuromancer*, she substitutes Winter; and so on. More generally, Acker's criminal partners, Abhor and Thivai, the former evidently herself a cybernetic "construct," the latter ambiguously the offspring either of an alien or a robot (1988:34, 154–5), echo not only Gibson's Molly and Case, but also the cyberpunk thematics of human-computer symbiosis in general. More generally still, the world of *Empire of the Senseless*, dominated by omnipotent multinationals and intelligence organizations, is that of cyberpunk (but also, as we have seen, that of Pynchon's fiction), while its cityscapes of post-apocalyptic ruin mingle cyberpunk models (e.g. Shirley's *Eclipse*, 1985) with those of mainstream postmodernist fiction and film (e.g. Paris in Fuentes's *Terra nostra* and Goytisolo's *Paisajes después de la batalla*, London in Kureishi's film *Sammy and Rosie Get Laid*). Postmodernized SF mingling with postmodernism: here we see just how tight the feedback loop has become, just how rapid the traffic between high and low.

It is as a consequence of this ever-tightening feedback loop between SF "genre" fiction and state-of-the-art mainstream fiction that the poetics of mainstream postmodernism and the poetics of the latest wave of SF have come to overlap to such an unprecedented degree. This high degree of overlap, this shared repertoire of motifs and strategies, what I called above *aesthetic contemporaneity*, is one of the necessary conditions for admission of SF to the high-culture canon, without which the legitimacy newly granted it by canonical authorities such as the *Columbia Literary History* would be impossible.

This is not, however, a *sufficient* condition for SF's legitimation. Other preliminary conditions have had also to be met, including the weakening and dilution of the authority of the literary canon itself, and a corresponding receptivity on the part of the literary institution to formerly marginalized writing; the accession to positions of influence of literary "mediators" (reviewers, critics, editors, university lecturers) with an intellectual commitment to popular culture; the necessity felt by educational institutions to cater for students with ever shallower backgrounds in "elite" culture; and so on. In short, the sufficient conditions for SF's legitimation are to be found not in SF poetics, but in shifts in the literary institution that lie outside the scope of the present essay.

INTERFACE FICTION

It would be convenient if the story I have been telling about the interaction and feedback between cultural strata were the whole story, so far as the apparent convergence between cyberpunk and postmodernist poetics is concerned. Unfortunately, literary history is seldom tidy, and this case is no exception. For, supplementing and to some extent cutting across the phenomenon of mutual interaction and feedback, there is a second mechanism, whose logic is quite different though its effects augment those of the feedback loop. This is the phenomenon of *independent but parallel development* in SF and postmodernist fiction.

This phenomenon accounts for the appearance, in an earlier phase, of texts such as Beckett's *The Lost Ones* (1972; in French, *Le Depeupleur*, 1971), which seems to exploit SF formulas (that of the multiple-generation space voyage, for instance) but almost certainly does not, its true sources being high-culture models (Dante) and Beckett's own individual repertoire of motifs and procedures (see Porush 1985:157–71; McHale 1987:62–5). Especially striking, in this context, is the emergence during the 1980s of what might be called "interface fiction," postmodernist fiction of the cybernetic interface, that is, texts which register the first, often traumatic encounters between "literary" culture (high culture generally) and the transformative possibilities of computer technology.[14] Christine Brooke-Rose's fictions of the 1980s and early 1990s – *Amalgamemnon* (1984), *Xorandor* (1986), and *Verbivore* (1990), three-quarters of a projected "computer tetralogy" – are exemplary in this regard. In the first of these, the encounter with computers is tentative and anxious, but already by the second, *Xorandor*, the literary repertoire has been reconfigured so as to begin to accommodate, right down to the "micro" level of verbal detail, the realities of computer technology.[15]

Some of these cybernetic interface motifs can be seen as emerging directly from earlier postmodernist topoi, in particular the topos of the act of writing, or what Ronald Sukenick calls "the truth of the page" (Sukenick 1985a:25; see McHale 1987:197–9). This topos involves the inscription of the writing situation, the moment of writing and/or the physical act of writing *in* the written text itself, and amounts to a kind of postmodernist hyper-realism in which the fictional frame is broken and ontological levels are telescoped. Of all the topoi in the postmodernist repertoire, this is the one which is most directly responsive to changes in the technology of writing, for obvious reasons. Thus, earlier versions of the topos (Beckett's *Texts for Nothing*, early texts of the surfictionists Sukenick, Federman, and Katz, not to mention *Tristram Shandy*) reflect traditional, "low-tech" writing practice – the writer at his or her desk, pen or pencil in hand. Later versions register the changes in the physical act of writing introduced by electric typewriters (e.g. Federman's *The Voice in the Closet*, 1979) and tape-recorders (stories in Sukenick's *Death of the Novel and Other Stories*, 1969, and *The Endless Short Story*, 1986, and in Barth's *Lost in the Funhouse*, 1969). From here it is a logical extension of the topos to adapt it so as to reflect the newest writing technology, that of personal computers and word-processing. This is precisely what we find in "interface fictions" such as Russell Hoban's *The Medusa Frequency* (1987), James McConkey's *Kayo* (1987), William Vollmann's *You Bright and Risen Angels* (1987), and Umberto Eco's *Il pendolo di Foucault* (1988).[16]

Postmodernist interface fictions often have the "look" and "feel" of cyberpunk SF, that is, they seem to share some of cyberpunk's characteristic motifs, materials, and even stylistic effects, e.g., the effect of incongruous juxtaposition of high- and low-tech, of "elite" culture and the hacker subculture, etc. Nevertheless, except in rare case (notably that of Brooke-Rose, and possibly Hoban), I think we can assume that these motifs and effects have emerged more or less independently of any significant contact with the SF genre. Exploring in their own postmodernist terms the literary implications of computer technology, mainstream interface fiction such as *Xorandor*, *The Medusa Frequency* and *You Bright and Risen Angels* have in effect arrived independently at a position *parallel to* the one occupied by the cyberpunks in the adjacent SF tradition.

WHEN IT CHANGED

Transformation is a science fiction cliché. The climactic metamorphosis of the human race into some "posthuman" form of being belongs to the traditional repertoire of the genre; its classic treatments include Arthur C. Clarke's *Childhood's End* or his and Kubrick's *2001: A Space Odyssey*.

The endings of some of these cyberpunk texts, notably Bear's *Blood Music*, clearly allude to the Clarke formula. Other cyberpunk endings involve other variations on the metamorphosis theme. Gibson's characters at the end of *Mona Lisa Overdrive* have left their organic bodies behind (if they ever had any to begin with) and opted for a different mode of existence on the cyberspace plane. Similarly, Sterling's hero Abelard Lindsay leaves his body at the end of *Schismatrix* in order to go adventuring through the cosmos with an alien Presence, while Rucker's characters metamorphose into dolphins at the end of *Wetware*, and so on.[17] I choose to read into these transformations an element of self-reflection, as though it were cyberpunk SF itself that was undergoing the sea-change.

Into what, though? Presumably something rich and strange; presumably a future writing in which "mainstream" and "genre" categories, "low" science fiction and "high" postmodernism, will be entangled even more intricately than they already are in cyberpunk SF.

At the end of *Breakfast of Champions* (1973), Kurt Vonnegut liberates his fictional alter ego, the imaginary SF writer Kilgore Trout, releasing him from the obligation to be a character in Vonnegut's own novels. (Of course Vonnegut would later renege on Trout's manumission in *Jailbird*, but that's another story.) In effect, with this gesture Vonnegut bids farewell to SF once and for all: from here on out, it will be mainstream postmodernism for him. At the end of *Schismatrix*, on the other hand, Bruce Sterling's alter ego Abelard Lindsay allows himself to be absorbed by a mysterious, alien Presence that has been shadowing him (and the novel in which he appears) for some time. *Schismatrix* can in this respect be read as a kind of answer (no doubt unintended) to *Breakfast of Champions*. Vonnegut dispenses with an unwanted self; Lindsay acquires a new one, a symbiote. Vonnegut puts SF behind him; perhaps Bruce Sterling takes on something new – could it be postmodernism?

In fact, Sterling actually has gone on to acquire a kind of "symbiote" in the person of William Gibson, and the two of them have adventured deeper into postmodernism in their collaborative novel *The Difference Engine* (1991; see Porush 1991), a hybrid (or symbiosis) of historical fiction and "parallel worlds" SF. In combining a classic SF topos, that of the parallel or alternative world (see, e.g., Dick's *Man in the High Castle*), with the typical postmodernist form of historical novel which Hutcheon has called "historiographic metafiction," Gibson and Sterling have in effect corroborated Jameson's (1982) analysis, according to which SF is the successor and functional equivalent of historical fiction. In literary-historical terms, SF takes up, according to Jameson, just where and when the historical novel leaves off (1982:150), and SF accomplishes for our imaginations the sorts of things that historical fiction once used to accomplish; in particular, it helps us historicize our present by reimagining it as the *past of a determinate future*, just as historical fiction once helped us in a similar way by reimagining the present as the *future of a determinate past* (1982:152). Gibson and Sterling show us, through their *tour de force* pastiche of a Victorian novel which is *at the same time* a cyberpunk SF novel, that in postmodern culture historical fiction and SF are not only functionally equivalent but can actually be made to *occupy the same textual space*.

APPENDIX 10.1

Neuromancer

Case hit the simstim switch. And flipped into the agony of broken bone. Molly was braced against the blank gray wall of a long corridor, her breath coming ragged and uneven. Case was back in the matrix instantly, a white hot line of pain fading in his left thigh.

Case forced himself to flip back. She was leaning against the wall taking all of her weight on her right leg. She fumbled through the contents of the suit's kangaroo pocket and withdrew a sheet of plastic studded with a rainbow of dermadisks. She selected three and thumbed them hard against her left wrist over the veins. Six thousand micrograms of endrophin analog came down on the pain like a hammer, shattering it. Her back arched convulsively. Pink waves of warmth lapped up her thighs. She sighed and slowly relaxed.

Case flipped into the matrix and pulled the trodes from his forehead. He was drenched with sweat. He wiped his forehead with a towel, took a quick sip of water from the bicycle bottle beside the Hosaka, and checked the map of the library displayed on the screen. A pulsing red cursor crept through the outline of a doorway. Only millimeters from the green dot that indicated the location of the Dixie Flatline's construct. He wondered what it was doing to her leg, to walk on it that way. With enough endorphin analog, she could walk on a pair of bloody stumps. He tightened the nylon harness that held him in the chair and replaced the trodes.

(Gibson 1984:64–5)

Molly was snoring on the temperfoam. A transparent cast ran from her knee to a few millimeters below her crotch, the skin beneath the rigid micropore mottled with bruises, the black shading into ugly yellow. Eight derms, each a different size and color, ran in a neat line down her left wrist. An Akai transdermal unit lay beside her, its fine red leads connected to input trodes under the cast.

(Gibson 1984:78)

Empire of the Senseless

After I left the doctor and returned home, what I called home, which was better than I had ever had, Abhor had gotten there before me and was waiting for me, so to speak. Asleep. Naked. I saw her. A transparent cast ran from her knee to a few millimetres below her crotch, the skin mottled by blue purple and green patches which looked like bruises but weren't. Black spots on the nails, finger and toe, shaded into gold. Eight derms, each a different colour size and form, ran in a neat line down her right wrist and down the vein of the right upper thigh. A transdermal unit, separated from her body, connected to the input trodes under the cast by means of thin red leads. A construct.

(Acker 1988:33–4)

She told me again. "All I know is we're looking for a certain construct. Somewhere. Nothing else matters." A pulsing red then black cursor crept through the outline of a doorway. With enough endorphin analogue, Abhor could walk on a pair of bloody stumps. "You don't matter and reality doesn't matter."

(Acker 1988:34)

The cunt was hurt. I realized that when I awoke. The terrorists said. Six thousand micrograms of endorphin analogue, however, were coming, down on the pain like a hammer, shattering it. Her back, like a cat's, was arching in convulsions. Pink warm waves were lapping her thighs.

(Acker 1988:38)

APPENDIX 10.2

Neuromancer

Smith, it developed, had had a supplier known as Jimmy. Jimmy was a burglar and other things as well, and just back from a year in high orbit, having carried certain things back down the gravity well. The most unusual thing Jimmy had managed to score on his swing through the archipelago was a head, an intricately worked bust, cloisonné over platinum, studded with seedpearls and lapis. Smith, sighing, had put down his pocket microscope and advised Jimmy to melt the thing down. It was contemporary, not an antique, and had no value to the collector. Jimmy laughed. The thing was a computer terminal, he said. It could talk. And not in a synth-voice, but with a beautiful arrangement of gears and miniature organ pipes. It was a baroque thing for anyone to have constructed, a perverse thing, because synth-voice chips cost next to nothing. It was a curiosity. Smith jacked the head into his computer and listened as the melodious, inhuman voice piped the figures of last year's tax return.

Smith's clientele included a Tokyo billionaire whose passion for clockwork automata approached fetishism. Smith shrugged, showing Jimmy his upturned palms in a gesture old as pawn shops. He could try, he said, but he doubted he could get much for it.

When Jimmy had gone, leaving the head, Smith went over it carefully, discovering certain hallmarks. Eventually he'd been able to trace it to an unlikely collaboration between two Zurich artisans, an enamel specialist in Paris, a Dutch jeweler, and a California chip designer. It had been commissioned, he discovered, by a Tessier-Ashpool S.A.

Smith began to make preliminary passes at the Tokyo collector, hinting that he was on the track of something noteworthy.

And then he had a visitor, a visitor unannounced, one who walked in through the elaborate maze of Smith's security as though it didn't exist. A small man, Japanese, enormously polite, who bore all the marks of a vatgrown ninja assassin. Smith sat very still, staring into the calm brown eyes of death across a polished table of Vietnamese rosewood. Gently, almost apologetically, the cloned killer explained that it was his duty to find and return a certain artwork, a mechanism of great beauty, which had been taken from the house of his master. It had come to his attention, the ninja said, that Smith might know of the whereabouts of this object.

Smith told the man that he had no wish to die, and produced the head. And how much, his visitor asked, did you expect to obtain through the sale of this object? Smith named a figure far lower than the price he'd intended to set. The ninja produced a credit chip and keyed Smith that amount out of a numbered Swiss account. And who, the man asked, brought you this piece? Smith told him. Within days, Smith learned of Jimmy's death.   (Gibson 1984:74–5)

Empire of the Senseless

' "My newest burglar is a rat who goes by the name of Ratso. Since rats are very intelligent, Ratso had a fondness for art objects. The rat craves art. His latest work-of-art, his newest find, find-and-keep so-to-speak, is a head. Not any head. It's a dead head and death is done up in pearls. Despite the obvious value of this work of art, its humanity, not being a humanist, I advised Ratso to get rid of it. These days times are so hard that heads are worthless.

' "At that moment I remembered I knew a head freak. A head freak who was rich. And liked to spend it.

"I accepted the rat's human head. Upon minute careful inspection, this head revealed the trademarks of the AI, American Intelligence, who're backing the AMA. Next to the military, the American medical industry take in the largest amounts of legal profit in the western hemisphere. No wonder the head was dead.

' "At the very moment I realized this, a gulag came through my door.

A block, a dunderhead, a lump of cement, a lobotomized mongoloid. A man who acted like he had all the muscle in the world because he owned everything in the world. A man who didn't need to walk as if he owned the place because he owned the place. There are people like that. I don't know them. I knew he was a real man because I knew I was staring into the eyes of death.

' "The weight-lifter carefully explained he had come for his head. I explained I don't give head. He explained that he thought I might be able to give it to him.

' "Not having the desire to get closer to death, though I find lack of desire strange and inhuman, I produced my head.

' "How much does a human head cost? These days?' the owner of the world asked me.

' "I named the price of a masticated piece of bubble-gum. One piece, or stick; not two. I got what I asked for. On credit.

' "Two days later I learned the rat had gotten his price. Death."

(Acker 1988:40)

Chapter 11

Towards a poetics of cyberpunk

"CYBERWHATSIS"

that old chestnut *cyberwhatsis*, or whatever it was, he couldn't remember . . .

(Pat Cadigan 1991:87)

What is cyberpunk, anyway? The question itself is wrong-headed, presupposing as it does that cyberpunk "is" some one thing or other, that it is some kind of "object" about which demonstrably true or false statements could be made. Nevertheless, wrong-headed though it may be, the question "What is cyberpunk?" does admit of an answer – or rather several answers, all different, none of them necessarily reducible to any of the others.

No doubt cyberpunk is, as its critics within the science-fiction (SF) community insist, a barefaced marketing device of SF publishers. But, if it is anything more than that (as I believe it is), then cyberpunk SF must, first of all, be a generational and "school" phenomenon. It has its own "school" institutions – manifestoes and literary polemics, group anthologies, fan magazines, panels at SF conventions, etc. – and its forms of "school" solidarity; e.g. cyberpunks write jacket blurbs for one another's books and otherwise promote the careers and reputations of fellow members of the school.[1] There does exist (as I shall undertake to demonstrate below) a shared cyberpunk poetics, but this is to some extent a consequence of membership in the cyberpunk group rather than the other way around. That is, the initial question to be asked about cyberpunk SF is not so much "*What* is it?" as "*Who* are the cyberpunks?" As with other school phenomena, we can identify an inner circle of "hard-core" cyberpunks – including Bruce Sterling, its leading propagandist, William Gibson, John Shirley, Rudy Rucker, and Lewis Shiner – and a more fluid outer circle of writers who have at some point or to some degree affiliated themselves with the cyberpunk group, or have had such an affiliation thrust upon them by others. This outer circle might include, among others,

Greg Bear, Pat Cadigan, Richard Kadrey, Marc Laidlaw, Tom Maddox, Lucius Shepard, Michael Swanwick, and Walter Jon Williams.

A Child's History of Science Fiction[2]

Secondly, cyberpunk is the latest in the succession of phases or "waves" constituting the modern history of the SF genre. The SF genre, Jameson (1982:149) reminds us, has "a complex and interesting formal history of its own . . . with its own dynamic, which is not that of high culture, but which stands in a complementary and dialectical relationship to high culture or modernism as such." Malmgren (1988b:30–4) has usefully suggested that an account of the genre's history in the twentieth century might be structured around the oscillation between two modes or types of science-fiction world-building, which, adapting familiar terminology of SF criticism, he calls "extrapolation" and "speculation." Extrapolative SF begins with the current state of the empirical world, in particular the current state of scientific knowledge, and proceeds, in logical and linear fashion, to construct a world which might be a future extension or consequence of the current state of affairs. Speculative world-building, by contrast, involves an imaginative leap, positing one or more disjunctions with the empirical world which cannot be linearly extrapolated from the current state of affairs. Worlds constructed by extrapolation, one might say, stand in a metonymic relation to the current empirical world, while worlds constructed by speculation stand in a metaphorical or analogical relation to it. These categories partly (but only partly) coincide with the distinction which has often been drawn in SF criticism between "hard" and "soft" SF (i.e. between SF based on the "hard" or physical sciences and SF based on the "soft" or human sciences); "hard" SF, says Malmgren, has certain "affinities" with extrapolation, "soft" SF with speculation.[3]

Naturally, these two modes of SF world-building are not mutually exclusive, either in historical periods or in individual texts. That is, extrapolation and speculation can coexist in the same text, and certainly in the same period of SF history, though in every case one of the two modes is likely to be relatively more salient or more central than the other. In other words, to label a text or period "extrapolative" or "speculative" is not to identify the presence of one mode and the corresponding absence of the other, but rather to specify the structural-functional *dominant* of the text or period (see Jakobson 1971a). Consequently, an internal history of the SF genre which utilizes these categories will be a history of the successive shifts of dominance between extrapolation and speculation.

According to one widely-accepted version, the history of modern SF commences (or recommences, if one counts H.G. Wells as its founding father) with the pulp-magazine fiction edited by Hugo Gernsback in the 1920s and 1930s. Gernsback's so-called "scientifiction" had extrapolative world-building as its dominant, and thereafter each successive phase or wave of SF has reacted against the dominant of the preceding phase, swinging toward the opposite pole of the extrapolation/speculation polarity. Thus, Gernsback's extrapolative "scientifiction" provoked, by way of reaction, a swing to speculative "space opera" and space fantasy (E.E. Smith, Edgar Rice Burroughs), which in turn provoked a counter-reaction against speculation and back to extrapolation in the so-called "Golden Age" magazine SF of the 1940s and 1950s. The "New Wave" SF of the 1960s clearly marks a return to the speculative dominant, in reaction against the extrapolative dominant of the preceding phase. This speculative phase has prolonged itself into the 1970s and 1980s, partly through the rise, in the aftermath of Tolkien's neo-fantasy trilogy *Lord of the Rings*, of hybrid "science fantasy" writing, a new sub-genre which seems likely to secede from SF altogether (if it has not already done so (see Malmgren 1988a)).

These successive shifts of dominance do not entail any simple return to or recovery of the poetics of the phase before the last; rather, some part of the poetics of the preceding phase is preserved and integrated in the new phase, even while other parts are rejected and replaced by elements retrieved from an earlier phase. Thus, the latest wave of SF writing rejects the speculative dominant of 1960s New Wave SF, and swings back to extrapolative world-building, while at the same time retaining certain elements of New Wave poetics. "When I was starting out," the cyberpunk novelist William Gibson explains, "I simply tried to go in the opposite direction from most of the stuff I was reading" (McCaffery 1990b:228): this might be taken as a typical (though atypically frank) expression of the relation between successive generations of SF writing in general, and between the generation of the 1980s and its predecessors in particular. This newest phase includes neo-extrapolative "hard" SF writers (e.g. Gregory Benford, David Brin) as well as, problematically, cyberpunk SF – problematically because, while the cyberpunks themselves describe their own world-building practice as extrapolative, other extrapolative SF writers tend to regard them as continuators of the New Wave, more preoccupied with style and "texture" than with extrapolation.[4]

Repertoires

Finally, whatever else cyberpunk may be, it is also, as I sought to demonstrate in the preceding chapter, a convenient name for the kind of writing that springs up where the converging trajectories of SF poetics and postmodernist poetics finally cross. It arises, in other words, from the interaction and mutual interference of SF and mainstream postmodernist writing. Consequently, no attempt to describe the repertoire of cyberpunk motifs would be adequate that failed to take into account cyberpunk's relations with both the SF repertoire and the postmodernist repertoire.

From the point of view of the SF repertoire, there are few, if any, absolute novelties in cyberpunk SF. Most cyberpunk motifs have precedents in earlier SF; some, indeed (e.g. the renegade robot motif), are among the hoariest of SF clichés. Cyberpunk's critics within the SF community have sometimes adduced this fact as counter-evidence to cyberpunk propagandists' excessive claims for the novelty and "breakthrough" character of cyberpunk. There is, nevertheless, an important sense in which cyberpunk is innovative despite the familiarity or formulaic character of its SF motifs. What is new in cyberpunk is, first of all, the conspicuousness of certain selected motifs rather than others, their foregrounding relative to other motifs from the SF repertoire; and, secondly, the co-occurrence of certain motifs in the same texts, the solidarity among these motifs, the way they mutually corroborate and reinforce each other to create a motif complex which is distinctive of the cyberpunk wave of SF, even if every one of the individual items making up the complex can be traced back to earlier SF phases. The novelty of cyberpunk, in other words, lies not in the absolute newness of any particular component or components, but in a shift of dominance or center of gravity reflected in the combination of components and their relative conspicuousness in cyberpunk texts.

Cyberpunk's relation to "elite" postmodernist poetics is rather different. In what follows I undertake to demonstrate and substantiate the overlap between the postmodernist poetics of fiction and cyberpunk poetics. It is worth noting right at the outset, however, that the shared motifs I identify typically occur at different levels of textual organization in postmodernism and cyberpunk. That is, what typically occurs as a configuration of narrative structure or a pattern of language in postmodernist fiction tends to occur as an element of the fictional world in cyberpunk. Cyberpunk, one might say, translates or transcodes postmodernist motifs from the level of form (the verbal continuum, narrative strategies) to the level of content or "world."[5] To put it differently, cyberpunk tends to "literalize" or "actualize" what in postmodernist fiction occurs as metaphor – metaphor not so much in the narrow sense of a verbal trope (though that is also a possibility), but in the extended sense in which a narrative strategy or a particular pattern of language use may be understood as a figurative reflection of an "idea" or theme. In this respect, too, cyberpunk practice is clearly a continuation or extension of SF practice generally, for SF often generates elements of its worlds by literalizing metaphors from everyday discourse or mainstream fiction and poetry (see Todorov 1975:76–7; Delany 1977; Lem 1984).

There are three large bundles or complexes of motifs which cyberpunk SF shares with mainsteam postmodernist fiction: motifs of what might be called "worldness"; motifs of the centrifugal self; and motifs of death, both individual and collective.

COWBOYS AND SUNDOGS

Isn't this an "interface" here? a meeting surface for two worlds . . . sure, but *which two*?

(Thomas Pynchon 1973:668)

Both science fiction and mainstream postmodernist fiction possess repertoires of strategies and motifs designed to raise and explore ontological issues. Here is the ultimate basis for the overlap between the poetics of postmodernist fiction and SF poetics in general, including cyberpunk poetics in particular. SF, that is, like postmodernist fiction, is governed by an ontological dominant, by contrast with modernist fiction or, among the genres of "genre" fiction, detective fiction, both of which raise and explore issues of epistemology and thus are governed by an epistemological dominant. Thus, while epistemologically-oriented fiction (modernism, detective fiction) is preoccupied with questions such as: what is there to know about the world? Who knows it, and how reliably? How is knowledge transmitted, to whom, and how reliably? etc., ontologically-oriented fiction (postmodernism, SF) is preoccupied with questions such as: what is a world? How is a world constituted? Are there alternative worlds, and if so how are they constituted? How do different worlds, and different kinds of world, differ, and what happens when one passes from one world to another? etc.[6]

To explore such ontological issues, both SF and postmodernist fiction naturally use and adapt the resources common to all varieties of fiction, in particular the universal fictional resource of presentation of virtual space. If all fictional texts project virtual spaces, not many of them foreground and exploit the spatial dimension to the degree that SF and postmodernist texts do.[7] This shared poetics of space is partly to be explained by the common historical origins of both SF and postmodernist fiction in romance. In medieval romance the category of "world," normally the unrepresentable, absolute horizon of all experience and perception, is itself made an object of representation through a particular metaphorical use of enclosed spaces *within* the romance world: castles, enchanted forests, walled gardens and bowers, etc. Such symbolic enclosures, functioning as scale-models or miniature analogues of worlds, bring into view the normally invisible horizons of world, the very "worldness" of world (see Jameson 1975 and 1981:103–50; cf. Harvey 1989:240–1). Space, in other words, becomes in medieval romance an all-purpose tool for "doing" ontology – a means of exploring ontology *in* fiction, as well as (potentially at least) the ontology *of* fiction.

And this is true not only of medieval romance itself, but of its "heirs" as well, including both SF and postmodernist fiction. SF in particular has developed in the course of its history as a genre an entire repertoire of "microworlds," scale-model worlds designed to bring into view the "worldness" of the category "world" itself. Ultimately derived from the castles, forests and bowers of medieval romance, these SF microworlds – domed space colonies, orbiting space-stations, subterranean cities, "cities in flight," and the like – recur throughout the genre's history. They recur yet again in cyberpunk SF, but with a new intensity of emphasis, sharpness of focus, and functional centrality.

Microworlds

The typical cyberpunk microworld uses the familiar motifs of outer-space fiction as building-blocks: orbiting space-stations or platforms, domed space colonies and the like. However, if the basic construction materials are SF clichés, the treatment of these materials in the cyberpunk context is typically revisionist or parodic. Where space-stations and space-colonies of traditional SF are glamorous showcases of high technology (think of Kubrick's *2001*), those of cyberpunk SF are likely to be orbiting slums – shabby, neglected, unsuccessful, technologically outdated, as in Gibson and Sterling's "Red Star, Winter Orbit," Shiner's *Frontera* (1984), or Shirley's *Eclipse* (1985). Alternatively, for the miniature liberal-egalitarian democracies of traditional SF (think of *Star Trek*), cyberpunk substitutes off-world havens of privilege, orbiting penthouses to which the wealthy and powerful withdraw to escape the poverty and danger of the planet surface, as in Gibson's *Neuromancer* (1984) and *Count Zero* (1986), or Williams's *Hardwired* (1986).

Moreover, the cyberpunk adaptations of these familiar motifs heighten precisely the "worldness" of outer-space microworlds. This tendency is particularly conspicuous in Sterling's *Schismatrix* (1986a), Swanwick's *Vacuum Flowers* (1987) and Williams's *Voice of the Whirlwind* (1987). These texts extrapolate a future in which the human race, having evacuated planet Earth (partially in Williams, totally in Sterling and Swanwick), lives dispersed throughout the solar system in artificial planets and space-colonies (on asteroids, the moons of other planets, etc.). Not only do these orbiting city-states differ from one another in the ways that nations differ in our world – in language, culture, political systems, etc. – but they also differ in much more basic, indeed ontological, ways – in light, gravity, temperature, strains of bacteria, etc. They differ, in other words, as worlds differ, and their differences heighten the world-modeling function of these enclosures.

Another cyberpunk variant brings these microworlds down out of orbit to the terrestrial surface and superimposes them on the current map of the world. In Marc Laidlaw's *Dad's Nuke* (1985) and Williams's *Hardwired*, for example, the United States of the near future has been balkanized (or, I suppose, "lebanonized"), that is, it has disintegrated into self-contained, warring enclaves sustained (in Laidlaw, less so in Williams) by disparate and competing ideologies and epistemologies. In Lucius Shepard's *Life During Wartime* (1987) and Lewis Shiner's *Deserted Cities of the Heart* (1988) it is Mexico and Central America that have disintegrated in this way; in Shirley's *Eclipse* it is Europe. These extrapolated near-futures literalize a familiar metaphor in the sociology of knowledge (see, e.g., Berger and Luckmann 1966), that of the multiple, competing "subuniverses" or "enclaves" of meaning into which complex (post)modern societies have diversified. Here the diversification of knowledge is literal and geographical, and Berger and Luckmann's epistemological enclaves have erected barbed-wire perimeter fences and armed themselves with the latest military hardware against their epistemological competitors.

Alternatively, microworlds appear as islands: the artificial island of Freezone in Shirley's *Eclipse* (symmetrically mirroring and balancing the orbiting space-station FirStep in the same text), or the islands of Sterling's "Green Days in Brunei" (1985) and *Islands in the Net* (1988). Some of Sterling's islands are fully integrated "in the net" of global communications and information, while other island enclaves, some of them literally islands (Grenada, Singapore, Brunei), others only figuratively so (renegade guerrilla bands, African pocket dictatorships), remain defiantly outside the net. It is these latter islands – disparate, marginalized, renegade, resisting integration into the homogenizing world-system – that most strongly foreground the "worldness" of island microworlds.

It is especially with these enclave and island microworlds that cyberpunk SF returns to its distant historical roots in the kinds of romance world-spaces that Jameson has described. Cyberpunk also returns to its romance roots through its use of wandering adventurer-heroes as a device for foregrounding its microworlds. "Worldness" in medieval romance (and in later subliterary derivatives, such as the Western) was heightened by the narrative device of the conventional knight-errant's itinerary, which took him from microworld to microworld – from castle to enchanted forest to cave to bower to another castle, and so on. Freely crossing world-boundaries, the knight-errant thus served to expose the differences among (micro)worlds.

How conscious cyberpunk is of the adventurer-hero tradition is suggested by the nickname of Williams's hero in *Hardwired*, who smuggles contraband across the internal frontiers of what used to be the United States: he is (what else?) Cowboy. Space-traveling versions of the knight-errant or cowboy abound in cyberpunk; Swanwick's Rebel Mudlark (*Vacuum Flowers*) is one, Sterling's Abelard Lindsay (*Schismatrix*) another, Williams's Etienne Steward (*Voice of the Whirlwind*) yet another. Sterling even coins a name for them: they are "sundogs" (by analogy, I suppose, with "seadogs," another adventurer-hero model), and the interplanetary spaces they traverse on their itineraries from microworld to microworld are "sundog zones."

In the zone

When Sterling calls these interplanetary spaces "sundog zones," he alludes to similar multiple-world spaces projected by postmodernist texts, in particular the "Zone" of Pynchon's *Gravity's Rainbow* and William Burroughs's "Interzone." All these spaces, cyberpunk and postmodernist alike, are instances of what Michel Foucault called "heterotopia," the impossible space in which fragments of disparate discursive orders (actualized in cyberpunk as disparate microworlds) are merely juxtaposed, without any attempt to reduce them to a common order.

In its terrestrial versions, this cyberpunk Zone typically takes one of two forms. One form is that of the War Zone, the familiar spaces of our world fragmented and "reconfigured" (Pynchon 1973:520), sometimes literally, by the impact of war – whether guerrilla war, as in Shepard's *Life During Wartime* and Shiner's *Deserted Cities*, tactical nuclear war, as in Shirley's *Eclipse*, or unconventional forms of so-called "conventional" warfare, as in Williams's *Hardwired*. The model of Pynchon's Zone of postwar occupied Germany is a strong presence in some of these texts (e.g. *Eclipse*); in others, especially those involving tropical jungle warfare (*Life During Wartime*, *Deserted Cities*), the model is rather Michael Herr's Vietnam War journalism in *Dispatches* (1978), or the fictionalized version in his screenplay for Coppola's *Apocalypse Now*.

The other typical cyberpunk Zone, and the source of what is perhaps the most characteristic cyberpunk imagery, is the Urban Zone. This is, so to speak, an "imploded" Zone: instead of microworlds spaced out along a narrative itinerary, here they have been collapsed together in the heterotopian space of a future megalopolis where "fragments of a large number of possible orders glitter separately in the dimension, without law or geometry, of the *heteroclite*" (Foucault 1970:xviii). The most characteristic and most influential example of this cyberpunk Zone is the "Sprawl," the near-future cityscape of Gibson's stories ("Johnny Mnemonic," "New Rose Hotel," "Burning Chrome") and novels (*Neuromancer, Count Zero, Mona Lisa Overdrive*). Similar Urban Zones occupy the backgrounds and sometimes the foregrounds (e.g. L.A. in Richard Kadrey's *Metrophage*, 1988, and Cadigan's *Synners*, 1991) of many other cyberpunk novels. They have even been projected into outer space to become the slummy asteroid-belt "tank towns" and the "cislunar sprawl" of "orbital hongkongs" in Swanwick's *Vacuum Flowers*.

The compositional principle of the Sprawl and its cognates, terrestrial and extraterrestrial, is maximally intimate juxtaposition of maximally diverse and heterogeneous cultural materials (Japanese, Western, and Third World, high-tech and low-tech, elite and popular, mainstream "official" culture and youth or criminal subcultures, etc.). The Sprawl is an image of the carnivalized city, the city as permanent carnival. Kadrey makes this explicit when, in *Metrophage*, he introduces in the background of his narrative a literal carnival, that of the Día de los Muertos, which serves to mirror *en abyme* the carnivalesque structure of the "reconfigured" Los Angeles of his near-future world.

At the center of this imploded multiple-world space – though "center" is a rather infelicitous term for a space whose organizational principle is precisely centerlessness – one typically finds an even more compact zone of cultural heterogeneity and juxtaposition, a kind of dense node of collapsed microworlds. This zone-within-the-Zone – red-light district, ghetto or barrio, sometimes a single building – can be read as a synecdoche (*pars pro toto*) or *mise-en-abyme* of the broader Zone that surrounds it. Examples include the multi-storey flea-market, the Hypermart, of Gibson's *Count Zero*; OmeGaity, the homosexual cruising warren on Shirley's island-city Freezone, with its "strange vibe of stratification: claustrophobia layered under agoraphobia" (Shirley 1987:129); the Iron Barrio prison-camp of Shepard's *Life During Wartime*; and the Golden Age of Hollywood Pavilion of Kadrey's *Metrophage*, an "enormous tented structure" housing reconstructions of classic Hollywood movie sets, left over from a world's fair and now home to a floating population of vagrants and squatters.

Cyberspace

All the strategies of "worldness" described so far have involved juxtapositions among microworlds occupying the same ontological plane and arranged along the same horizontal axis. It is also possible, however, to foreground the "worldness" of world by juxtaposing worlds not, as in all these cases, in series, on a horizontal axis, but rather *in parallel*, on a *vertical* axis; that is, it is possible to juxtapose worlds occupying *different* ontological planes – worlds and meta-worlds, or worlds and inset worlds (worlds-within-worlds).

The characteristic cyberpunk form of inset world is "cyberspace" (Gibson's coinage), the computer-generated space mentally experienced by computer operators whose nervous systems are directly interfaced with the computer system. According to the fictitious history developed in cyberpunk novels, cyberspace evolved from the "virtual worlds" of military simulations, but its real origin (as Gibson has cheerfully admitted in an interview) is less glamorous, namely, contemporary video-arcade games and computer-graphics programs (McCaffery 1990b:138). More generally, the cyberspace motif arises from the potent illusion, experienced (I suppose) by all computer-users, sophisticated and unsophisticated alike, of gazing into (or even moving around inside) some space lying somehow "within" or "behind" the flat screen of the computer monitor.[8] And of course, apart from its immediate experiential source in illusions of this kind, cyberspace also has a long SF pedigree, including all the many variations on the SF motif of "paraspace": parallel worlds, other "dimensions," worlds of unactualized historical possibility, etc.

Gibson's cyberspace, also called the "matrix," is a three-dimensional grid ("a 3–D chessboard, infinite and perfectly transparent" (Gibson 1987a:168)) in which concentrations of data (those stored by corporations, government agencies, the military, etc.) are represented by color-coded geometrical shapes: "the stepped scarlet pyramid of the Eastern Seaboard Fission Authority burning beyond the green cubes of Mitsubishi Bank of America, and high and very far away . . . the spiral arms of military systems" (Gibson 1984:52). The user of this system has the illusion of moving among these representations as through a landscape, but a landscape entirely mental and virtual. The matrix is a "consensual hallucination," that is, exactly the same hallucinatory landscape is experienced by everyone who "jacks into" any one of the system's terminals.

Apart from this second plane of shared cyberspace reality, parallel to the primary reality plane, Gibson's fictional world also incorporates a number of "private" paraspaces, limited-access worlds-within-the-world. The billionaire Virek, for instance (*Count Zero*), whose sickly body is kept alive in a vat, has had a private mental reality constructed for himself, one that simulates the city of Barcelona, while Bobby Newmark (*Mona Lisa Overdrive*) is permanently jacked into a unit that contains its own separate cyberspace world-construct ("an *approximation of everything*" (Gibson 1988:128)). These private paraspaces are not, however, hermetically sealed, but may be entered not only from the primary reality plane but even, in extraordinary circumstances, from other inset worlds: Bobby Newmark, for instance, penetrates Virek's world-construct from the cyberspace matrix at the climax of *Count Zero*. It is possible, in other words, to adventure from parallel world to parallel world on the vertical axis, just as one can from microworld to microworld on the horizontal axis of the primary reality plane.

Where texts such as *Neuromancer*, Cadigan's *Mindplayers* (1987) and Laidlaw's *Dad's Nuke* construct a two-tier ontology (see Pavel 1980) by juxtaposing a primary reality plane with an inset cyberspace world, other cyberpunk texts do so by juxtaposing the primary reality plane with a parallel realm of mythic archetypes. Examples include Shiner's *Frontera*, whose protagonist, Kane, acts out the hero "monomyth" simultaneously in the real world and the myth-world, to which he has access in dreams and hallucinations; Shiner's *Deserted Cities of the Heart*, where the myth being re-enacted is the Mesoamerican one of Kukulcan/Quetzlcoatl; and Shepard's *Green Eyes* (1984), where the parallel myth-world is that of voodoo divinities. In other words, these texts literalize or actualize the kinds of mythological materials that function metaphorically in modernist texts such as *Ulysses* and *Doktor Faustus*. While Joyce's Leopold Bloom "is" Odysseus only figuratively, in a kind of extended metaphor, Shiner's Kane *really* is the Hero with a Thousand Faces on a different but parallel plane of reality.[9]

The paraspace motif, including cyberspace and its functional equivalent, the myth-world, not only serves to bring into view the "worldness" of world; it also offers opportunities for reflecting concretely on world-making itself, and on science fiction world-making in particular. For paraspace is, at least potentially, a scale-model of the fictional world itself, a fictional-world-within-the-fictional-world or *mise-en-abyme* of the text's world. The paraspace motif makes possible, in other words, metafictional reflection *by* the text on its own ontological procedures.

Cyberpunk texts often foreground this metafictional potential of paraspace. For instance, they develop an analogy between the author of the text, who has written the fictional world into being, and the "author" of the cyberspace or paraspace world. In Gibson's *Mona Lisa Overdrive*, this subsidiary "author," the real author's fictional double, is evidently the artificial intelligence Continuity, who intervenes in and manipulates the cyberspace world. Continuity is described as "writing a book . . . *always* writing it" (Gibson 1988:42); is this "book" cyberspace, one wonders queasily, or *Mona Lisa Overdrive* itself? Similarly, in Shepard's *Green Eyes*, it is the protagonist Donnell who seems to be the "author" of paraspace, for the paraspace myth-world first manifests itself in stories (fictions-within-the-fiction) he has written. Later this myth-world will acquire independent ontological status, so that Donnell's role comes to be that of a subsidiary world-builder in his own right, uncannily doubling his own author.

SIMSTIM

> Which world is this? What is to be done in it? Which of my selves is to do it?
>
> (Dick Higgins 1978:101)

Postmodernism's shift of focus to ontological issues and themes has radical consequences for literary models of the self. A poetics in which the category "world" is plural, unstable and problematic would seem to entail a model of the self which is correspondingly plural, unstable, and problematic. If we posit a plurality of worlds, then conceivably "my" self exists in more than one of them; if the world is ontologically unstable

(self-contradictory, hypothetical or fictional, infiltrated by other realities)
then so perhaps am "I." Dick Higgins's first question would seem to entail
his last: if we can ask, "Which world is this?", then it follows that
eventually we must also get around to asking, "Which of my selves . . . ?"

Modernist perspectivism (e.g. *Ulysses*, *The Sound and the Fury*, *To the
Lighthouse*, *Les Faux-monnayeurs*) multiplied points of view on the world,
but without, for the most part, undermining the underlying unity of the
self. Though in modernist fiction the perspectives on the world are many,
and each differs from all the others, nevertheless each perspective is lodged
in a subjectivity which is itself relatively coherent, relatively centered and
stable; and this is true even of those modernist texts (e.g. *A la recherche
du temps perdu*, *La coscienza di Zeno*, *Die Mann ohne Eigenschaften*) in
which the unity and continuity of the self is problematized. Still, perspectivism does exert considerable centrifugal pressure on the self, and there are
tendencies in modernism toward fragmentation and decentering. Never
brought to full fruition during the modernist period, these centrifugal
tendencies could not be fully realized until the emergence of a postmodernist poetics exploring and problematizing the ontologies of worlds and texts
(see Docherty 1982, Margolin 1986).

For the most part, fragmentation and dispersal of the self occurs in
postmodernist fiction at the levels of language, narrative structure, and the
material medium (the printed book), or between these levels, rather than
at the level of the fictional world. In other words, postmodernist fiction
prefers to represent the disintegration of the self figuratively, through
linguistic, structual, or visual metaphors, rather than literally, in the persons of characters who undergo some kind of literal disintegrative experience. There are exceptions. Pynchon and Sukenick, for instance, have both
produced characters who fracture or distintegrate not at all metaphorically
(psychologically), but ontologically. In *Gravity's Rainbow*, for instance,
Pirate Prentice is literally a medium, a "fantasist-surrogate" possessed by
alternate selves, while the novel's supposed hero, Tyrone Slothrop, undergoes disassembly and "scattering," entirely disappearing from the world
by the closing episodes. Similarly, there are characters in Sukenick's texts
who, before our eyes so to speak, "peel off" from other characters (Roland
Sycamore in *Out*), "split" into two (Boris Ccrab in *Blown Away*), infiltrate
and take possession of other characters by "a kind of psychic osmosis"
(*Blown Away*), and so on.

Ontologically oriented like postmodernist fiction, science fiction has
also developed a repertoire of strategies for asking, "Which world is this?",
yet it has for the most part managed to avoid asking the corollary question,
"Which of my selves?" It has, in other words, appeared to evade the
consequences of its ontological pluralism and experimentalism for its
model of the self. Or rather, SF has tended to neutralize the issue of
the (re)presentation of self by keeping characterization generally "thin,"

"shallow," and impoverished, strictly subordinated to the foreground category of "world." In this respect we might even say, paradoxically, that traditional SF, otherwise so "pre-modernist" in its orientation, has always been postmodernist. "The disappearance of character (in the traditional sense) from contemporary ('postmodern') fiction," writes Christine Brooke-Rose (1981:102), "is one of the ways in which SF and the more 'serious,' experimental fiction have come close together"; character, newly absent from "serious" fiction, has always been absent from SF!

Cyberpunk practice, here as elsewhere, is to actualize or literalize what in postmodernist poetics normally appears as a metaphor at the level of language, structure, or the material medium. Where postmodernism has figurative representations of disintegration, cyberpunk texts typically project fictional worlds which include (fictional) objects and (fictional) phenomena embodying and illustrating the problematics of selfhood: human-machine symbiosis, artificial intelligences, biologically-engineered alter egos, and so on.

Since cyberpunk handles the centrifugal self at the level of fictional world rather than, as postmodernist fiction prefers to do, at one or more of the formal levels of the text, its motifs of dispersion and decentering fall naturally into categories based on the types of fictional objects and phenomena represented. Here we can turn to Sterling's fiction for a convenient taxonomy. In a series of five stories published between 1982 and 1984 (and now reprinted in *Crystal Express*, 1989), culminating in his 1985 novel *Schismatrix*, Sterling projects a future history in which humankind divides into two "posthuman" species in competition with one another, each species employing a different range of technologies to enhance and transform itself so as to improve its own chances for success. The "Mechanists," or "Mechs," use electronic and biomechanical means to augment themselves: prostheses to enhance the body, but with the side-effect of violating its integrity; brain-computer interfacing to extend the mind, but with the side-effect of attenuating and dispersing it. Their rivals, the "Shapers," use bio-engineering techniques – cloning, genetic engineering – to achieve the same ends, and with similar side-effects: who am "I" if I am a member of a "congenetic clan" of identical cloned individuals? These two technological options – the Mech option and the Shaper option[10] – define alternative ranges of representational motifs of the centrifugal self. We might call the first set, corresponding to the Mech option, cyberpunk proper, and the second set, corresponding to the Shaper option, "biopunk."

Riding the eye-face

The traditional SF iconography of the humanoid robot, as developed by Čapek, Binder, Asimov and others, is relatively rare in cyberpunk; only

Rudy Rucker (*Software*, 1982; *Wetware*, 1988) has exploited it in any very ambitious way. More typical of cyberpunk are its artificial intelligences (AIs), software surrogate humans, i.e. programs, rather than the hardware robots (or "wetware" androids) of traditional SF. Examples include Cadigan's AI "character" Artie Fish (*Synners*) and Gibson's Wintermute and Neuromancer, AIs who merge at the end of *Neuromancer* but by the time of its sequel, *Count Zero*, have already broken up into multiple software "selves." All of these variants on the robot motif serve to raise the classic SF question, who (or what) is human? At what point does a machine cease being a "mere" machine and begin to count as a human being?

This same question is also raised, but in inverted form, by the cyberpunk motif of prosthesis: at what point does a human being cease to be a human being and begin to count as a machine? The Mechanists of Sterling's Shaper/Mechanist cycle present an entire range of prosthetic possibilities, from biomechanical arms and legs, through remote-control "waldos" that enable human beings to extend their presence into unlivably hostile environments (deep space, ocean abysses), to "wireheads" who, abandoning their organic bodies entirely, survive as software ghosts in electronic machines. Less total prostheses are recurrent motifs in Gibson, Kadrey (*Metrophage*) and Williams (*Hardwired*, *Voice of the Whirlwind*), especially artificial eyes and surgically-implanted weapons, and even, in Kadrey, prosthetic genitalia!

Prosthetic augmentation is possible for mental capacities as well as for the body's physical capacities. There are minimal forms of this mental-augmentation motif, in which units ("microsofts," "augs") introduced permanently or temporarily into the nervous system supply specialized knowledge or preprogrammed technical skills when needed. Maximally, as in Swanwick's *Vacuum Flowers* and Cadigan's *Mindplayers*, mental augmentation takes the form of temporary programming of individuals with any of a whole range of useful or desirable personality constructs ("personas"), either for the sake of the specialized skills which these latter possess (doctor, police, skilled worker, weapons operator), or simply for reasons of entertainment and fashion.

At some hard-to-define point prosthetic augmentation shades off into a complete human-machine symbiosis or fusion, and the borders of the self blur and erode. The image of a human being coupled with a machine – "jacked-in," "riding the eye-face" (i.e. the "I-face," or human-machine interface) – recurs in many variations throughout cyberpunk; it is, indeed, the most characteristic piece of cyberpunk iconography. In these postures of fusion, the human partner in the symbiosis may experience an exhilarating expansion of self, as Williams's protagonist Cowboy does when he plugs into his armored vehicle, or, alternatively, an identity-threatening dilution or attenuation, as does, for instance, Williams's part-human, part-prosthetic character, Reno, or the "wirehead" Ryumin in *Schismatrix*. In extreme cases, the human self may be entirely absorbed into the machine. Williams's Reno, for instance, who begins as part prosthetic, ends by being a literally centrifugal self, diffused throughout the worldwide information network; similarly, Cadigan's Visual Mark (*Synners*), interfaced with the electronic network through skull-sockets, finally abandons his ravaged body ("the meat," as he contemptuously calls it) and "spreads" into the system. Rucker's Cobb Anderson persists as disembodied, taped "software" capable of being booted up in a variety of "hardware" vehicles, custom-made bodies as well as machines. Both in Rucker's two cyberpunk novels and in Swanwick's *Vacuum Flowers*, renegade cybernetic systems aspire to absorb the entire human race into a collective group-mind incorporating human and machine intelligences alike – the ultimate form of human-machine symbiosis.

Zombies

The "bio-punk" sub-variety of cyberpunk SF makes available an entirely different, though complementary, range of motifs of the centrifugal self. Where machine-oriented cyberpunk produces electronic and mechanical surrogates of human beings (robots, AIs), the bio-punk variety "grows" new human individuals in vats, or clones identical multiples of the "same" individual, literally pluralizing the self. Where the machine-oriented variety augments and extends human capacities through mechanical means (prostheses, "waldos"), bio-punk accomplishes the same thing through bio-techniques, engineering new, reconfigured human types: "angels" (*Schismatrix*, *Wetware*), or mermaids and mermen (Shiner's "Till Human Voices Wake Us"). Finally, where the machine-oriented variety threatens the individual human self with diffusion throughout an electronic network, bio-punk threatens bodily fusion with other individuals (the effect of the drug "merge" in *Wetware*) and, ultimately, physical diffusion and loss of differentiation (the woman grotesquely reconfigured as a wall of undifferentiated tissue, the "Wallmother," in *Schismatrix*, the planet-wide biomass in Greg Bear's *Blood Music*).

It is not hard to see that these bio-punk motifs revise, update and rationalize classic Gothic-horror motifs of bodily invasion and disruption. This is especially the case with the bio-punk variations on the classic B-movie Gothic-horror motif of the zombie. The traditional zombie, of course, is a corpse reanimated by powerful voodoo magic to do the magician's will. In its various bio-punk adaptations, the zombie is rarely a corpse, more often a living human being "possessed" by some alien self, or under the irresistible control of some other human being. The technologies of possession and control vary.

One variant, for instance, extrapolates from the familiar capacity of present-day drugs to induce in the drug-user temporary personality changes of a regular and to some extent predictable kind, changes in effect "coded" in the chemical structure of the drug. These extrapolated "designer drugs" of the future temporarily efface the "real" self and induce, for instance, a prostitute-self (Gibson's "meat puppets"), or a soldier-self (Shepard's "samurai," the name both of the drug and the personality it induces; Williams's "hardfire"). In one sophisticated version, found in Sterling's *Islands in the Net*, the capacity for transformation into an assassin personality is chemically preprogrammed into the individual, requiring only an enzyme trigger to activate it: merely eating a carton of yoghurt turns a personable Rastafarian into a "killing machine." Clearly, this military use of drugs to induce a soldier personality is functionally equivalent to the motif of human-machine symbiosis in which the pilot directly interfaces with his weapons system, as in Swanwick and Gibson's "Dogfight," Williams's *Hardwired*, and many other cyberpunk texts.

A second bio-punk variant on the zombie motif extrapolates from a classic paranoid theme, what Pynchon (1973:542) calls "the old Radio-Control-Implanted-In-the-Head-At-Birth problem." In other words, this variant involves biotechnological devices, such as surgically-implanted radio receivers, by means of which the individual self is subjected to some irresistible remote control by others. Shiner's hero Kane, in *Frontera*, for instance, is subjected to just this sort of biotechnological control, while the "spook" (i.e. secret agent) of Sterling's story by that name (1983) has been transformed into a human weapon, a "psychopath in harness" (Sterling 1990:177), by the introduction of a "Veil" over his cerebral cortex that, disrupting his personality, leaves him vulnerable to manipulation by his masters and handlers. Shepard (*Life During Wartime*) even has an entire radio-controlled zombie army. Rucker, in *Wetware*, elaborates a range of horrible baroque variations on this control motif, including a "zombie box" which, affixed to the spine, turns a human being into a remote-controlled zombie; a miniaturized "robot rat" which replaces the right half of the human brain, transforming a human being into a puppet-like "meatie"; and a robot "Happy Cloak" which, draped around a vat-grown, mindless cloned body, is capable of animating it and inducing in it a semblance of sentience. Here, obviously, the distinction between machine-oriented cyberpunk motifs and bio-punk motifs has become a purely notional one, and biotechnological control devices such as those found in *Wetware* shade imperceptibly into the range of techniques for superimposing personalities which we have already mentioned in connection with *Vacuum Flowers* and *Mindplayers*.[11]

Finally, closest of all in some ways to the traditional zombie of horror fiction and movies, is what might be called the motif of the cellular-level self. In *Green Eyes*, Lucius Shepard's self-concious revision of the zombie myth, a particular strain of bacteria introduced into the brain of a fresh corpse generates there a short-lived ersatz personality (a "Bacterially

Induced Artificial Personality"). Under these bizarre circumstances, the self is literally plural and decentered, literally "a disease in a borrowed brain" (Shepard 1984:89).[12] The ultimate elaboration of this variant of the centrifugal self is to be found in Greg Bear's *Blood Music* (1985), in which the cells of the human body acquire their own collective intelligence, like that of an ant hill, wholly independent of the intelligence of their human "host." Seizing control of their "environment" – in the first instance, the bodies of their hosts, ultimately the entire planet – and reshaping it to their needs, they transform Earth into a vast, constantly metamorphosing biomass, possessing a single collective selfhood. Simultaneously the one and the many, centripetal and centrifugal, Bear's cellular-level intelligence mirrors the world-spanning symbiotic human-machine intelligences of Rucker and Swanwick.[13]

Simstim

The theme of the centrifugal self, and the representational motifs through which it is manifested in cyberpunk SF, are essentially incompatible with the perspectivist narrative strategies of modernist fiction. Such modernist strategies (multiple limited points of view, "parallax" of perspectives, etc.) rest, as I have already suggested, on the assumption of relatively centered, relatively stable subjectivities. Recognizing this, postmodernist writers have either sought to "background" these strategies, relegating them to a subordinate and ancillary role, or have, like Pynchon in *Gravity's Rainbow*, deployed them in ways that undermine the modernist assumptions upon which they rest, in effect parodying modernist perspectivism. But Pynchon's is a difficult precedent to emulate, and cyberpunk writers have all too often ended up falling back on perspectivist structural clichés inherited from modernist poetics (either directly, or indirectly by way of SF's own modernist generation, the so-called "New Wave" SF of the 1960s). This is true, for instance, of Shiner's *Frontera*, Shirley's *Eclipse*, Gibson's *Count Zero* and *Mona Lisa Overdrive*, Cadigan's *Synners*, and other cyberpunk novels composed on the modernist model of multiple, shifting points of view.

But the modernist assumptions underlying perspectivism can be countered, and in ways that are distinctively cyberpunk rather than weak imitations of Pynchon's postmodernism. How this can be achieved is best demonstrated by Gibson's *Neuromancer*.[14] Gibson's world includes an extrapolated communications and entertainment medium called "simulated stimulus," or "simstim," involving not only audio and visual sensory channels, as televison presently does, but the entire range of senses, the full human sensorium. As an entertainment medium, Gibson's simstim is a cross between the "feelies" of Huxley's *Brave New World* and American commercial television's egregious *Lifestyles of the Rich and Famous*:

simstim stars travel, interview celebrities, and enjoy the good life while wearing equipment that records the full range of their sensory experience for broadcast (appropriately edited, of course) to consumers who re-experience vicariously through simstim receivers at home what the stars have directly experienced in real life. Typical SF extrapolated technology, in other words – but with interesting implications for literary perspectivism.

Twice in the course of *Neuromancer* – once when she breaks into the Sense/Net corporate headquarters, and again during her raid on the Tessier-Ashpool refuge of Villa Staylight – Molly the female ninja wears a simstim broadcast rig, enabling her partner Case to accompany her on the raid vicariously, as it were. Using simstim technology, Case can occupy Molly's point of view at will, literally at the flip of a switch. The action in these episodes unfolds simultaneously on two "planes," three if one counts cyberspace, for Case shifts back and forth among his own point of view on the primary reality plane, Molly's point of view, and the secondary, cyberspace reality plane. The effect is that of "split-screen" cinema or television – or indeed, that of multiple-point-of-view fiction.[15]

This is, in one sense, a purely formal solution ingeniously motivated by a representational motif at the level of the fictional world. The text of *Neuromancer* is consistently focalized through Case, but in these episodes Case is not at the center of the action, or rather he does not occupy its only center; the action involving Molly is at least as important and engaging. The simstim motif allows Gibson to introduce Molly's experience without violating the basic point of view convention of the text.

Ingenious though it may be, this is not, however, *only* a characteristically cyberpunk solution to a formal problem. It is also a subversive gesture, implicitly undermining the model of the centered, centripetal self upon which modernist perspectivism rests. For with the flip of a switch Case is able to experience another's body, "other flesh," *from within*. He experiences another's physical pain when he shifts into Molly's sensorium a moment after she has had her leg broken (Gibson 1984:64). He even has the opportunity to see himself from another point of view, literally *through another's eyes* (or eye, in fact):

> [He] found himself staring down, through Molly's one good eye, at a white-faced, wasted figure, afloat in a loose fetal crouch, a cyberspace deck between its thighs, a band of silver [elec]trodes above closed, shadowed eyes. The man's cheeks were hollowed with a day's growth of dark beard, his face slick with sweat.
> He was looking at himself.
>
> (Gibson 1984:256)

And of course finally, and perhaps most radically of all, when Case flips the switch that displaces him into Molly's point of view, he literally *changes gender*: he inhabits, if only temporarily, a woman's body. "So now you get to find out just how tight those jeans really are, huh?" wisecracks the Finn after he finishes explaining the simstim hook-up to Case (Gibson 1984:53), and this witty, subversive literalization of male clichés of sexual conquest ("I wouldn't mind getting into *her* pants!") suggests just how disorienting this motif can be, at least potentially. As a vehicle for imagining what it would be like to *be* a centrifugal self – to be in two places at once, to occupy two different points of view and two different bodies simultaneously, to change genders at the flip of a switch – the characteristic cyberpunk motif of simstim gives fresh, concrete, and radical meaning to Dick Higgins's question, "Which of my selves is to do it?"

THE FINAL FRONTIER

> His whole psychology, his point of orientation, is to dabble with death and yet somehow surmount it.
>
> (Philip K. Dick)

The ultimate ontological boundary, the one that no one can help but cross, is of course the boundary between life and death, between being and not-being. It is only to be expected, then, that an ontologically-oriented poetics such as that of postmodernist fiction should be preoccupied with death. Perhaps, though, it would be more accurate to put this the other way around, and say rather that the ontologically-oriented poetics of postmodernism is the latest, renewed manifestation of our culture's protracted struggle to represent, and thus symbolically to master, death. Either way, postmodernist fiction might somewhat reductively be characterized as one long, resourceful, highly diversified, obsessive meditation on the intolerable fact of personal extinction – your death, my death, our collective death (see McHale 1987:227–35).

Pynchon (1984:5) has remarked that in science fiction "mortality is . . . seldom an issue," and that this mark of the genre's immaturity helps to explain its appeal for immature readers. This is unfair; there are a number of SF writers (Philip K. Dick and Thomas Disch, among others) who have been as seriously preoccupied with mortality as any "mainstream" writer, and who have used SF conventions and formulas to explore death in ways not open to writers outside the SF genre. Nevertheless, it could be argued that no generation or group of SF writers has made the exploration of death its special province until the emergence of the cyberpunk "wave" in the 1980s.

There is one important exception to this generalization, and this has to do with a particular variant of the theme of death which has been a special province of SF writing in general since 1945 (and in fact before), namely the theme of nuclear holocaust. If late-twentieth-century literature in general, including postmodernist fiction, has turned with renewed attention to the perennial human preoccupation with death, no doubt this is in part because for the first time in history human beings feel threatened with "double" death: inevitable personal extinction, as always, but also the probable global self-destruction of the race and its posterity through nuclear war (or, alternatively, some ecological disaster). To SF writing in particular has fallen the task of feeding our imaginations with images and scenarios of our impending global extinction.[16] This task has been inherited in due course by the cyberpunk generation of SF writers, who have stamped their own distinctive mark and emphases on the nuclear-war theme.

Dad's nuke

A distinguishing mark of cyberpunk SF, writes Bruce Sterling, is its "boredom with Apocalypse" (in Gibson 1987a:xi; cf. Sterling 1991), which does not mean that cyberpunk disregards the nuclear war theme but rather that, like its SF and postmodernist precursors, it seeks ways of renewing and de-familiarizing it.

Thus, for instance, John Shirley prefaces his *Eclipse* (1985) with an alarming and enigmatic "note from the author":

> This is not a post-holocaust novel.
> Nor is this a novel about nuclear war.
> It may well be that this is a *pre*-holocaust novel.

Distancing himself in this way from familiar SF nuclear war motifs (those of the "post-holocaust novel"), Shirley prepares us for his revisionist treatment of nuclear war, for what follows is a representation of the nuclear apocalypse as a long drawn-out agony, a tactical nuclear war of attrition in Europe. In other words, Shirley challenges the image of apocalypse as a punctual, transformative, irreversible event, substituting for it an image of "slow-motion" apocalypse, an endlessly protracted "pre-holocaust" from which the world never emerges into a transformed, post-holocaust future.

Bruce Sterling's *Islands in the Net* (1988) de-familiarizes the nuclear threat in a particularly powerful and subtle way. Projecting a near-future world from which nuclear weapons have supposedly been abolished, Sterling has his heroine Laura, the quintessentially normal citizen of this world, uncover a cabal of renegades armed with atomic weapons and intent on nuclear blackmail. Before our eyes, as it were, her nuclear-free world is shockingly transformed into our own brink-of-apocalypse world. The effect is that of a double de-familiarization: Laura's nuclear-free world, alien to us but familiar to her, is abruptly transformed into a state of affairs utterly alien to her but only too familiar to us, yet, since it is through Laura's eyes and from her alien perspective that we view this familiar state of affairs, it jolts us with a shock of de-familiarized recognition.

Another powerful de-familiarizing strategy of cyberpunk nuclear war fiction is what might be called the motif of "backyard apocalypse." The nuclear threat is literally reduced to backyard dimensions in Marc Laidlaw's satirical *Dad's Nuke* (1985), where suburban neighbors in an embattled Neighborhood enclave compete over who possesses the most advanced family arsenal: when the neighbor across the street acquires his own backyard tactical nuclear missile system, Dad responds by installing a miniature nuclear reactor in the garage! Sterling exploits a version of this same motif in *Schismatrix* (1985), where he de-familiarizes nuclear war by reducing its dimensions and making it a universally available option. In a future in which "world" has been reduced to the dimensions of orbiting "microworlds," the threat of annihilation becomes correspondingly small-scale: every orbital microworld is vulnerable to instant micro-apocalypse through the simple puncturing of its airtight outer shell. Furthermore anyone, even a crew of pirates, can possess technology sufficient to destroy such a world:

> *Worlds could burst.* The walls held life itself, and outside those locks and bulkheads loomed utterly pitiless darkness, the lethal nothingness of naked space . . . . There was no true safety. There had never been any. There were a hundred ways to kill a world: fire, explosion, poison, sabotage . . . , The power of destruction was in the hands of anyone and everyone. Anyone and everyone shared the burden of responsibility. The specter of destruction had shaped the moral paradigm of every world and every ideology.
>
> (Sterling 1986a:79–80)

Scaling it down to microworld proportions in this way restores to the motif of nuclear apocalypse its power to shock and haunt: Sterling's microworlds are transparently scale-models of our world, his micro-apocalypses displaced versions of the collective death we face.

Certain critics (e.g. Sontag 1966:223–5; Wagar 1982:70) have suggested that the literary representation of nuclear war is itself a displacement, that, in fact, every image of collective death is only a kind of metaphor for personal death. Perhaps so; in any case, it is striking that in cyberpunk SF motifs of apocalypse and motifs of personal extinction co-occur, mutually corroborating and reinforcing each other. If anything, though, it is at the level of personal extinction, rather than that of collective disaster, that the cyberpunk meditation on death is most innovative, most resourceful, and most persistent. "The spectre haunting all c[yber]-p[unk]," as McCaffery (1988a:15) has observed, is *the* Spectre, the spectre of death.

Excluded middles

Life and death form a binary opposition, of course. As Pynchon reminds us in *Vineland* (1990), returning to a metaphor from his earlier *The Crying of Lot 49* (1966), ours is "a world based on the one and zero of life and death" (Pynchon 1990:72). Between life and death there is no third option, no middle state; the law of the excluded middle applies. But, as we know from *The Crying of Lot 49*, excluded middles are "bad shit, to be avoided" (Pynchon 1967:136), so in *Vineland* Pynchon tries to imagine a middle state of "mediated death" (1990:218) occupied by beings called Thanatoids who, because of some "karmic imbalance" (1990:173), are not permitted fully to die but must linger on in an ambiguous condition "like death, only different" (1990:170).[17] Pynchon's is one version of the postmodernist modeling of the ontological frontier between life and death. Other, parallel versions are to be found in SF, for instance the "half-life" state upon which Dick's *Ubik* (1969) is premised, and the many other SF variations on the theme of "suspended animation."

Fusing the SF and postmodernist strategies for modeling death, cyberpunk, too, seeks to imagine some middle state beyond or outside biological life yet not a state of non-being, not death itself. Here, as in the case of other cyberpunk motifs, the range of motifs for exploring this middle or half-life state divides along the lines laid down in Sterling's future history of the "posthuman" race: on one side, the Mechanist options, or cyberpunk proper, that is, electronic means of "resurrection" and persistence beyond death; on the other side, the Shaper or "bio-punk" options, that is, bio-engineered means of "posthumous" survival.

We might take as the paradigm of cyberpunk motifs of death and machine-mediated resurrection a cinematic rather than literary example: the death of the policeman Murphy and his "resurrection" as the hybrid RoboCop in Paul Verhoeven's film of that name (1987). In this extraordinary sequence, Murphy's death on the operating table is represented from his subjective point of view. Emergency procedures fail to save him, the doctors declare him dead, the screen goes black; then, after a moment of darkness, the subjective "camera-eye" perspective returns, this time framed as in a camera viewfinder, and with LED numbers flashing in one corner of the screen: Murphy has been "revived" as RoboCop, part human being, part machine.[18] This same interior perspective on the experience of dying and being posthumously "booted up" in a machine, so graphically represented in the *RoboCop* sequence, is persistently explored by Rudy Rucker in *Software* and its sequel *Wetware*. Throughout Rucker's texts, intelligences both human and machine face death and experience the disorienting transition to a new mechanical or biological body and the limbo state between existing in one body and existing in another. This is, in a sense, the focus or dominant of Rucker's poetics, and he is relentless in his experimentation with means of representing the subjective experience of death and resurrection.

If Rucker seems particularly obsessive in his exploration of this theme, his preoccupation with death is by no means unique in cyberpunk writing. For instance, Cadigan (in *Synners*) has one character who dies and revives not once but twice – once when he leaves his body to enter the electronic network, a second time *within* the network – and another character, literally a death addict, who wills himself to die over and over, having acquired implants that allow him to shut down his metabolism temporarily (to "flatline") and then restart it again to return to life. Plural deaths is also a leitmotif of Swanwick's *Vacuum Flowers*. His heroine Rebel Mudlark survives her first death thanks to her personality having been taped, and "dies" a second time when that taped personality is superimposed over another personality – or was it the other who died? The former personality (called Eucrasia) has not, in any case, been wholly obliterated but persists "under" the Rebel-personality as a kind of "ghost" self, "haunting" Rebel from within. Similar variations on the motif of the "ghost" self and "haunting" from within recur throughout Cadigan's *Mindplayers*, where residues of the personalities of the dead persist within the minds of the living, thanks to mind-to-mind contact mediated by machines.

In fact, "ghosts" of various kinds, both in and out of machines, abound in cyberpunk. There are, for instance, the "wireheads" of Sterling's *Schismatrix*, Williams's *Hardwired*, and Cadigan's *Synners*, human selves persisting outside their natural bodies as configurations of information in computer and communication networks; and the "personality constructs" of Gibson's trilogy, ROM units preserving the selves of deceased characters. In both these variants, the dead manifest themselves to the living as uncanny posthumous voices like those of certain postmodernist texts (e.g. Flann O'Brien's *The Third Policeman*, 1940/1967; Russell Hoban's *Pilgermann*, 1983; Thomas Disch's *The Businessman*, 1984); this effect is exploited particularly powerfully by Williams in *Hardwired*. Gibson actually calls certain beings in his *Mona Lisa Overdrive* "ghosts." These, however, are not posthumous selves but constructs, computer-simulated selves who have never existed as biological organisms in the first place, but spring full-grown from artificial-intelligence programs – ghosts *from* the machine. Another version of the ghost from the machine appears in Swanwick's *Vacuum Flowers*, in the form of "interactive ALIs," or Artificial Limited Intelligences, short-lived computer simulations of human beings. In one of its formats, the ALI is agonizingly aware of its brief life-span and imminent death; in another, however, its memories are recorded and made available to a successor ALI, ensuring "a kind of serial immortality" (Swanwick 1987:242).

At the end of his trilogy, in the closing pages of *Mona Lisa Overdrive*,

Gibson assembles representatives of all his posthumous or out-of-body types on the cyberspace plane: a computer-simulated "ghost," a posthumous ROM personality construct, three human beings who have "died into" the cyberspace matrix. We had already, as early as the end of *Neuromancer*, had intimations of the possibility of posthumous survival in cyberspace, but here the association is confirmed: cyberspace is the machine-mediated version of the World to Come, and in this function bears a certain resemblance to some of the postmodernist variations on the World-to-Come topos (e.g. Christine Brooke-Rose's *Such*, 1966; Alasdair Gray's *Lanark*, 1981; and especially the double-agents' Hell of *Gravity's Rainbow* (Pynchon 1973:537–48)). "There's dying, then there's dying," as one of Gibson's characters somewhat unhelpfully explains (Gibson 1988:252); there's dying the death of the organic body, then there's dying into the half-life of cyberspace.

The "bio-punk" versions of the death and half-life motif do not figure so conspicuously in cyberpunk writing as do the machine-mediated versions. Nevertheless, it is striking that several of the essentially machine-oriented treatments of this theme have a strong body-oriented component, a strain or undercurrent of Gothic-hōrror imagery of the disrupted, exploded, or dismembered body. This is the case, for instance, with Cadigan's *Mindplayers*, where, in one episode, the heroine must make contact with the mind of a deceased poetess whose brain has been extracted and preserved in "stay-juice" – a typical Gothic-horror image. It is also true of Kadrey's *Metrophage*, where the crime-boss Conover maintains, in an off-limits precinct of his house, a grisly "farm" of multiple clones of his own body, alter egos from whom he "harvests" transplant organs in order to keep himself alive: a case of "Suicide and murder all rolled into one package" (Kadrey 1988:215). Rucker's two cyberpunk novels, too, abound in Gothic-horror imagery of dismemberment, cannibalism, necrophilia, and so on; *Wetware* in particular alludes explicitly, and appositely, to Edgar Allan Poe.

Specifically bio-punk equivalents of the various machine-oriented motifs include cloning, which serves the same function that booting up a software self in a new body does in the machine-mediated variants: it ensures "serial immortality." Thus Steward, at the beginning of Williams's *Voice of the Whirlwind*, is already a "Beta," i.e., the clone of his dead "Alpha" self; later he will die and "return" yet again as his own "Gamma," the clone of his cloned self! Similarly, a character who dies in the first pages of *Schismatrix* "returns" near its close, many decades later, as a cloned *Doppelgänger* of herself. Sterling also exploits the familiar SF motifs of suspended animation and extreme longevity, especially the latter. In the course of *Schismatrix*, only one natural death is recorded; otherwise, characters live on and on, either dying by violence or, in extreme old age, "fading" into an ambiguous half-life state.

The bio-punk equivalent of "wirehead" survival, i.e., posthumous existence as a configuration of information in a cybernetic system, occurs in
Bear's *Blood Music*. Here human selves are encoded as information at
the level of the component cells of their own bodies; thus, when the
body is dissolved and its component cells dispersed, the original self can
nevertheless be posthumously reconstituted from the information encoded
at the cellular level. This, eerily, is what happens late in *Blood Music* to
an entire family who are physically dissolved into undifferentiated tissue
and then reconstituted as "themselves," returning to "haunt" (benignly)
the surviving family member.

If Bear thus gives a distinctively bio-punk twist to the ghost motif,
Shepard does the same with the zombie motif. In his *Green Eyes*, posthumous life is induced in corpses through the introduction of a strain of
bacteria. The life span of these "Bacterially Induced Artificial Personalities" ranges from a norm of a few minutes or hours, to several months
in extraordinary cases, so-called "slow-burners." Shepard, especially in the
early parts of the novel, explores the subjective experience of posthumous
life in "slow-burners": their struggles to gain control of their new bodies,
their growing awareness of the imminence and inevitability of their own
second deaths. He gives us, in other words, the bio-punk version of the
death and half-life of Verhoeven's RoboCop.

In its preoccupation with the representation of death, both in its
machine-oriented and its bio-punk forms, cyberpunk shows to what degree
it has converged with mainstream postmodernist fiction, and how far
it has outstripped all the earlier "waves" of science fiction, where the
representation of death, even in the boldest and most sophisticated New
Wave examples (e.g. Dick's *Ubik*, Disch's *On Wings of Song*), seems
somewhat primitive and flatfooted by comparison. The cyberpunk writers
(and film-makers) demonstrate that conventional "old-wave" science
fiction of the *Star Trek* type has it all wrong: death, not space, is the
final frontier of the imagination, beyond which only the most innovative
adventurers boldly go.

Notes

INTRODUCING CONSTRUCTING

1 Connor (1989:126) objects to what he characterizes as my "serene belief in the givenness of the category of literature, or the 'literary system' " in *Postmodernist Fiction*. At the same time, he also objects to my having treated the category of literature as "an elastic form which expands obediently to contain every kind of subversion" (*ibid.*). Apart from the tendentious adverb "obediently," I find I can endorse this second characterization, which describes, it seems to me, a constructivist approach to the category of literature. If I believe anything about literature (serenely or otherwise), it is that it is constructed – and elastically constructible and re-constructible – not given.

Connor tends to prefer Linda Hutcheon's approach which, he says, undermines the category "literature" (1989:126–8), though he allows himself to wonder for whom this "subversion" of literature is subversive, thus inadvertently corroborating my more "elastic" approach. For the subversion of literature is itself a literary phenomenon, and the category of literature has shown itself to be sufficiently elastic to contain – more accurately, *to be constructible in such a way as to contain* – just about every kind of subversion one could imagine.

2 In particular, I have preserved unchanged the formulations of postmodernism in the earliest essays reprinted here, " 'You Used to Know What These Words Mean' " and especially "Modernist Reading, Postmodernist Text," even though in some respects I would no longer endorse them. On the other hand, in preparing the revised and updated versions of these earlier essays, I was pleased to find in "Modernist Reading" an emphasis that corresponds closely with my current position, and which I would happily endorse. This is its skepticism toward insufficiently nuanced and self-critical models of change in literary history, in particular toward the narrative of the apocalyptic "rupture" between modernism and postmodernism. There seems to be a clear continuity, though one I had been unaware of, between these expressions of skepticism and the retelling of the "breakthrough narrative" in the key of "as if" which is to be found in "Telling Postmodernist Stories," written nearly a decade later.

3 See, e.g., Chatman 1978, 1990; Prince 1982, 1987; Rimmon-Kenan 1983; Bal 1985; Martin 1986; Cohan and Shires 1988.

4 See, e.g., *Poetics Today*, special issues "Narratology I, II, III," 1980–1, and "Narratology Revisited I, II, III," 1990–1.

5 It is the ethical and political dimension of the narrative turn that has particularly recommended narrative to Brown (1987) and Rorty (1989). Brown advocates

the return of narrative in public discourse, because it is the only medium capable of integrating the manifold information of everyday life in the postmodern world with our moral existence (Brown 1987:159). Moreover, it is "radically democratic," the only adequate mode of "civic communication" in a "democratic political community" (1987:157, 164, 169): "Narrative enables us to understand . . . others . . . because it is through narrative that we live and understand our own existence . . . . The intelligibility of our moral and public life depends on the restoration of narrative discourse" (Brown 1987:165, 170). This is very close to Rorty's language when he speaks of narrative forms such as ethnography and the novel as the principal vehicles of imaginative solidarity with "others," and hence of moral change and progress, in contemporary liberal democracies (1989:xvi). Furthermore, as Brown goes on to say, narrative persists as the mode of intelligibility of last resort when other modes are called into question, or call *each other* into question. When paradigms clash, their mutual intelligibility and the eventual success of one paradigm over the other are mediated by narrative form: "paradigm shift" is essentially a narrative concept, essentially a story about how we passed from one world-version to another (Brown 1987:168). Here Brown approaches Tyler's more radical sense of (narrative) ethnography as the superordinate discourse in which all others find their meaning and justification.

6 A useful corrective to overstatements (such as these) of narrative's centrality to "real life" is Bell (1990). Bell objects to the tendency in various disciplines to conflate "narrative" and "life," arguing that this destroys the meaningfulness of narrative, which lies precisely in its dialectical tension with the reader's "real world." Narratives are significantly, and often self-consciously (e.g. *Don Quixote*) both like *and* unlike the reader's world; conflate the two, and the potential for significant difference is lost.

7 All of this tends to contradict Brown, who believes narrative to be an "endangered species" (1987:144) in contemporary culture, and in need of rescue; but then, he seems not to have been looking in the right places for it.

8 For other spatialized representations of the opposition between modernism and postmodernism, see, e.g., Venturi, *et al.* (1977), Hassan (1975a), Jencks (1980), Wollen (1982), and Fokkema (1984). Actually, Lethen's two-column array is not so much a representation of literary history as a pastiche of the binary schemes typical of postmodernist criticism. His argument is that *both* terms of these oppositions were already operative *within* modernism, and that only by cutting modernism in half, retrospectively, could we ever have arrived at a picture of literary history in which the first terms of the oppositions (the left-hand column) characterized modernism while the second terms (the right-hand column) characterized postmodernism; see below, "Constructing (post)modernism."

9 " 'The king died and then the queen died' is a story. 'The king died and then the queen died of grief' is a plot" (Forster 1963:93).

10 For an unsympathetic, but not inaccurate retelling of my story, see Mepham (1991:150–2).

11 Jameson, it seems, is always there ahead of one, his own claim clearly staked, no matter what topic in postmodern culture one has set out to investigate, so that one seems always compelled to deal with Jameson first before beginning to deal with the matter at hand. Try as I might to prevent this book from turning into a discussion of Jameson on postmodernism, it will be seen that his name crops up often, especially in Chapters 5, 7 and 11.

12 Period, *oeuvre*, career, author – these are all suspect terms, over-charged with

literary ideology (or indeed, several mutually incompatible literary ideologies). They are used here only as heuristic fictions, provisional constructs, on the understanding that such constructs are always made, not found, and are susceptible of being unmade and remade, "customized" to meet immediate, specific needs. The "author," in particular, is not necessarily dead, but neither is she or he a "given," to be taken for granted as some kind of ineluctable fact of literary history. Rather, the "author," and "authority" generally, is another convenient fiction of literary-historical discourse, a tool for carving up and organizing the literary continuum, useful when used circumspectly, to be taken or left according to need.

13 Two other McElroy novels, *Ancient History* (1971) and the most recent one, *The Letter Left to Me* (1988), are mentioned only in passing.

14 My essay on McElroy's fiction overlaps in certain striking ways with an essay on McElroy by Harry Mathews (Mathews 1990). Our essays were written entirely independently of one another; far from being distressed by the similarities, I was gratified, when the two essays appeared side-by-side in the special McElroy number of *Review of Contemporary Fiction* (10, 1:199–226 and 227–47), to find how closely they corroborated each other. Nothing could please me better than evidence that I was thinking on the same wavelength as a writer I admire as much as I do Harry Mathews.

15 I would like to be able to cite the Brooke-Rose essay as counter-evidence to the charge, lodged by one reviewer against *Postmodernist Fiction*, that I totally neglect women postmodernists. However, I doubt that one chapter devoted to a woman writer out of eleven would persuade anyone, least of all the reviewer in question, who managed not to notice any of the women writers I discussed in *Postmodernist Fiction*, some of them quite conspicuously, including Angela Carter, Monique Wittig, Brigid Brophy, Muriel Spark and of course Brooke-Rose. Perhaps my mistake was in not confining them to a ghetto clearly signposted "Women's Writing."

Leaving aside the issue of male critics' blindness (or alleged blindness) to women writers, there is a deeper issue here (which I would not presume to address) concerning the reasons for the relative under-representation of women writers in the postmodernist field; see, e.g., Hutcheon 1989; Suleiman 1990; Brooke-Rose 1991:223–34 and 250–64; Sherzer 1991.

1 TELLING POSTMODERNIST STORIES

1 In a later text, Lyotard has somewhat qualified his position on the role of narrative in epistemology and legitimation. He now regrets, he says, having exaggerated the importance of narrative at the expense of other genres of discourse; in particular, he distances himself from what he now sees as his too complete identification of narrative with knowledge in general (Lyotard 1986:40, 45). He also complains about an uncritical and "metaphysical" tendency among narratologists to exempt "little narratives" from the legitimation crisis. Insofar as "little narratives" are immune from the crisis, this is only because they never possessed any legitimating power in the first place; but insofar as they possess the power of legitimation, they are no more exempt from the crisis of incredulity than the "grand narratives" are (1986:41).

2 It is Rorty, of course, who, in an analysis paralleling Lyotard's, has sought to demonstrate that objectivity, the search for Truth, is itself only a character in the metanarrative of Western philosophy since Descartes, and that this metanarrative has ceased to be relevant and compelling and ought to be abandoned in

favor of local, provisional sense-conferring stories (Rorty 1979, 1982; see Norris 1985:139–66).

3 Utopian versions of the breakthrough myth include, for example, Hassan (1975a, 1980) and Docherty (1982); dystopian versions include Newman (1984) and West (1985). Newman has sought to portray the postmodernist breakthrough as a whimpery minor apocalypse, but his manifest intentions are betrayed by his own high-pitched, over-the-top rhetoric, which has the effect of inflating postmodernism to the proportions of a major disaster.

4 Apocalyptic rhetoric also comes on strong in Cornel West's version of the breakthrough narrative:

> In the eyes of many, we live among the ruins of North Atlantic civilization. Major philosophical figures such as Hannah Arendt, Walter Benjamin, Martin Heidegger, Alasdair MacIntyre and Ludwig Wittgenstein echo this Spenglerian theme. Possible nuclear holocaust hovers over us. Rampant racism, persistent patriarchy, extensive class inequality, brutal state repression, subtle bureaucratic surveillance, and technological abuse of nature pervade capitalist, communist, and neocolonial countries. The once vital tradition of bourgeois humanism has become vapid and sterile. The emancipatory intent of revolutionary Marxism has been aborted and discredited. The shock effect of Catastrophic nihilism is now boring and uninteresting. As we approach the end of the twentieth century, the rich intellectual resources of the West are in disarray and a frightening future awaits us.
>
> (West 1985:259)

For a skeptical retelling of the apocalyptic "breakthrough" narrative (or the "decisive seismic event," as he calls it), see Mepham (1991:138–9).

5 A striking exception is Frank Kermode (1968), who managed to challenge the idea of a breakthrough to postmodernism without inadvertently evoking the myth of the postmodernist breakthrough in the process. But, then again, Kermode was writing rather early in the history of the postmodernist controversy; a few years later he might have found the lure of the breakthrough metanarrative harder to resist. More recently, Helmut Lethen (1986) has succeeded in getting outside the postmodernist breakthrough narrative by relocating both the "before" and "after" of the breakthrough *within* modernism itself. The polar thinking that gives rise to such a narrative of discontinuity, he argues, is itself typically modernist; a genuinely "new" postmodernism would abandon the myth of breakthrough altogether! Lyotard (1986:120–1) has made a similar point, as have Harvey (1989:339–42) and Herman (1991:57).

6 Some of the storytellers who have narrated one or other version of the postmodernist breakthrough narrative have managed to keep it in the key of "as if"; others conspicuously have not. Thus, for example, Malcolm Bradbury (1983) and Ron Sukenick (1985b (1972)) both insist on the ultimate fictionality of their stories about the discontinuity between modernism and postmodernism. Even Ihab Hassan, for all his over-heated apocalypticism, treats the categories "modernist" and "postmodernist" circumspectly. If he draws up parallel columns of modernist and postmodernist characteristics, he also recognizes that other schemas are always possible: "Make Your Own List," he invites us (1975a:48). On the other hand, we find the architectural critic Charles Jencks in a recent book (Jencks 1986) grimly berating other critics and theorists for having "illicitly" conflated late-modernist architecture with postmodernism – as though such categories could actually be found lying around "out there" in the world, so that verifiably true or false statements could be made about

them, instead of their having been *constructed* by the discourses of writers like Jencks himself. On Jencks's lapse into "realistic illusion," i.e. the illusion that his constructs are *real*, see Calinescu (1987a:287, 1990).

7 See Calvino's speculative essay (Calvino 1986) on one such combinatorial system.

8 Interestingly, Borges had actually raised the possibility of this form of narrative exhaustion at the beginning of "Tlön":

> Bioy Casares had dined with me that night and talked to us at length about a great scheme for writing a novel in the first person, using a narrator who omitted or corrupted what happened, and who ran into various contradictions, so that only a handful of readers, a very small handful, would be able to decipher the horrible or banal reality behind the novel.
>
> (Borges 1962c:17)

The difference is that in *Pale Fire* the "very small handful" of successful decipherers dwindles to none.

9 The parallel or alternative world is of course a venerable topos of science fiction; classic examples are Edwin A. Abbott's *Flatland* (1884), Ward Moore's *Bring the Jubilee* (1955), Philip K. Dick's *The Man in the High Castle* (1962), and now William Gibson and Bruce Sterling's *The Difference Engine* (1991).

10 I am being somewhat unfair to Barth, of course: in 1967, with the publication of *Ada* still two years in the future, there was no possibility of his taking it into account. Nevertheless, in the "Replenishment" essay of 1979, having had a decade to consider the anomalous case of *Ada*, Barth continues to locate Nabokov in the exhausted camp.

11 John Barth, in "The Literature of Exhaustion" of 1967, offers as evidence of literature's exhaustion the "experimental" works published by the Something Else Press, which he sneeringly dismisses as "a swinging outfit" (1984b:65). That "outfit" was Dick Higgins, founder and publisher of Something Else.

12 Barth is righter than he knows when, intending to be snide, he observes of the Something Else Press publications that in them the "traditional notion of the artist" as "the Aristotelian conscious agent who achieves with technique and cunning the artistic effect" (1984b:65) is conspicuous by its absence; this is precisely what Higgins means by "postcognitive." (See Higgins 1978:3–9, 93–101, 156–66 and 1984:5–6, 71–81.)

13 Higgins is not alone in telling the postmodernist breakthrough story this way; others have told it in roughly comparable terms: cf. Ron Sukenick's account, in an interview with Larry McCaffery dating from February 1981, of the displacement of "epistemology" (Higgins's "cognition") from the center of literary interest (LeClair and McCaffery 1983:286); or William S. Wilson's story of how he came to came to give up asking the "central question 'How do I know?' " in his own modernist art (Wilson 1989:19–20); or Matei Calinescu's story of the transition from modernist "monism" (roughly, Higgins's "cognitivism") to postmodernist "pluralism" (roughly, "postcognitivism"; Calinescu 1983:267); or my own story of the shift of dominant from epistemology to ontology in postmodernist writing (McHale 1987).

14 Again, this is somewhat unfair to Barth: writing in 1967 he could not have anticipated Beckett's continuing productivity, manifested in such late masterpieces as "The Lost Ones" (1971/72) and "Company" (1980). Higgins himself (1984:71), it should be noted, tends to treat Beckett's writing as still predominantly cognitivist.

15 Moreover, by naming his second author-character "Joyce Carol," and making

her a writer of gothic romances, Apple opens up another dimension of ontological tension in his text. For these details are clearly designed to tease the reader into expecting a *roman à clef*, in which the fictional heroine is modelled on the real-world novelist Joyce Carol *Oates*, sometime author of Gothic romance pastiches. *Roman à clef*, of course, incorporates sharp ontological tension between real-world persons and events and their fictional surrogates as one of its defining characteristics, and Apple has exploited this characteristic of *roman à clef* in such texts as "The Oranging of America" (1976) and its expanded version, *The Propheteers* (1987).

2 CONSTRUCTING (POST)MODERNISM: THE CASE OF *ULYSSES*

1 Which chapter a critic identifies as the "epitome" or "microcosm" or *mise-en-abyme* of *Ulysses* can serve as a useful benchmark of his or her literary-historical allegiances. Goldberg could not even see how anyone could seriously propose "Wandering Rocks" (a chapter much closer to the conservative modernist poetics he valued) as an epitome of *Ulysses*; his candidate would have been "Hades" (1963:139, 271). Ellmann (1972:91) evidently would have selected "Wandering Rocks," though with reservations; Beebe (1974:184) would have nominated "Penelope"; both choices place these critics in the modernist camp alongside Wilson and Goldberg. At the other extreme, Tempera (1986:199) has proposed "Circe" as "a *mise-en-abyme* of the whole novel," which would seem to align her with postmodernists such as Iser and Lawrence. Revealingly, the standard teaching anthologies tend to follow the Wilson–Goldberg (modernist) line: the *Norton Anthology* has reprinted "Proteus" (which Iser, for one, has explicitly *disqualified* from functioning as an epitome of *Ulysses*, 1974:211) and "Lestrygonians" through five editions, while the *Oxford* offers "Nausicaa." We will know that the postmodernist *Ulysses* has really arrived when the *Norton Anthology* reprints "Sirens" or "Cyclops," say, instead of "Proteus" and "Lestrygonians."

2 By contrast with earlier, modernist-oriented critics, whose attitudes toward *Finnegans Wake* ranged from outright hostility (Goldberg) to straining to keep an open mind (Wilson), recent critics not only value the *Wake* but emphasize the ways in which various late chapters of *Ulysses* anticipate its techniques, for instance, "Sirens" (Lawrence 1981:96 fn. 15; Attridge 1988:172), "Eumaeus" (Kenner 1978:37; Attridge 1988:183), or "Ithaca" (Lawrence 1981:198, 207).

3 The key words here are Karen Lawrence's. In "Aeolus," she writes,

> The book turns back on itself to comment on and *parody* its own assumptions, explicitly in the way the headings "comment" on or rewrite the [narrative], and implicitly in the way the chapter *exceeds* and incorporates the novel we have read in the early chapters.
>
> (1981:69; my emphases)

See also Lawrence 1981:102, 208.

4 As many commentators have remarked, the norm of "integrated" direct interior monologue persists even in such stylistically extravagant chapters as "Aeolus," "Scylla and Charybdis," and "Sirens," and only disappears after "Sirens," to resurface one final time in the latter part of "Nausicaa" (see, e.g., Lawrence 1981:99 fn. 18).

5 On "Eumaeus," see below. Stanzel (1971:133–6) distinguishes between the style of "Nausicaa," where the discourse of sentimental fiction which "masks" the authorial voice also contaminates the characters' consciousness, and that of "Eumaeus," where the "mask" remains at the level of the authorial medium

and does not penetrate to the characters' consciousness; see also Lawrence (1981:169). Bašić (1986–7:36–7) describes the style of "Eumaeus" as a parody of free indirect discourse, a view congenial to my own.

Kenner's (1978:16–21) celebrated "Uncle Charles Principle" of Joyce's prose, namely the principle that "the narrative idiom need not be the narrator's" (18) but may be that of the nearest character, proves on inspection to be none other than a description of free indirect discourse (or "combined discourse"). Far from being, as Kenner claims, "apparently something new in fiction" (17), original with Joyce, the Uncle Charles Principle is of course ubiquitous in nineteenth- and twentieth-century fiction; he need not have looked farther for examples than *Madame Bovary*, discussed in the preceding chapter of his book. Nothing is more revealing of the continuing insularity of Anglo-American literary criticism than the fact that the device of free indirect discourse, a staple of Continental critical discourse on the novel, should continue to go largely unrecognized as such at least among Joyceans, while the Uncle Charles Principle has passed into the Joycean critical vocabulary.

6　All subsequent references to *Ulysses*, incorporated parenthetically in the body of the text, will follow this format, giving chapter number and line numbers in the Gabler reading text, which is identical with the line-numbering by episodes of the Gabler critical edition.

7　Some commentators have preferred to see in "Wandering Rocks" a swerve away from the "narrative norm" of modernist poetics, but I regard it as exemplifying a particularly heightened form of modernist parallax; in other words, I side with Kenner (1980) on this, against Lawrence (1981).

8　E.g. Fokkema and Ibsch (1987:70) strain to assimilate such chapters as "Oxen of the Sun" and "Ithaca" to their modernist code by attributing to them a "metalingual" function. Unquestionably these chapters *do* have a metalingual function, but this seems a strikingly meager and inadequate motivation for what are, after all, massive and densely wrought chapters.

9　Cf. Lawrence (1981:124): "Depending on how annoyed or lulled we are by the screen of language, we can read right past certain events that *do* occur in the chapter (or, at least, miss salient aspects of these events)"; see also Iser (1974:179–95).

10　Kenner (1980:36) wants to make Mulligan responsible for *all* the Gothic special effects in this passage, not just the frame-tale but the poison, the secret panel, the sensationalistic confession, and all the rest. This seems to me an unjustified "naturalization" of the episode, and one at variance with Joyce's general technique in "Oxen." Are we to extrapolate from this passage and assume that each of the various pastiche styles is to be attributed to some one or other of the characters present in the "real" scene? I think not.

11　A comparable case from "Proteus" is Stephen's (non)visit to his relatives, the Gouldings (see, e.g., Benstock 1974:95; Kenner 1980:38–9). Developed at some length and in some detail, the entire vignette of Goulding domestic life suddenly collapses into unreality, becoming merely part of Stephen's subjective subworld: "I have passed the way to aunt Sara's. Am I not going there? Seems not" (3.158–9). Momentarily disoriented, we quickly recover, reassured by the definiteness of the end-frame which separates Stephen's subworld from the *Ulysses* world. Not so in "Circe": here frames dissolve, hallucinations and "reality" mingle as promiscuously as the whores and their clients, and we will never know for sure whether Boylan was "really" there or not.

12　Cf. Kenner (1980:98): "the break-up of a seamless book after 'Wandering

Rocks' is apparent merely. It was fissured already, and the microplanes of its surface minutely canted."

13 The match-up between style and its possessor in "Nausicaa" falters at only one point, the transition or "hinge" between Gerty's half of the chapter and Bloom's. Here, for the space of a paragraph, *two* characters' consciousnesses mingle with the narratorial medium in the same sentences:

> Leopold Bloom (for it is he) stands silent, with bowed head before those young guileless eyes. What a brute he had been! At it again? A fair unsullied soul had called to him and, wretch that he was, how had he answered? An utter cad he had been. He of all men! But there was an infinite store of mercy in those eyes, for him too a word of pardon even though he had erred and sinned and wandered. Should a girl tell? No, a thousand times no. That was their secret, only theirs, alone in the hiding twilight and there was none to know or tell save the little bat that flew so softly through the evening to and fro and little bats don't tell.

The language, clearly, is still that of Gerty's women's-magazine models, but Bloom's consciousness must also be presented here, for who else could know enough about Bloom's intimate life to be in a position to think, "At it *again?*" (see McHale 1983:35–7).

14 Bersani refuses to be drawn into any of the controversies over the various cruxes of voice and perspective in *Ulysses* (including the crux of the "Eumaeus" style), because he believes that the critical practice of tracking down and (if possible) explaining away anomalies ("stylistic intrusions," "perspectival agitations," 1990:158, 161) only plays into Joyce's hands, implicating the narratologist-critic in a ritual endorsement of and submission to the author's authority and superiority:

> the intrusions, confusions, and discontinuities of point of view in *Ulysses* must, I think, be read as an important element in the strategic centering of the narrator's authority. That is, they should be read as part of his aggressively demonstrated superiority to the patterns and models of representation he insists that we recognize and analytically elaborate while he himself partially neglects them.
>
> (Bersani 1990:160–1)

Presumably the present essay falls under Bersani's strictures, and Joyce is playing me for a sucker as he has so many other critics before me (including the ones whose readings I have cited throughout these pages). My only defense is that I am not interested either in the narratological cruxes of *Ulysses* or their solutions *per se*, but only in how they have been *differently recuperated* at different times, and what the different modes of recuperation tell us about the different literary-historical periods (modernist and postmodernist, respectively) in which they have been practiced.

15 Relatively early on Stanzel (1971:136) queasily recognized that there was something anomalous in the last paragraph of "Eumaeus," quoted above, but without being able to account for it.

16 On the "conflict of discourses" in "Cyclops," see Topia (1984:116–24). See also MacCabe's analysis of the two disparate accounts of Alf Bergan's entrance, one in a medieval pastiche (12.244–8), the other in the first-person narrator's discourse (12.249–56). Objects which are admissible in one discourse are inadmissible in the other: "each object can only be identified in a discourse which already exists, and that identification is dependent on the possible distinctions available in the discourse" (MacCabe 1978:92). Cf. Lawrence: "style creates a

certain type of fictional role for the character, and in a larger sense, creates a
particular type of fictional world in which the character belongs" (1981:132);
"the various styles contain their own systems of values; because events are
narrated in certain styles, they are apt to be altered by the style chosen"
(1981:136). Lawrence is actually referring to "Oxen of the Sun" here, but her
observations are readily applicable to "Cyclops" and other chapters of the
second half as well.

17 Fokkema and Ibsch are corroborated by Kenner (1980:80–1) when he compares
Ulysses to the detective story, the genre of epistemological quest *par excellence*.

18 "*Ulysses* is a post-epistemological novel: it does not answer the epistemologist's
questions but it 'unpacks' many of them, and it moves us from doubts about
our knowledge to knowledge about our doubts" (Perl 1984:210). On Dick
Higgins's opposition between "cogntive" and "postcognitive" art, see above,
"Telling postmodernist stories"; and on the shift from a modernist poetics
of epistemology to a postmodernist poetics of "post-epistemology" (in fact,
ontology), see McHale (1987:3–25).

19 According to Beebe (1974:184), *Ulysses* recapitulates the three historical stages
of modernism, from impressionism ("the external world *as seen*") to the foregrounding of the observer, finally to "complete immersion within the internal
consciousness of the 'I' "; and he sees "Penelope," which belongs to this final
stage, as the high-water mark of aesthetic radicalism in *Ulysses*. Beebe also,
incidentally, suggests that "Penelope" anticipates postmodernism (1974:187),
but it seems clear that the meaning he gives this term is far from its meaning
in the present essay, indeed closer to "anti-modernism."

20 Lethen's insight is certainly borne out by the practice of recent literary historians of modernism. Fokkema and Ibsch, for instance, explicitly exclude the
European avant-garde movements – Expressionism, Surrealism, Futurism –
from consideration in their account of the modernist "mainstream" (1987:1–2).
In their defense, however, it should be remembered that it has long been the
practice on the Continent (less so in Britain or the United States) to distinguish
between modernism and the avant-garde (see Calinescu 1987a:140–1).

21 Beebe (1974:165–6) identifies four characteristics of modernist writing: (1)
formalism and aesthetic autonomy; (2) detachment and irony; (3) myth used
as an arbitrary ordering principle; and (4) solipsism and reflexivism. Frow's
first and second characteristics seem to correspond to Beebe's "reflexivism";
his third can perhaps be seen as a radicalization of Beebe's "irony"; but where
in Frow's list is anything corresponding to Beebe's "formalism" or "myth"?
Similarly, Frow's first characteristic corresponds to the feature of "metalingual
reflexion" in Fokkema and Ibsch's account of the modernist code (1987:30–47
and *passim*, recapitulated 318), but apart from that there is no overlap betwen
their construction of modernism and Frow's.

22 I have been paraphrasing here Thomas Kuhn's account of the incommensurability of rival scientific paradigms. The analogies between Kuhnian paradigms
and the alternative constructions of literary history are, I hope, obvious.

23 This, too, is borne out by the practice of literary historians of modernism.
Stein is conspicuous by her absence from Quinone's (1985) "map" of modernism, while Fokkema and Ibsch, though they do acknowlege her modernism,
nevertheless exclude her from their modernist canon on the grounds that she
is an American, and American literary history "follows a somewhat different
course" (1987:17) from that of Europe in the modernist decades. Equally telling
is the case of Kafka, another writer in excess of modernism: Fokkema and
Ibsch (1987:39) exclude him from consideration for his absence of metalingual

reflexion, for them a key identifying mark of modernism; Quinones ostensibly includes Kafka in his modernist canon (1985:9, 18), but in fact has little to say about him, and at one point is forced to admit how anomalous and marginal is Kafka's alleged "modernism" (276 n. 26).

3 MODERNIST READING, POSTMODERNIST TEXT: THE CASE OF GRAVITY'S RAINBOW (1979)

1 Pynchon 1973:3. All subsequent references will be to this edition, and will be noted parenthetically in the body of the text, thus: (GR:00). Bracketed ellipses in the quotations from Gravity's Rainbow are mine; those without brackets, Pynchon's.

2 The "realism" of this opening dream-episode – the fact that it cannot be distinguished on internal evidence from "real" episodes – has been remarked by a number of critics, including Siegel (1976:51–2) and Seed (1976:79).

3 Since these words were first published, it has become an option for a reader to mean, when evoking postmodernism, not this "writerly" model of text (which has come increasingly to be identified with a "late" or residual modernism) but a renewed "readerly" model, or a "double-coded" model which superimposes legibility and writerliness (see, e.g., Barth 1984c; Hutcheon 1988).

4 On Pynchon's relative readability, see Slade, who takes the extreme position that, despite his innovations, Pynchon is "a remarkably conventional writer, as evidenced by his preference for the ominiscient narrator, the skillfully orchestrated leitmotif, the archetype, the picaresque plot, and the epic sweep of narrative" (Slade 1990:222). For a more judicious account of the ways in which Pynchon is "conventionally" readable, see Hume (1987).

5 Actually, The Crying of Lot 49 is formally closer to James's The Ambassadors than to What Maisie Knew. Oedipa Maas, like Lambert Strether but unlike Maisie, is articulate to the same degree as the novel's narrator; the gap between her voice and the narrator's is so small as to be negligible. Indeed, the novel goes out of its way to motivate several of the most important and extravagant metaphors at the level of the narrator's discourse as plausibly emanating from Oedipa herself (Pynchon 1967:13, 15, 93, 95–6, 136–7).

6 Whether this phenomenon (not only in V. but elsewhere in contemporary North American fiction) is best described as "parody" or "self-conscious exploitation" (i.e. stylization, imitation) has been discussed at some length by Brooke-Rose (1991:191–203). Van Delden (1990) pertinently applies to V. Huyssen's (1986) thesis that postmodernism rejects not modernist poetics per se but rather the "domesticated" or institutionalized modernism of New Critical orthodoxy: "Pynchon's parodic re-working of modernist conventions [in V.] takes as its point of departure a view of modernism largely shaped by the concerns of the New Critics" (1990: 134).

7 This baring of the device had already been anticipated in Pynchon's short story "Entropy" (1960; reprinted in Pynchon 1984), in which a character dictates his memoirs in the third person; The Education of Henry Adams is explicitly identified as the model for this strategy in "Entropy"; a postmodernist equivalent can be found in Mailer's The Armies of the Night.

8 The strategy's self-consciousness is all the more striking when one compares this chapter of V. (Chapter 3, "In which Stencil, a quick-change artist, does eight impersonations") with the earlier short story on which it is based, "Under the Rose" (1961; reprinted in Pynchon 1984). In the story, this same espionage melodrama had originally been rendered from a unitary, "omniscient" narratorial point of view (see Cowart 1977).

9 The general perspective underlying my approach here is best formulated in the admirable chapter on "Convention and Naturalization" in Culler (1975:131–60).

10 On the "code" of modernist poetics, with which a reader must be conversant in order properly to process a modernist text, see Fokkema and Ibsch (1987).

11 For an account of ontological reliability and unreliability in the "Circe" chapter somewhat at odds with the present one, see above, "Constructing (post)modernism: the case of *Ulysses*."

12 This experience of the reader's in *Gravity's Rainbow* is anticipated by Pynchon's earlier novels. The career of V. in the novel of that name is an imaginative projection by one Herbert Stencil on the basis of doubtful and fragmentary information. The information, we are told, has been "Stencilized":

> Around each seed of a dossier [. . .] had developed a nacreous mass of inference, poetic licence, forcible dislocation of personality into a past he didn't remember and had no right in, save the right of imaginative anxiety or historical care [. . .] The rest was impersonation and dream.
>
> (Pynchon 1964:50–1)

In *The Crying of Lot 49*, the ontological embarrassments are transferred to the heroine, Oedipa, something of a literary critic herself, whose difficulties in reconstructing the reality of the Tristero System the reader shares.

13 Another option, exemplified by Clerc (1983b:126), is to treat the incest scene as irresolvably ambiguous between fantasy and actuality, but I don't see that this reading is any better sustained by the textual evidence than the "real incest" reading. For corroboration of my account of the "amazing incest" passage, see, e.g., Clark (1985:24).

14 In fact, this possibility had been anticipated from the beginning, although only in the form of unreliable speculation by a minor character, one Teddy Bloat (*GR*:19).

15 For a sharp critique of my account of the "two" Mrs. Quoads, see McHoul and Wills (1990:45–6); details of McHoul and Wills's position may be found in the Appendix to this chapter. For corroboration of my account, see Duyfhuizen (1981b).

16 The Schwarzkommando themselves are sensitive to the implausibility of their own existence. As Enzian the Nguarorerue, their leader, tells Slothrop:

> There are even now powerful factions in Paris who don't believe we exist. And most of the time I'm not so sure myself [. . .] I think we're here, but only in a statistical way. Something like that rock over there is just about 100% certain – it knows it's there, so does everybody else. But our own chances of being right here right now are only a little better than even – the slightest shift in the probabilities and we're gone – schnapp! like that.
>
> (*GR*:361–2)

One rubs one's eyes a bit at that phrase "powerful factions in Paris," for which, moreover, there is no particular motivation in the fictional terms (no enemies of the Schwarkommando explicitly identified with Paris). But what better site for those who would place the Schwarzkommando *sous rature*?

17 The theme of concretization of fantasy had already been anticipated in *The Crying of Lot 49*, where Driblette the theatrical director describes himself as "the projector at the planetarium, all the closed little universe visible in the circle of that stage is coming out of my mouth, eyes, sometimes other orifices also" (Pynchon 1967:56). Oedipa takes over his metaphor along with his ontology: "*Shall I project a world?*" (Pynchon, 1967:59).

18 Such verbal blurring or hedging of reality is of course a major stylistic device of Faulkner's prose. For these purposes Faulkner favors the conjunction *or* and conditional adverbs such as *possibly, likely, probably, doubtless, maybe, perhaps*: see especially *Light in August* (1932) and *Absalom, Absalom!* (1936). Pynchon had already used such a device to comic effect in *The Crying of Lot 49*:

> Popov did send out a ship, either the corvette "Bogatir" or the clipper "Gaidamak," to see what it could see. Off the coast of either what is now Carmel-by-the-sea, or what is now Pismo Beach, around noon or possibly toward dusk, the two ships sighted each other. One of them may have fired; if it did then the other responded; but both were out of range so neither showed a scar afterward to prove anything.
>
> (Pynchon 1967:32)

19 Anomalously, Bersani (1990:193) claims to find no recuperative uses for Prentice's talent anywhere in *Gravity's Rainbow*. This represents an almost unique case of *under reading* of this particular motif.

20 This is not as fanciful an outcome as it might seem. After all, what else has Bruce Morrissette done but apply precisely this reductive naturalization to Robbe-Grillet's novels, locating each within the mind of a protagonist whose particular psychopathology manifests itself in the novel's structure (Morrissette 1963; see Culler 1975:200; Brooke-Rose 1981:291–310)?

21 Other naturalizations are possible, however. Byron's story is said to be dictated to one Eddie Pensiero, who is able to "read" shivers, through the "muscular modulations" of the soldier cranking the generator that supplies Byron with power (*GR*:640–2, 647). Since Pensiero is also identified as a benzedrine user, perhaps this authorizes us to locate Byron's story within Pensiero's hallucination. A more disorienting possibility is that we are meant to incorporate Byron in the "real" world of *Gravity's Rainbow*. This may be indicated by the recurrence throughout the novel, in contexts of varying reliability, of other sentient inanimate objects: ball-bearings (*GR*:583–5), rocks (*GR*:612–3), even other light-bulbs (*GR*:464).

22 Certain materials in these passages, in fact, seem to resist this naturalization. Some elements of the "Komical Kamikaze" episodes obviously relate to Pirate Prentice's experience, and could not plausibly emanate from Slothrop's mind (*GR*:698). Other elements (*GR*:691–2) derive from a hallucination once suffered by a certain Geza Rózsavölgyi (*GR*:634–5), hence are equally inaccessible to Slothrop; unless, that is, we give credence to Roger Mexico's paranoid fear of merging minds with Rózsavölgyi (*GR*:634). If with Mexico, why not with Slothrop?

23 For an exemplary analysis of the motivation of transitions in a typical nineteenth-century realist text, see Harshav [Hrushovski] (1988). My own approach draws upon the general theory of the literary text outlined in Harshav's paper, which originally appeared in 1976.

24 This transition by triangulation in Virginia Woolf was already noticed long ago by Daiches (1963 (1947)). I owe this reference to W.J. Bronzwaer, who has had to wait over a decade for this long-delayed acknowledgement.

25 When this paper was first published in 1979, I was able to cite as evidence of Pynchon's preeminence in this mode of postmodernism only the case of Tom Robbins, an epigonic writer whose poetics, in a novel such as *Even Cowgirls Get the Blues* (1976), seems clearly to have derived from that of *Gravity's Rainbow*. Since then, many other writers in Pynchon's mode have emerged or

have come to my attention, including weakly epigonic ones such as Robert Shea and Robert Anton Wilson (*Illuminatus!*, 1975), and more robustly independent ones such as Joseph McElroy (in *Lookout Cartridge*, 1974), Don DeLillo (*Ratner's Star*, 1976; *Running Dog*, 1978; *The Names*, 1982), Ted Mooney (*Easy Travel to Other Planets*, 1981), Steve Erickson (*Tours of the Black Clock*, 1989), and William Vollmann (*You Bright and Risen Angels*, 1987; *The Rainbow Stories*, 1989), as well as an entire school of science-fiction writing, so-called cyberpunk SF, which is undisguisedly modeled on elements of Pynchon's poetics. In some cyberpunk texts, the debt to Pynchon is openly acknowledged; see especially Rudy Rucker's *Software* (1982) and *Wetware* (1988), and Walter Jon Williams's *Hardwired* (1986). For more on Pynchon's relation to cyberpunk, see below, "POSTcyberMODERNpunkISM."

26 See Van Delden (1990), who specifies that these are the norms of New Critical (i.e. institutionalized, pedagogical) modernism. And cf. Jameson, who has argued that the various postmodernisms

> emerge as specific reactions against the established forms of high modernism, against this or that dominant high modernism . . . This means that there will be as many different forms of postmodernism as there were high modernisms in place, since the former are at least initially specific and local reactions *against* those models . . . the unity of this new impulse – if it has one – is given not in itself but in the very modernism it seeks to displace.
>
> (Jameson 1983:111–12)

(Incidentally, this passage does not appear in the version of this paper reprinted in Jameson 1991b.)

27 For more on this apocalyptic narrative of literary change, and alternatives to it, see above, "Telling postmodernist stories."

4 "YOU USED TO KNOW WHAT THESE WORDS MEAN": MISREADING *GRAVITY'S RAINBOW* (1985)

1 Pynchon 1973:207. All subsequent references will be to this edition, and will be incorporated in the body of the text, thus: (*GR*:00). Bracketed ellipses are my own; Pynchon's are without brackets.

2 Schuber (1984:74) finds it "curious" that Pynchon criticism has failed to "highlight parallels between Slothrop's problems with reading and those of readers reading." This was not even true in 1984; but since then, the parallelism between the reading practices of Pynchon's characters and those of his readers has become something of a commonplace of Pynchon criticism; (see, e.g., Hite 1983a:17; Russell 1983:254–5; O'Donnell 1986).

3 This is somewhat less true now than it was when this paper was originally published; see, for examples of a more negatively capable approach to Pynchon, the papers in the February 1984 special issue of *Pynchon Notes*, "Deconstructing *Gravity's Rainbow*," edited by Bernard Duyfhuizen, and especially McHoul and Wills (1990).

4 Or almost always: the case of impersonal *you*, which defies this generalization, is discussed below.

5 Banfield (following Benveniste 1966) begins from the controversial premise that not every sentence necessarily implies an act of communication, and that some sentences in a narrative text may be, strictly speaking, "narratorless." She challenges, in other words, the communication model that has been the basis of most theories of narrative. This is not the place to argue my differences with Banfield; I have, in any case, done that elsewhere (see McHale 1983).

6 The same goes, *mutatis mutandis*, for the implied author's presumed opposite number, the "implied reader," a term which designates the reader's hypothetical reconstruction of the empirical author's anticipations of his or her readers' norms and values.

7 I have placed "he" and "she" between quotation marks here because the extradiegetic narrator is typically genderless.

8 Banfield (1982) claims that the second person is excluded from free indirect discourse, both as a surface form and as an underlying pronoun, in such forms as the subjectless imperative or addressee-oriented adverbials (*personally, honestly, candidly, confidentially*, and others). She would appear to be wrong about the exclusion of forms with an underlying second person, for counterexamples to this generalization abound: e.g. (1) subjectless imperative in FID: "How she could eat in those days. She'd give anything now to have an appetite like that. Health was better than all the money in the world. *Look* at Rockefeller" (Dahlberg 1976:336); (2) addressee-oriented adverbials in FID:

> he certainly did feel, and no denying it [. . .], a certain kind of admiration for a man who had actually brandished a knife, cold steel, with the courage of his political convictions though, *personally*, he would never be a party to any such thing.
>
> (Joyce 1973:562)

"*Honestly*, she was surprised when Susan Gillespie came up to her when they were getting their wraps to go home and giggled, 'My dear, you were the belle of the ball' " (Dos Passos n.d.:258). Banfield would seem to be right, however, about the impossibility of the second person pronoun itself appearing in FID; or at least, I have found no counter-examples.

9 An instance occurs, for example, in "The Haunted Mind," one of Hawthorne's *Twice-Told Tales* of 1842.

10 Among the other possible transgressions that will *not* be considered here are, for instance, (1) the narratee turning the tables on the narrator and addressing him or her in return (as in Sterne's *Tristram Shandy* or Federman's *Take It or Leave It*); or (2) the characters presuming to address their narrator (as in Unamuno's *Niebla*, Flann O'Brien's *At Swim-Two-Birds*, Muriel Spark's *The Comforters* or Kurt Vonnegut's *Breakfast of Champions*); or (3) the narrator addressing himself or herself in the catechetical, question-and-answer mode (which is presumably the case in the "Ithaca" chapter of Joyce's *Ulysses*); or even (4) the character addressing the empirical author, as Molly Bloom seems to do in the "Penelope" chapter of *Ulysses*: "O Jamesy let me up out of this" (Joyce 1973:691).

11 Morrissette is anxious to distinguish as sharply as possible between the "pure narrative you" and the second person of "rhetoric" and "oratory," that is, cases in which *you* is "addressed frankly to an audience" (1985b:115). Nevertheless, he is forced to admit that the "rhetorical cast . . . never . . . disappears entirely from the [second-person] mode, even when it becomes unmistakably narrative" (1985b:121).

12 Butor (1964) has described second-person narrative in similar terms, as a didactic situation in which a character is told his own story by someone else. He draws an analogy with a police interrogation in which the interrogator reconstructs for the criminal actions to which the latter refuses to confess, so that the interrogator in effect forces the narrative upon him. This analogy is, as we shall see, directly relevant to several of the cases of second-person narrative in *Gravity's Rainbow*.

13 Morrissette (1985b:118–26) has collected a number of earlier examples, mainly from modernist fiction, including passages from Faulkner's *Absalom, Absalom!*, Hemingway's *A Farewell to Arms*, and Robert Penn Warren's *All the King's Men*.

14 Smetak (1987) is among those who have suggested that the *Gravity's Rainbow* narrator *is*, in some sense, a character-narrator. The question here, of course, is "In *what* sense?"; for this narrator is clearly not a personified character (he could not possibly be " 'found' [. . .] in the conventional sense of 'positively identified and detained,' " as the text will eventually say of Slothrop (*GR*:712), and his only claim to character status is his renunciation of the supposed narratorial prerogative of omniscience: "the 'Over Voice' [i.e. narrator] functions not as an omniscient narrator but as a virtual first person narrator, in other words, as just another 'voice' in this fragmentary universe" (Smetak 1987:101). At the other extreme, Schaub (1981), against whose interpretation Smetak is reacting here, posits an unbounded, omnipresent, omnicompetent "Orphic voice" of narration in *Gravity's Rainbow*.

This narrator can only be a *"virtual* first person narrator" because he never actually advertises his presence by using the first-person pronoun *I*, although he does command the first-person plural *we*. *We* in Gravity's Rainbow behaves in many respects analogously to *you*, raising many of the same problems; e.g.:

An organ grinder plays Rossini's overture to *La Gazza Ladra* (which, as we shall see later, in Berlin, marks a high point in music which everybody ignored. . . .)

(*GR*:273)

We drank the blood of our enemies. The blood of our friends, we cherished.

(*GR*:739)

It was difficult even for us, old fans who've always been at the movies (haven't we?).

(*GR*:760)

Who is *we* here? Is it inclusive ("I and you")? exclusive ("I and they")? both? neither?

15 Cf. Duyfhuizen (1981b:26): "Pynchon's narrator constantly berates his readers, and often he catches us in our 'unhealthily obsessed' readings: 'Ha, ha! Caught *you* with your hand in your pants!' " See also Seed (1988:216).

16 Morrissette (1985b:122, 126 and *passim*) observes that the more fully particularized and individualized the narrated events, the more closely will the second person approach what he calls "pure narrative you," and the less will it be contaminated with "rhetorical" elements. In our terms, this means that when events are fully particularized (e.g. "the moment of sun-silence inside the white tile greasy-spoon"), the second person is more likely to be character-oriented than narratee-oriented. This is certainly borne out by Hawkes's *The Lime Twig* and Calvino's *If on a Winter's Night a Traveler*, both of which begin as second-person narratives sufficiently general and unparticularized to accommodate any *you*, but gradually become more specific and individualized until the referent of *you* has been narrowed to exclude everyone except one particular individual (Hencher in Hawkes, the anonymous but richly personified Reader in Calvino).

17 Here, according to Smith (1982:30), "Pynchon intrudes to address his readers."

18 The main formal criterion for free indirect discourse is the back-shifting of the present-tense verbs of sentences of reported speech to conform with the past-tense verbs of the narrative context (see McHale 1978). But the narrative

context in *Gravity's Rainbow* is cast almost entirely in the present tense; consequently, back-shifting of tenses cannot occur, and free indirect discourse, in the strict sense, is excluded. This contradicts Smetak (1987), who argues that *Gravity's Rainbow* is written almost entirely in free indirect discourse; but she must have in mind some looser sense of "combined discourse" or multiple-voice text, not free indirect discourse as a syntactical type.

19 Here, according to Fowler (1980:88), we hear "Pynchon's voice, heavy with sensual intimacy," that is, presumably, the extra-diegetic narrator apostrophizing "his" character – not the most persuasive of readings.

20 Unless Blicero is already broadcasting to him over the radio-link that has been specially provided:

> In one of his ears, a tiny speaker has been surgically implanted [. . .] The data link runs through the radio-guidance system, and the words of Weissmann [i.e. Blicero] are to be, for a while, multiplexed with the error-corrections sent out to the Rocket.
>
> (*GR*.751)

21 Not in the sense that one is *absent from* oneself, but in the sense that one's self is, from a communicative point of view, an inappropriate addressee: there is no "real," i.e. extra-mental, communicative circuit here.

22 Doury's solutions to the problem of translating Pynchon's second-person pronouns are not very consistent or systematic. He will, for instance, translate *you* by *on* at the beginning of a passage, but switch to *vous* by the end (e.g. Doury 1975:367; cf. *GR*:419). Often enough he will simply omit the problematical second-person sentence altogether (e.g. Doury 1975:333; cf. *GR*:379). Although hardly the most responsible of solutions, the practice of simple omitting "untranslatable" passages is by no means unheard of among translators. It does, however, rather strikingly contradict the claim by an unnamed source (reported in Siegel 1978:126, n. 12) that Pynchon "allowed only a few word changes to be made in the new French translation."

23 But see Wilson (1990:196), who does identify the "you" of this passage with Slothrop, confusing (I think) The White Visitation, which is located well outside of London, on the Kentish coast, with St. Veronica's Hospital in the London's East End, where Slothrop is for a time held for experimental observation.

24 See, e.g., Clerc (1983c:17): the narrative voice "speaks pointedly to the reader ('You will want cause and effect. All right.') . . . and on rare occasions gives parenthetical advice, like its recommendation that the reader check out Ishmael Reed. . . ."

25 Cf. Purdy (1988:13): "When speaker and spoken to are not clearly identified, there is always the threat of a 'you' or a 'we' getting out of the textual representation and inescapably including *me*. Pynchon repeatedly presses this threat."

26 And of *we*: the first-person plural is also conspicuously present in this passage. See note 14 above.

27 An interesting counter-example to this generalization is Caesar (1984), who *does* read the Advent vespers episode in the light of a general interpretive hypothesis about the text, proposing a connection between the second-person mode in general, and the vespers passage in particular, and the textual logic of "waste." However, far from exemplifying the drive for certitude among Pynchon's critics, this essay seems to me one of the all-too-rare instances of negatively capable reading in the Pynchon literature.

28 Somewhat problematic, from the point of view of this attribution of these

second-person pronouns to Slothrop, is the phrase "you used to know what these words mean," occurring as it does parenthetically in a sentence in which Slothrop is referred to in the third person ("Of course Slothrop lost her," etc.) By the logic of an argument I used above, in the third section ("The second person of *Gravity's Rainbow*"), when describing contextual disambiguation in second-person passages which might ambiguously be ascribed to a character-addressee or to the narratee, the third-person reference to Slothrop here should eliminate him as potential addressee of *you*, leaving only the narratee to fill that role.

29 Rosenheim (1985:48) writes, for instance, that while many of the second-person passages scattered throughout *Gravity's Rainbow* "may not refer to the reader, exactly," the one in which Slothrop takes leave of Bianca "does, unmistakably." Rosenheim's reasoning would seem to be that, precisely because this passage is particularly offensive to the reader (accusing him, e.g., of masturbating in public), this makes its effect of direct address particularly strong and indelible. This corroborates an argument I proposed at the end of the third section, above. On the other hand, the specificity of the experience that *you* is supposed to have undergone (he has seen the film German Expressionist film *Alpdrücken*, has masturbated while viewing it, etc.) would appear to be a factor weighing against an unequivocal identification of *you* with the narratee. As Morrissette has argued, and various postmodernist examples confirm (see note 16 above), the more concrete and detailed the experiences ascribed to *you*, the more likely that *you* designates a character rather than the narratee.

30 Hite's version is perhaps slightly to be preferred over Seed's, not because it is in any sense "truer," but just because it is a useful corrective to the sentimental readings to which Pynchon's critics are prone. A case in point is Werner's (1986:93–4) startling, but nevertheless exemplary, misreading of a second-person passage apparently involving displaced children in "St. Veronica's Downtown Bus Station": "You feel her exhaustion, feel the impossible vastness of all the sleeping countryside at her back, and for the moment you really are selfless, sexless . . . considering only how to shelter her, you are the Traveler's Aid" (*GR*:50–1). Werner identifies this *you* as being addressed to "the reader," and interprets it as an "outreach for love." Hite (1983b:61) correctly observes that the likeliest candidate for the referent of this *you* is the sinister Mr. Pointsman, and that in this passage he appears to be contemplating picking up waifs for sexual purposes! Cf. also Smetak (1987:98–9), who reads this passage much the way Hite does. (In fact, it seems to me that the entire passage is better understood not as a literal scene of child-molestation, nor even as Pointsman's sexual fantasy, but rather as an extended metaphor for the latter's unwholesome experimental interest in the rocket-bomb victims recuperating in St. Veronica's Hospital.)

31 Purdy (1988) proposes yet another global hypothesis bearing on the leavetaking passage, namely that throughout *Gravity's Rainbow* the second-person pronoun forms a nexus with recurrent motifs of death and childhood. I have left this hypothesis out of my account because, like Caesar's (1984) reading of the Advent vespers episode, it seems to me not a certitude-hungry interpretation at all, but one of the rare negatively capable readings.

32 The reference (*GR*:49) to "the rows either side" (that is, both rows of beds in a hospital ward and rows of seats in a theater) helps gloss the otherwise rather puzzling allusion to "rookwise row or diagonal" in *GR*:472. Here, as also in *GR*:543, where Prentice is accosted from a "bishopwise seat" in an all-

night cinema, the arrangement of seats in a movie house is seen as analogous to a chessboard, with ranks, files, and diagonals.

33 As early as 1982, Smith (1982:36 n. 11) was already calling the global interpretation of *Gravity's Rainbow* as a film "almost a commonplace of Pynchon criticism." If it was already almost a commonplace then, what shall we call it by now? See also Simmon (1974:57 and *passim*); Schwarzbach (1978:66); Wolfley (1977:873); Tate (1983:5–6); Clerc (1983b:112); Kharpertian (1990:137); etc.

34 This functional equivalence between reading *Gravity's Rainbow* as "one whole dream" or hallucination and reading it as "one whole film" has been noticed by McHoul and Wills (1990:38, 45).

35 On this motif of the reversal of processes, which Weisenburger identifies with the classical trope of *hysteron proteron*, see Friedman (1983:82–5) and Weisenburger (1988:36–7 and *passim*). A number of other postmodernist texts have experimented with this trope; see, e.g., Carpentier's "Vuelta a la semilla" ("Journey to the Source") and Merwin's "Unchopping a Tree" (in *The Miner's Pale Children*).

36 The pointing finger is a recurrent gesture of threat in *Gravity's Rainbow*; see, e.g., Slothrop's encounter with the fearsome Major Marvy:

> "There he is," in a great roar, indicating Slothrop with a trembling finger, "by God the limey sonofabitch go *git* him, boys!" Go *git him*, boys? Slothrop continuing to gaze a moment here at this finger, illuminated in cute flourishes and curlicues of cherubic fat.
>
> (*GR*:308)

The nightmarish turning face also recurs; see, e.g., Geza Rózsavölgyi's encounter with what appears to be a figure from a hallucination:

> The pilot is turning to Rószavölgyi, who is still strapped in safety harness behind him. The face is covered with helmet, goggles that reflect too much light, oxygen mask – a face of metal, leather, isinglass. But now the pilot is raising the goggles, slowly, and whose eyes are these, so familiar, smiling hello, I know you, don't you know me? Don't you *really* know me?
>
> (*GR*:635)

See also *GR*:22, *GR*:714, and *GR*:196, 222 (Katje's "Face That Is No Face," turned three-quarters away from Slothrop), as well as Pynchon (1967:36) (the metaphorical stripper who comes back down the runway to stare into Oedipa's face). Pynchon's "turning face" motif can perhaps be seen as the postmodernist reversal of the characteristic modernist motif (found in James) of the semiotically-charged "turned back" (see White 1981).

5 ZAPPING, THE ART OF SWITCHING CHANNELS: ON *VINELAND*

1 My title was inspired by that of Richard Shusterman's essay, "The Fine of Art of Rap" (Shusterman 1991). There is much that could be said about the relations between the practice of channel-switching ("zapping") and "sampling" in rap music; unfortunately, it will have to be said elsewhere.

2 Pynchon 1990:11–12. All subsequent page references will be to this edition, and will be incorporated in the body of the text, thus: (*V*:00).

3 Compare Lucifer Amp, a subsidiary character who "makes a spectacle of himself" for a living in *Gravity's Rainbow*. Amp's chosen medium, however, is the newsreel film, television not being available yet (Pynchon 1973:542–3). All subsequent page references will be to this edition and will be incorporated in the body of the text, thus: (*GR*:00).

4 Examples include: *Phil Donahue* (V:103, 160, 373), celebrity talk-show; *Jeopardy* (V:9) and *Wheel of Fortune* (V:12–13), game-shows; *Gilligan's Island* (V:33, 368), *The Brady Bunch* (V:33, 198), *I Love Lucy* (V:67), *Bewitched* (V:198), and *Love Boat* (V:174), situation comedies; *Hawaii Five-O* (V:59, 60, 62, 99), *CHiPs* (V:83), *Police Woman* (V:327), *Hill Street Blues, Ironside*, and *Mod Squad* (V:345), cop-shows; *Wonder Woman* (V:327), *Bionic Woman* (V:165–6, 327), *The Invaders* (V:234), and *Star Trek* (V:11, 40, 110, 176, 345, 285, 370), science-fiction "action" programs; Sylvester and Tweety-Pie (V:22), *The Flintstones* (V:26), Porky Pig (V:46), *The Smurfs* (V:53, 341), the Roadrunner (V:153), Daffy Duck and Bugs Bunny (V:255), and *The Care Bears* (V:341), cartoon characters and programs.

5 Compare Oedipa Maas's hallucination of Uncle Sam in the familiar army-recruiting pose, "his finger pointing between her eyes. I want you" (Pynchon 1967:7; see above, " 'You used to know what these words mean,' " note 36; all subsequent page references to *The Crying of Lot 49* will be to this edition and will be incorporated in the body of the text, thus: (*Lot*:00)).

The obvious model for this ominous address from the TV screen is of course *Nineteen Eighty-Four* – *Vineland*, after all, is set in the year 1984 – but the immediate source for Pynchon's motif of the accidental broadcast would appear to be the notorious gaffe by Ronald Reagan when, as President of the United States, he jokingly announced the abolition of the Soviet Union, and the "joke" inadvertently went out over the broadcast media.

6 See, among others, Cowart (1980:31–62); Simmon (1981:124–39); Smith (1982); Clerc (1983b); Tate (1983); Marriott (1985); McHoul and Wills (1990:38–45); and see above, " 'You used to know what these words mean.' "

7 It is in the context of these flashback episodes that we find movie-based idioms and figures equivalent to the TV-based language of the present-day (1984) episodes; e.g. "Frenesi found she'd been switching her eyes back and forth, as if cutting together reverse shots of two actors" (V:80–1).

8 It is entirely likely that the critics' sense that *Gravity's Rainbow* draws on the more durable elements of popular culture rests on a kind of optical illusion: i.e., because we critics are only familiar with the more canonical popular-culture items in Pynchon's repertoire, these are the only ones we actually notice; allusions of the more "ephemeral" kind we either misidentify or, more often, simply fail to notice altogether. In this respect, Weisenburger's (1988) annotations of the comic-book and especially the many radio allusions in *Gravity's Rainbow* come as a welcome corrective to our collective critical myopia.

9 "Attention" is associated with film and correct film-viewing: the revolutionary film collective's political program involves "learning how to pay attention" (V:195); Frenesi's political education begins when she learns how to pay correct attention to credits when viewing movies on TV (V:81–2). It is also associated with the Sisterhood of Kunoichi Attentives, an order of female ninjas who are positive figures in this novel: learning kunoichi discipline "takes a serious attention span" (V:112; see also V:154, 155). For other positive contexts of "attention/attend," see V:121, 296, 317, 381.

10 See Leverenz's (1976:244–5) insight, apropos *Gravity's Rainbow*, into Pynchon's language of natural description, which simultaneously calls attention to its own intrusiveness yet leaves us with a sense of nature persisting unimpaired despite the intrusions of human language.

11 For other typical examples of TV jeremiads, see Crary (1984:283–94) and Solomon (1988). On the jeremiad rhetoric of recent education-reform docu-

ments, see Gottlieb and Cornbleth (1989). On Pynchon's affinities with the jeremiad genre, see Smith and Tölölyan (1981).

12 Equivocation is only to be expected of the author of *Gravity's Rainbow*. Critics have regularly sought to organize the various values of *Gravity's Rainbow* into more or less tidy axiological systems, sets of antinomies or binary oppositions, (e.g. Gravity vs the Rainbow, Fathers vs Sons, North vs South, Metropolis vs King Kong, Zero vs One, Christian vs Pagan, White vs Non-White, Elect vs Preterite, etc.), where one term is alleged to be negative, the other positive (see, e.g. Leverenz 1976; Fowler 1980:47–51 and *passim*; Bass 1983:32–3; Hume 1987:118–35 and *passim*). Unfortunately, the harder we scrutinize the polar terms of such oppositions, the more evidence we find that each is already contaminated with its opposite: positively-valued terms "leak" or "bleed" into negatively-valued terms, and vice versa, leaving us anxiously uncertain about where exactly the text's sympathies are supposed to lie (see Schaub 1981:60, 133–6; Hayles and Eiser 1985).

13 See McHale 1987:128–30. Postmodernist representations of the process of *producing* movies occur in such texts as Fuentes's *Zona sagrada*, McElroy's *Lookout Cartridge*, Barth's *LETTERS*, Brodeur's *The Stunt Man*, and Sukenick's *Blown Away*. Representations of the act of *consuming* movies can be found in Simon's *Triptyque*, DeLillo's *Running Dog*, and Coover's *A Night at the Movies*. Cinema functions more diffusely as cultural model or pervasive cultural discourse in Cabrera Infante's *Tres tristes tigres*, Puig's *Kiss of the Spider Woman*, Robbe-Grillet's *Projet pour une révolution à New York*, Rushdie's *Midnight's Children*, and many other postmodernist texts.

14 The idea of simulacral war has been anticipated by the science fiction writer Philip K. Dick, in his novel *The Penultimate Truth* (1964), and later by Pynchon in *Gravity's Rainbow*, in which Enzian discovers that bomb-damage to a chemical works is not real bomb-damage after all, but simulated ruin (*GR*: 520), and where Allied propagandists' simulation of black African rocket-troops in the Third Reich uncannily "precedes" their realization (see above, "Modernist reading, postmodernist text"). For a strikingly Baudrillardian analysis of simulacral crime in science-fiction terms, see Bruce Sterling's "cyberpunk" SF novel *Islands in the Net* (1988). Sterling extrapolates a near future in which, nuclear weapons having been abolished, terrorism remains the only threat to world peace, and the policing of terrorism mainly involves censoring the mass-media so as to deny to terrorist acts their simulacral existence.

15 Another strategy for foregrounding this interpenetration of TV worlds and the real world is illustrated by *The Crying of Lot 49*, where a series of elaborate exchanges are transacted across the porous ontological membrane of the TV screen: e.g. Metzger, formerly a child-actor, whose movies can still occasionally be seen on TV, is currently a lawyer; his friend Manny DiPresso, formerly a lawyer but currently a TV actor, has starred in a TV pilot based on the life of Metzger; and so on. Compare a similar structure of exchange in *Vineland*, in which the actor Millard Hobbs begins by acting the part of the "Marquis de Sod" in TV commercials for a lawn-care company by that name, then, because so many viewers mistake him for the owner, buys into the company, eventually becoming its *real* owner (*V*:46–7).

16 Abish in fact specifies a *movie* screen (see immediately below), but I can only see this is a a kind of anachronism on his part. Abish's example of a simulacrum, "Mannix," is after all a TV show, not a film, and the entire phenomenon of simulation, in the aggravated, reality-sapping form that his text addresses,

belongs to the era of electronic mediation much more than it does to the cinema era.

17 Compare the exploration of the precession of simulacra in Philip K. Dick's science fiction novels and stories (e.g. *The Penultimate Truth*, 1964; *The Simulacra*, 1964; "Faith of Our Fathers," 1967) and more recently in so-called cyberpunk SF, e.g. Bruce Sterling's *The Artificial Kid* (1980), William Gibson's trilogy of *Neuromancer* (1984), *Count Zero* (1986), and *Mona Lisa Overdrive* (1988), and Pat Cadigan's *Synners* (1991). On the relationship between postmodernist fiction and cyberpunk SF, see below, "POSTcyberMODERNpunkISM."

18 The literature on *mise-en-abyme* in poetics is extensive; see, e.g., Morrissette (1985a [1971]); Dällenbach (1977); Bal (1978); Ron (1987); McHale (1987:124–8); and Füredy (1989).

19 There is also in the penultimate chapter of *White Noise* a faintly uncanny shift of register from the discourse of television, recurrent throughout this text, to, of all things, the discourse of angelology. For more on postmodernist angelology, see below, "Women and Men and Angels."

20 For the distinguished career that this memorable sentence has gone on to have in cyberpunk SF, see below, "POSTcyberMODERNpunkISM."

Cf. also the icon that associates TV with death in Pynchon's sole excursion into journalism, "A Journey into the Mind of Watts":

> In one corner was this old, busted, hollow TV set with a rabbit-ears antenna on top; inside, where its picture tube should have been, gazing out with scorched wiring threaded like electronic ivy among its crevices and sockets, was a human skull. The name of the piece was "The Late, Late, Late Show."
> (Pynchon 1966:84)

21 On the postmodernist poetics of MTV, see Kaplan (1987). In commercial TV practices such as Music Television (MTV), the gap between commercial art and avant-garde video is narrowed or even closed, corroborating Polan's observation (1986:182) that "mass culture today takes on the form generally attributed to experimental art."

22 For a description of this passage, see above, " 'You used to know what these words mean.' " See also Clark (1985:27–8).

23 Nor is Takeshi the only character to return in *Vineland*, for Mucho Maas, too, returns, after having last been heard of as long ago as *The Crying of Lot 49*. Moreover, there is oblique reference to a character who, though not actually present in *Vineland*, nevertheless leaves indelible traces in it: Mucho, we are told, had by 1967 passed through "a divorce remarkable even in that more innocent time for its geniality" (*V*:309). That divorce could only have been from Oedipa, and could only have taken place after the end of *The Crying of Lot 49*, which leads one to conclude that Oedipa must after all have survived the "crying of lot 49" on that novel's closing page! – startling news for any devotee of Pynchon's fiction.

24 Already conventional in realist and modernist fiction (e.g. Balzac, Faulkner), *retour des personnages*, i.e. the persistence of characters from novel to novel, is a "postmodernist" device only in the sense that postmodernist writers such as Barth, Durrell (in the *Avignon Quintet*), Brooke-Rose, and others, have exploited it for its potentially disorienting ontological effects. Characters who exist *inter*textually, "between" texts, seem to approach (but at the same time serve to defamiliarize) the ontological status of beings who exist *extra*-textually, *outside* texts. On *retour des personnages* in Brooke-Rose's *Verbivore* (1990)

(which reprises characters from both *Amalgamemnon*, 1984, and *Xorandor*, 1986), see below, " 'I draw the line as a rule ...' " On postmodernist *retour des personnages* in general, see McHale (1987:56–8).

25 This partitioning of the world into regions based on different pop-culture genres is already anticipated in *Gravity's Rainbow*; see Henkle (1983).

26 Compare the many episodes of *Gravity's Rainbow* that allude to the worlds of animated cartoons, in particular the episodes involving anthropomorphic inanimate objects: talking melanocytes (*GR*:148–9), animate pinballs (*GR*:583–5), and let's not forget Byron the Bulb (*GR*:647–55).

27 This is the sort of incongruity that was so memorably exploited by the film *Who Framed Roger Rabbit?*; see also Robert Coover's story "Cartoon" from *A Night at the Movies* (1987).

28 None of them in this text, however, approaches the scale of the hypertrophied monster-metaphors of *Gravity's Rainbow*, truly self-contained worlds-within-the-world (see McHale 1987:128–9, 139–40).

29 The "images ... rolling in and out of the frame" here represent the normal "programming flow" of commercial TV, and the heightened "flow" of zapping, but there is an explicit analogy here with the scene, cited above, in which Takeshi zaps through the channels (*V*:160–1). DL watches TV while waiting to assassinate Brock Vond; Takeshi watches TV *after* DL has mistakenly administered to him the delayed-action death-blow intended for Vond. The two scenes of TV-viewing are thus symmetrical, one mirroring the other.

30 Episodes of dream or hallucination in *Vineland* include Zoyd's dream, with which the novel actually opens (*V*:3); Takeshi's acid trip (*V*:159); Frenesi's dream (*V*:255–6); Brock Vond's dream (*V*:274–5); Zoyd's trip (*V*:285); and Sasha's, Weed's, Frenesi's, and Zoyd's dreams (*V*:362, 365–6, 370 and 374 respectively). Strangest of all is the episode of collective "lucid dreaming" in which the children of Van Meter's household arrange to rendezvous, in their respective dreams, in the same shared dream landscape, the same "alternate world" (*V*:223).

31 Visits (often parodic) to heaven or to the underworld are a staple of postmodernist fiction; see, e.g., Flann O'Brien's *The Third Policeman* (1940/67), Christine Brooke-Rose's *Such* (1966), Ishmael Reed's *The Last Days of Louisiana Red* (1974) and *The Terrible Twos* (1982), R.M. Koster's *The Dissertation* (1975), Stanley Elkin's *The Living End* (1979), and William T. Vollman's *The Ice-Shirt* (1990).

32 See also Prairie's fantasy of an alternative scenario, not realized in the real world, in which her mother had not given birth to her but had had an abortion instead, Prairie returning as a ghost (if that's the right word) to haunt the woman who *would have been* her mother (*V*:334). See below, "I draw the line as a rule ... ," on Brooke-Rose's "non-actualizing" narrative fiction, *Amalgamemnon*.

33 On the relation between "angelic" motifs and their updated science-fiction versions, see below, "Women and men and angels."

34 Motifs of individual death in postmodernist fiction are often linked to themes of collective death – nuclear apocalypse, environmental disaster – reflecting the conditions under which postmodern lives are lived out; see, e.g., DeLillo's *White Noise*; and see below, "The (post)modernism of *The Name of the Rose*." Apocalyptic motifs enter *Vineland*, however, only obliquely: the student revolutionaries from the College of the Surf are spirited away to concentration camps along secret highways originally designed for evacuating the cities in case of nuclear attack (*V*:249). Traveling on those secret highways evokes

proleptic images of the day when they will be used for the purpose for which they were designed: "the sudden light from behind, the unbearable sight in the mirror" (V:252).

35 The ones and zeroes of life and death would seem to exhaust the range of ontological options, but, as Oedipa would come to understand in *The Crying of Lot 49*, "excluded middles [. . .] were bad shit, to be avoided" (*Lot*:136).

36 Cf. Thomas Disch's experiments with represented states of half-death, or modes of being dead, in *The Businessman* – an exercise, parallel to Pynchon's, in attempting to think what most eludes thought, to represent what eludes representation. Corroborating my own analysis, Pfeil (1988:62) draws an analogy between the ontological fluidity of *The Businessman* and TV "flow."

6 THE (POST)MODERNISM OF *THE NAME OF THE ROSE*

1 Both reprinted in Barth 1984a:62–76, 193–206. See above, "Telling postmodernist stories."

2 For application of the concept of "double coding" to literary postmodernism, see Hutcheon (1988).

3 See above, "Telling postmodernist stories."

4 This argument contradicts that of Holquist (1971), who has sought to identify the detective story not with modernism but with postmodernism. Actually, Holquist's account and mine converge in their respective analyses; it is only in *terminology* that they differ. The texts which Holquist analyzes as postmodernist versions of the detective story – especially Robbe-Grillet's *Le Voyeur* and *Les Gommes* and Nabokov's *Lolita* and *Pale Fire*, more problematically Borges's fictions – I would describe as modernist (or late-modernist) texts; while the texts which I would consider postmodernist *sub*versions of the detective story do not appear in his account.

5 On McElroy's fiction, see below, "Women and men and angels."

6 Eco 1983:243. All subsequent references will be to this translation, and will be incorporated parenthetically in the text, thus: (*NR*:00).

7 It is hard not to hear a Proustian echo in Adso's rueful characterization of his own narrative quest as "a sinful succumbing to the terrestrial passion of recollection, a foolish attempt to elude the flow of time, and death" (*NR*:281). Only the word "sinful" would be out of place in a Proustian context. Other modernist models for *The Name of the Rose* explicitly acknowledged by Eco include *Ulysses* and *Der Zauberberg* (Eco 1984:30).

8 Calinescu (1987a:13–92) has demonstrated the historical continuity between *modernus* (a medieval coinage) in the opposition between "modern" and "ancient," and the "modern" of twentieth-century modernism and postmodernism.

9 See, for instance, Levao's (1985) account of the perspectivism of Nicholas Cusanus, a fifteenth-century figure, so a century later than Eco's fictional William of Baskerville. According to Levao, Cusanus, a kind of proto-epistemologist or late-medieval Wallace Stevens, tries to reconstruct Anselm's ontological assumptions in terms of a perspectivist cosmology – the reverse process to the one by which postmodernism deconstructs modernist perspectivism. Strikingly, Cusanus's term for fiction (in the broad sense) is "conjecture" (as in his treatise *De coniecturis*, 1440–4), the very word Eco uses to descibe the detective-story structure of *The Name of the Rose*.

10 Spanos's class of anti-detective stories comprises a rather eccentric collection, ranging from Kafka's *The Trial* and Eliot's *Sweeney Agonistes*, through Greene's *Brighton Rock* and Beckett's *Watt* and *Molloy*, to Robbe-Grillet and

Nathalie Sarraute, stopping short in the 1950s. See also Tani (1984), who distinguishes among three types of anti-detective story: the "innovative" type (including *The Name of the Rose*), in which "the conventional rules of detective fiction are freely used or twisted but not subverted" and "some partially satisfying solution is still present" (Tani 1984:43); the "deconstructive" type, e.g. *The Crying of Lot 49*; and the "metafictional" type, e.g. *If on a Winter's Night a Traveller, Pale Fire*.

11 A characteristic recent example is Paul Auster's *New York Trilogy* (*City of Glass*, 1985; *Ghosts*, 1986; *The Locked Room*, 1986). Here all the "mysteries" are left unsolved, and detectives, clients and suspects under investigation swap roles dizzyingly. Auster's detectives are literally "absorbed" in their respective cases, coming to identify so completely with the suspects as to lose all sense of their own identities; or they renounce their quests just short of the final revelation, and the role of cognitive hero is transferred to the author – or to *an* author, for author-characters and surrogate authors (including one named "Paul Auster") abound. In Tani's terms (see note 10 above), Auster's trilogy combines at least the "deconstructive" and "metafictional" types of anti-detective fiction, if not all three types.

Auster's precursors in the anti-detective "genre" (if that's what it is) include Borges's "Death and the Compass" (see below, "Ways of world-making") and Pynchon's *The Crying of Lot 49*. Other characteristic recent examples of anti-detective fiction (apart from those mentioned above in the text) include Sebastien Japrisot's *Piège pour Cendrillon*, Giles Gordon's *Girl with Red Hair*, Maggie Gee's *Dying, in Other Words*, John Fowles's *A Maggot*, and Steve Katz's parodic "Death of the Band."

12 I am grateful to Claude Gandelman for calling my attention to the fact that these topical allusions were especially added in the English translation, and are not present in the Italian original. The *roman-à-clef* dimension is one feature of Eco's novel which the film version does preserve, minimally but conspicuously: examining a book in the library, Sean Connery as William remarks that it contains annotations by "Umberto of Bologna."

13 Cf. Coletti (1988:189): "The Babel of languages by, or perhaps in spite of, which Salvatore communicates is an image of dialogic heteroglossia."

14 This catalogue seems reminiscent of Pynchon's account, in *Gravity's Rainbow*, of the Zone, that space of stateless anarchy opened in the months after the fall of the Third Reich:

> The Nationalities are on the move. It is a great frontierless streaming out here. Volksdeutsch from across the Oder, moved out by the Poles and headed for the camp at Rostock, Poles fleeing the Lublin regime, others going back home . . . Estonians, Letts, and Lithuanians trekking north again . . . Sudetens and East Prussians shuttling between Berlin and the DP camps in Mecklenburg, Czechs and Slovaks, Croats and Serbs, Tosks and Ghegs, Macedonians, Magyars, Vlachs, Circassians, Spaniols, Bulgars. . . .
>
> (Pynchon 1973:549)

15 See Coletti (1988:112–41). Claude Gandelman discussed the iconography of the "world turned upside-down" at the 1988 *Name of the Rose* symposium at Hebrew University in a paper entitled, "The Semiotics of Heresies/Heresies as Semiotics in *The Name of the Rose*." On Adso's vision of the *Coena Cypriani*, see Parker 1985.

16 We might also add, as a further layer or frame not acknowledged by the preface, William Weaver's English translation of Eco's transcription of Vallet's translation, etc.

17 On *mise-en-abyme*, see, among others, Morrissette (1985a [1971]), Dällenbach (1977), Bal (1978), Ron (1987).

18 Compare the complexly-embedded structure *en abyme* at the core of *Gravity's Rainbow* (Pynchon 1973:680–1): an amphitheater on whose stage is enacted the world in which the amphitheater itself is located. "The chances for any paradox here, really, are less than you think," says Pynchon's narrator; he is lying.

19 For a precocious example of a postmodernist spatial sensibility, see Harbison 1977 (written 1973–4). Harbison discusses, among many other things, Piranesi, baroque space, the architectural spaces of gothic fiction, space in Kafka and Pynchon, and museums and their catalogues.

20 Eco rightly observes that the labyrinth he has constructed is a "mannerist" one, that is, a solvable puzzle, while the world-system which it serves to model is a labyrinth of a different kind, namely a "net" or "rhizome" (the terms come from Deleuze and Guattari), which "has no center, no periphery, no exit, because it is potentially infinite" (Eco 1984:57). For an attempt at a more direct modeling of the postmodernist world-net one would need to turn to the newest "wave" of science fiction writing, so-called "cyberpunk" SF, for instance William Gibson's trilogy (*Neuromancer*, *Count Zero*, *Mona Lisa Overdrive*) or, better yet, Bruce Sterling's *Islands in the Net*.

21 See above, " 'You used to know what these words mean.' "

22 This representational problem is strictly parallel to the problem of representing the Nazi genocide of the Jews, and postmodernist writers have developed parallel strategies of displacement: for instance, Pynchon's displacement of the Jewish Holocaust onto the Hereros in *Gravity's Rainbow*, or D.M. Thomas's displacement of it into the fantastic mode in *The White Hotel*, or Raymond Federman's various metafictional displacements in *Double or Nothing*, *Take It or Leave*, *The Voice in the Closet*, and *The Twofold Vibration*. On the analogy between Holocaust fiction and nuclear apocalypse fiction, see Dowling (1987:147–9).

23 For surveys of nuclear holocaust fiction, see Morrissey (1984), Dowling (1987) and Dorris and Erdrich (1988).

24 Examples include J.G. Ballard's apocalyptic tetralogy based on the four elements of air (*The Wind from Nowhere*), water (*The Drowned World*), fire (*The Drought*), and earth (*The Crystal World*); Rudy Wurlitzer's *Quake*; and Kurt Vonnegut's *Cat's Cradle*, Christine Brooke-Rose's *Out*, and William Burroughs's *The Wild Boys*, all based on nonnuclear manmade disasters. On apocalyptic fiction generally, nuclear and nonnuclear, see Wagar (1982) and Sontag (1966); and for nineteenth-century disaster scenarios, see Landow (1982). The classic text on literary apocalypse is still Kermode (1967).

25 For an example of displacement to the (near) past, see (in addition to *Gravity's Rainbow*) Vonnegut's *Slaughterhouse-Five*; for displacement to a distant future and a distant planet as well, see Samuel Delany's *Stars in My Pocket Like Grains of Sand*.

26 Another example, nearly as complex as these, is Denis Johnson's *Fiskadoro*, set, like Miller's and Hoban's texts, in a post-apocalyptic future. In *Fiskadoro*, the "End of the World" repeats and (as it were) anticipates itself in various forms: in Mr. Cheung's epileptic seizures, during which he experiences a vision of the Bomb; in his aged grandmother's memories of the proto-apocalyptic fall of Saigon; in the communal reading aloud of a rediscovered book about the bombing of Nagasaki ("Was this the first bomb? Was this the last bomb?"); etc. "Everything we have, all we are, will meet its end, will be overcome, taken

up, washed away. But everything came to an end before. Now it will happen again. Many times. Again and again" (Johnson 1985:219).

27 Peter Sagamore glosses his own text:

> When, in a story, nothing happens next, that is the thing that happens next: The nothing becomes a thing, which, we may be sure, the author will quickly cause to be followed by the *next* thing, a more conventionally dramatic thing, and on goes the story. Whereas ... in fact, nothing is no thing, and our story does not at all necessarily go on, for the reason that our lives are not stories.
>
> (Barth 1987:142)

On apocalyptic metafiction, see Dowling (1987:12–14, 185–9).

28 An example from *Fiskadoro*:

> "Que dice – mwe pa hen-yeh – what es?" Towanda said [. . .] "Mean, 'I got no family to speak for me,' " Ms. Chicago said. "Es exactly proper wording de la Voodoo. Go find me that tooth, Belinda. Maybe go he a loa para tu."
>
> (Johnson 1985:136)

Another text, though not precisely an apocalyptic one, which displaces the nuclear threat into a reconfigured form of English is Christine Brooke-Rose's *Xorandor*.

29 One of the disappointments of the film version of *The Name of the Rose*, it seems to me, is its muting of the novel's apocalyptic dimension. In the film, but not in the novel, the burning of the library must compete for attention with the parallel burning of the Inquisition's victims. Inevitably, in the face of this horror, the loss of a mere library dwindles in importance, and the apocalyptic theme, conceivably Eco's largest and most urgent "message," is all but lost sight of.

30 Note that the abbey in general, and not just the library or the Aedificium in particular, is repeatedly spoken of as a microcosm (*NR*:196, 400, 401) and as a "speculum mundi" (*NR*:120), so it is only appropriate that the abbey as a whole be consumed in the "ecpyrosis," and not the library alone.

31 Compare the final post-apocalyptic image of *The Name of the Rose* with that of Maggie Gee's *Dying, in Other Words*:

> This is a city, though who is there here who can tell. For miles there is nothing left standing: light falls upon miles and miles of litter and ice and ice and litter and chaos, miles of grey litter and silent miles of dust and such sightless dullness that even the gross bleached ice-floes of dusty glass lack teeth to glitter: no lips and no heart, though who is there here who remembers what these things were. No speech, and no stories. The last great story was death: someone failed to tell it, or else no-one wanted to hear.
>
> (Gee 1981:213)

The difference, of course, is that no text and no world will rise from the ruins of Maggie Gee's world.

32 I have told a similar story about Joyce, and parallel stories about the careers of Beckett, Robbe-Grillet, Fuentes, Nabokov, Coover, and Pynchon (McHale 1987:12–25, 233–5).

7 WAYS OF WORLD-MAKING: ON *FOUCAULT'S PENDULIM*

1 On the Borges intertext in *The Name of the Rose*, see Solotorevsky (1989) and Corry (forthcoming).
2 Eco 1989:617. All subsequent references will be to this translation, and will be incorporated parenthetically in the text, thus: (*FP*:00).
3 This account of *The Name of the Rose* converges with Eco's own account of Borges's anti-detective stories (including "Death and the Compass") in Eco (1990).
4 When Casaubon complains about the repetitiveness of Diabolical texts, his employer, Signor Garamond, replies: "They confirm one another; therefore they're true" (*FP*:276). So authentically has he captured the spirit of Diabolical thought that in the end Garamond joins the Diabolicals.
5 On the mingling of apparently apocryphal (but true) facts and apparently true (but apocryphal) fictions, Schaub writes, "The real world of the reader is part of Pynchon's fiction; the two, which at first seem so far apart, become inseparable in the act of informed reading" (Schaub 1981:116).
6 For a typical exercise in extrapolating Pynchon's conspiracy theories to real-world conspiracies, see McHale (1981); for a typical exercise in reading Pynchon's biography paranoiacally, see Winston (1976). Winston writes,

> It goes without saying that the Pynchon family history contains many . . . coincidences [such as that of Pynchon being distantly related to the authors of books on chemical physics and the aviation industry]; in Pynchonland one may almost presume that *"everything is connected."*
>
> (Winston 1976:256)

See also Schwan (1987), a parody of paranoid Pynchon scholarship, but one that comes uncomfortably close to the real thing.
7 For a decidedly un-naive reading of Pynchon, see McHoul and Wills (1990), perhaps the first reading successfully to resist being swamped by Pynchon's paranoia. For a classic account of the "transference" (in a psychoanalytic sense) of a text's obsessions to its critics, see Felman (1977).
8 Belbo would, much later, change his mind and, without saying so in so many words, endorse the saint's idealism: "If the problem is this absence of being and if what *is* is what is said, then the more we talk, the more being there is" (*FP*:530).
9 Cf. Lia's skeptical account of Freudianism:

> Imagine that a Viennese prankster, to amuse his friends, invented the whole business of the id and Oedipus, and made up dreams he had never dreamed and little Hanses he had never met . . . And what happened? Millions of people were out there, all ready and waiting to become neurotic in earnest. And thousands were ready to make money treating them.

To which Casaubon can only respond, "Lia, you're paranoid" (*FP*:532–3).
10 For more on "Tlön," see above, "Telling postmodernist stories."
11 Ardenti is A, the first link in the chain of conspiracy-theories constituting The Plan; unless it is Abulafia, Belbo's personal computer. Belbo, Casaubon, Diotallevi are, of course, B, C, and D, respectively. Who, then, is E, do you suppose?
12 See Linda Hutcheon's (1988) construction of *The Name of the Rose* as "historiographic metafiction," a genre which actualizes Jencks's criterion of "double coding."
13 For more on cyberpunk, see below, "POSTcyberMODERNpunkISM." There

is in the SF genre a venerable tradition of conspiracy paranoia, of which the most distinguished practitioner (and the one to whom the cyberpunks obviously owe the most) is Philip K. Dick. Almost any of Dick's novels or stories might be cited as an example, but see, e.g., his masterpiece of paranoid SF, the novella "Faith of Our Fathers" (1967).

14 On the "cross-over" of motifs from popular to "advanced" fiction generally, see below, "POSTcyberMODERNpunkISM." On DeLillo's use, in *Running Dog*, of thriller motifs in particular, see Frow (1986:139–47).

15 In Pavić's *Dictionary*, other-worldly agents ("devils") evidently conspire against the inhabitants of our world, contriving throughout the centuries to suppress the *Dictionary of the Khazars* itself. Similarly, in *Gravity's Rainbow*, the conspiracy spans world-boundaries, and other-worldly and this-worldly conspirators collaborate: the Nazi directors of IG Farben seek advice from the spirit of Walther Rathenau (Pynchon 1973:164–7); some agency on the "other side" feeds Kekulé in a dream the key he needs in order to unlock the secret of the carbon molecule and launch organic chemistry (Pynchon 1973:410–412); the capitalist conspirator Tyro Bland, a student of the Masonic Mysteries, leaves his body by astral projection, never to return (Pynchon 1973:588–90); etc. For an early version of this motif of the persistence of secret societies or conspiracies into the world-to-come, see Pierre Klossowski's *Le Baphomet* (1965), a strange text, defying classification (philosophical tale? pornography? fantastic novel? postmodernist precursor?), that is actually cited in *Foucault's Pendulum* (*FP*:82).

16 By way of example, Jameson notes how DePalma's *Blowout*, presumably because of its representations of video and audio taping, can be seen as the postmodernist equivalent of Antonioni's modernist *Blowup* (1991a:37). Further cinematic examples of the thematics of mechanical reproduction spring readily to mind: movies about movie technology itself (*The Stunt Man*, *F/X*, *Who Framed Roger Rabbit?*), movies about video-taping and televison broadcasting (*Network*, *The Osterman Weekend*, Soderberg's *sex, lies, & videotape*), movies about audio-taping (Beneix's *Diva*, Coppola's *The Conversation*), even futuristic films about the entire integrated system of reproduction, simulation, storage, and retrieval technologies (Verhoeven's *Robocop*, Badham's *Blue Thunder*). Note how many of these films (in fact, all of them except Soderberg's) are also conspiracy fictions. One of the few examples on commercial TV of the thematics of mechanical reproduction is the short-lived *Max Headroom* television series (see Solomon 1988:136–41).

17 Cf. also Manuel Puig's *Kiss of the Spider-Woman*, with its fusion of the thematics of mechanical reproduction (the movies) with terrorist and counter-terrorist conspiracy motifs.

18 On representations of film and television in postmodernist fiction generally, see above, " 'You used to know what these words mean' " and "Zapping, the art of switching channels."

19 Indeed, the narrative situation in *You Bright and Risen Angels* is even more complicated than that, for this is a case (Nabokov's *Ada* is another) of *dual* narration: the primary narrator, a computer programmer, ostensibly types this text on a computer keyboard and enters it into a mainframe computer's memory; meanwhile, his input is being continuously monitored and presumably censored by a second narrator, the programmer's supervisor, leaving the reader unable to disentangle the primary narrator's narrative from the supervisor's interventions.

20 For another version of "mediatized" or "technologized" point-of-view shift,

see Gibson's *Neuromancer*, described below in "Towards a poetics of cyber-punk."

8 WOMEN AND MEN AND ANGELS: ON JOSEPH McELROY'S FICTION

1 He also meant, of course, to scandalize literary historians by upsetting the hierarchy of "central" and "marginal" figures – a strategy which still has some teeth in it (see, e.g., Attridge 1988:236).

2 Cf. Walsh's (1988:264) description of *Women and Men* as "[a]n extension and rewriting of McElroy's earlier novels, and a nearly complete assortment of his themes and subjects recycled and transfigured."

3 See, e.g., Wilson (1931), Goldberg (1963), MacCabe (1978) and Lawrence (1981); and see above, "Constructing (post)modernism: the case of *Ulysses*."

4 McElroy (1987:947). All subsequent references will be to this edition and will be incorporated parenthetically in the body of the text, thus: (*WM*:00).

5 The primacy of the metaphoric process in the literary schools of romanticism and symbolism has been repeatedly acknowledged, but it is still insufficiently realized that it is the predominance of metonymy which underlies and actu-ally predetermines the so-called 'realistic' trend . . . Following the path of contiguous relationships, the realist author metonymically digresses from the plot to the atmosphere and from the characters to the setting in space and time. He is fond of synecdochic details.

(Jakobson 1971d:255)

6 Bredin (1984:58), it should be noted, is skeptical about claims for metonymy as constitutive or distinctive of realist prose.

7 McElroy 1986:104; cf. 381. All subsequent references to *A Smuggler's Bible* will be to this edition and will be incorporated parenthetically in the body of the text, thus: (*SB*:00).

8 McElroy corroborates this metonymic orientation when he describes *A Smug-gler's Bible* in terms of "connections" and "gaps," the "coexistence of conti-nuity and discontinuity," and compares it to the "widening rings of relation" in Butor's *Degrees* (McElroy 1975).

9 See McElroy's remarks on Pynchon and paranoia (1975:216–17). Jameson has pertinently described the thematics of conspiracy as an (unsatisfactory) attempt to model or "map" the late-capitalist world system for the use of imagination; see Jameson 1988:356, 1991a:37–8 and see above, "Ways of world-making: on *Foucault's Pendulum*."

10 Anxiety for a daughter implicated in some kind of conspiracy is a motif already explored by McElroy in *Lookout Cartridge*.

11 On Lodge's story, and his abandonment of it upon reaching postmodernism, see McHale (1982) and "Telling postmodernist stories," above.

12 On the concept of the dominant, see Jakobson (1971a).

13 On the epistemological dominant of modernist fiction, see Krysinski (1981), McHale (1987:4–25), Fokkema and Ibsch (1987), and Wilson (1989:19–20). Porter (1981) proposes a Marxist understanding of the epistemological dominant in terms of reification, the structure of detached observer confronting a reified object-world. This reification structure undergoes a precocious development in American literature beginning with Emerson, but reaches its crisis in modernists such as Henry James and, especially, Faulkner.

14 "[W]ho or what is missing becomes the core around which McElroy's stories

turn," writes Walsh; and he describes *Women and Men* in particular as "a virtuosic fiction focused on what is missing" (1988:263, 264).

15 On the "investigative form" of Faulkner's fiction, see Kinney (1978:33–4) and *passim*; and on the detective-story model in modernist poetics generally, see above, "The (post)modernism of *The Name of the Rose*."

16 "McElroy's interest," writes Tanner (1987:200), "is in the very structure of perception – how do you see the coherent field of objects, *if* you do? If not, what is it to perceive incoherence?" Cf. Mathews (1990:217 and *passim*).

17 These include first-person narration (parts IV and V), third-person "free indirect discourse" (part I) and a present-tense variant of FID (part III), multiple, juxtaposed first-person monologues (part II) and multiple shifts of point of view in the third person (part VI), and even the epistolary form (part VII).

18 This "filtering" process is particularly conspicuous in the "free indirect" report of other characters' speech, where we "hear" not what Cartwright's interlocutor says but rather Cartwright's own *act of hearing*:

> I asked if he was with Queen Films, he said No though he'd heard of them. Our film didn't include Coventry, did it – or had I said I know someone in Coventry.
> An engineer, but I don't think I mentioned him to you.
> . . .
> He'd come in from London this morning, he said.
> I said I'd guessed that.
> He took another sip and said he'd learned – in London – that a film I'd made was very interesting and that I hadn't sold it yet.
> I said we'd lost most of it so there was virtually nothing to sell.
> He said according to his information we still had some signficiant footage.
> I said what could you do with a few minutes of 16 mill?
>
> (McElroy 1985:73)

19 Towards the end of the first of his monologues, Jimmy suddenly "acquires" the first-person pronoun, his "I" (*WM*: 476), and begins to use it sporadically thereafter. Jimmy's monologues are insistently epistemological in orientation, as their titles, "known bits I, II, III," suggest; key words in the opening pages of "known bits I" include "definitely" and "not definitely," "probable" and "probably": "Probable is not definite, not known for sure, not fact" (*WM*:465).

20 McElroy had already experimented with the representation of telepathic communication in the last chapter of *Plus*.

21 Yet another perspective is provided, after an interval of some 250 pages, by Jimmy Banks, who catches sight of the women through the window of the cafe in which they are sitting (*WM*:471).

22 Cf. Kinney (1978:101): "the epistemological emphasis in Faulkner's narrative poetics is finally on the reader."

23 In *Women and Men*, writes Mathews,

> the proliferation of senses attached to words and moving *between* words . . . colors the surface of the whole book . . . The use of language in *Women and Men* makes us sense that behind words other words lie in wait, that a word may lead us to all other words.
>
> (1990:205, 206)

Incidentally, Mathews has used strikingly similar formulations to describe his *own* linguistic practice (see Mathews 1986:126).

24 For evidence that the parallelism between Brooke-Rose's discourse and

McElroy's is more than merely coincidental, see Brooke-Rose's essay on *Plus* (Brooke-Rose 1981:268–88).

25 See Mathews (1990:200–1 and *passim*). The case of McElroy's anomalous first-person plural in *Women and Men* has much in common with that of the second-person pronoun of *Gravity's Rainbow*; see above, " 'You used to know what these words mean.' "

26 Among other things, Moore observes that Theroux's angel lore derives in large part from Davidson (1967). So, too, does Barthelme's angelology and, I suppose, that of many of the other recent angelologists as well.

27 The presence of Wyndham Lewis in this list points to the role played in the revival of angelology by certain transitional figures, modernists (or at any rate contemporaries of the high modernists) who late in their careers seemed to swerve in a direction that we have only recently learned to think of as postmodernism. Apart from Wyndham Lewis, I have in mind, for instance, Kenneth Patchen (*The Journal of Albion Moonlight*, 1941), H.D. (*Tribute to the Angels*, 1945), and Isak Dinesen ("The Diver," in *Anecdotes of Destiny*, 1953). We need also to find room in our account for Mark Twain, whose late, fragmentary *Mysterious Stranger* texts read, in retrospect, like postmodernist angelology before the fact – a case of a pre-modernist writer anticipating postmodernist developments?

Altogether more problematic is the angel who makes an appearance in Gide's *Les Faux-monnayeurs* (1925). *Les Faux-monnayeurs* is generally recognized, of course, as a typically or even normatively high-modernist text (e.g. Fokkema and Ibsch call it a "touchstone" of modernism (1987:204)); nevertheless, in Chapter 14 of this novel an angel intervenes to reform the profligate Bernard Profitendeu. Moreover, the angel's intervention here correlates, in a way typical of *post*modernist fiction, with various ontological cruxes: the angel may be only a kind of literalized Biblical allusion (when Bernard recounts his conversion experience to Edouard he says, "I wrestled over it all night," alluding obliquely to Jacob's encounter with the angel, Genesis 32), so that it "hovers" ambiguously between figurative and literal status; and it may function as a surrogate for the author, who here can be seen to intervene metafictionally in the narrated world to "redeem" one of his characters arbitrarily. Could we see this anomalous Gidean angel as a premature irruption of postmodernism into an otherwise modernist text?

28 On the parallels between Pynchon and Merrill, see Berger (1983). Merrill's angelology, drawing heavily on Dante's, is more traditional than Pynchon's, but still far from orthodox. Pynchon's angels owe much to Rilke, of course, especially to Rilke's remark, in a famous letter to his Polish translator, that the angels of the *Duino Elegies* are less Christian than Islamic; Pynchon's angels, too, are modeled on the "star-blotting Moslem angels" (Pynchon 1973:341) more than on those of Christian iconography. But there is also a surprising element of kabbalistic and other apocryphal lore in Pynchon's angelology; for instance, Pynchon's "watchmen of world's edge" seem to echo the fallen "Watcher" angels (the *grigori* or *egregori*) of the apocrypha; see Davidson (1967:311–12 (entry for "Watchers")), and Forsyth (1987:160–81). See also Pynchon (1973:478, 584, 680, 734, 747–8, 753). On Pynchon's angelology in general, see McLaughlin (1988).

29 And from the "top" of the cultural hierarchy to its lower reaches: it is easy to trace the diffusion of postmodernist angelology from "advanced" and "difficult" texts such as *Gravity's Rainbow* or *The Changing Light at Sandover* outward and downward into other markets and other media – performance

art, film, rock video. Examples include Ping Chong's performance piece, *The Angels of Swedenborg* (first performed 1985), based on material from Borges's *Book of Imaginary Beings*; Laurie Anderson's song, "Gravity's Angel" (recorded on her 1984 album, *Mr. Heartbreak*, and performed in her film *Home of the Brave*), a gloss on *Gravity's Rainbow* which also seems to echo (deliberately or fortuitously?) imagery from Rilke's *Duino Elegies*; Wim Wenders's film, *Wings of Desire* (1987, scripted by Wenders and Peter Handke); and even MTV rock-videos such as David Bowie's "Day In Day Out," which features a pair of guardian angels, one black, one white, equipped with video cameras, or R.E.M.'s "Losing My Religion," in which an aged angel (García Márquez's "Very Old Man with Enormous Wings"?) falls to earth and loses his wings, amid visual allusions to Renaissance painting styles and Maxfield Parrish poster art.

30 Sophisticated examples include the alien "guests" of *Solaris*, both Stanislaw Lem's novel (1961) and the film version by Andrei Tarkovsky; and the alien murderer/rescuer of Slava Tsukerman's film, *Liquid Sky* (1982). Less sophisticated versions of the angelic alien include the otherworldly slab of Arthur Clarke and Stanley Kubrick's *2001: A Space Odyssey*, and the extraterrestrials of Spielberg's *Close Encounters of the Third Kind* and *E.T.*; least sophisticated of all, of course, are the everyday-or-garden-variety aliens which are the staple of *National Enquirer* UFO stories. Joanna Russ has explicitly made the connection between angels and aliens in her story "Souls" (from *Extra(Ordinary) People*, 1984), as has John Fowles in *A Maggot* (1985) and, more obliquely, Don DeLillo in *White Noise*.

31 On the persistence of the angel-function and its transformations, see Forsyth (1987) and Zaleski (1987).

32 Or, to use terminology developed above in "Zapping, the art of switching channels," they function as "ontological pluralizers."

33 On plurality of worlds, see Goodman (1978), Calinescu (1983), Davies (1980), and McHale (1987:26–40 and *passim*)

34 In several recent "cyberpunk" science-fictions, cybernetic or genetically-engineered "post-humans" are called "angels" or given angelic physiognomies and powers; see, e.g., Bruce Sterling's *Schismatrix* (1985) and Rudy Rucker's *Wetware* (1988).

35 Here, too, contemporary angelology seems to have reinvented a piece of ancient angel lore: according to apocryphal texts (with meager corroboration in canonical Scripture), the stars and planets were to be regarded as angels. If stars and planets, why not orbiting satellites? See Davidson (1967:111–12, 279 (entries on "Fallen Angels" and "Stars")) and Forsyth (1987:252, 353–4).

36 See *Sonnets to Orpheus* (II.12). McElroy's immediate allusion may be to Pynchon, however, who quotes from this sonnet in *Gravity's Rainbow* (Pynchon 1973:97).

37 Grace's meditation is corroborated by other characters – by Luisa, the diva: "angels already are *in* her, welcomed by her as they come and go . . . like interior clothes" (*WM*:325); by Larry:

> lately he thinks of invaders in his bloodstream (maybe they're good) but then they aren't the We his mother Sue's always speaking in – (We feel that only through money can we achieve power) but (God, maybe) his *own* We, but does that make him wacko or a vehicle for these bloodstream visitors to . . . feel, not think.

> (*WM*:349)

38 There is a striking parallel here with the interchapters of McElroy's first novel,

A Smuggler's Bible, where another voice, asserting its first-person privileges over David Brooke's third-person "free indirect" discourse, can be discerned behind or within David's: his alter ego? the voice of his author, Joseph McElroy himself? The indeterminacies of the discursive situation of *A Smuggler's Bible* in turn echo those of Borges's classic short text, "Borges y yo" (see Walsh 1988:269).

39 Apart from "angels" and "colloids," the text's other master-metaphor for discursive consciousness is the *weather*, which, like both angels and colloids, is ubiquitous yet largely subliminal, fluidly washing over and between everything and penetrating everywhere (see *WM*:892, 911–12 and *passim*; cf. Mathews 1990:201, 209–10). Strikingly, a similar correlation between weather pattern and discursive "collective consciousness" occurs in John Dos Passos's *The 42nd Parallel* (1930), whose title refers to the median of paths traced by storms as they traverse the North American continent from west to east.

40 Cf. Kinney on Faulkner:

> Faulkner's meanings come not simply in the narrative consciousness of one or more characters ... but in our *constitutive consciousness* as readers, the integrated sum of our awareness of the structure of the work and the perceptions of all the characters whose thoughts are explicitly or implicitly provided for us ... The increased possibilities [made available by blending omniscient narration with stream of consciousness and multiple perspectives] are what give to Faulkner's work its distinctive quality of seeming to be both inside and outside the characters, inside and outside events simultaneously.
> (Kinney 1978:101)

41 This paragraph reflects, though in no very systematic way, various phenomenological approaches to the literary work of art. It merges (no doubt irresponsibly) the two major strains of phenomenological literary theory: on the one hand, the Geneva School model of reading, wherein the reader appears as a passive figure, possessed by the consciousness "incarnated" in the text; on the other hand, Ingarden's more dynamic model, in which the reader is called upon actively to reconstruct and realize the literary work of art. See Ingarden (1973a (1968) and 1973b (1931)); and for a convenient introduction to the Geneva School, see Lawall (1968).

42 See above, "Telling postmodernist stories" and "The (post)modernism of *The Name of the Rose*."

43 I see no reason to alter this account of McElroy's poetics in the light of the publication of his latest novel, *The Letter Left to Me* (1988). This text seems unproblematically to fit the paradigm of late-modernist explorations of epistemological and phenomenological issues.

9 "I DRAW THE LINE AS A RULE BETWEEN ONE SOLAR SYSTEM AND ANOTHER": THE POSTMODERNISM(S) OF CHRISTINE BROOKE-ROSE

1 Hawkes zigzags from the precocious postmodernism of *The Cannibal* (1949) to the modernism (or "late-modernism") of the novels from *The Beetle Leg* (1951) through *The Passion Artist* (1979), then back to postmodernism in *Virginie: Her Two Lives* (1981), then back again to modernism in *Adventures in the Alaskan Skin Trade* (1985); Barth, from the postmodernism of *LETTERS* (1979) to the late-modernism of *Sabbatical* (1982), back to postmodernism again in *The Tidewater Tales* (1987); Abish seems to "retreat" from postmodernism to modernist poetics in *How German Is It* (1980), García Márquez in

Chronicle of a Death Foretold (1981), and Fuentes in *La cabeza de la hidra* (1978).

2 The *nouveau roman* can be seen, according to Brooke-Rose's account, as a kind of displaced form of the fantastic. Thus, for instance, Robbe-Grillet's novels are said to "produce *an* effect of the uncanny [i.e. the explicable fantastic] if not the same effect" as the one described by Todorov (Brooke-Rose 1981:310); they yield "an eerie effect close to the fantastic, or, in Todorov's terms, to the uncanny" (1981:336); and so on.

3 See Jameson's account of Claude Simon's "alternation between a Faulknerian evocation of perception and a neo-novelistic practice of textualization" (1991b:135); and cf. Harvey (1989:339–42) on modernism and postmodernism as permanent alternatives within capitalism, expressing its internal contradictions, rather than as successive historical periods.

4 With apologies to Ihab Hassan (see Hassan 1975b).

5 Brooke-Rose herself would presumably not want to see her novels described as either "modernist" or "postmodernist," at least on the evidence of her unprociono of dicontictaction with these terms (1981:141–51). However, in a 1987 interview she explicitly identifies herself with "the writers of the postmodern movement" (Friedman and Fuchs 1989:88).

For Brooke-Rose's own (partial) narrative of the zigs and zags of her novelistic career, which partly corroborates my account of it, see Brooke-Rose (1991:5–15).

6 Brooke-Rose 1986:17, 67. All subsequent references to *Out* and the other three novels (*Such, Between, Thru*) will be to this omnibus edition and will be noted parenthetically in the body of the text, thus: (*O*:00), (*S*:00), (*B*:00), (*T*:00).

7 What distinguishes *Out* from the *nouveau roman* of Robbe-Grillet, as Brooke-Rose observes, is precisely its science fiction premise, for the *nouveau roman* never undertook to construct alternative realities like those of science fiction (1986:102). Martin, writing of *Out*, suggests that science fiction convention relieves the writer of any responsibility to adhere to norms of verisimilitude (Martin 1989:114–15), but this is surely wrong, for conventional science fiction, as Brooke-Rose herself notes, "always is realistically anchored" (Friedman and Fuchs 1989:88; cf. Brooke-Rose 1981:72–102). That is, science fiction normally extrapolates a *new* level or standard of verisimilitude, different in certain respects from present-day standards, to which it then faithfully adheres. With rare exceptions (e.g. Philip K. Dick), science fiction does not introduce epistemological uncertainties of the kind that Brooke-Rose introduces in *Out*; consequently, science fiction's extrapolated verisimilitude typically serves to *resolve* uncertainty rather than to *heighten* it as Brooke-Rose's science fiction premise does in this novel.

8 Other examples of this topos include Flann O'Brien's *The Third Policeman* (1940/1967), Muriel Spark's *The Hothouse by the East River* (1973), Thomas Pynchon's *Gravity's Rainbow* (1973) and *Vineland* (1990), Ishmael Reed's *The Last Days of Louisiana Red* (1974) and *The Terrible Twos* (1982), R.M. Koster's *The Dissertation* (1975), Stanley Elkin's *The Living End* (1979), Alasdair Gray's *Lanark* (1981), Peter Carey's *Bliss* (1981), Russell Hoban's *Pilgermann* (1983), David Carkeet's *I Been There Before* (1985), and William Burroughs's *The Western Lands* (1987). Of all these versions of the world-to-come, perhaps the closest to Brooke-Rose's is one which is not strictly speaking a world-to-come at all, namely Slothrop's hallucinatory descent into the cloacal underworld in Pynchon's *Gravity's Rainbow* (1973:60–71). For an account of the poetics of

what is nowadays called "near-death experience" narratives, with many striking parallels to Larry's experience in *Such*, see Zaleski (1987).

9 Brooke-Rose, personal communication, 14 November 1990.

10 See above, "Constructing (post)modernism: the case of *Ulysses*."

11 Brooke-Rose has denied any direct influence of Sarraute on her own writing (Friedman and Fuchs 1989:82), and there seems little reason to doubt her; for one thing, the "submicroscopic" and "giant-telescopic" metaphors which she describes in this passage, and which occur throughout *Such*, are actually rare in Sarraute. However, here is one instance:

> Tout autour de lui se rétrécit, rapetisse, devient inconsistant, léger – [. . .] le ciel tourne au-dessus de lui, les astres bougent, il voit se déplacer les planètes, un vertige, une angoisse, un sentiment de panique le prend, tout bascule d'un coup, se renverse . . . elle-même s'éloigne, elle disparaît de l'autre côté.
> (Sarraute 1959:270; bracketed ellipsis is mine)

> Everything about him is shrinking, growing smaller, becoming inconsistent, light [. . .] the sky is turning above his head, the stars are moving, he sees planets travelling from place to place, a sensation of dizziness, of anguish, a feeling of panic seizes him, everything is toppling, overturning, at once . . . she herself is moving away, she disappears on the other side.
> (Sarraute 1965:191)

12 For instance, even Martin (1989:116–17), in his attentive and sympathetic survey of Brooke-Rose's fiction, fails to mention the global constraint on the copula in *Between*.

13 For further examples of heterogeneous fictional worlds produced by "appropriating" characters from other texts, see Carpentier's *El recurso del metodo* (1974), Fuentes's *Terra Nostra* (1975), Timothy Findley's *Famous Last Words* (1981), Kathy Acker's *Great Expectations* (1983), *Don Quixote* (1986), and *In Memoriam to Identity* (1990), Coover's *A Night at the Movies* (1987), Barth's *The Tidewater Tales* (1987), and Robert Steiner's *Matinee* (1989).

14 On Brooke-Rose's fascination with and use of technical jargons, see Friedman and Fuchs (1989:83–4, 88), and Brooke-Rose (1989:104, 105). Other writers whose use of technical discourses invites comparison with Brooke-Rose include the British poet J.H. Prynne and the American novelists Thomas Pynchon and Joseph McElroy.

15 Brooke-Rose's model for the use of future tense in *Amalgamemnon* is very likely Maurice Roche's *Compact* (1966); see her discussion of this text's "transgressive" future tense (Brooke-Rose 1981:329). A parallel case is that of Carlos Fuentes's *La muerte de Artemio Cruz* (1962). Incidentally, as in the case of the blanket ban on *to be* in *Between*, here too the constitutive constraint of the text has gone largely unnoticed by its readers, and in particular its reviewers; see Brooke-Rose, "Illicitations" (1989:103). An example is Ihab Hassan's review of *Amalgamemnon* in the *New York Times Book Review* (Hassan 1985): not a word here about "nonrealizing" tenses and moods.

16 In *Amalgamemnon*, writes Martin (1989:119), "the archetypical phrase of fiction 'as if' becomes a thematic motif." The phrase "to go on as if," in a sense the kernel from which the whole of *Amalgamemnon* springs, had already appeared conspicuously in *Thru* (*T*:603); for that matter, it also appears in *A Rhetoric of the Unreal* (Brooke-Rose 1981:6).

This, incidentally, is an instance of the convergence between Brooke-Rose's poetics and that of American surfiction on which Brooke-Rose herself has remarked (1981:416). Raymond Federman, too, has written a hypothetical-conditional fiction, *Smiles on Washington Square* (1985), though he has not undertaken to conform all of his sentences to the dominant conditional mood, as Brooke-Rose has, contenting himself with framing the events of his story in an overall perspective of conditionality. A related case is Ronald Sukenick's short text, "Aziff" from his *Endless Short Story*, in which the phrase "as if" materializes as a character:

> Then Aziff appeared in a gout of steam from the radiator . . . It was as if present company were excepted . . . As if the room became an absence . . . As if it were embraced with dark soft wings . . . As if we were all smoothed and soothed . . . It was as if. As if. Aziff.
>
> (Sukenick 1986:4)

I note, too, that Walter Abish has announced that his forthcoming novel is to be entitled *As If*.

17 Though Brooke-Rose herself casually describes *Xorandor* as "a science fiction" (Brooke-Rose 1989:104), the novel frequently distances itself from SF conventions: "Martians! Martians have gone out even of science fiction long ago"; "Pure science fiction, Diggles snapped"; "The myth of little green men dies hard" (Brooke-Rose 1987:59, 102, 201). This, however, is an example of the strategy Empson once called "self-parody to disarm criticism," and in fact is typical of many postmodernist texts that exploit SF conventions but distance themselves from SF at the same time, including Alasdair Gray's *Lanark* (1981), Raymond Federman's *The Twofold Vibration* (1982), and Carlos Fuentes's *Terra Nostra*.

18 Cf. the use of SF novelties to motivate formal solutions to comparable problems of point of view in the newest "wave" of SF writing, so-called "cyberpunk" fiction, e.g. William Gibson's *Neuromancer* (1984) and Bruce Sterling's *Islands in the Net* (1988). See below, "Towards a poetics of cyberpunk."

19 See above, "The (post)modernism of *The Name of the Rose*."

20 "Science fiction, although about the future, commonly postdates its narration" (Brooke-Rose 1981:329). Brooke-Rose also expands on a remark by Raymond Williams concerning the "subjunctivity" of utopian fiction: "SF," she writes, "is written in a subjunctive mood, not a future but an 'as if,' a 'what if' " (1981:393 n. 2). Cf. also Friedman and Fuchs (1989:85) and Brooke-Rose (1989:103).

21 In what seems to be an interesting anticipation of *Xorandor*, Brooke-Rose in *A Rhetoric of the Unreal* reacts with disapproval to Mas'ud Zavarzadeh's remark, in a 1978 MLA conference paper, that Joseph McElroy's *Plus* (1977) is written in "computer language" (Brooke-Rose 1981:288). She is, of course, correct: if anything, the strange language of *Plus* derives not from computer language but from the mission-control radio-communications language made familiar by the manned space-exploration programs. But one can't help but wonder whether Zavarzadeh's mistake about *Plus* might have planted the seed of Brooke-Rose's own later large-scale use of computer language in *Xorandor*.

22 Susan E. Hawkins suggests that *Xorandor* explores the impact that computers are beginning to have on our notions of language and of speech and writing, and even our very notion of self: "the subject is . . . becoming a technological production." Appositely enough, she cites Philip K. Dick's "obsession with the inevitable conflation of the human and the technetronic" (Hawkins 1989:143). Indeed, this exploration of the radical impact of computer technology on subjectivity has been pursued by SF writers like Dick and the so-called "cyberpunks" (Gibson, Sterling, Rucker, Cadigan, Shiner, Shirley, and others) at least as vigorously as it has by "mainstream" (non-SF) postmodernists.

23 See below, "POSTcyberMODERNpunkISM."
24 See Brooke-Rose (1981:60–1), on the return of romance – including SF, a modern manifestation of romance – in contemporary fiction. Cf. also Brooke-Rose's remarks (1981:415 n. 1) on the convergence of postmodernism and SF in the fiction of Pynchon and Delany, a case of convergence pursued further by Ebert (1980) and Mathieson (1985).

10 POSTcyberMODERNpunkISM

1 I have adapted from Ihab Hassan (1975b) this typographic means of signalling what I take to be the relationship between postmodernism and cyberpunk. Other titles in this chapter incorporate titles or phrases stolen from Leslie Fiedler (first section), Tom LeClair (third and fourth sections), and Joanna Russ and William Gibson (sixth section). My apologies to them all.

2 My skepticism about the alleged erosion of the high/low divide in postmodernism has been anticipated by Luckhurst (1991). His canny readings of postmodernist theories of SF (including Jameson's, Ebert's, Pfeil's and my own) pinpoint places where high/low boundaries, supposedly abolished, are surreptitiously reintroduced. This movement of "erasure followed by reinscription" (Luckhurst 1991:36) suggests to Luckhurst that cultural hierarchy cannot merely be wished away, leading him to conclude that, rather than seeking to efface boundaries (if only by rhetorical fiat) we would do better to make them the objects of our inquiry: "What is required is not the evasion of borders but a constant attention to their productivity of meaning, on the one hand, and how they are implicated in construction of value on the other" (1991:365). I could not agree more.

3 For an updated view, see the November 1991 special issue of *Science Fiction Studies* on postmodernism and science fiction.

4 See Luckhurst:

> the "mainstream" is a fantasy projection *by* SF, the construction of its own "outside." This fantasy, frequently discussed in terms of difference of character, representation, or mode is, I would suggest, intimately connected with the displaced factors of institutional and canonical power, the processes of inclusion and exclusion by which SF has been traditionally dismissed.
>
> (Luckhurst 1991:365)

5 It should be noted that the analysis that follows restricts itself to the situation of SF in the U.S. and U.K. almost exclusively. Elsewhere, notably in the former Soviet Union, SF production is situated in a literary system organized along such different lines that it would be impractical to try to integrate it with the present model, even if the present writer were capable of undertaking such an integration.

6 Luckhurst (1991:362–3) objects to accounts that treat SF as a perpetually "backward" and belated imitation of mainstream writing. My account escapes this stricture by making the belatedness *mutual*: if SF is backward relative to mainstream poetics, mainstream writing is backward relative to SF. The traffic is two-way.

7 Other postmodernist examples include Carter's *The Passion of New Eve* (1977), Harry Mathews's *The Sinking of the Odradek Stadium* (1971–72), Steve Katz's *Saw* (1972), Carlos Fuentes's *Terra Nostra* (1975), Don DeLillo's *Ratner's Star* (1976), Joseph McElroy's *Plus* (1976), William S. Wilson's *Why I Don't Write Like Franz Kafka* (1977), Russell Hoban's *Riddley Walker* (1980), and Ted Mooney's *Easy Travel to Other Planets* (1981) (see McHale 1987:65–8).

8 Evidence of Kadrey's awareness of Burroughs includes, for instance, the phrase "algebra of need" (Kadrey 1989:100, 209), a Burroughs leitmotif (and the title of Eric Mottram's landmark study of Burroughs's fiction, (Mottram 1977)), and a sly passing reference to the "Boys of Tangier gang" who trade in illicit immunotoxins (Kadrey 1989:47).

9 Confirmation of the Burroughs connection is to be found in combinations of Burroughs's "lost civilization" motif with unrelated motifs from elsewhere in Burroughs's repertoire. In Sterling's "Spook" (1983), for instance, Mayan insurgents of the near future revive ancient methods of thought-manipulation as a means of resisting domination by powerful industrial cartels. While these Mayans and their thought-control techniques seem to have derived from Burroughs's "lost civilization" motif, their adversary, the "spook" (i.e. secret agent) of the title, derives from a different Burroughs motif. For the spook's tactic of provoking "cognitive dissonance" among the insurgents, thus destroying their resistance movement from within, is traceable to similar tactics practiced by the interplanetary "Nova criminals" of Burroughs' *Nova Express* (1964).

Further corroborating this connection, the short-story collection in which Sterling has reprinted his Burroughs-influenced story "Spook" is entitled *Crystal Express* (1989), seemingly a direct allusion to Burroughs's *Nova Express*. Moreover, the collection reprints another story, "Twenty Evocations" (1984), in which Sterling uses Burroughs' cut-up technique on the characteristically cyberpunk materials of his own Shaper/Mechanist story cycle. On Sterling's Shaper/Mechanist cycle, see below, "Towards a poetics of cyberpunk."

10 Other versions of Gibson's sentence have appeared, e.g., in Williams's *Voice of the Whirlwind* and Kadrey's *Metrophage*: "Steward hung suspended beneath a sky the color of wet slate" (Williams 1989:1; first sentence of the text);

> They came upon a young girl kneeling in the corridor, bathed in the blue light of an ancient portable television, tying off with a hachimaka. When she saw them, the girl gathered up her works and took off. She left the television, which was slowly rolling a dead channel of snow.
>
> (Kadrey 1989:73)

Moreover, McCaffery quotes Gibson's sentence verbatim as the epigraph of his chapter on "The Fictions of the Present" in the *Columbia Literary History* (McCaffery 1988b:1161).

11 Acker's treatment of these monster movies seems likely to have been influenced by Susan Sontag's well-known essay on post-Hiroshima SF films, "The Imagination of Disaster" (Sontag 1966).

12 See below, "Towards a poetics of cyberpunk."

13 "Back-broke sentences" is Donald Barthelme's phrase; for a discussion, see McHale (1987:154–5).

14 Precursors of 1980s cybernetic interface fiction include John Barth's *Giles Goat-Boy* (1966) and Joseph McElroy's *Plus* (1977). See Porush (1985, 1991:383).

15 See above, " 'I draw the line as a rule . . . ' "

16 On *Foucault's Pendulum* as (in part) an "interface fiction," see above, "Ways of world-making."

17 Actually, the metamorphosis at the end of *Wetware* constitutes a particularly elegant formal closure of the paired novels *Wetware* and *Software*: the dolphin-like creatures into which the three characters are transformed in the last sentences of *Wetware* recall the dolphins sighted by Cobb Anderson in the opening sentence of *Software*, thus closing the circle and bringing us "by a commodius vicus of recirculation" back to the beginning.

11 TOWARDS A POETICS OF CYBERPUNK

1 On cyberpunk "school" institutions, see Bruce Sterling's introductions to Sterling (1986b) and Gibson (1987a); McCaffery (1988b); and McCaffery's interviews with Gibson and Sterling in McCaffery (1990a:130–50, 211–32).
2 The joke is Dick Higgins's; see his "A Child's History of Fluxus."
3 Malmgren's proposal of alternating phases of extrapolative and speculative dominance in the history of twentieth-century SF seems to echo David Lodge's (1977) account of alternating phases of metaphorical and metonymic dominance in the history of "mainstream" fiction in our century. But, if the rhythm of historical change in SF parallels that of mainstream fiction, it does so only in principle. For the pendulum-swings in the history of SF are not synchronized with those of mainstream fiction: SF does not shift from an extrapolative to a speculative dominant when mainstream fiction swings from its metonymic to its metaphorical pole, or from speculation back to extrapolation when mainstream fiction swings from metaphor to metonymy. Nor, for that matter, is SF history simply mainstream fiction's inverse, speculative when the latter is metonymic, extrapolative when it is metaphoric. Out of synch with each other, the two cycles do interact, but in a more complex rhythm of influence, counter-influence, and feedback (see above, "POSTcyberMODERNpunk-ISM").
4 For cyberpunk claims to extrapolation, again see Sterling's introductions to Sterling (1986) and to Gibson (1987a). For expressions of skepticism from "hard" SF writers, see Benford's and Brin's contributions to McCaffery 1988:18–27. It is perhaps paradoxical that one of Gibson's earliest stories, "The Gernsback Continuum" (reprinted in both Sterling 1986b and Gibson 1987a), involves a parody and explicit critique of Gernsback-style extrapolative "scientifiction." On the one hand, this might be read as an unconcealed manifestation of "anxiety of influence," Gibson's attempt to get the SF "Great Tradition" off his back. On the other hand, it aptly demonstrates the principle of no simple "return" to an earlier phase; rather, each return, e.g. of 1930s-style extrapolation in the 1980s, is inevitably a return with a difference.
5 Underlying my rather casual use of "levels" here is Harshav's (1979) three-dimensional model of the text.
6 See Calinescu (1983) and McHale (1987); and see above, "The (post)modernism of *The Name of the Rose*."
7 On space in postmodernist fiction, see Malmgren (1985); on the "spatial turn" of postmodernism in general, see Harvey (1989), Soja (1989), and Jameson (1991b:16, 154–7, 364–76 and *passim*); on the spatial dominant in SF, see Jameson (1987:53–8).
8 Computer technology is rapidly outstripping science fiction, for actual, functioning versions of computer-simulated "virtual reality" closely resembling Gibson's fictional "cyberspace" are currently under development (see, e.g. Stewart 1991).
9 Literalization of modernist-style mythic archetypes is also a motif of postmodernist writing; see, e.g., Donald Barthelme's *Snow White* (1967), *The Dead Father* (1974), and *The King* (1990), Robert Coover's *Pricksongs and Descants* (1969), Italo Calvino's *The Castle of Crossed Destinies* (1969/1973), Günter Grass's *The Flounder* (1977), Angela Carter's *The Bloody Chamber* (1979), John Fowles's *Mantissa* (1982), and especially the fiction of John Barth, including *Giles Goat-Boy* (1966), *Lost in the Funhouse* (1968), *Chimera* (1972), and *The Tidewater Tales* (1987). Barth puts the case for literalizing mythic archetypes in quite explicit terms: "to write realistic fictions which point always to

mythic archetypes is in my opinion to take the wrong end of the mythopoeic stick, however meritorious such fiction may be in other respects. Better to address the archetypes directly" (Barth 1973:207–8).

10 See Maddox in McCaffery (1988a:237–44); and Bukatman (1991). Swanwick, in *Vacuum Flowers*, offers a parallel future history and an alternative pair of categories; in his version, the division is between the "wettechnic civilization" (roughly, the Mech option) of the solar system proper and the bioprogramming technologies (roughly, the Shaper option) of the comet worlds.

11 Also related is the motif of telepathic mind-control, a much more conventional SF motif, to be found in Shepard's *Life During Wartime* alongside the more distinctively cyberpunk variants of the drug-induced personality and the radio-controlled zombie.

12 It seems likely that Shepard's motif of bacterially-induced personality owes something to Thomas Disch's New Wave SF novel *Camp Concentration* (1968), in which, in a medical experiment on prison inmates, a strain of syphilis is introduced which produces a temporary heightening of intelligence.

13 Another bio-punk version of the motif of collective selfhood is Sterling's "Swarm" (1982), the first of the Shaper/Mechanist stories, featuring an anthill-like collective organism (the Swarm of the title) that horribly absorbs one human interloper and establishes a symbiotic relation with another.

14 Other striking examples of the use of extrapolated technologies to motivate modernist-style perspectivism can be found in Sterling's *Islands in the Net* and Kadrey's *Metrophage*. In the former, agents of a multinational corporation wear broadcast rigs which allow their colleagues throughout the world to occupy their points of view electronically. In the latter, the modernist techniques of flashback and involuntary memory are technologically literalized through prosthetic eyes which enable the user to record and play back past scenes.

15 See above, "POSTcyberMODERNpunkISM," on Kathy Acker's rewriting of one of these simstim episodes from *Neuromancer*.

16 See Wagar (1982) and Dowling (1987); and see above, "The (post)modernism of *The Name of the Rose*."

17 See above, "Zapping, the art of switching channels."

18 Compare the premise of the *Max Headroom* television series (in the United States, ABC, spring 1987), in which a television journalist named Edison Carter, the victim of foul play, is "resurrected" as his manic alter ego, the computer simulation Max Headroom. It transpires that Carter isn't really dead after all, so that Max doesn't replace but merely mirrors (however distortedly) his human "original." A postmodernist analogue is McElroy's *Plus* (1976), in which the supposedly deceased human protagonist, who has allowed his brain to be reused as the control system for an orbiting satellite, feeds on cosmic radiation and gradually regenerates "himself," recovering piece by piece his supposedly "lost" memories and identity.

References

Abish, Walter (1977) "Ardor/Awe/Atrocity," in *In the Future Perfect*, New York: New Directions.

Acker, Kathy (1986) *Don Quixote, which was a dream*, New York: Grove Press.

Acker, Kathy (1988) *Empire of the Senseless*, New York: Grove Press.

Adams, Hazard (1990 (1986)) "Critical Constitution of the Literary Text: The Example of *Ulysses*," in *Antithetical Essays in Literary Criticism and Liberal Education*, Tallahassee: Florida State University Press, 90–110.

Altman, Rick (1986) "Television/Sound," in Modleski 1986, 39–54.

Apple, Max (1984) *Free Agents*, New York: Harper & Row.

Ashbery, John (1981) "Paradoxes and Oxymorons," in *Shadow Train*, Harmondsworth: Penguin.

Attridge, Derek (1988) *Peculiar Language: Literature as Difference from the Renaissance to James Joyce*, London: Methuen.

Attridge, Derek and Daniel Ferrer (eds) (1984a) "Introduction: Highly continental évènements," in Attridge and Ferrer 1984b, 1–13.

Attridge, Derek and Daniel Ferrer (eds) (1984b) *Post-structuralist Joyce: Essays from the French*, Cambridge, London and New York: Cambridge University Press.

Bal, Mieke (1978) "Mise en abyme et iconicité," *Littérature* 29, 116–28.

Bal, Mieke (1981) "The Laughing Mice, or: On Focalization," *Poetics Today* 2, 2:202–10.

Bal, Mieke (1985) *Narratology: Introduction to the Theory of Narrative*, Toronto: University of Toronto Press.

Bal, Mieke (1990) "The Point of Narratology," *Poetics Today* 11, 4:727–53.

Banfield, Ann (1982) *Unspeakable Sentences: Narration and Representation in the Language of Fiction*, London: Routledge & Kegan Paul.

Barker, Francis (1984) *The Tremulous Private Body*, London and New York: Methuen.

Barry, Jackson G. (1990) "Narratology's Centrifugal Force: A Literary Perspective on the Extensions of Narrative Theory," *Poetics Today* 11, 4:295–307.

Barth, John (1969) "Life-Story," in *Lost in the Funhouse*, New York: Bantam.

Barth, John (1973) *Chimera*, New York: Fawcett.

Barth, John (1984a) *The Friday Book: Essays and Other Nonfiction*, New York: Putnam's.

Barth, John (1984b(1967)) "The Literature of Exhaustion," in Barth 1984a, 62–76.

Barth, John (1984c(1979)) "The Literature of Replenishment," in Barth 1984a, 193–206.

Barth, John (1987) *The Tidewater Tales: A Novel*, New York: Putnam's.

Barthelme, Donald (1976(1975)) *The Dead Father*, New York: Pocket Books.
Barthelme, Donald (1982a(1968)) "The Indian Uprising," in Barthelme 1982d, 108–14.
Barthelme, Donald (1982b(1975)) "A Manual for Sons," in Barthelme 1982d, 249–71.
Barthelme, Donald (1982c(1970)) "On Angels," in Barthelme 1982d, 135–7.
Barthelme, Donald (1982d) *Sixty Stories*, New York: Dutton.
Barthes, Roland (1964) *Essais critiques*, Paris: Seuil.
Barthes, Roland (1975) *The Pleasure of the Text*, trans. Richard Miller, New York: Hill & Wang.
Barthes, Roland (1977) "From Work to Text," in *Image – Music – Text*, trans. Stephen Heath, New York: Hill & Wang, 155–64.
Bašić, Sonja (1986–7) "The Narrative of Joyce's *Ulysses*: Modernist Mainstream, Postmodernist Source," *Studia Romanica et Anglica Zagrabiensia* 31–2, 33–46.
Bass, Thomas A. (1983) "*Gravity's Rainbow* as Orphic Text," *Pynchon Notes* 13, 25–46.
Baudrillard, Jean (1983a) "The Ecstasy of Communication," in Foster 1983.
Baudrillard, Jean (1983b(1981)) "The Precession of Simulacra," in *Simulations*, trans. Paul Foss, Paul Patton and Philip Beitchman, New York: Semiotext(e), 1–79; repr. (in a different version) as Baudrillard 1988.
Baudrillard, Jean (1988) "Simulacra and Simulations," in *Selected Writings*, ed. Mark Postman, Stanford, CA: Stanford University Press, 166–84.
Bear, Greg (1986(1985)) *Blood Music*, New York: Ace Science Fiction.
Beckett, Samuel (1970(1953)) *Watt*, New York: Grove Press.
Beebe, Maurice (1974) "*Ulysses* and the Age of Modernism," in Staley 1974, 172–88.
Bell, Michael (1990) "How Primordial is Narrative?" in Nash 1990, 172–98.
Benstock, Bernard (1974) "*Ulysses* without Dublin," in Staley 1974, 90–117.
Benveniste, Emile (1966) *Problèmes de linguistique générale*, Paris: Gallimard.
Bercovitch, Sacvan (1978) *The American Jeremiad*, Madison: University of Wisconsin Press.
Berger, Charles (1983) "Merrill and Pynchon: Our Apocalyptic Scribes," in David Lehman and Charles Berger (eds), *James Merrill: Essays in Criticism*, Ithaca, NY and London: Cornell University Press, 282–97.
Berger, Peter L. and Thomas Luckmann (1966) *The Social Construction of Reality: A Treatise in the Sociology of Knowledge*, Garden City, NY: Doubleday.
Bernstein, J.M. (1990) "Self-Knowledge as Praxis: Narrative and Narration in Psychoanalysis," in Nash 1990, 51–77.
Berryman, John (1976) "One Answer to a Question: Changes (1965)," in *The Freedom of the Poet*, New York: Farrar Straus & Giroux.
Bersani, Leo (1990) *The Culture of Redemption*, Cambridge MA and London: Harvard University Press.
Bester, Alfred (1979(1955)) *Tiger! Tiger!* (U.S. title: *The Stars My Destination*), Harmondsworth: Penguin.
Boorstin, Daniel J. (1985(1961)) *The Image: A Guide to Pseudo-Events in America*, repr. New York: Atheneum.
Borges, Jorge Luis (1962a(1944)) "Death and the Compass," in Borges 1962b, 129–41.
Borges, Jorge Luis (1962b) *Ficciones*, trans. Anthony Kerrigan, New York: Grove Press.
Borges, Jorge Luis (1962c(1941)) "Tlön, Uqbar, Orbis Tertius," in Borges 1962b, 17–35.

Borges, Jorge Luis (1968) *A Personal Anthology*, trans. Anthony Kerrigan, London: Jonathan Cape.

Borradori, Giovanna (1987/8), " 'Weak Thought' and Postmodernism: The Italian Departure from Deconstruction," *SocialText* 18, 39–49

Bosinelli, Rosa Maria, Paola Pugliatti, and Romana Zacchi (eds) (1986) *Myriad-minded Man: Jottings on Joyce*, Bologna: CLUEB.

Bradbury, Malcolm (1983) "Modernisms/Postmodernisms," in Hassan and Hassan 1983, 311–27.

Bredin, Hugh (1984) "Metonymy," *Poetics Today* 5, 1:45–58.

Brooke-Rose, Christine (1981) *A Rhetoric of the Unreal: Studies in Narrative and Structure, Especially of the Fantastic*, Cambridge and New York: Cambridge University Press.

Brooke-Rose, Christine (1984) *Amalgamemnon*, Manchester: Carcanet Press.

Brooke-Rose, Christine (1986) *The Christine Brooke-Rose Omnibus: Four Novels*, Manchester and New York: Carcanet Press, 1986.

Brooke-Rose, Christine (1987) *Xorandor*, London: Paladin.

Brooke-Rose, Christine (1989) "Illicitations," *Review of Contemporary Fiction* 9, 3:101–9.

Brooke-Rose, Christine (1991) *Stories, Theories and Things*, Cambridge and New York: Cambridge University Press.

Brown, Richard Harvey (1987) *Society as Text: Essays on Rhetoric, Reason and Reality*, Chicago and London: University of Chicago Press.

Bruner, Jerome (1986) *Actual Minds, Possible Worlds*, Cambridge, MA and London: Harvard University Press.

Bukatman, Scott (1991) "Postcards from the Posthuman Solar System," *Science-Fiction Studies* 18, 343–57.

Butor, Michel (1964) "L'Usage des pronoms personnels dans le roman," in *Essais sur le roman*, Paris: Gallimard, 73–88.

Cadigan, Pat (1987) *Mindplayers*, Toronto, New York, London: Bantam.

Cadigan, Pat (1991) *Synners*, New York, London, Toronto: Bantam.

Caesar, Terry (1984) " 'Trapped inside Their frame with your wastes piling up': Mindless Pleasure in *Gravity's Rainbow*," *Pynchon Notes* 14, 39–48.

Calinescu, Matei (1983) "From the One to the Many: Pluralism in Today's Thought," in Hassan and Hassan 1983, 263–88.

Calinescu, Matei (1987a) *Five Faces of Modernity: Modernism, Avant-Garde, Decadence, Kitsch, Postmodernism*, Durham NC: Duke University Press.

Calinescu, Matei (1987b) "Introductory Remarks: Postmodernism, the Mimetic and Theatrical Fallacies," in Calinescu and Fokkema 1987, 3–16.

Calinescu, Matei (1990) "Modernism, Late Modernism, Postmodernism," in Danuta Zadworna-Fjellestad and Lennard Björk (eds), *Criticism in the Twilight Zone: Postmodern Perspectives on Literature and Politics*, Stockholm: Almqvist & Wiksell, 52–61.

Calinescu, Matei and Douwe Fokkema (eds) (1987) *Exploring Postmodernism*, Amsterdam and Philadelphia: John Benjamins.

Calvino, Italo (1978(1973)) *The Castle of Crossed Destinies*, trans. William Weaver, London: Pan.

Calvino, Italo (1986) "Prose and Anticombinatorics," in Motte 1986, 143–52.

Chambers, Ross (1984) *Story and Situation: Narrative Seduction and the Power of Fiction*, Minneapolis: University of Minnesota Press.

Chatman, Seymour (1978) *Story and Discourse: Narrative Structure in Fiction and Film*, Ithaca, NY: Cornell University Press.

Chatman, Seymour (1990) *Coming to Terms*, Ithaca, NY: Cornell University Press.

Clark, Beverley Lyon (1985) "Realizing *Gravity*'s Fantasy," *Pynchon Notes* 17, 15–34.

Clerc, Charles (ed.) (1983a) *Approaches to Gravity's Rainbow*, Columbus: Ohio State University Press.

Clerc, Charles (1983b) "Film in *Gravity's Rainbow*," in Clerc 1983a, 103–51.

Clerc, Charles (1983c) "Introduction," in Clerc 1983a, 3–30.

Cohan, Steven and Linda Shires (1988) *Telling Stories: A Theoretical Analysis of Narrative Fiction*, New York and London: Routledge.

Cohn, Dorrit (1978) *Transparent Minds: Narrative Modes for Presenting Consciousness in Fiction*, Princeton, NY: Princeton University Press.

Coletti, Theresa (1988) *Naming the Rose: Eco, Medieval Signs, and Modern Theory*, Ithaca, NY and London: Cornell University Press.

Connor, Steven (1989) *Postmodernist Culture: An Introduction to Theories of the Contemporary*, Oxford and New York: Basil Blackwell.

Conrad, Joseph (1971) *Under Western Eyes*, Harmondsworth: Penguin.

Corry, Leo (forthcoming) "Jorge Borges, Author of *The Name of the Rose*," *Poetics Today*.

Cowart, David (1977) "Love and Death: Variations on a Theme in Pynchon's Early Fiction," *Journal of Narrative Technique* 7, 157–69.

Cowart, David (1980) *Thomas Pynchon: The Art of Allusion*, Carbondale: Southern Illinois University Press.

Crary, Jonathan (1984) "Eclipse of the Spectacle," in Brian Wallis (ed.), *Art after Modernism: Rethinking Representation*, New York: New Museum of Contemporary Art/Boston: Godine, 283–94.

Culler, Jonathan (1975) *Structuralist Poetics: Structuralism, Linguistics and the Study of Literature*, London: Routledge & Kegan Paul.

Culler, Jonathan (1981) "Apostrophe," in *The Pursuit of Signs: Semiotics, Literature, Deconstruction*, London: Routledge & Kegan Paul, 135–54.

Dahlberg, Edward (1976) *From Flushing to Calvary*, in *Bottom Dogs, From Flushing to Calvary, Those Who Perish, and Hitherto Unpublished and Uncollected Works*, New York: Minerva Press.

Daiches, David (1963(1947)) *Virgina Woolf*, New York: New Directions.

Dällenbach, Lucien (1977) *Le Récit spéculaire: Essai sur la mise en abyme*, Paris: Seuil.

Davidson, Gustav (1967) *A Dictionary of Angels, including the Fallen Angels*, New York and London: Macmillan/The Free Press.

Davies, Paul (1980) *Other Worlds*, London: J.M. Dent.

Delany, Samuel (1977) "Shadows," in *The Jewel-Hinged Jaw: Notes on the Language of Science-Fiction*, Elizabethtown, NY: Dragon Press, 88–98.

De Lauretis, Teresa (1985) "Gaudy Rose: Eco and Narcissism," *SubStance* 47, 13–29.

DeLillo, Don (1984(1977)) *Players*, New York: Vintage.

DeLillo, Don (1985) *White Noise*, New York: Viking Penguin.

Derrida, Jacques (1984) "No Apocalypse, Not Now (full speed ahead, seven missiles, seven missives)," *Diacritics* 14, 2:20–31.

Dickens, Charles (1971) *Bleak House*, ed. Norman Page, Harmondsworth: Penguin.

Dillard, Annie (1982) *Living by Fiction*, New York: Harper & Row.

Docherty, Thomas (1982) *Reading (Absent) Character: Towards a Theory of Characterization in Fiction*, Oxford: Oxford University Press.

Dorris, Michael and Louise Erdrich (1988), "Bangs and Whimpers: Novelists at Armageddon," *New York Times Book Review*, 13 March, 21 5.

Dos Passos, John (n.d.) *U.S.A.*, New York: Modern Library.

Doury, Michel (trans.) (1975) *Rainbow*, Paris: Plon.

Dowling, David (1987) *Fictions of Nuclear Disaster*, London: Macmillan.

Duyfhuizen, Bernard (1981a) "A Long View of V 2," *Pynchon Notes* 5, 17–19.

Duyfhuizen, Bernard (1981b) "Starry-Eyed Semiotics: Learning to Read Slothrop's Map and *Gravity's Rainbow*," *Pynchon Notes* 6, 5–33.

Ebert, Teresa L. (1980) "The Convergence of Postmodern Innovative Fiction and Science Fiction: An Encounter with Samuel R. Delany's Technotopia," *Poetics Today* 1, 4:91–104.

Eco, Umberto (1979) "*Lector in Fabula*: Pragmatic Strategy in a Metanarrative Text," in *The Role of the Reader: Explorations in the Semiotics of Texts*, Bloomington and London: Indiana University Press, 200–60.

Eco, Umberto (1983(1980)) *The Name of the Rose* (*Il nome della rosa*), trans. William Weaver, San Diego, New York, London: Harcourt Brace Jovanovich.

Eco, Umberto (1984(1983)) *Postscript to The Name of the Rose* (*Postille a Il nome della rosa*), trans. William Weaver, San Diego, New York, London: Harcourt Brace Jovanovich.

Eco, Umberto (1989(1988)) *Foucault's Pendulum* (*Il pendolo di Foucault*), trans. William Weaver, San Diego, New York, London: Harcourt Brace Jovanovich.

Eco, Umberto (1990(1983)) "Abduction in Uqbar," in *The Limits of Interpretation*, Bloomington and Indianapolis: Indiana University Press.

Ellmann, Richard (1972) *Ulysses on the Liffey*, London: Faber & Faber.

Even-Zohar, Itamar (1990a) "Polysystem Studies," special issue of *Poetics Today* 11, 1.

Even-Zohar, Itamar (1990b(1980)) " 'Reality' and Realemes in Narrative," in Even-Zohar 1990a, 207–18.

Felman, Shoshana (1977) "Turning the Screw of Interpretation," *Yale French Studies* 55–6, 94–207.

Ferrer, Daniel (1984(1975)) "Circe, Regret and Regression," in Attridge and Ferrer (eds) 1984b, 127–44.

Fielding, Henry (1974) *The History of Tom Jones, A Foundling*, ed. Martin Battestin and Fredson Bowers, Oxford: Oxford University Press.

Fokkema, Douwe (1984) *Literary History, Modernism, and Postmodernism*, Amsterdam and Philadelphia, PA: John Benjamins.

Fokkema, Douwe and Elrud Ibsch (1987) *Modernist Conjectures: A Mainstream of European Literature*, London: C. Hurst.

Fokkema, Douwe, and Hans Bertens (eds) (1986) *Approaching Postmodernism*, Amsterdam and Philadelphia, PA: John Benjamins.

Forster, E.M. (1963(1927)) *Aspects of the Novel*, Harmondsworth: Penguin.

Forsyth, Neil (1987) *The Old Enemy: Satan and the Combat Myth*, Princeton, NJ: Princeton University Press.

Foster, Hal (ed.) (1983) *The Anti-Aesthetic: Essays on Postmodern Culture*, Port Townsend WA: Bay Press.

Foucault, Michel (1970) *The Order of Things: An Archeology of the Human Sciences*, New York: Pantheon.

Fowler, Douglas (1980) *A Reader's Guide to "Gravity's Rainbow"*, Ann Arbor, MI: Ardis.

Friedman, Alan J. (1983) "Science and Technology," in Clerc 1983a, 69–102.

Friedman, Ellen G. and Miriam Fuchs (1989) "A Conversation with Christine Brooke-Rose," *Review of Contemporary Fiction* 9, 3:81–90.

Frow, John (1986) *Marxism and Literary History*, Cambridge, MA: Harvard University Press.

Füredy, Viveca (1989) "A Structural Model of Phenomena with Embedding in Literature and Other Arts," *Poetics Today* 10, 4:745–69.

Gass, William H. (1968) *Willie Master's Lonesome Wife*, Evanston, IL: Northwestern University Press.

Gee, Maggie (1981) *Dying, in Other Words*, Brighton: Harvester.

Genette, Gérard (1983) *Nouveau discours du récit*, Paris: Seuil.

Gibson, William (1984) *Neuromancer*, New York: Ace Science Fiction.

Gibson, William (1987a(1986)) *Burning Chrome* (stories), New York: Ace Science Fiction.

Gibson, William (1987b(1986)) *Count Zero*, New York: Ace Science Fiction.

Gibson, William (1988) *Mona Lisa Overdrive*, Toronto, New York, London: Bantam.

Gibson, William and Bruce Sterling (1991) *The Difference Engine*, New York, Toronto, London: Bantam.

Gifford, Don, with Robert J. Seidman (1974) *Notes for Joyce: An Annotation of James Joyce's "Ulysses"*, New York: E.P. Dutton.

Goldberg, S.L. (1963) *The Classical Temper: A Study of James Joyce's "Ulysses"*, London: Chatto & Windus.

Goodman, Nelson (1978) *Ways of Worldmaking*, Indianapolis, IN and Cambridge: Hackett.

Gorak, Jan (1987) *God the Artist: American Novelists in a Post-Realist Age*, Urbana and Chicago: University of Illinois Press.

Gottlieb, E.E. and C. Cornbleth (1989) "The Professionalization of *Tomorrow's Teachers*: An Analysis of US Teacher-Education Reform Rhetoric," *Journal of Education for Teaching* 15, 1:3–15.

Graff, Gerald (1979) *Literature Against Itself: Literary Ideas in Modern Society*, Chicago and London: University of Chicago Press.

Greene, Thomas (1963) *The Descent from Heaven: A Study in Epic Continuity*, New Haven, CT and London: Yale University Press.

Guillén, Claudio (1971) *Literature as System: Essays towards the Theory of Literary History*, Princeton, NY: Princeton University Press.

Harbison, Robert (1988(1977)) *Eccentric Spaces*, Boston: Godine.

Harshav (Hrushovski), Benjamin (1979) "The Structure of Semiotic Objects: A Three-Dimensional Model," *Poetics Today* 1, 1–2:365–76; repr. in Wendy Steiner (ed.), *The Sign in Music and Literature*, Austin: University of Texas Press, 1981.

Harshav (Hrushovski), Benjamin (1988(1976)) "Theory of the Literary Text and the Structure of Non-Narrative Fiction: In the First Episode of *War and Peace*," *Poetics Today* 9, 3:635–66.

Harvey, David (1989) *The Condition of Postmodernity: An Enquiry into the Origins of Cultural Change*, Oxford and Cambridge, MA: Basil Blackwell.

Hassan, Ihab (1975a) *Paracriticisms: Seven Speculations of the Times*, Urbana: University of Illinois Press.

Hassan, Ihab (1975b) "POSTmodernISM: A Paracritical Bibliography," in Hassan 1975a, 39–59.

Hassan, Ihab (1980) *The Right Promethean Fire: Imagination, Science, and Cultural Change*, Urbana: University of Illinois Press.

Hassan, Ihab (1985) "Revillusionary Panorama" (review of Christine Brooke-Rose, *Amalgamemnon*), *New York Times Book Review*, 8 September, 20.

Hassan, Ihab and Sally Hassan (eds) (1983) *Innovation/ Renovation: New Perspectives on the Humanities*, Madison and London: University of Wisconsin Press.

Hawkins, Susan E. (1989) "Memory and Discourse: Fictionalizing the Present in *Xorandor*," *Review of Contemporary Fiction* 9, 3:138–44.

Hayles, N. Katherine, and Mary B. Eiser (1985) "Coloring *Gravity's Rainbow*," *Pynchon Notes* 16, 3–24.

Hayman, David (1987) *Re-Forming the Narrative: Toward a Mechanics of Modernist Fiction*, Ithaca, NY and London: Cornell University Press.

Hemingway, Ernest (1958) *In Our Time*, New York: Scribner's.

Henkle, Roger B. (1983) "The Morning and Evening Funnies," in Clerc 1983a, 273–90.

Herman, David J. (1991) "Modernism and Postmodernism: Towards an Analytic Distinction," *Poetics Today* 12, 1:55–86.

Herr, Michael (1978) *Dispatches*, New York: Avon.

Higgins, Dick (1978) *A Dialectic of Centuries: Notes towards a Theory of the New Arts*, New York and Barton, VT: Printed Editions.

Higgins, Dick (1984) *Horizons: The Poetics and Theory of the Intermedia*, Carbondale and Edwardsville: Southern Illinois University Press.

Hite, Molly (1983a) *Ideas of Order in the Novel of Thomas Pynchon*, Columbus: Ohio State University Press.

Hite, Molly (1983b) "Influence, Parallels, Filiations," Review of *Paradoxical Resolutions* by Craig Werner, *Pynchon Notes* 11, 57–62.

Hofstadter, Richard (1967) "The Paranoid Style in American Politics" (1963/64), repr. in *The Paranoid Style in American Politics and Other Essays*, New York: Vintage, 3–40.

Holquist, Michael (1971) "Whodunit and Other Questions: Metaphysical Detective Stories in Post-war Fiction," *New Literary History* 3, 1:135–56.

Howard, Richard (1986) "Smuggling a Score," in McElroy 1986, n.p.

Hume, Kathryn (1987) *Pynchon's Mythography: An Approach to "Gravity's Rainbow,"* Carbondale and Edwardsville: Southern Illinois University Press.

Hutcheon, Linda (1988) *A Poetics of Postmodernism: History, Theory, Fiction*, New York and London: Routledge.

Hutcheon, Linda (1989) *The Politics of Postmodernism*, New York and London: Routledge.

Huyssen, Andreas (1986) *After the Great Divide: Modernism, Mass Culture, Postmodernism*, Bloomington: Indiana University Press.

Ingarden, Roman (1973a (1968)) *The Cognition of the Literary Work of Art*, trans. Ruth Ann Crowley and Kenneth R. Olson, Evanston: Northwestern University Press.

Ingarden, Roman (1973b (1931)) *The Literary Work of Art*, Evanston, IL: Northwestern University Press.

Iser, Wolfgang (1974) *The Implied Reader: Patterns of Communication in Prose Fiction from Bunyan to Beckett*, Baltimore, MD and London: Johns Hopkins University Press.

Jakobson, Roman (1971a) "The dominant," in Ladislav Matejka and Krystyna Pomorska (eds), *Readings in Russian Poetics: Formalist and Structuralist Views*, Cambridge, MA and London: MIT Press, 105–10.

Jakobson, Roman (1971b) *Selected Writings: Word and Language*, The Hague: Mouton, II.

Jakobson, Roman (1971c) "Shifters, Verbal Categories, and the Russian Verb," in Jakobson 1971b, 130–47.

Jakobson, Roman (1971d) "Two Aspects of Language and Two Types of Aphasic Disturbances," in Jakobson 1971b, 239–59.

Jameson, Fredric (1975) "Magical Narratives: Romance as Genre," *New Literary History* 7, 1:135–63.

Jameson, Fredric (1979) *Fables of Aggression: Wyndham Lewis, the Modernist as Fascist*, Berkeley, Los Angeles, London: University of California Press.

Jameson, Fredric (1981) *The Political Unconscious: Narrative as a Socially Symbolic Act*, Ithaca, NY: Cornell University Press.

Jameson, Fredric (1982) "Progress Versus Utopia; or, Can We Imagine the Future?," *Science-Fiction Studies* 9, 2:147–58.

Jameson, Fredric (1983) "Postmodernism and Consumer Society," in Foster 1983, 111–25; repr. in Kaplan 1988b, 13–29.

Jameson, Fredric (1987) "Science Fiction as a Spatial Genre: Generic Discontinuities and the Problem of Figuration in Vonda McIntyre's *The Exile Waiting*," *Science-Fiction Studies* 14, 1: 44–59.

Jameson, Fredric (1988) "Cognitive Mapping," in Cary Nelson and Lawrence Grossberg (eds), *Marxism and the Interpretation of Culture*, Urbana and Chicago: University of Illinois Press, 347–57.

Jameson, Fredric (1989) "Afterword – Marxism and Postmodernism," in Douglas Kellner (ed.), *Postmodernism/Jameson/Critique*, Washington, D.C.: Maisonneuve Press, 369–87.

Jameson, Fredric (1991a(1984)) "The Cultural Logic of Late Capitalism," in Jameson 1991b, 1–54.

Jameson, Fredric (1991b) *Postmodernism, or, The Cultural Logic of Late Capitalism*, Durham, NC: Duke University Press.

Jameson, Fredric (1991c), "Spatial Equivalents in the World System," in Jameson 1991b, 97–129.

Janusko, Robert (1983) *The Sources and Structures of James Joyce's "Oxen"*, Ann Arbor: UMI Research.

Jencks, Charles (1980) *Late-Modern Architecture and Other Essays*, London: Academy Editions/New York: Rizzoli.

Jencks, Charles (1984) *The Language of Post-Modern Architecture*, 4th rev. edn., London: Academy Editions.

Jencks, Charles (1986) *What is Post-Modernism?*, London: Art and Design.

Johnson, B.S. (1973), "Introduction," in *Aren't You Rather Young to be Writing Your Memoirs?*, London: Hutchinson, 11–31.

Johnson, Denis (1985) *Fiskadoro*, New York: Knopf.

Joyce, James (1973) *Ulysses*, Harmondsworth: Penguin.

Joyce, James (1986) *Ulysses*, ed. Hans Walter Gabler with Wolfhard Steppe and Claus Melchior, London: The Bodley Head.

Kadrey, Richard (1989(1988)) *Metrophage*, London: Gollancz.

Kaplan, E. Ann (1987) *Rocking Around the Clock: Music, Televison, Postmodernism, and Consumer Culture*, New York and London: Methuen.

Kaplan, E. Ann (1988a) "Introduction," in Kaplan 1988b.

Kaplan, E. Ann (ed.) (1988b) *Postmodernism and Its Discontents: Theories, Practices*, London and New York: Verso.

Kaufman, Marjorie (1976) "Brunhilde and the Chemists: Women in *Gravity's Rainbow*," in Levine and Leverenz 1976b, 197–227.

Kenner, Hugh (1964) "Art in a Closed Field," in Robert Scholes (ed.), *Learners and Discerners: A Newer Criticism*, Charlottesville, VA: University Press of Virginia, 109–33.

Kenner, Hugh (1978) *Joyce's Voices*, London: Faber & Faber.

Kenner, Hugh (1980) *Ulysses*, London: George Allen & Unwin.

Kermode, Frank (1967) *The Sense of an Ending: Studies in the Theory of Fiction*, New York: Oxford University Press.

Kermode, Frank (1968) "Modernisms," in *Continuities*, London: Routledge & Kegan Paul, 1–27.

Kharpertian, Theodore D. (1990) *A Hand to Turn the Time: The Menippean Satires of Thomas Pynchon*, Rutherford, Madison and Teanecks: Fairleigh Dickinson University Press/London and Toronto: Associated University Presses.

Kinney, Arthur F. (1978) *Faulkner's Narrative Poetics: Style as Vision*, Amherst: University of Mississippi Press.

Kiš, Danilo (1989(1983)) *The Encyclopedia of the Dead*, trans. Michael Henry Heim, New York: Farrar Straus Giroux.

Kroker, Arthur and David Cook (1986) "Television and the Triumph of Culture," in *The Postmodern Scene: Excremental Culture and Hyper-Aesthetics*, New York: St. Martin's Press, 267–79.

Krysinski, Wladimir (1981) *Carrefours de signes: Essais sur le roman moderne*, The Hague: Mouton.

Kurzon, Dennis (1989) "*Nomen Rosae*: Latin and 'The Ambience of the Period' in Eco's Novel," *Hebrew University Studies in Literature and the Arts* 17, 36–51.

LaCapra, Dominick (1985) *History and Criticism*, Ithaca, NY and London: Cornell University Press.

Laidlaw, Marc (1986(1985)) *Dad's Nuke*, London: Gollancz.

Landow, George P. (1982) *Images of Crisis: Literary Iconology, 1750 to the Present*, Boston, London, Henley: Routledge & Kegan Paul.

Lawall, Sarah N. (1968) *Critics of Consciousness: The Existential Structures of Literature*, Cambridge, MA: Harvard University Press.

Lawrence, Karen (1981) *The Odyssey of Style in "Ulysses"*, Princeton, NY: Princeton University Press.

Lawson, Hilary and Lisa Appignanesi (eds) (1989) *Dismantling Truth: Reality in the Post-Modern World*, New York: St Martin's Press.

LeClair, Tom and Larry McCaffery (eds) (1983) *Anything Can Happen: Interviews with Contemporary American Novelists*, Urbana, Chicago, London: University of Illinois Press.

Lem, Stanislaw (1984) "Todorov's Fantastic Theory of Literature," in *Microworlds: Writings on Science Fiction and Fantasy*, San Diego, New York, London: Harcourt Brace Jovanovich, 209–32.

Lethen, Helmut (1986) "Modernism Cut in Half: The Exclusion of the Avant-Garde and the Debate on Postmodernism," in Fokkema and Bertens 1986, 233–8.

Levao, Ronald (1985) *Renaissance Minds and Their Fictions: Cusanus, Sidney, Shakespeare*, Berkeley, Los Angeles, London: University of California Press.

Leverenz, David (1976) "On Trying to Read *Gravity's Rainbow*," in Levine and Leverenz 1976b, 229–49.

Levine, George (1976) "Risking the Moment: Anarchy and Possibility in Pynchon's Fiction," in Levine and Leverenz 1976b, 113–36.

Levine, George (1978) "V-2," in Mendelson 1978b, 178–91.

Levine, George and David Leverenz (1976a) "Introduction: Mindful Pleasures," in Levine and Leverenz 1976b, 3–11.

Levine, George and David Leverenz (eds) (1976b) *Mindful Pleasures: Essays on Thomas Pynchon*, Boston: Little, Brown.

Lippman, Bertram (1977) "The Reader of Movies: Thomas Pynchon's *Gravity's Rainbow*," *The Denver Quarterly* 12, 1–46.

Lodge, David (1977) *The Modes of Modern Writing: Metaphor, Metonymy, and the Typology of Modern Literature*, London: Edward Arnold.

Lodge, David (1981) "Modernism, Antimodernism and Postmodernism," in *Working with Structuralism: Essays and Reviews on Nineteenth- and Twentieth-Century Literature*, London: Routledge & Kegan Paul, 3–16.

Luckhurst, Roger (1991) "Border Policing: Postmodernism and Science Fiction," *Science-Fiction Studies* 18, 358–66.

Lyotard, Jean-François (1984a) "Appendix: Answering the Question: What is Postmodernism?" in Lyotard 1984b, 71–82.

Lyotard, Jean-François (1984b(1979)) *The Postmodern Condition: A Report on Knowledge*, Minneapolis: University of Minnesota Press.

Lyotard, Jean-Francois (1986) *Le Postmoderne expliqué aux enfants: Correspondance 1982–1985*, Paris: Galilee.

MacCabe, Colin (1978) *James Joyce and the Revolution of the Word*, London: Macmillan.

McCaffery, Larry (ed.) (1988a) Special issue, "The Cyberpunk Controversy," *Mississippi Review 47/48* 16, 2–3.

McCaffery, Larry (1988b) "The Fictions of the Present," in *Columbia Literary History of the United States*, general ed. Emory Elliot, New York: Columbia University Press, 1161–77.

McCaffery, Larry (1990a) *Across the Wounded Galaxies: Interviews with Contemporary American Science Fiction Writers*, Urbana and Chicago: University of Illinois Press.

McCaffery, Larry (1990b) "An Interview with William Gibson," in McCaffery 1990a, 130–50.

McCloskey, Donald N. (1990) "Storytelling in Economics," in Nash 1990, 5–22.

McConnell, Frank D. (1977) *Four Postwar American Novelists: Bellow, Mailer, Barth and Pynchon*, Chicago: University of Chicago Press.

McElroy, Joseph (1975) "Neural neighborhoods and other concrete abstractions," *TriQuarterly* 34, 201–17.

McElroy, Joseph (1985(1974)) *Lookout Cartridge*, New York: Carroll & Graf.

McElroy, Joseph (ed.) (1986(1966)) *A Smuggler's Bible*, New York: Carroll & Graf.

McElroy, Joseph (1987) *Women and Men*, New York: Alfred A. Knopf.

McHale, Brian (1978) "Free Indirect Discourse: A Survey of Recent Accounts," *PTL* 3, 2:249–87.

McHale, Brian (1981) "On Moral Fiction: One Use of *Gravity's Rainbow*," *Pynchon Notes* 6, 34–9.

McHale, Brian (1982) "Writing about Postmodern Writing," *Poetics Today* 3, 3:211–27.

McHale, Brian (1983) "Unspeakable Sentences, Unnatural Acts: Linguistics and Poetics Revisited," *Poetics Today* 4, 1:17–45.

McHale, Brian (1987) *Postmodernist Fiction*, New York and London: Methuen.

McHoul, Alec (1987) "*Gravity's Rainbow*'s Golden Sections," *Pynchon Notes* 20–1, 31–8.

McHoul, Alec and David Wills (1990) *Writing Pynchon: Strategies in Fictional Analysis*, Urbana and Chicago: University of Illinois Press.

McLaughlin, Robert L. (1988) "Pynchon's Angels and Supernatural Systems in *Gravity's Rainbow*," *Pynchon Notes* 22–3, 25–33.

Major, Clarence (1975) *Reflex and Bone Structure*, New York: Fiction Collective.

Malmgren, Carl D. (1985) *Fictional Space in the Modernist and Postmodernist American Novel*, Lewisburg, PA: Bucknell University Press.

Malmgren, Carl D. (1988a) "Toward a Definition of Science Fantasy," *Science-Fiction Studies* 15, 3:259–81.

Malmgren, Carl D. (1988b) "Worlds Apart: A Theory of Science Fiction," in Arno Heller, Walter Höbling, and Waldemar Zacharasiewicz (eds), *Utopian Thought in American Literature: Untersuchungen zur literarischen Utopie und Dystopie in den USA*, Tübingen: Gunter Narr, 25–42.

Margolin, Uri (1986) "Dispersing/Voiding the Subject: A Narratological Perspective," *Texte* 5/6, 181–210.

Márquez, Gabriel García (1977 (1967)) *One Hundred Years of Solitude*, trans. Gregory Rabassa, Harmondsworth: Penguin.

Marriott, David (1985) "Moviegoing," *Pynchon Notes* 16, 46–77.

Martin, Richard (1989) " 'Just Words on a Page': The Novels of Christine Brooke-Rose," *Review of Contemporary Fiction* 9, 3:110–23.

Martin, Wallace (1986) *Recent Theories of Narrative*, Ithaca, NY and London: Cornell University Press.

Mathews, Harry (1986(1981)) "Mathews' Algorithm," in Motte 1986, 126–39.

Mathews, Harry (1990) "We for One: An Introduction to Joseph McElroy's *Women and Men*," *Review of Contemporary Fiction* 10, 1:199–226.

Mathieson, Kenneth (1985) "The Influence of Science Fiction in the Contemporary American Novel," *Science-Fiction Studies* 12, 1:22–31.

Mendelson, Edward (1976) "Gravity's Encyclopedia," in Levine and Leverenz 1976b, 161–95.

Mendelson, Edward (1978a) "Introduction," in Mendelson 1978b, 1–15.

Mendelson, Edward (ed.) (1978b) *Pynchon: A Collection of Critical Essays*, Englewood Cliffs, NJ: Prentice-Hall.

Mepham, John (1991) "Narratives of Postmodernism," in Smyth 1991, 138–55.

Merwin, W.S. (1970) "The Second Person," in *The Miner's Pale Children*, New York: Atheneum.

Modleski, Tania (ed.) (1986) *Studies in Entertainment: Critical Approaches to Mass Culture*, Bloomington and Indianapolis: Indiana University Press.

Montag, Warren (1988) "What is at Stake in the Debate on Postmodernism?" in Kaplan 1988b, 88–103.

Moore, Steven (1986) "Alexander Theroux's *Darconville's Cat* and the Tradition of Learned Wit," *Contemporary Literature* 27, 2:233–45.

Morrissey, Thomas (1984) "Armageddon from Huxley to Hoban," *Extrapolations* 25, 3:197–213.

Morrissette, Bruce (1963) *Les Romans de Robbe-Grillet*, Paris: Editions de Minuit.

Morrissette, Bruce (1985a(1971)) "Interior Duplication," in Morrissette 1985c, 141–56.

Morrissette, Bruce (1985b(1965)) "Narrative 'You'," in Morrissette 1985c, 108–40.

Morrissette, Bruce (1985c) *Novel and Film: Essays in Two Genres*, Chicago and London: University of Chicago Press.

Morse, Margaret (1986) "The Televison News Personality and Credibility: Reflections on the News in Transition," in Modleski 1986, 55–79.

Motte, Warren F. (ed. and trans.) (1986) *Oulipo: A Primer of Potential Literature*, Lincoln and London: University of Nebraska Press.

Mottram, Eric (1977) *William Burroughs: The Algebra of Need*, London: Marion Boyars.

Nabokov, Vladimir (1970(1969)) *Ada, or Ardor: A Family Chronicle*, Greenwich, CT: Fawcett Crest.

Nash, Cristopher (ed.) (1990) *Narrative in Culture: The Uses of Storytelling in the Sciences, Philosophy, and Literature*, London and New York: Routledge.

Nevo, Ruth (1982) "*The Waste Land*: Ur-Text of Deconstruction," *New Literary History* 13, 3:453–61.

Newman, Charles (1984) "The Post-Modern Aura: The Act of Fiction in an Age of Inflation," *Salmagundi* 63–4, 3–199.

Newman, Robert D. (1986) *Understanding Thomas Pynchon*, Columbia, SC: University of South Carolina Press.

Norris, Christopher (1985) *The Contest of Faculties: Philosophy and Theory after Deconstruction*, London and New York: Methuen.

O'Donnell, Patrick (1986) " 'A Book of Traces': *Gravity's Rainbow*," in *Passionate Doubts: Designs of Interpretation in Contemporary American Fiction*, Iowa City: University of Iowa Press, 73–94.

Parker, Douglas (1985) "The Curious Case of Pharaoh's Polyp, and Related Matters," *SubStance* 47, 74–85.

Passias, Katherine (1976) "Deep and Surface Structure of the Narrative Pronoun *Vous* in Butor's *La Modification* and Its Relationship to Free Indirect Style," *Language and Style* 9, 3:197–212.

Patteson, Richard (1974) "What Stencil Knew. Structure and Certitude in Pynchon's *V.*," *Critique* 16, 30–44.

Pavel, Thomas (1980) "Narrative Domains," *Poetics Today* 1, 4:105–14; repr. in *Fictional Worlds*, Cambridge, MA: Harvard University Press, 1986.

Pearce, Richard (ed.) (1981) *Critical Essays on Thomas Pynchon*, Boston: Hall.

Perl, Jeffrey M. (1984) *The Tradition of Return: The Implicit History of Modern Literature*, Princeton, NY: Princeton University Press.

Perry, Menachem (1968) "Analogy and its Role as a Structural Principle in the Novels of Mendele Moykher-Sforim" (in Hebrew), *Hasifrut* 1, 65–100.

Pfeil, Fred (1988) "Potholders and Subincisions: On *The Businessman, Fiskadoro*, and Postmodern Paradise," in Kaplan 1988b, 59–78.

Piwowarczyk, Mary Ann (1976) "The Narratee and the Situation of Enunciation: A Reconsideration of Prince's Theory," *Genre* 9, 2:161–77.

Plater, William M. (1978) *The Grim Phoenix: Reconstructing Thomas Pynchon*, Bloomington: Indiana University Press.

Poirier, Richard (1973) "Rocket Power," in Mendelson 1978b, 167–78.

Poirier, Richard (1976) "The Importance of Thomas Pynchon," in Levine and Leverenz 1976b, 15–29.

Polan, Dana (1986) "Brief Encounters: Mass Culture and the Evacuation of Sense," in Modleski 1986, 167–87.

Polan, Dana (1988) "Postmodernism and Cultural Analysis Today," in Kaplan 1988b, 45–58.

Porter, Carolyn (1981) *Seeing and Being: The Plight of the Participant Observer in Emerson, James, Adams, and Faulkner*, Middletown, CT: Wesleyan University Press.

Porush, David (1985) *The Soft Machine: Cybernetic Fiction*, New York and London: Methuen.

Porush, David (1991) "Prigogine, Chaos, and Contemporary Science Fiction," *Science-Fiction Studies* 18, 367–86.

Postman, Neil (1985) *Amusing Ourselves to Death: Public Discourse in the Age of Show Business*, New York: Viking Penguin.

Prince, Gerald (1973) "Introduction a l'étude du narrataire," *Poétique* 14, 178–96.

Prince, Gerald (1982) *Narratology: The Form and Functioning of Narrative*, Berlin: Mouton.

Prince, Gerald (1987) *A Dictionary of Narratology*, Lincoln and London: University of Nebraska Press.

Purdy, Strother (1988) "*Gravity's Rainbow* and the Culture of Childhood," *Pynchon Notes* 22–3, 7–23.

Pynchon, Thomas (1964) *V.: A Novel*, New York: Bantam.

Pynchon, Thomas (1966) "A Journey into the Mind of Watts," *The New York Times Magazine*, 12 June, 34–5, 78, 80–2, 84.

Pynchon, Thomas (1967) *The Crying of Lot 49*, New York: Bantam.

Pynchon, Thomas (1973) *Gravity's Rainbow*, New York: Viking.

Pynchon, Thomas (1984) *Slow Learner: Early Stories*, Boston and Toronto: Little, Brown.

Pynchon, Thomas (1990) *Vineland*, Boston, Toronto, London: Little, Brown.

Quilligan, Maureen (1979) *The Language of Allegory: Defining the Genre*, Ithaca, NY: Cornell University Press.

Quinones, Ricardo J. (1985) *Mapping Literary Modernism: Time and Development*, Princeton, NJ: Princeton University Press.

Rabinowitz, Peter (1977) "Truth in Fiction: A Reexamination of Audiences," *Critical Inquiry* 4, 1:121–41.

Rajchman, John, and Cornel West (eds) (1985) *Post-Analytic Philosophy*, New York: Columbia University Press.

Reed, Ishmael (1973 (1972)) *Mumbo Jumbo*, New York: Bantam.

Reiss, Timothy (1982) *The Discourse of Modernism*, Ithaca, NY and London: Cornell University Press.

Reynolds, David S. (1988) *Beneath the American Renaissance: The Subversive Imagination in the Age of Emerson and Melville*, New York: Alfred A. Knopf.

Rimmon-Kenan, Shlomith (1982) "Ambiguity and Narrative Levels: Christine Brooke-Rose's *Thru*," *Poetics Today* 3, 1:21–32.

Rimmon-Kenan, Shlomith (1983) *Narrative Fiction: Contemporary Poetics*, London and New York: Methuen.

Roberts, Marie (1990) *Gothic Immortals: The Fiction of the Brotherhood of the Rosy Cross*, London and New York: Routledge.

Ron, Moshe (1987) "The Restricted Abyss: Nine Problems in the Theory of *Mise-en-Abyme*," *Poetics Today* 8, 2:417–38.

Rorty, Richard (1979) *Philosophy and the Mirror of Nature*, Princteon, NJ: Princeton University Press.

Rorty, Richard (1982) *Consequences of Pragmatism: Essays 1972–1980*, Minneapolis: University of Minnesota Press.

Rorty, Richard (1985) "Solidarity or Objectivity?" in Rajchman and West 1985, 3–19.

Rorty, Richard (1989) *Contingency, Irony, and Solidarity*, Cambridge and New York: Cambridge University Press.

Rosenbaum, Jonathan (1976) "A Reply," in Mendelson 1978b, 67–8.

Rosenheim, Laurence (1985) "Letter to Richard Pearce in Response to 'Pynchon's Endings,'" *Pynchon Notes* 17, 35–50.

Rosso, Stefano (1987) "Postmodern Italy: Notes on the 'Crisis of Reason,' 'Weak Thought,' and *The Name of the Rose*," in Calinescu and Fokkema 1987, 79–92.

Rucker, Rudy (1985(1982)) *Software*, Harmondsworth: Penguin.

Rucker, Rudy (1988) *Wetware*, New York: Avon Books, 1988.

Rushdie, Salman (1988) *The Satanic Verses*, London and New York: Viking.

Rushdie, Salman (1989) "An Interview by Catherine Bush," *Conjunctions* 14, 7–20.

Russell, Charles (1983) "Pynchon's Language: Signs, Systems, and Subversion," in Clerc (1983a), 251–72.

Sanders, Scott (1976) "Pynchon's Paranoid History," in Levine and Leverenz 1976b, 139–59.

Sarraute, Nathalie (1959) *Le Planétarium*, Paris: Gallimard.

Sarraute, Nathalie (1965) *The Planetarium*, trans. Maria Jolas, London: John Calder.

Schaub, Thomas H. (1981) *Pynchon: The Voice of Ambiguity*, Urbana and Chicago: University of Illinois Press.

Schmidt, S.J. (1984) "The Fiction Is that Reality Exists: A Constructivist Model of Reality," *Poetics Today* 5, 2:253–74.

Schmidt, S.J. (1985) "On Writing Histories of Literature: Some Remarks from a Constructivist Point of View," *Poetics* 14, 279–301.

Scholes, Robert (1974) "*Ulysses*: A Structuralist Perspective," in *Structuralism in Literature*, New Haven, CT: Yale University Press, 180–90.

Schuber, Stephen P. (1984) "Textual Orbits/Orbiting Criticism: Deconstructing *Gravity's Rainbow*," *Pynchon Notes* 14, 65–74.

Schwan, Helke (1987) "The Light Bulb Fake," *Pynchon Notes* 20–1, 121–33.

Schwarzbach, F.S. (1978) "A Matter of Gravity," in Mendelson 1978b, 56–67.

Seed, David (1976) "The Fictional Labyrinths of Thomas Pynchon," *Critical Quarterly* 18, 4:73–81.

Seed, David (1988) *The Fictional Labyrinths of Thomas Pynchon*, Iowa City: University of Iowa Press.

Shepard, Lucius (1984) *Green Eyes*, New York: Ace Science Fiction.

Shepard, Lucius (1987) *Life During Wartime*, Toronto, New York, London: Bantam.

Sherzer, Dina (1991) "Postmodernism and Feminisms," in Smyth 1991, 156–68.

Shiner, Lewis (1984) *Frontera*, New York: Baen.

Shiner, Lewis (1989(1988)) *Deserted Cities of the Heart*, Toronto, New York, London: Bantam.

Shirley, John (1987(1985)) *Eclipse*, New York: Popular Library/Warner Books.

Shusterman, Richard (1991) "The Fine Art of Rap," *New Literary History* 22, 613–32.

Sidney, Sir Philip (1963) *The Countesse of Pembrokes Arcadia*, in *The Prose Works of Sir Philip Sidney*, ed. Albert Feuillerat, Cambridge: Cambridge University Press.

Siegel, Mark R. (1976) "Creative Paranoia: Understanding the System of *Gravity's Rainbow*," *Critique* 18:39–54.

Siegel, Mark R. (1978) *Pynchon: Creative Paranoia in "Gravity's Rainbow*," Port Washington, NY: Kennikat Press.

Simmon, Scott (1974) "*Gravity's Rainbow* Described," *Critique* 16, 2:54–67.

Simmon, Scott (1981) "Beyond the Theater of War: *Gravity's Rainbow* as Film," in Pearce 1981, 124–39.

Slade, Joseph W. (1983) "Religion, Psychology, Sex and Love in *Gravity's Rainbow*," in Clerc 1983a, 153–98.

Slade, Joseph (1990 (1974)) *Thomas Pynchon*, New York and Bern: Peter Lang.

Smetak, Jacqueline R. (1987) "Who's Talking Here: Finding the Voice in *Gravity's Rainbow*," *Pynchon Notes* 20–1, 93–103.

Smith, Mack (1982) "The Paracinematic Reality of *Gravity's Rainbow*," *Pynchon Notes* 9, 17–37.

Smith, Marcus and Khachig Tölölyan (1981) "The New Jeremiad: *Gravity's Rainbow*," in Pearce 1981, 169–86.

Smyth, Edumnd J. (ed.) (1991) *Postmodernism and Contemporary Fiction*, London: Batsford.

Soja, Edward W. (1989) *Postmodern Geographies: The Reassertion of Space in Critical Social Theory*, London and New York: Verso.

Solomon, Jack (1988) "Reading the Tube: The Semiotics of Television," in *The*

Signs of Our Times. Semiotics: The Hidden Messages of Environments, Objects, and Cultural Images, Los Angeles: Jeremy P. Tarcher, 123–46.

Solotorevsky, Myrna (1989) "The Borgesian Intertext as an Object of Parody in Eco's *The Name of the Rose*," *Hebrew University Studies in Literature and Art* 17, 82–97.

Sontag, Susan (1966) "The Imagination of Disaster," in *Against Interpretation and Other Essays*, New York: Dell, 209–25.

Spanos, William (1972) "The Detective and the Boundary: Some Notes on the Postmodern Literary Imagination," *boundary 2* 1, 1:146–68.

Spence, Donald (1982) *Narrative Truth and Historical Truth: Meanings and Interpretation in Psychoanalysis*, New York: Norton.

Spinalbelli, Rosalba (1986) "Molly 'live,' " in Bosinelli *et al.* (eds) 173–84.

Staley, Thomas F. (ed.) (1974) *Ulysses: Fifty Years*, Bloomington and London: Indiana University Press.

Stanzel, Franz (1971) *Narrative Situations in the Novel: "Tom Jones," "Moby-Dick," "The Ambassadors," "Ulysses"*, trans. James P. Pusack, Bloomington and London: Indiana University Press.

Sterling, Bruce (1986a (1985)) *Schismatrix*, New York: Ace Science Fiction.

Sterling, Bruce (ed.) (1986b) *Mirrorshades: The Cyberpunk Anthology*, New York: Arbor House.

Sterling, Bruce (1988) *Islands in the Net*, New York: Arbor House/ William Morrow.

Sterling, Bruce (1990) *Crystal Express* (stories), New York: Ace.

Sterling, Bruce (1991) "Get the Bomb Off My Back," *New York Times*, October 13, Op-Ed page.

Sternberg, Meir (1970) "The Compositional Principles of Faulkner's *Light in August* and the Poetics of the Modern Novel" (in Hebrew), *Hasifrut* 2, 498–537.

Stewart, Doug (1991) "Through the Looking Glass into an Artificial World – via Computer," *The Smithsonian* 21, 10:36–45.

Sukenick, Ronald (1969) "The Death of the Novel," in *The Death of the Novel and Other Stories*, New York: Dial.

Sukenick, Ronald (1985a) *In Form: Digressions on the Act of Fiction*, Carbondale and Edwardsville: Southern Illinois University Press.

Sukenick, Ronald (1985b (1972)) "The New Tradition," in Sukenick 1985a, 201–13.

Sukenick, Ronald (1986) *The Endless Short Story*, New York: Fiction Collective, 1986.

Suleiman, Susan (1990) *Subversive Intent: Gender, Politics, and the Avant-Garde*, Cambridge, MA and London: Harvard University Press.

Swanwick, Michael (1987) *Vacuum Flowers*, New York: Arbor House.

Tamir, Nomi (1976) "Personal Narrative and Its Linguistic Foundation," *PTL* 1, 3:403–29.

Tani, Stefano (1984) *The Doomed Detective: The Contribution of the Detective Novel to Postmodern American and Italian Fiction*, Carbondale and Edwardsville: Southern Illinois University Press.

Tanner, Tony (1974) "V. & V-2," in Mendelson 1978b, 47–55.

Tanner, Tony (1982) *Thomas Pynchon*, London: Methuen.

Tanner, Tony (1987) "Toward an ultimate topography: the work of Joseph McElroy," in *Scenes of Nature, Signs of Men*, Cambridge: Cambridge University Press, 206–237.

Tate, J.O. (1983) "*Gravity's Rainbow*: The Original Soundtrack," *Pynchon Notes* 13, 3–24.

Tempera, Mariangela (1986) "A Battle of Voices: The Authorship of the Stage Directions in 'Circe,' " in Bosinelli *et al.* (eds) 1986, 195–207.

Thiher, Alan (1984) *Words in Reflection: Modern Language Theory and Postmodern Fiction*, Chicago and London: University of Chicago Press.

Todorov, Tzvetan (1975) *The Fantastic: A Structural Approach to a Literary Genre*, trans. Richard Howard, Ithaca, NY: Cornell University Press.

Tölölyan, Khachig (1983) "War as Background in *Gravity's Rainbow*," in Clerc 1983a, 31–67.

Topia, André (1984 (1976)) "The Matrix and the Echo: Intertexuality in *Ulysses*," in Attridge and Ferrer 1984b, 102–25.

Tsur, Reuven (1975) "Two Critical Attitudes: Quest for Certitude and Negative Capability," *College English* 36: 777–88.

Tyler, Stephen A. (1987) "Postmodern Ethnography: From Document of the Occult to Occult Document," in *The Unspeakable: Discourse, Dialogue, and Rhetoric in the Postmodern World*, Madison and London: University of Wisconsin Press, 199–216.

Vaihinger, Hans (1965 (1935)) *The Philosophy of "As If": A System of the Theoretical, Practical and Religious Fictions of Mankind*, trans. C.K. Ogden, London: Routledge & Kegan Paul.

Vance, Eugene (1986) *Mervelous Signals: Poetics and Sign Theory in the Middle Ages*, Lincoln and London: University of Nebraska Press.

van Delden, Maarten (1990) "Modernism, the New Criticism and Thomas Pynchon's *V.*," *Novel* 23, 2:117–36.

Venturi, Robert (1977 (1966)) *Complexity and Contradiction in Architecture*, New York: The Museum of Modern Art.

Venturi, Robert, Denise Scott Brown and Steven Izenour (1977 (1972)) *Learning from Las Vegas: The Forgotten Symbolism of Architectural Form*, Cambridge, MA and London: MIT Press.

Wagar, W. Warren (1982) *Terminal Visions: The Literature of Last Things*, Bloomington: Indiana University Press.

Walsh, Robert (1988) " 'A Wind Rose': Joseph McElroy's *Women and Men*," in Heide Ziegler (ed.), *Facing Texts: Encounters between Contemporary Writers and Critics*, Durham, NC and London: Duke University Press, 263–72.

Weisenburger, Steven (1981) "The End of History? Thomas Pynchon and the Uses of the Past," in Pearce 1981, 140–56.

Weisenburger, Steven (1988) *A "Gravity's Rainbow" Companion: Sources and Context for Pynchon's Novel*, Athens: University of Georgia Press.

Werner, Craig Hansen (1986 (1982)) "Recognizing Reality, Realizing Responsibility," in Harold Bloom (ed.), *Modern Critical Interpretations: Thomas Pynchon's "Gravity's Rainbow"*, New York, New Haven, CT, and Philadelphia, PA: Chelsea House, 85–96.

West, Cornel (1985) "Afterword: The Politics of American Neo-Pragmatism," in Rajchman and West 1985, 259–72.

White, Allon (1981) *The Uses of Obscurity: The Fiction of Early Modernism*, London: Routledge & Kegan Paul.

White, Hayden (1987) *The Content of the Form: Narrative Discourse and Historical Representation*, Baltimore, MD, and London: Johns Hopkins University Press.

Wilde, Alan (1981) *Horizons of Assent: Modernism, Postmodernism, and the Ironic Imagination*, Baltimore, MD and London: Johns Hopkins University Press.

Williams, Raymond (1974) *Television: Technology and Cultural Form*, New York: Schocken.

Williams, Walter Jon (1988 (1986)) *Hardwired*, London and Sydney: Futura.

Williams, Walter Jon (1989 (1987)) *Voice of the Whirlwind*, London and Sydney: Futura.

Wilson, Edmund (1931) *Axel's Castle: A Study in the Imaginative Literature of 1870–1930*, New York: Scribner's.

Wilson, R. Rawdon (1990) *In Palamedes' Shadow: Explorations in Play, Game, and Narrative Theory*, Boston: Northeastern University Press.

Wilson, William S. (1989) "And/Or: One or the Other, or Both," in Julia Ballerini (ed.), *Sequence (con)Sequence: (sub)Versions of Photography in the 80s*, Bard College: Edith C. Blum Art Institute/Aperature Foundation, 11–31.

Winston, Mathew (1976) "Appendix: The Quest for Pynchon," in Levine and Leverenz 1976b, 251–63.

Wolfley, Lawrence C. (1977) "Repression's Rainbow: The Presence of Norman O. Brown in Pynchon's Big Novel," *PMLA* 92, 5:873–9.

Wollen, Peter (1982) "Godard and Counter Cinema: *Vent d'Est*," in *Readings and Writings: Semiotic Counter-Strategies*, London: Verso, 79–91.

Woolf, Virginia (1971) *Mrs. Dalloway*, Harmondsworth: Penguin.

Woolf, Virginia (1974) *To the Lighthouse*, Harmondsworth: Penguin.

Zaleski, Carol (1987) *Otherworld Journeys: Accounts of Near-Death Experience in Medieval and Modern Times*, New York and Oxford: Oxford University Press.

Ziff, Larzer (1981) *Literary Democracy: The Declaration of Cultural Independence in America*, New York: Viking.

Index